## Collins

# Student Book

# CAMBRIDGE IGCSE® CHEMISTRY

Chris Sunley and Sam Goodman

William Collins' dream of knowledge for all began with the publication of his first book in 1819. A self-educated mill worker, he not only enriched millions of lives, but also founded a flourishing publishing house. Today, staying true to this spirit, Collins books are packed with inspiration, innovation and practical expertise. They place you at the centre of a world of possibility and give you exactly what you need to explore it.

Collins. Freedom to teach

Published by Collins
An imprint of HarperCollins*Publishers*
The News Building
1 London Bridge Street
London
SE1 9GF

Browse the complete Collins catalogue at:
www.collins.co.uk

Commissioned by **Letitia Luff**
Managed by **Caroline Green**
Project managed by **Alicia Higgins**
Proofread by **Tony Clappison**
Illustrations by
**Jouve India Private Limited and Ann Paganuzzi**
Typeset by **Jouve India Private Limited**
Indexed by **Indexing Specialists (UK) Ltd**
Cover design by **Angela English**
Production by **Rachel Weaver**
Printed and bound by **Grafica Veneta S.p.A., Italy**

Fully safety checked but not trialled
by CLEAPSS

Many thanks to Andrew Young, Head Science Technician of Stewards Academy, for his safety testing and reviewing of all practical activities.

The syllabus content is reproduced by permission of Cambridge International Examinations.

Exam-style questions and sample answers have been written by the author.

® IGCSE is the registered trademark of Cambridge International Examinations.

# Acknowledgements

The publishers wish to thank the following for permission to reproduce photographs. Every effort has been made to trace copyright holders and to obtain their permission for the use of copyright materials. The publishers will gladly receive any information enabling them to rectify any error or omission at the first opportunity.

(t = top, c = centre, b = bottom, r = right, l = left)

Cover and title page image ©nikkytok/Shutterstock pp 8-9 Denis Vrublevski/Shutterstock, 10 (t) jele/Shutterstock, p 10 (b) Achim Baque/Shutterstock, p 14 cobalt88/Shutterstock, p 15 (l) Andrew Lambert Photography/Science Photo Library, p 15 (r) Andrew Lambert Photography/Science Photo Library, p 15 (b) Andrew Lambert Photography/Science Photo Library, p 18 Lightspring/Shutterstock, p 21 Charles D. Winters/Science Photo Library, p 22 haveseen/Shutterstock, p 23 Andrew Lambert Photography/Science Photo Library, p 25 Martyn F. Chillmaid/Science Photo Library, p 26 Leslie Garland Picture Library/Alamy, p 30 FikMik/Shutterstock, p 33 United States Navy, p 34 David Parker & Julian Baum/Science Photo Library, p 37 Ho Philip/Shutterstock, p 38 Andrew Lambert Photography/Science Photo Library, p 43 Smit/Shutterstock, p 46 Blaz Kure/Shutterstock, p 47 jordache/Shutterstock, p 48 (l) Travis Manley/Shutterstock, p 48 (r) Marc Dietrich/Shutterstock, p 51 Voronin76/Shutterstock, p 57 (t) broukoid/Shutterstock, p 57 (b) Tyler Boyes/Shutterstock, p 58 (t) Dmitry Kalinovsky/Shutterstock, p 58 (b) Tatiana Grozetskaya/Shutterstock, p 62 demarcomedia/Shutterstock, p 64 Feraru Nicolae/Shutterstock, p 67 Martyn F. Chillmaid/Science Photo Library, p 73 Leslie Garland Picture Library/Alamy, p 74 Andrew Lambert Photography/Science Photo Library, p 77 (l) Phototake Inc./Alamy, p 77 (r) Picsfive/Shutterstock, p 80 Andrew Lambert Photography/Science Photo Library, p 85 Arena Creative/Shutterstock, p 92 Science Photo Library, p 104-105 Galyna Andrushko/Shutterstock, p 106 Maximilian Stock Ltd/Science Photo Library, p 110 Charles D. Winters/Science Photo Library, p 119 (l) Marafona/Shutterstock, p 119 (r) Matt Valentine/Shutterstock, p 122 EdBockStock/Shutterstock, p 131 badahos/Shutterstock, p 140 (t) Iakov Kalinin/Shutterstock, p 140 (b) John T. Fowler/Alamy, p 142 (t) Mattes/WikiMedia Commons, p 142 (b) MCT/Getty Images, p 143 Friedrcih Saurer/Science Photo Library, p 147 Anna Baburkina/Shutterstock, p 157 Martyn F. Chillmaid/Science Photo Library, p 158 (l) dgmata/Shutterstock, p 158 (r) Ken Brown/iStockphoto, p 159 Charles D. Winters/Science Photo Library, p 164 Martyn F. Chillmaid/Science Photo Library, p 166 Andrew Lambert Photography/Science Photo Library, p 171 Cyril Hou/Shutterstock, p 174 Andrew Lambert Photography/Science Photo Library, p 179 Phil Degginger/Alamy, p 179 Martyn F. Chillmaid/Science Photo Library, p 184 (l) Andrew Lambert Photography/Science Photo Library, p 184 (r) Andrew Lambert Photography/Science Photo Library, p 186 (l) Blaz Kure/Shutterstock, p 186 (r) Andrew Lambert Photography/Science Photo Library, p 189 Charles D. Winters/Science Photo Library, p 192 jcwait/Shutterstock, p 196 Johann Helgason/Shutterstock, p 197 (t) Robert Pickett, p 197 (b) Andrew Lambert Photography/Science Photo Library, p 201 Andrew Lambert Photography/Science Photo Library, p 214-215 Piotr Zajc/Shutterstock, p 216 Shebeko/Shutterstock, p 223 Andrew Lambert Photography/Science Photo Library, p 224 Charles D. Winters/Science Photo Library, p 226 Andrew Lambert Photography/Science Photo Library, p 227 design56/Shutterstock, p 230 Andrew Lambert Photography/Science Photo Library, p 239 Slaven/Shutterstock, p 244 Centrill Media/Shutterstock, p 246 mffoto/Shutterstock, p 248 (l) Lawrence Migdale/Science Photo Library, p 248 (r) Richard Treptow/Science Photo Library, p 248 (b) Julia Reschke/Shutterstock, p 254 (l) kilukilu/Shutterstock, p 254 (r) Fokin Oleg/Shutterstock, p 255 (l) Parnumas Na Phatthalung/Shutterstock, p 255 (r) Holly Kuchera/Shutterstock, p 255 (b) Danicek/Shutterstock, p 259 David_Monniaux, p 260 Joe Gough/Shutterstock, p 265 Brian Jeffery Beggerly/Shutterstock, p 266 Martyn F. Chillmaid/Science Photo Library, p 268 Jackiso/Shutterstock, p 271 Meryll/Shutterstock, p 272 (t) Ratikova/Shutterstock, p 272 (b) sciencephotos/Alamy, p 274 Nando Machado/Shutterstock, p 277 muzsy/Shutterstock, p 279 Prixel Creative/Shutterstock, p 287 beboy/Shutterstock, p 290 Rigamondis/Shutterstock, p 293 AISPIX by Image Source/Shutterstock, p 295 Francois Etienne du Plessis/Shutterstock, p 302-303 1971yes/Shutterstock, p 308 Paul Rapson/Science Photo Library, p 309 Bestweb/Shutterstock, p 314 Dawid Zagorski/Shutterstock, p 318 Yvan/Shutterstock, p 319 speedpix/Alamy, p 320 Leslie Garland Picture Library/Alamy, p 321 Joe Gough/Shutterstock, p 322 Rick Decker/Alamy, p 326 Gwoeii/Shutterstock, p 329 JoLin/Shutterstock, p 333 Tonis Valing/Shutterstock, p 335 David R. Frazier Photolibrary, Inc./Alamy, p 339 Jim Parkin/Alamy, p 342 Goran Bogicevic/Shutterstock, p 347 Dmitry Yashkin/Shutterstock, p 349 kaband/Shutterstock, p 350 EpicStockMedia/Shutterstock, p 352 (l) Lya_Cattel/iStockphoto, p 352 (r) Green Stock Media/Alamy, p 370 Ed Phillips/Shutterstock.

# Contents

# Getting the best from the book

Welcome to Collins *Cambridge IGCSE Chemistry*.

This textbook has been designed to help you understand all of the requirements needed to succeed in the Cambridge IGCSE Chemistry course. The book has taken the Cambridge IGCSE syllabus and split each of the topics across four main sections of study: Principles of chemistry, Physical chemistry, Inorganic chemistry and Organic chemistry.

Each topic in the textbook covers the essential knowledge and skills you need. The textbook also has some very useful features which have been designed to really help you understand all the aspects of Chemistry which you will need to know for this syllabus.

## SAFETY IN THE SCIENCE LESSON

This book is a textbook, not a laboratory or practical manual. As such, you should not interpret any information in this book that relates to practical work as including comprehensive safety instructions. Your teachers will provide full guidance for practical work and cover rules that are specific to your school.

A brief introduction to the section to give context to the science covered in the section.

Starting points will help you to revise previous learning and see what you already know about the ideas to be covered in the section.

The section contents shows the separate topics to be studied matching the syllabus order.

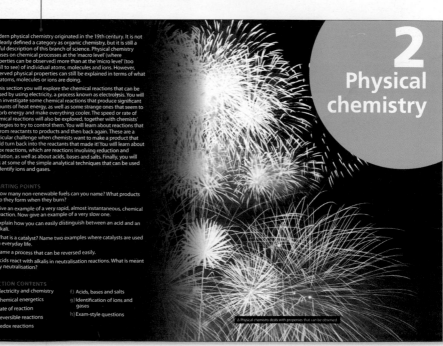

Modern physical chemistry originated in the 19th century. It is not as clearly defined a category as organic chemistry, but it is still a useful description of this branch of science. Physical chemistry focuses on chemical processes at the 'macro level' (where properties can be observed) more than at the 'micro level' (too small to see) of individual atoms, molecules and ions. However, observed physical properties can still be explained in terms of what the atoms, molecules or ions are doing.

In this section you will explore the chemical reactions that can be caused by using electricity, a process known as electrolysis. You will then investigate some chemical reactions that produce significant amounts of heat energy, as well as some strange ones that seem to absorb energy and make everything cooler. The speed or rate of chemical reactions will also be explored, together with chemists' strategies to try to control them. You will learn about reactions that go from reactants to products and then back again. These are a particular challenge when chemists want to make a product that could turn back into the reactants that made it! You will learn about redox reactions, which are reactions involving reduction and oxidation, as well as about acids, bases and salts. Finally, you will look at some of the simple analytical techniques that can be used to identify ions and gases.

**STARTING POINTS**

1. How many non-renewable fuels can you name? What products do they form when they burn?

2. Give an example of a very rapid, almost instantaneous, chemical reaction. Now give an example of a very slow one.

3. Explain how you can easily distinguish between an acid and an alkali.

4. What is a catalyst? Name two examples where catalysts are used in everyday life.

5. Name a process that can be reversed easily.

6. Acids react with alkalis in neutralisation reactions. What is meant by neutralisation?

**SECTION CONTENTS**

a) Electricity and chemistry
b) Chemical energetics
c) Rate of reaction
d) Reversible reactions
e) Redox reactions

f) Acids, bases and salts
g) Identification of ions and gases
h) Exam-style questions

## 2
### Physical chemistry

△ Physical chemistry deals with properties that can be observed

Knowledge check shows the ideas you should have already encountered in previous work before starting the topic.

Learning objectives cover what you need to learn in this topic.

Examples of investigations are included with questions matched to the investigative skills you will need to learn.

# Getting the best from the book *continued*

Remember boxes provide tips and guidance to help you during your course and to prepare for examination.

Science in context boxes put the ideas you are learning into real-life context. It is not necessary for you to learn the content of these boxes as they do not form part of the syllabus. However, they do provide interesting examples of scientific application that are designed to enhance your understanding.

Clearly differentiated Extended material takes your learning even further.

Learn to apply formulae through worked examples.

Questions to check your understanding.

End of topic questions allow you to apply the knowledge and understanding you have learned in the topic to answer the questions.

A full checklist of all the information you need to cover the complete syllabus requirements for each topic.

## End of topic checklist

### Key terms

Avogadro constant, Avogadro's law, chemical formula, chemical symbol, concentration, decomposition, diatomic, element, empirical formula, ionic equation, mole, molecular formula, percentage yield, percentage purity, product, radical, reactant, relative atomic mass ($A_r$), relative formula mass ($M_r$), relative molecular mass ($M_r$) solution, solvent, spectator ions, yield

### During your study of this topic you should have learned:

○ How to use the symbols of the elements to write the formulae of simple compounds.

○ How to deduce the formula of a simple compound from the numbers of atoms present.

○ How to deduce the formula of a simple compound from a model or a diagrammatic representation.

○ How to construct word equations and simple balanced chemical equations.

○ The definition of relative atomic mass ($A_r$).

○ The definition of relative molecular mass ($M_r$) as the sum of the relative atomic masses.

○ That relative formula mass ($M_r$) is used for compounds.

○ How to use simple proportion to work out reacting masses.

○ EXTENDED How to determine the formula of an ionic compound from the charges on the ions present.

○ EXTENDED How to construct equations with state symbols, including ionic equations.

○ EXTENDED How to deduce the balanced equation for a chemical reaction, given relevant information.

○ EXTENDED The definition of the mole and the Avogadro constant.

○ EXTENDED How to use the molar gas volume (24 dm³ at room temperature and pressure).

○ EXTENDED How to calculate stoichiometric reacting masses and volumes of gases and solutions.

○ EXTENDED That solution concentrations are expressed in g/dm³ and mol/dm³(M).

○ EXTENDED How to calculate empirical formulae and molecular formulae.

○ EXTENDED How to calculate percentage yield and percentage purity.

## End of topic questions

*Note: The marks awarded for these questions indicate the level of detail required in the answers. In the examination, the number of marks awarded to questions like these may be different.*

**1.** Work out the chemical formulae of the following compounds:

a) sodium chloride (1 mark)

b) magnesium fluoride (1 mark)

c) aluminium nitride (1 mark)

d) lithium oxide (1 mark)

e) carbon (IV) oxide (carbon dioxide). (1 mark)

**2.** Work out the chemical formulae of the following compounds:

a) iron(III) oxide (1 mark)

b) phosphorus(V) chloride (1 mark)

c) chromium(III) bromide (1 mark)

d) sulfur(VI) oxide (sulfur trioxide) (1 mark)

e) sulfur(IV) oxide (sulfur dioxide). (1 mark)

**3.** Work out the chemical formulae of the following compounds:

a) potassium carbonate (1 mark)

b) ammonium chloride (1 mark)

c) sulfuric acid (1 mark)

d) magnesium hydroxide (1 mark)

e) ammonium sulfate. (1 mark)

**4.** Write symbol equations from the following word equations:

a) carbon + oxygen → carbon dioxide (1 mark)

b) iron + oxygen → iron(III) oxide (1 mark)

c) iron(III) oxide + carbon → iron + carbon dioxide (1 mark)

d) calcium carbonate + hydrochloric acid → calcium chloride + carbon dioxide + water. (1 mark)

**5.** What is the formula mass of:

a) ethene, $C_2H_4$ (1 mark)

b) sulfur dioxide, $SO_2$ (1 mark)

c) methanol, $CH_3OH$? (1 mark)

($A_r$: H = 1; C = 12; O = 16; S = 32)

---

Each section includes exam-style questions to help you prepare for your exam in a focussed way and get the best results.

## Exam-style questions
### Sample student answer

*The questions, sample answers and marks in this section have been written by the authors as a guide only. The marks awarded for these questions indicate the level of detail required in the answers. In the examination, the number of marks awarded to questions like these may be different.*

### Question 1

Solutions of lead(II) nitrate and potassium iodide react together to make the insoluble substance lead(II) iodide.

The equation for the reaction is

$Pb(NO_3)_2(aq) + 2KI(aq) \rightarrow 2KNO_3(aq) + PbI_2(s)$

An investigation was carried out to find how much precipitate formed with different volumes of lead(II) nitrate solution.

A student measured out 15 cm³ of potassium iodide solution using a measuring cylinder.

He poured this solution in to a clean boiling tube.

Using a clean measuring cylinder, he measured out 2 cm³ of lead(II) nitrate solution (of the same concentration as the potassium iodide solution). He added this to the potassium iodide solution.

A cloudy yellow mixture formed and the precipitate was left to settle.

The student then measured the height (in cm) of the precipitate using a ruler.

The student repeated the experiment using different volumes of lead(II) nitrate solution. The graph shows the results obtained.

### TEACHER'S COMMENTS

a) i) Correct point marked.

ii) Correct explanation. Also correct would be tube not being vertical when being set up so precipitate not level.

b) i) Correct response.

ii) Correct response – also correct is 'lead(II) nitrate in excess'.

c) i) Correct reading of ruler.

ii) Answer is 3.9 cm³ – the candidate has misread the horizontal axis scale.

d) i) Correct response.

ii) Correct – this is the purpose of the experiment.

e) 2 marks have been lost here because the filtered-off precipitate needs to be washed (1) and 'dried' (1) before being weighed.

---

a) i) On the graph, circle the point that seems to be anomalous. (1)

ii) Explain two things that the student may have done in the experiment to give this anomalous result.

*Precipitate not settled* ✓ ① *Because not left long enough* ✓ ① (2)

iii) Why must the graph line go through (0, 0)?

*Cannot have a precipitate if no lead nitrate added yet.* ✓ ① (1)

b) Suggest a reason why the height of the precipitate stops increasing.

*No more potassium iodide left to react.* ✓ ① (1)

c) i) How much precipitate has been made in the tube drawn on the right?

*1.5 cm* ✓ ① (1)

ii) Use the graph to find the volume of lead(II) nitrate solution needed to make this amount of precipitate.

*2.9 cm³* ✗ (1)

d) After he had plotted the graph, the student decided he should obtain some more results.

i) Suggest what volumes of lead(II) nitrate solution he should use.

*Between 6 cm³ and 10 cm³* ✓ ① (1)

ii) Explain why he should use these volumes.

*Need to know exactly where the graph levels off* ✓ ① (1)

e) Suggest a different method for measuring the amount of precipitate formed.

*Filter* ✓ ① *off each precipitate and weigh it* ✓ ① (4)

(Total 13 marks)

⑩⁄₁₃

The first question is a student sample with teacher's comments to show best practice.

---

GETTING THE BEST FROM THE BOOK

**7**

This section provides the basic ideas that the rest of your course is built on. You may have covered some aspects in your previous work, but it is important to understand the key principles thoroughly before seeing how these can be applied across all the other sections. The section covers some of the experimental techniques you will meet in your course.

First you will look at the existing evidence for the particulate nature of matter. Next, you will consider the structure of an atom and why the atoms of different elements have different properties. You will look at the different ways that atoms of elements join together when they form compounds, and how the method of combination will determine the properties of the compound formed. You will develop your skills in writing word and symbol equations; and, as well as being able to use an equation to work out the products of a reaction, you will be able to calculate how much of the product can be made in the reaction. These quantitative aspects of chemistry are crucially important in the chemical industry.

## STARTING POINTS

1. What is an atom?

2. Name some of the particles that are found in an atom.

3. What name is given to a particle formed when two atoms combine together?

4. You will be learning about the states of matter. Do you know what these states are?

5. One type of chemical bonding you will study is called ionic bonding. Find out what an ion is.

6. Diamond and graphite are both covalent substances. They contain the same atoms but have very different structures and properties. What do you know about what diamond and graphite are used for?

## SECTION CONTENTS

a) The particulate nature of matter

b) Experimental techniques

c) Atomic structure and the Periodic Table

d) Ions and ionic bonds

e) Molecules and covalent bonds

f) Metallic bonding

g) Stoichiometry

h) Exam-style questions

# 1
# Principles of chemistry

△ Diamond and graphite are both forms of carbon but have quite different properties

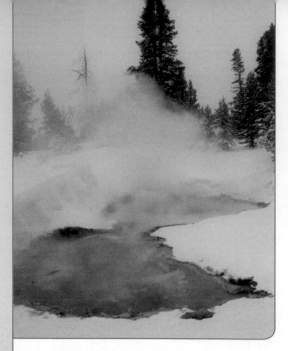

△ Fig. 1.1 Water in all its states of matter.

# The particulate nature of matter

## INTRODUCTION

Nearly all substances may be classified as solid, liquid or gas – the states of matter. In science these states are often shown in shorthand as (s), (l) and (g) after the formula or symbol (these are called **state symbols**). The kinetic particle theory is based on the idea that all substances are made up of extremely tiny particles. The particles in these three states are arranged differently and have different types of movement and different energies. In many cases, matter changes into different states quite easily. The names of many of these processes are in everyday use, such as melting and condensing. Using simple models of the particles in solids, liquids and gases can help to explain what happens when a substance changes state.

## KNOWLEDGE CHECK

✓ Be able to classify substances as solid, liquid or gas.
✓ Be familiar with some of the simple properties of solids, liquids and gases.
✓ Know that all substances are made up of particles.

## LEARNING OBJECTIVES

✓ Be able to state the distinguishing properties of solids, liquids and gases.
✓ Be able to describe the structure of solids, liquids and gases in terms of particle separation, arrangement and types of motion.
✓ Be able to describe the changes of state in terms of melting, boiling, evaporation, freezing, condensation and sublimation.
✓ Be able to describe qualitatively the pressure and temperature of a gas in terms of the motion of its particles.
✓ Be able to show an understanding of the random motion of particles in a suspension (sometimes known as Brownian motion) as evidence for the kinetic particle (atoms, molecules or ions) model of matter.
✓ Be able to describe and explain diffusion.

✓ **EXTENDED** Be able to explain changes of state in terms of the kinetic theory.

✓ **EXTENDED** Be able to describe and explain Brownian motion in terms of random molecular bombardment.

✓ **EXTENDED** Be able to state evidence for Brownian motion.

✓ **EXTENDED** Be able to describe the dependence of rate of diffusion on molecular mass.

△ Fig. 1.2 Water covers nearly four-fifths of the Earth's surface. In this photo you can see that all three states of matter can exist together: solid water (the ice) is floating in liquid water (the ocean), and the surrounding air contains water vapour (clouds).

## HOW DO SOLIDS, LIQUIDS AND GASES DIFFER?

The three states of matter each have different properties, depending on how strongly the particles are held together.

- **Solids** have a fixed volume and shape.
- **Liquids** have a fixed volume but no definite shape. They take up the shape of the container in which they are held.
- **Gases** have no fixed volume or shape. They spread out to fill whatever container or space they are in.

Substances don't always exist in the same state; depending on the physical conditions, they change from one state to another (interconvert).

Some substances can exist in all three states in the natural world. A good example of this is water.

## QUESTIONS

**1.** What is the state symbol for a liquid?

**2.** Which is the only state of matter that has a fixed shape?

**3.** In what ways does fine sand behave like a liquid?

### Why do solids, liquids and gases behave differently?

The behaviour of solids, liquids and gases can be explained if we think of all matter as being made up of very small particles that are in constant motion. This idea has been summarised in the **kinetic theory** of matter.

In solids, the particles are held tightly together in a fixed position, so solids have a definite shape. However, the particles are vibrating about their fixed positions because they have energy.

In liquids, the particles are held tightly together but have enough energy to move around. Liquids have no definite shape and will take on the shape of the container they are in.

In gases, the particles are further apart with enough energy to move apart from each other and are constantly moving. Gas particles can spread apart to fill the container they are in.

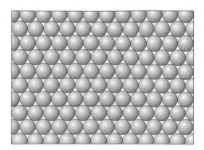

△ Fig. 1.3 Particles in a solid.

△ Fig. 1.4 Particles in a liquid.

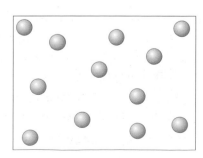

△ Fig. 1.5 Particles in a gas.

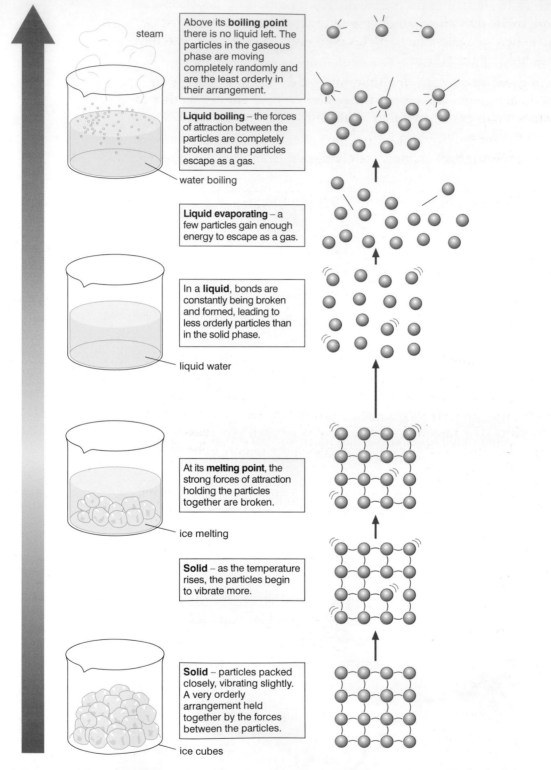

Above its **boiling point** there is no liquid left. The particles in the gaseous phase are moving completely randomly and are the least orderly in their arrangement.

steam

**Liquid boiling** – the forces of attraction between the particles are completely broken and the particles escape as a gas.

water boiling

**Liquid evaporating** – a few particles gain enough energy to escape as a gas.

In a **liquid**, bonds are constantly being broken and formed, leading to less orderly particles than in the solid phase.

liquid water

At its **melting point**, the strong forces of attraction holding the particles together are broken.

ice melting

**Solid** – as the temperature rises, the particles begin to vibrate more.

**Solid** – particles packed closely, vibrating slightly. A very orderly arrangement held together by the forces between the particles.

ice cubes

Δ Fig. 1.6 Particles in the different states of matter.

# HOW DO SUBSTANCES CHANGE FROM ONE STATE TO ANOTHER?

To change solids into liquids and then into gases, heat energy must be put in. The heat provides the particles with enough energy to overcome the forces holding them together.

To change gases into liquids and then into solids involves cooling, so removing heat energy. This makes the particles come closer together as the substance changes from gas to liquid and the particles bond together as the liquid becomes a solid.

The temperatures at which one state changes to another have specific names:

| Name of temperature | Change of state |
| --- | --- |
| **Melting** point | Solid to liquid |
| **Boiling** point | Liquid to gas |
| **Freezing** point | Liquid to solid |
| **Condensation** point | Gas to liquid |

△ Table 1.1 Changes of state.

The particles in a liquid can move around. They have different energies, so some are moving faster than others. The faster particles have enough energy to escape from the surface of the liquid and it changes into the gas state (also called **vapour** particles). This process is **evaporation**. The rate of evaporation increases with increasing temperature because heat gives more particles the energy to be able to escape from the surface.

Fig. 1.7 summarises the changes in states of matter. Note that melting and freezing happen at the same temperature – as do boiling and condensing.

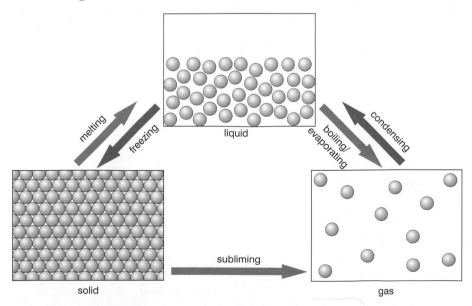

△ Fig. 1.7 Changes of state. Note that melting and freezing happen at the same temperature – as do boiling and condensing.

# THE STATES OF MATTER

There are three states of matter – or are there? To complicate this simple idea, some substances show the properties of two different states of matter. Some examples are given below.

## Liquid crystals

Liquid crystals are commonly used in displays in computers and televisions. Within particular temperature ranges the particles of the liquid crystal can flow like a liquid, but remain arranged in a pattern in which the particles cannot rotate.

△ Fig. 1.8 An LCD (liquid crystal display) television.

### Superfluids

When some liquids are cooled to very low temperatures they form a second liquid state, described as a *superfluid* state. Liquid helium at just above absolute zero has infinite fluidity and will 'climb out' of its container when left undisturbed – at this temperature the liquid has zero viscosity. (You may like to look up 'fluidity' and 'viscosity'.)

### Plasma

Plasmas, or ionised gases, can exist at temperatures of several thousand degrees Celsius. An example of a plasma is the charged air produced by lightning. Stars like our Sun also produce plasma. Like a gas, a plasma does not have a definite shape or volume but the strong forces between its particles give it unusual properties, such as conducting electricity. Because of this combination of properties, plasma is sometimes called the fourth state of matter.

The **pressure** exerted by a gas is caused by the gas particles bombarding the sides of the container the gas is in. If a gas is compressed into a smaller volume, the number of gas particles hitting the sides of the container every second will increase (there is less space for them to move in). The increase in the number of collisions per second causes the increase in pressure. If the **temperature** of a gas is increased, the gas particles have more energy and will move faster. Again there will be more collisions with the sides of the container each second and so the gas will exert a greater pressure.

1. What type of movement do the particles in a solid have?

2. In which state are the particles held together more strongly: in solid water, liquid water or water vapour?

3. What is the name of the process that occurs when the faster-moving particles in a liquid escape from its surface?

4. What name is given to the temperature at which a solid changes into a liquid?

## DIFFUSION EXPERIMENTS

Scientists have confidence in the kinetic theory because of the evidence from simple experiments.

The random mixing and moving of particles in liquids and gases is known as **diffusion**. The examples given below show the effects of diffusion.

### Dissolving crystals in water

Fig. 1.9 shows purple crystals of potassium manganate(VII) dissolving in water.

△ Fig. 1.9 Crystals of potassium manganate(VII) dissolving in water. The picture on the left shows the water immediately after the crystal was added; the picture on the right shows the water 1 hour later.

There are no water currents, so only the kinetic theory can explain this. The particles of the crystal gradually move into the water and mix with the water particles.

### Mixing gases

These photos show a jar of air and a jar of bromine gas. Bromine gas is red-brown and heavier than air. The jar of air has been placed on top of the jar of bromine and the lids removed so the gases can mix (left-hand part of Fig.1.10).

After about 24 hours the bromine gas and the air have spread throughout both jars. Kinetic theory says that the particles of

△ Fig. 1.10 Diffusion of bromine.

bromine gas can move around randomly so that they can fill both gas jars. This also occurs with hydrogen and air Fig. 1.11.

Δ Fig. 1.11 Demonstration of diffusion with a jar of oxygen and a jar of hydrogen.

## BROWNIAN MOTION

The Scottish scientist Robert Brown looked at pollen in water using a microscope. He saw that the pollen grains were always moving.

Kinetic theory explains this as the pollen grains being pushed around by water molecules that are always moving. You can also see **Brownian motion** in a smoke cell. The smoke particles move about because they are constantly pushed around by the tiny, invisible air molecules.

Δ Fig. 1.12 Brownian motion in a smoke cell.

The molecules of different gases do not all move at the same speed at room temperature. The rate at which gases diffuse depends on their molecular mass – the larger their molecular mass, the lower their rate of diffusion. For example hydrogen, which has the lowest molecular mass of any gas, will diffuse much more rapidly than carbon dioxide which has a molecular mass 22 times that of hydrogen.

## Developing investigative skills

Two students set up the experiment shown in Fig. 1.13. They carefully clamped the long glass tube horizontally. At the same time, they inserted the cotton wool plugs soaked in the two solutions at each end of the tube and replaced the rubber bungs.

white ring where gases A+B meet

cotton wool soaked in concentrated ammonia solution

cotton wool soaked in concentrated hydrochloric acid

△ Fig. 1.13 Results of experiment.

After about 15 minutes a white ring was seen in the tube.

*Note*: The white ring was formed where the ammonia gas from the concentrated ammonia solution met the hydrogen chloride gas from the concentrated hydrochloric acid. Together they formed a white substance called ammonium chloride.

### Using and organising techniques, apparatus and materials

**The concentrated ammonia solution is corrosive – it burns and is dangerous to the eyes. Concentrated hydrochloric acid is corrosive – it burns and its vapour irritates the lungs.**

❶ How should the cotton wool plugs have been handled when putting them into the tube?

❷ What other safety precaution(s) should the two students have used?

### Observing, measuring and recording

❸ Which gas moved furthest in the 15 minutes before the ring formed?

❹ Approximately how much further did this gas travel compared to the other gas?

### Handling experimental observations and data

❺ The rate of diffusion of a gas depends on the mass of its particles. What conclusion can you draw about the relative masses of the two gases in this experiment?

## ELEMENTS, ATOMS AND MOLECULES

All matter is made from **elements**. Elements are substances that cannot be broken down into anything simpler, because they are made up of only one kind of the same small particle. These small particles are called **atoms**.

Almost always, the atoms in an element combine with other atoms to form molecules. For example, the particles in water are molecules containing two hydrogen atoms joined up with one oxygen atom. The formula is therefore $H_2O$. There are also particles called ions (see page 43).

△ Fig. 1.14 Model of a water molecule.

## QUESTIONS

1. What is *diffusion*?

2. Explain how the purple colour of the potassium manganate(VII) shown in Fig. 1.9 spreads through the water.

3. A bottle of perfume is broken at one end of a room. Explain why the perfume can soon be smelled all over the room.

4. What is the name of the particle that is found in all elements?

5. **EXTENDED** Brownian motion can be observed in a laboratory using a smoke cell:

   a) In what situation was Brownian motion first observed?

   b) In the smoke cell, what causes the random motion of the smoke particles?

# End of topic checklist

## Key terms

atom, boiling, Brownian motion, condensation, diffusion, element, evaporation, freezing, gas, kinetic theory, liquid, melting, pressure, solid, state symbols, temperature, vapour

## During your study of this topic you should have learned:

○ About the different properties of solids, liquids and gases.

○ How to describe the structure of solids, liquids and gases in terms of particle separation, arrangement and types of motion.

○ How to describe changes of state in terms of melting, boiling, evaporation, freezing, condensation and sublimation.

○ How to describe the pressure and temperature of a gas in terms of the motion of its particles.

○ An understanding of the random motion of particles in a suspension (Brownian motion) as evidence for the kinetic particle (atoms, molecules or ions) model of matter.

○ How to describe and explain diffusion.

○ **EXTENDED** How to explain changes of state in terms of the kinetic theory.

○ **EXTENDED** How to describe and explain Brownian motion in terms of random molecular bombardment
  - about evidence for Brownian motion
  - how to describe how the rate of diffusion depends on molecular mass.

*Note: The marks awarded for these questions indicate the level of detail required in the answers. In the examination, the number of marks awarded to questions like these may be different.*

1. In which of the three states of matter are the particles moving fastest? **(1 mark)**

2. Describe the arrangement and movement of the particles in a liquid. **(2 marks)**

3. In which state of matter do the particles just vibrate about a fixed point? **(1 mark)**

4. Sodium (melting point 98 °C) and aluminium (melting point 660 °C) are both solids at room temperature. From their melting points, what can you conclude about the forces of attraction between the particles in the two metals? **(1 mark)**

5. What is the name of the process involved in each of the following changes of state:

   **a)** $Fe(s) \rightarrow Fe(l)$? **(1 mark)**

   **b)** $H_2O(l) \rightarrow H_2O(g)$? **(1 mark)**

   **c)** $H_2O(g) \rightarrow H_2O(l)$? **(1 mark)**

   **d)** $H_2O(l) \rightarrow H_2O(s)$? **(1 mark)**

6. Ethanol liquid turns into ethanol vapour at 78 °C. What is the name of this temperature? **(1 mark)**

7. Explain how water in the Earth's polar regions can produce water vapour even when the temperature is very low. **(2 marks)**

8. A student wrote in her exercise book, 'The particle arrangement in a liquid is more like the arrangement in a solid than in a gas'. Do you agree with this statement? Explain your reasoning. **(2 marks)**

9. What word is used to describe the rapid mixing and moving of particles in gases? **(1 mark)**

10. Look at Fig. 1.10 showing gas jars of air and bromine. Explain why bromine gas fills the top gas jar even though it is denser than air. **(2 marks)**

11. **EXTENDED a)** What would you see if you observed illuminated smoke particles in a smoke cell? **(1 mark)**

    **b)** What causes what you observe? **(1 mark)**

12. **EXTENDED** The molecular masses of some gases are shown in the table:

    Which gas would diffuse at the greatest rate? Explain your answer. **(2 marks)**

| Gas | Molecular mass |
|---|---|
| Oxygen | 32 |
| Nitrogen | 28 |
| Chlorine | 71 |

# Experimental techniques

## INTRODUCTION

Practical work is a very important part of studying chemistry. In your practical work you will need to develop your skills so that you can safely, correctly and methodically use and organise techniques, apparatus and materials. This involves being able to use appropriate apparatus for measurement to give readings to the required degree of accuracy. It is important to be able to use techniques that will determine the purity of a substance and, if necessary, techniques that can be used to purify mixtures of substances.

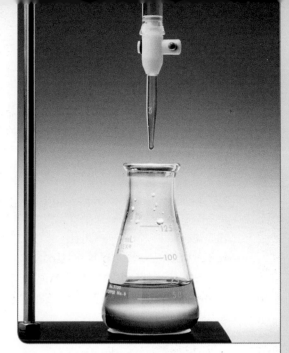

△ Fig. 1.15 Using the neutralisation method for a titration.

## KNOWLEDGE CHECK

✓ Be familiar with some simple equipment for measuring time, temperature, mass and volume.
✓ Know that some substances are mixtures of a number of different components.

## LEARNING OBJECTIVES

✓ Be able to name appropriate apparatus for accurate measurement of time, temperature, mass and volume.
✓ Be able to describe paper chromatography.
✓ Be able to interpret simple chromatograms.
✓ Be able to identify substances and assess their purity from the melting point and boiling point.
✓ Understand the importance of purity in substances in everyday life.
✓ **EXTENDED** Be able to use $R_f$ values in interpreting simple chromatograms.

✓ **EXTENDED** Be able to outline how chromatography techniques can be applied to colourless substances by exposing chromatograms to substances called locating agents.
✓ Be able to describe methods of purification by the use of a suitable solvent, filtration, crystallisation and distillation.
✓ Be able to suggest suitable purification techniques, given information about the substances involved.

## MEASUREMENT

In your study of chemistry you will carry out practical work. It is essential to use the right apparatus for the task.

*Time* is measured with clocks, such as a wall clock. The clock should be accurate to about 1 second. You may be able to use your own wristwatch or a stopclock.

*Temperature* is measured using a thermometer. The range of the thermometer is commonly −10 °C to +110 °C with intervals of 1 °C.

*Mass* is measured with a balance or scales.

*Volume* of liquids can be measured with burettes, pipettes and measuring cylinders.

△ Fig. 1.16 Measuring equipment.

## CRITERIA OF PURITY

### Paper chromatography

Paper **chromatography** is a way of separating solutions or liquids that are mixed together.

Black ink is a mixture of different coloured inks. The diagrams in Fig. 1.17 show how paper chromatography is used to find the colours that make up a black ink.

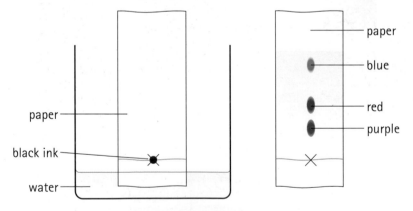

△ Fig. 1.17 Paper chromatography separates a solution to find the colours in black ink. The left part of the diagram shows the paper before the inks have been separated, and the right part shows the paper after the inks have been separated.

A spot of ink is placed on the × mark and the paper is suspended in water. As the water rises up the paper, the different dyes travel different distances and so are separated on the **chromatogram**.

Paper chromatography can be used to identify what an unknown liquid is made of. This is called to interpreting a chromatogram.

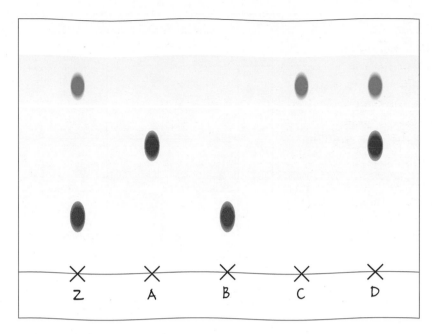

△ Fig. 1.18 A chromatogram.

The unknown liquid Z is compared with known liquids – in this case A to D.

Z must be made of B and C because the pattern of their dots matches the pattern shown by Z.

△ Fig. 1.19 A piece of filter paper is marked with black ink and dipped into water in a beaker.

△ Fig. 1.20 After a few minutes the chromatogram has been created by the action of the water on the ink.

Even colourless liquids can be separated using this technique. The difference is that the chromatogram paper is still white/colourless at the end. To see the pattern of dots, the paper is viewed under ultraviolet light or sprayed with a liquid **locating agent** that shows up the dots as colours.

△ Fig. 1.21 The $R_f$ value for the food additive E102 is 0.17.

### Retention factors

Substances can also be identified using chromatography by measuring their **retention factor** on the filter paper. The retention factor ($R_f$) for a particular substance compares the distance the substance has travelled up the filter paper with the distance travelled by the **solvent**. The retention factor can be calculated using the following formula:

$$R_f = \frac{\text{Distance moved by a substance from the baseline}}{\text{Distance moved by the solvent from the baseline}}$$

As the solvent will always travel further than the substance, $R_f$ values will always be less than 1.

### The purity of solids and liquids

It is very important that manufactured foods and drugs contain only the substances the manufacturers want in them – that is, they must not contain any contaminants.

The simplest way of checking the purity of solids and liquids is using heat to find the temperature at which they melt or boil.

An impure solid will have a lower melting point than the pure solid.

A liquid containing a dissolved solid (solute) will have a higher boiling point than the pure solvent.

The best examples to use to remember these facts are water and ice:

- Pure water boils at 100 °C – salted water for cooking vegetables boils at about 102 °C.
- Pure ice melts at 0 °C – ice with salt added to it melts at about –4 °C.

## QUESTIONS

1. The start line, or baseline, in chromatography should be drawn in pencil. Explain why.

2. In a chromatography experiment, why must the solvent level in the beaker be below the baseline?

**3.** In a chromatography experiment to compare the dyes in two different inks, one of the inks does not move at all from the baseline. Suggest a reason for this.

**4.** A sample of water contains some dissolved impurities. What would you expect the boiling point of the sample to be?

**5.** <u>EXTENDED</u> Look at the diagram in Fig. 1.21. Explain why the retention factor for the food additive E102 is 0.17.

## METHODS OF PURIFICATION

Techniques for purifying solids and liquids rely on finding different properties of the substances that make up the impure mixture.

### Purifying impure solids

The method is:

**1.** Add a solvent that the required solid is **soluble** in, and dissolve it.

**2.** Filter the mixture to remove the insoluble impurity.

**3.** Heat the solution to remove some solvent and leave it to crystallise.

**4.** Filter off the crystals, wash with a small amount of cold solvent and dry them – this is the pure solid.

△ Fig. 1.22 Filtration of copper (II) hydroxide.

An example of using this technique would be separating salt from 'rock salt' (the impure form of sodium chloride). Water is added to dissolve the salt but leave the other solids undissolved. Filter off the insoluble impurities, warm the salt solution and leave it to crystallise to form salt crystals.

filter off
excess solid

filter

mixture of salt
solution and solid
impurities

evaporating
dish

evaporate to
reduce volume
of solution

transfer hot
solution to dish

crystals form after
leaving to cool and
when solution is
saturated

△ Fig. 1.23 Separating impurities in rock salt.

## Purifying impure liquids

There are two methods:

**1.** Liquids contaminated with soluble solids dissolved in them.

The method is **distillation**.

The solution is heated, the solvent boils and turns into a vapour. It is condensed back to the pure liquid and collected.

This is the technique used in **desalination** plants, which produce pure drinking water from sea water. The solids are left behind after boiling off the water.

△ Fig.1.24 Distillation apparatus.

△ Fig. 1.25 Distillation of salt water.

**2.** Liquids contaminated with other liquids.

In this case the technique is **fractional distillation**, which uses the difference in boiling points of the different liquids mixed together.

The mixture is boiled, and the liquid with the lowest boiling point turns to a vapour first, rises up the fractionating column and is condensed back to liquid in the condenser. The next lowest boiling point liquid comes off, and so on until all the liquids have been separated. You can identify the fraction you want to collect by the temperature reading on the thermometer. The fractionating column increases the purity of the distilled product by reducing the amount of other substances in the vapour when it condenses.

Fractional distillation is the method used in the separation of crude oil and collecting ethanol from the fermentation mixture.

△ Fig. 1.26 Apparatus for fractional distillation of an alcohol/water mixture.

## QUESTIONS

**1.** What is a *solvent*?

**2.** What does the term *soluble* mean?

**3.** What method would you use to separate a pure liquid from a solution of a solid and the liquid?

**4.** To separate two liquids by fractional distillation they must have different:

**a)** melting points

**b)** boiling points

**c)** colours

**d)** viscosities.

# End of topic checklist

## Key terms

chromatogram, desalination, distillation, fractional distillation, locating agent, paper chromatography, retention factor, soluble, solvent

## During your study of this topic you should have learned:

○ About the appropriate apparatus for the measurement of time, temperature, mass and volume, including burettes, pipettes and measuring cylinders.

○ About the technique of paper chromatography.

○ How to interpret simple chromatograms.

○ How to identify substances and assess their purity from melting point and boiling point information.

○ About the importance of purity in substances in everyday life.

○ **EXTENDED** How to interpret simple chromatograms, including the use of $R_f$ values.

○ **EXTENDED** How to outline how chromatography techniques can be applied to colourless substances by exposing chromatograms to substances called locating agents.

○ How to describe methods of purification by the use of:

- a suitable solvent – to separate a soluble solid from an insoluble solid
- filtration – to separate a solid from a liquid
- crystallisation – to separate a solid from its solution
- distillation – to separate a solid and a liquid from a solution
- fractional distillation – to separate liquids with different boiling points.

○ How to suggest suitable purification techniques given information about the substances involved.

# End of topic questions

*Note: The marks awarded for these questions indicate the level of detail required in the answers. In the examination, the number of marks awarded to questions like these may be different.*

1. You are provided with four samples of black water-soluble inks. Two of the ink samples are identical. Describe how you would use paper chromatography to identify which two ink samples are the same. **(3 marks)**

2. You are trying to separate the dyes in a sample of ink using paper chromatography. You set up the apparatus as shown in Fig. 1.19. After 20 minutes the black spot is unchanged and the water has risen nearly to the top of the filter paper.

   a) Suggest a reason why the black spot has remained unchanged. **(1 mark)**

   b) What could you change that might lead to a successful separation of the dyes? **(1 mark)**

3. Pure ethanol has a boiling point at normal pressure of 78 °C. What temperature might a sample of ethanol contaminated with sugar boil at? **(1 mark)**

4. What effect will impurities have on the melting point of ice? **(1 mark)**

5. In the fractional distillation of ethanol and water, why does the ethanol vapour condense in the condenser? **(1 mark)**

6. Describe how you would produce crystals of sodium chloride from a sodium chloride solution. **(2 marks)**

7. What process could be used to separate the following mixtures:

   a) sand from a sand/water mixture? **(1 mark)**

   b) petrol from a petrol/diesel mixture? **(1 mark)**

   c) pure water from salt solution? **(1 mark)**

8. **EXTENDED** Look at the chromatogram produced when testing four food colouring compounds A, B, C and D.

   a) Which compound has the largest retention factor ($R_f$)? **(1 mark)**

   b) Which compound has the smallest $R_f$? **(1 mark)**

   c) Estimate the $R_f$ for compound C. Explain how you made the estimate. **(2 marks)**

   d) Why are all $R_f$ values less than 1.0? **(1 mark)**

△ Fig. 1.27

# Atomic structure and the Periodic Table

△ Fig. 1.28 A model showing molecular structure.

## INTRODUCTION

This topic is about the structure, or the makeup, of all substances. Some substances exist in nature as elements, others as compounds that are formed when elements combine chemically. The topic starts by considering the structure of the atoms that make up elements. It shows how the arrangement of elements in the Periodic Table is determined by the structure of their atoms. The properties of metals and non-metals are explained and an introduction to the combination of atoms forming compounds is provided. The following topics look in more detail at how atoms combine together to form ions and molecules, and the structure of metals.

## KNOWLEDGE CHECK

✓ Know the three states of matter and how to use the kinetic particle theory to explain the conversion of one state into another.
✓ Understand how diffusion experiments provide evidence for the existence of particles.
✓ Know that compounds are formed when elements combine together chemically.

## LEARNING OBJECTIVES

✓ Be able to state the relative charges and approximate relative masses of protons, neutrons and electrons.
✓ Be able to define *proton number* (atomic number) as the number of protons in the nucleus of an atom and *nucleon number* (mass number) as the total number of protons and and neutrons in the nucleus of an atom.
✓ Be able to use proton number and the simple structure of atoms to explain the basis of the Periodic Table, with special reference to the elements with proton numbers 1 to 20.
✓ Be able to define *isotopes* as atoms of the same element that have the same proton number but different nucleon number.
✓ **EXTENDED** Understand that isotopes have the same chemical properties because they have the same number of electrons in their outer shells.
✓ Be able to state the two types of isotopes as being radioactive and non-radioactive.
✓ Be able to state one medical and one industrial use of radioactive isotopes.
✓ Be able to describe the build-up of electrons in 'shells' around the nucleus and understand the significance of the noble gas electronic structures and of the outer shell electrons.
✓ Be able to describe the differences between elements, mixtures and compounds, and between metals and non-metals.
✓ Be able to describe an alloy, such as brass, as a mixture of a metal with other elements.

## ATOMIC THEORY

In 1808 the British chemist John Dalton published a book outlining his theory of atoms. These were the main points of his theory:

- All matter is made of small, indivisible spheres called atoms.
- All the atoms of a given element are identical and have the same mass.
- The atoms of different elements have different masses.
- Chemical compounds are formed when different atoms join together.

All the molecules of a chemical **compound** have the same type and number of atoms.

An element is the smallest part of a substance that can exist on its own. When two or more elements combine together a compound is formed.

Since 1808, atomic theory has developed considerably and yet many of Dalton's ideas are still correct. Modern theory is built on an understanding of the particles that make up atoms – the so-called sub-atomic particles.

## SUB-ATOMIC PARTICLES

The smallest amount of an element that still behaves like that element is an atom. Each element has its own unique type of atom. Atoms are made up of smaller, sub-atomic particles. The three main sub-atomic particles are **protons**, **neutrons** and **electrons**.

These particles are very small and have very little mass. However, it is possible to compare their masses using a relative scale. Their charges may also be compared in a similar way. The proton and neutron have the same mass, and the proton and electron have equal but opposite charges.

| Sub-atomic particle | Relative mass | Relative charge |
|---|---|---|
| Proton | 1 | +1 |
| Neutron | 1 | 0 |
| Electron | about $\dfrac{1}{2000}$ | −1 |

△ Table 1.2 Relative masses and charges of sub-atomic particles.

Protons and neutrons are found in the centre of the atom in a cluster called the **nucleus**. The electrons form a series of 'shells' around the nucleus.

◁ Fig. 1.29 Structure of an atom.

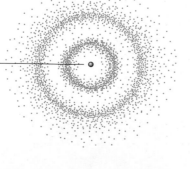

**Nucleus**
this is very small, it contains positively charged particles called protons and particles with no charge at all called neutrons

**Electrons**
are negatively charged particles that form a series of 'shells' around the nucleus

△ Fig. 1.30 Diagrams are another way of representing the structure of an atom.

## Proton number and nucleon number

In order to describe the numbers of protons, neutrons and electrons in an atom, scientists use two numbers. These are called the **proton number** (or **atomic number**) and the **nucleon number** (or **mass number**). The proton number, as you might expect, describes the number of protons in the atom. The nucleon number describes the number of particles in the nucleus of the atom – that is, the total number of protons and neutrons.

Proton numbers are used to arrange the elements in the Periodic Table. The atomic structures of the first ten elements in the Periodic Table are shown in Table 1.3.

Hydrogen is the only atom that has no neutrons.

NUCLEON NUMBER
(the number of
protons + neutrons)

symbol for
the element

$$^{A}_{Z}\textbf{X}$$

PROTON NUMBER
(the number of protons,
which equals the number
of electrons)

△ Fig. 1.31 Chemical symbol showing nucleon number and proton number.

| Element | Proton number | Nucleon number | Number of protons | Number of neutrons | Number of electrons |
|---|---|---|---|---|---|
| Hydrogen | 1 | 1 | 1 | 0 | 1 |
| Helium | 2 | 4 | 2 | 2 | 2 |
| Lithium | 3 | 7 | 3 | 4 | 3 |
| Beryllium | 4 | 9 | 4 | 5 | 4 |
| Boron | 5 | 11 | 5 | 6 | 5 |
| Carbon | 6 | 12 | 6 | 6 | 6 |
| Nitrogen | 7 | 14 | 7 | 7 | 7 |
| Oxygen | 8 | 16 | 8 | 8 | 8 |
| Fluorine | 9 | 19 | 9 | 10 | 9 |
| Neon | 10 | 20 | 10 | 10 | 10 |

△ Table 1.3 Atomic structures of the first ten elements.

1. Which sub-atomic particle has the smallest relative mass?

2. Why do atoms have the same number of protons as electrons?

3. An aluminium atom can be represented as $^{27}_{13}$Al.

   a) What is aluminium's nucleon number?

   b) How many neutrons does this atom of aluminium have?

## ISOTOPES

Atoms of the same element with the same number of protons and electrons but different numbers of neutrons are called **isotopes**. For example, there are two isotopes of chlorine:

| Symbol | Number of protons | Number of neutrons |
|---|---|---|
| $^{35}_{17}$Cl | 17 | 18 |
| $^{37}_{17}$Cl | 17 | 20 |

Δ Table 1.4 Isotopes of chlorine.

Isotopes have the same chemical properties but slightly different physical properties.

Some isotopes are **radioactive**. They emit radioactivity from the nucleus and decay — that is, if the radioactivity is alpha particles or beta particles, they change into other atoms with different numbers of protons and/or neutrons.

Isotopes that do not decay and do not emit radiation are classed as non-radioactive isotopes.

Radioactive isotopes emit radioactivity of one of the following types:

Δ Fig. 1.32 A gamma camera is an example of radioactive isotopes used in medicine.

Alpha particles ($\alpha$) are helium nuclei; they contain two protons and two neutrons.

Beta particles ($\beta$) are fast-moving electrons.

Gamma rays ($\gamma$) are high-energy electromagnetic rays.

In medicine, radioactive isotopes are used to sterilise equipment and in radiotherapy to treat cancer tumours.

Industry uses radioactive isotopes as 'tracers' to detect leaks in pipes.

## EXTENDED

The chemical properties of an element depend on the number of electrons in the outer electron shell. As isotopes of the same element have the same number of electrons they have the same chemical properties.

## END OF EXTENDED

## SUB-ATOMIC PARTICLES

△ Fig. 1.33 The Large Hadron Collider at CERN in Switzerland.

Protons, neutrons and electrons are the particles from which atoms are made. However, in the past 20 years or so scientists have discovered a number of other sub-atomic particles: quarks, leptons, muons, neutrinos, bosons and gluons. The properties of some of these particles have become well known, but there is still much to learn about the others. Finding out about these, and possibly other sub-atomic particles, is one of the challenges of the 21st century.

To study the smallest known particles, a particle accelerator has been built underground at CERN near Geneva, Switzerland. This giant instrument, called the Large Hadron Collider (LHC), has a circumference of 27 km. It attempts to recreate the conditions that existed just after the 'Big Bang' by colliding beams of particles at very high speed – only about 5 m/s slower than the speed of light. It promises to revolutionise scientific understanding of the nature of atoms. Who knows – school science in 10 or 20 years' time may be very different from your lessons today!

## QUESTIONS

1. What are *isotopes*?

2. What is the difference between a radioactive and a non-radioactive isotope?

3. Give three uses of radioactive isotopes.

# ARRANGEMENTS OF ELECTRONS IN THE ATOM

An atom's electrons are arranged in **shells** around the nucleus. These do not all contain the same number of electrons – the shell nearest to the nucleus can take only two electrons, whereas the next one out from the nucleus can take eight.

| Electron shell | Maximum number of electrons |
|---|---|
| 1 | 2 |
| 2 | 8 |
| 3 | 8 (initially, with up to 18 after element 20) |

Δ Table 1.5 Maximum number of electrons in a shell.

Oxygen has a proton number of 8, so it has 8 electrons. Of these, two are in the first shell and six are in the second shell. This arrangement is written 2,6. A phosphorus atom with a proton number of 15 has 15 electrons, arranged 2,8,5. The electrons in the outer electron shell that are involved in chemical bonding are known as the **valency electrons**.

## Atom diagrams

The atomic structure of an atom can be shown simply in a diagram.

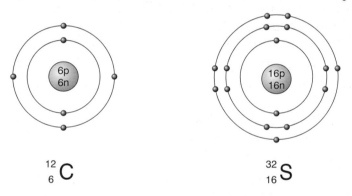

$$^{12}_{6}C \qquad\qquad ^{32}_{16}S$$

Δ Fig. 1.34 Atom diagrams for carbon and sulfur showing the numbers of protons and neutrons and the electron arrangements.

The arrangement of electrons in an atom is called its **electronic configuration**.

## Electronic configuration: The first 20 elements of the Periodic Table

There are over 100 different elements. They are arranged in the Periodic Table according to their chemical and physical properties.

The chemical properties of elements depend on the arrangement of electrons in their atoms. The electronic structure of the first 20 elements is shown in Table 1.6.

| Element | Symbol | Proton number | Electron number | Electronic configuration |
|---|---|---|---|---|
| Hydrogen | H | 1 | 1 | 1 |
| Helium | He | 2 | 2 | 2 |
| Lithium | Li | 3 | 3 | 2,1 |
| Beryllium | Be | 4 | 4 | 2,2 |
| Boron | B | 5 | 5 | 2,3 |
| Carbon | C | 6 | 6 | 2,4 |
| Nitrogen | N | 7 | 7 | 2,5 |
| Oxygen | O | 8 | 8 | 2,6 |
| Fluorine | F | 9 | 9 | 2,7 |
| Neon | Ne | 10 | 10 | 2,8 |
| Sodium | Na | 11 | 11 | 2,8,1 |
| Magnesium | Mg | 12 | 12 | 2,8,2 |
| Aluminium | Al | 13 | 13 | 2,8,3 |
| Silicon | Si | 14 | 14 | 2,8,4 |
| Phosphorus | P | 15 | 15 | 2,8,5 |
| Sulfur | S | 16 | 16 | 2,8,6 |
| Chlorine | Cl | 17 | 17 | 2,8,7 |
| Argon | Ar | 18 | 18 | 2,8,8 |
| Potassium | K | 19 | 19 | 2,8,8,1 |
| Calcium | Ca | 20 | 20 | 2,8,8,2 |

△ Table 1.6 Electronic structure of first 20 elements.

## Periodicity and electronic configuration

In the Periodic Table lithium, sodium and potassium are placed on the left, and neon and argon are placed on the right. The proton number increases from lithium to neon, moving through a section, or **period,** of the Periodic Table. The number of electrons in the outer shell increases. This is called **periodicity**.

## ELECTRONIC CONFIGURATION AND CHEMICAL PROPERTIES

Elements that have similar electronic configurations have similar chemical properties.

Lithium (2,1), sodium (2,8,1) and potassium (2,8,8,1) all have one electron in their outer shell. These are all highly reactive metals. They are called Group I elements.

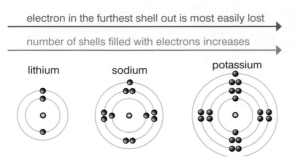

△ Fig. 1.35 Electronic configurations of lithium, sodium and potassium.

Fluorine (2,7), chlorine (2,8,7), bromine (2,8,18,7) and iodine (2,8,18,18,7) all have seven electrons in their outer shell. These elements are all highly reactive non-metals. They are called Group VII elements, or halogens.

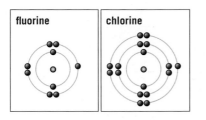

△ Fig. 1.36 Electronic configuration of fluorine and chlorine.

Similarly, all the elements in Group III of the Periodic Table have three electrons in their outer electron shell.

The elements helium (2), neon (2,8), argon (2,8,8), krypton (2,8,18,8) and xenon (2,8,18,18,8) either have a full outer shell or have eight electrons in their outer shell and therefore the atoms do not lose or gain electrons easily. This means that these gases are unreactive. They are called **noble gases**.

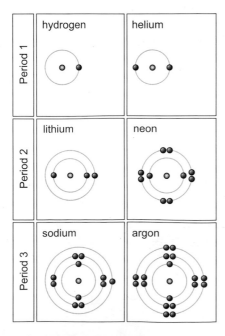

△ Fig. 1.37 Electronic configurations of helium, neon and argon.

△ Fig. 1.38 Neon lighting in Hong Kong.

1. **a)** How many electrons does magnesium have in its outer electron shell?

   **b)** Which group of the Periodic Table is magnesium in?

2. Draw atom diagrams for:

   **a)** aluminium

   **b)** calcium.

3. Why are noble gases unreactive?

## THE STRUCTURE OF MATTER

All matter can be classified into the three categories of elements, mixtures and compounds. As you have seen, the elements can be ordered in the Periodic Table. You will be learning how elements combine together to form compounds in the next two topics.

A **mixture** contains more than one substance (elements or compounds). In a mixture, the individual substances can be separated by simple means. This is because the substances in a mixture have not combined chemically.

Most elements can be classified as either **metals** or **non-metals**. In the Periodic Table, the metals are arranged on the left and in the middle, and the non-metals are on the right.

△ Fig. 1.39 Non-metals: from left: silicon, chlorine, sulfur.

Metals and non-metals have quite different physical and chemical properties.

Good conductors of electricity

High melting points

Good conductors of heat

**Typical properties of metals**

Shiny

**Malleable** can be hammered into shape

**Ductile** can be drawn into a wire

**Sonorous** ring when struck

*Exceptions:*
• The alkali metals have low melting points and are not sonorous.
• Mercury has a low melting point.

△ Fig. 1.40 Typical properties of metals.

Poor conductors of electricity

Low melting points

Poor conductors of heat

**Typical properties of non-metals**

Brittle

Dull

*Exceptions*
- Carbon in the form of graphite is a good conductor of electricity.
- Carbon and silicon have high melting points.

△ Fig.1.41 Typical properties of non-metals.

An **alloy** is formed when a metal is mixed with other elements. Common examples are:

| Alloy | Constituents |
|-------|--------------|
| Brass | Copper (70%), zinc (30%) |
| Bronze | Copper (90%), tin (10%) |
| Steel | Iron and small amounts of carbon |
| Solder | Tin (50%), lead (50%) |

△ Table 1.7 Common alloys.

## QUESTIONS

**1.** What is the difference between a *mixture* and a *compound*?

**2.** Metals are often *malleable*. What does this mean?

**3. a)** What is an *alloy*?

**b)** What elements are contained in the alloy brass?

# End of topic checklist

## Key terms

alloy, compound, electron, electronic configuration, isotopes, metal, mixture, neutron, noble gases, non-metal, nucleon number (mass number), nucleus, period, periodicity, proton, proton number (atomic number), radioactive, shell

## During your study of this topic you should have learned:

○ About the relative charges and approximate relative masses of protons, neutrons and electrons.

○ How to define *proton number* (atomic number) and *nucleon number* (mass number).

○ How to use proton numbers and the simple structure of atoms to explain the basis of the Periodic Table, with special reference to the elements with proton numbers 1 to 20.

○ That the arrangement of electrons in an atom can be worked out from the atom's position in the Periodic Table.

○ To describe the build-up of electrons in 'shells' and understand the significance of the noble gas electronic structures and of valency or outer electrons.

○ How to define *isotopes*.

○ **EXTENDED** Understand that isotopes have the same properties because they have the same number of electrons in their outer shell.

○ That the two types of isotope are *radioactive* and *non-radioactive*.

○ About one medical and one industrial use of radioactive isotopes.

○ How to describe the build-up of electrons in 'shells' and understand the significance of the noble gas electronic structures and of valency electrons.

○ About the differences between elements, mixtures and compounds, and between metals and non-metals.

○ That an alloy, such as brass, is a mixture of a metal with other elements.

# End of topic questions

*Note: The marks awarded for these questions indicate the level of detail required in the answers. In the examination, the number of marks awarded to questions like these may be different.*

1. What is the relative mass of a proton? (1 mark)

2. Explain the meaning of:

   **a)** *proton number* (atomic number) (1 mark)

   **b)** *nucleon number* (mass number). (1 mark)

3. Chlorine has two common isotopes, chlorine-35 and chlorine-37.

   **a)** What is an *isotope*? (1 mark)

   **b)** What are the numbers of protons, neutrons and electrons in each isotope? (2 marks)

4. Some isotopes are *radioactive*.

   **a)** Give one medical use of a radioactive isotope. (1 mark)

   **b)** Give one industrial use of a radioactive isotope. (1 mark)

5. Copy and complete the table. (4 marks)

| Atom | Number of protons | Number of neutrons | Number of electrons | Electron arrangement |
|---|---|---|---|---|
| $^{28}_{14}$Si | | | | |
| $^{24}_{12}$Mg | | | | |
| $^{32}_{16}$S | | | | |
| $^{40}_{18}$Ar | | | | |

# End of topic questions continued

**6.** The table shows information about the structure of six particles (A–F).

| Particle | Protons | Neutrons | Electrons |
|---|---|---|---|
| A | 8 | 8 | 10 |
| B | 12 | 12 | 10 |
| C | 6 | 6 | 6 |
| D | 8 | 10 | 10 |
| E | 6 | 8 | 6 |
| F | 11 | 12 | 11 |

**a)** In each of questions i) to v), choose one of the six particles A–F. Each letter may be used once, more than once or not at all.

Choose a particle that:

**i)** has a nucleon number of 12          **(1 mark)**

**ii)** has the highest nucleon number          **(1 mark)**

**iii)** has no overall charge          **(1 mark)**

**iv)** has an overall positive charge          **(1 mark)**

**v)** is the same element as particle E.          **(1 mark)**

**b)** Draw an atom diagram for particle E.          **(2 marks)**

**7.** Draw an atom diagram for:

**a)** oxygen          **(2 marks)**

**b)** potassium.          **(2 marks)**

**8.** For each of parts a) to d) say whether the statement is TRUE or FALSE.

There is a relationship between the group number of the first 20 elements in the Periodic Table and:

**a)** the number of protons in an atom of the element          **(1 mark)**

**b)** the number of neutrons in an atom of the element          **(1 mark)**

**c)** the number of electrons in an atom of the element          **(1 mark)**

**d)** the number of electrons in the outer electron shell of the element.          **(1 mark)**

**9.** **EXTENDED** There are two common isotopes of chlorine, chlorine-35 and chlorine-37. Explain why these different isotopes have exactly the same chemical properties.          **(2 marks)**

# Ions and ionic bonds

## INTRODUCTION

When the atoms of elements react and join together, they form compounds. When one of the reacting atoms is a metal, the compound formed is called an ionic compound. They do not contain molecules; instead they are made of particles called ions. Ionic compounds have similar physical properties, many of which are quite different from the properties of substances made up of atoms or molecules.

△ Fig. 1.42 Sodium chloride is an example of an ionic compound.

## KNOWLEDGE CHECK

✓ Understand that compounds are formed when the atoms of two or more elements combine together.
✓ Know that protons have a positive charge and are found in the nucleus of the atom.
✓ Know that electrons have a negative charge and are found in shells around the nucleus.
✓ Know that the number of outer electrons in an atom depends on its group in the Periodic Table.

## LEARNING OBJECTIVES

✓ Be able to describe the formation of ions by electron loss or gain.
✓ Be able to describe the formation of ionic bonds between elements from Groups I and VII.
✓ **EXTENDED** Be able to describe the formation of ionic bonds between metallic and non-metallic elements.
✓ **EXTENDED** Be able to describe the lattice structure of ionic compounds as a regular arrangement of alternating positive and negative ions.

## THE FORMATION OF IONS

Atoms bond with other atoms in a **chemical reaction** to make a compound. For example, sodium reacts with chlorine to make sodium chloride. **Ionic compounds** contain a metal combined with one or more non-metals. They are not made up of molecules – they are made up of **ions**.

Ions are formed from atoms by the gain or loss of electrons. Both metals and non-metals try to achieve complete (filled) outer electron shells or the electron configuration of the nearest noble gas.

Metals lose electrons from their outer shells and form positive ions. Non-metals gain electrons in their outer shells and form negative ions.

The bonding process can be represented in dot and cross diagrams. Look at the reaction between sodium and chlorine as an example.

| | |
|---|---|
| Sodium is a metal. It has a proton number of 11 and so has 11 electrons, arranged 2,8,1. Its atom diagram looks like this: | Chlorine is a non-metal. It has a proton number of 17 and so has 17 electrons, arranged 2,8,7. Its atom diagram looks like this: |

△ Fig. 1.43 Dot and cross diagrams for sodium and chlorine.

| | |
|---|---|
| Sodium has one electron in its outer shell. It can achieve a full outer shell by losing this electron. The sodium atom transfers its outermost electron to the chlorine atom. | Chlorine has seven electrons in its outer shell. It can achieve a full outer shell by gaining an extra electron. The chlorine atom accepts an electron from the sodium. |

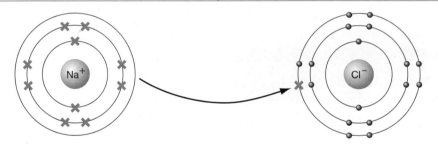

△ Fig. 1.44 Dot and cross diagram for sodium chloride, NaCl.

| | |
|---|---|
| The sodium is no longer an atom; it is now an ion. It does not have equal numbers of protons and electrons, so it is no longer neutral. It has one more proton than it has electrons, so it is a positive ion with a charge of 1+. The ion is written as $Na^+$. | The chlorine is no longer an atom; it is now an ion. It does not have equal numbers of protons and electrons, so it is no longer neutral. It has one more electron than it has protons, so it is a negative ion with a charge of 1−. The ion is written as $Cl^-$. |

## METALS CAN TRANSFER MORE THAN ONE ELECTRON TO A NON-METAL

Magnesium combines with oxygen to form magnesium oxide. The magnesium (electron arrangement 2,8,2) transfers two electrons to the oxygen (electron arrangement 2,6). Magnesium therefore forms an $Mg^{2+}$ ion and oxygen forms an $O^{2-}$ ion.

△ Fig. 1.45 Dot and cross diagram for magnesium oxide, MgO.

Aluminium has an electron arrangement 2,8,3. When it combines with fluorine with an electron arrangement 2,7, three fluorine atoms are needed for each aluminium atom. The formula of aluminium fluoride is therefore $AlF_3$.

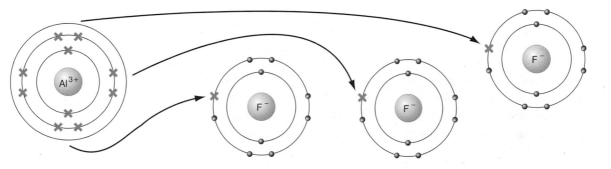

△ Fig. 1.46 Dot and cross diagram for aluminium fluoride, $AlF_3$.

### REMEMBER

Many students find it difficult to remember the difference between oxidation and reduction. In ionic bonding the atom that loses electrons is said to be *oxidised*. The atom that gains the electrons is said to be *reduced*. So, aluminium is oxidised and fluorine is reduced when aluminium fluoride is made.

### END OF EXTENDED

### QUESTIONS

1. Draw a dot and cross diagram to show how lithium and fluorine atoms combine to form lithium fluoride. You must show the starting atoms and the finishing ions. (Proton numbers: Li 3; F 9)

2. **EXTENDED** Draw a dot and cross diagram to show how calcium and sulfur atoms combine to form calcium sulfide. You must show the starting atoms and finishing ions. (Proton numbers: Ca 20; S 16)

3. **EXTENDED** How do you know that phosphorus oxide is not an ionic compound?

## ELECTRONIC CONFIGURATION AND IONIC CHARGE

When atoms form ions, they are trying to achieve the electronic configuration of their nearest noble gas. Some common ions and their electronic configurations are shown in Table 1.8.

| Ion | Electronic configuration |
|---|---|
| $Li^+$ | 2 |
| $Na^+$ | 2,8 |
| $Mg^{2+}$ | 2,8 |
| $F^-$ | 2,8 |
| $Cl^-$ | 2,8,8 |
| $O^{2-}$ | 2,8 |

△ Table 1.8 Electronic configurations of some ions.

**EXTENDED**

## PROPERTIES OF IONIC COMPOUNDS

Ionic compounds have high melting points and high boiling points because of strong electrostatic forces between the ions.

The strong electrostatic attraction between oppositely charged ions is called an **ionic bond**.

Ionic compounds form giant lattice structures. For example, when sodium chloride is formed by ionic bonding, the ions do not pair up. Each sodium ion is surrounded by six chloride ions, and each chloride ion is surrounded by six sodium ions.

The electrostatic attractions between the ions are very strong. The properties of sodium chloride can be explained using this model of its structure.

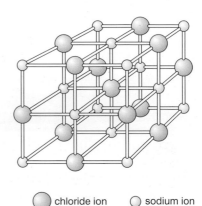

◯ chloride ion      ◯ sodium ion

△ Fig. 1.47 In solid sodium chloride, the ions are held firmly in place. All ionic compounds have giant ionic lattice structures like this.

△ Fig. 1.48 Crystals of sodium chloride.

| Properties of sodium chloride | Explanation in terms of structure |
|---|---|
| Hard crystals | Strong forces of attraction between the oppositely charged ions |
| High melting point (801 °C) | Strong forces of attraction between the oppositely charged ions |
| Dissolves in water | The water is also able to form strong electrostatic attractions with the ions – the ions are 'plucked' off the lattice structure |
| Does not conduct electricity when solid | Strong forces between the ions prevent them from moving |
| Conducts electricity when molten or dissolved in water | The strong forces between the ions have been broken down and so the ions are able to move |

△ Table 1.9 Properties of sodium chloride.

Magnesium oxide is another ionic compound. Its ionic formula is $Mg^{2+}O^{2-}$.

MgO has a much higher melting point and boiling point than NaCl because of the increased charges on the ions. The forces holding the ions together are stronger in MgO than in NaCl.

**END OF EXTENDED**

### SCIENCE IN CONTEXT **MAGNESIUM OXIDE**

Magnesium oxide is a very versatile compound. It is used extensively in the construction industry, both in making cement and in making fire-proof construction materials. The fact that it has a melting point of over 2800 °C makes it ideal for this use.

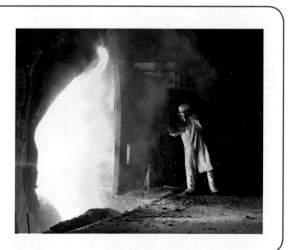

▷ Fig. 1.49 The heat resistance of magnesium oxide means that it is used to line furnaces.

## IONIC CRYSTALS

△ Fig. 1.50 Gemstones are examples of ionic crystals.

All ionic compounds form giant structures, and all have relatively high melting and boiling points. The charges on the ions determine the strength of the electrostatic attraction between the ions, and hence the melting and boiling points of the compound compared to others.

Another factor that affects the strength of the electrostatic attraction is the relative sizes of the positive and negative ions and how well they are able to pack together. The overall arrangement of the ions is determined by attractive forces between oppositely charged ions and repulsive forces between similarly charged ions. In sodium chloride, for example, six chloride ions fit around one sodium ion without the chloride ions getting too close together and repelling one another. Similarly, six sodium ions can fit around one chloride ion. This structure is sometimes called a 6:6 lattice (see Fig. 4.16 for a diagram of this structure).

Caesium is a metal in the same group of the Periodic Table as sodium, but caesium ions are much bigger than sodium ions. In the structure of caesium chloride, eight chloride ions can fit around each caesium ion. So although sodium and caesium are in the same group, their chlorides have different structures.

Some of the most valuable gemstones are ionic compounds. Rubies and sapphires, for example, are both aluminium oxide. The different colours of the gemstones are due to traces of other metals such as iron, titanium and chromium.

## QUESTIONS

1. **EXTENDED** Why does an ionic compound such as magnesium oxide not conduct electricity when it is solid?

2. **EXTENDED** Suggest a reason why magnesium oxide has a higher melting point than sodium chloride.

# End of topic checklist

## Key terms

chemical reaction, ion, ionic bond, ionic compound

## During your study of this topic you should have learned:

○ How to describe the formation of ions by electron loss or gain.

○ How to describe the formation of ionic bonds between elements from Groups I and VII.

○ **EXTENDED** How to describe the formation of ionic bonds between metallic and non-metallic elements.

○ **EXTENDED** How to describe the lattice structure of ionic compounds as a regular arrangement of alternating positive and negative ions.

# End of topic questions

*Note: The marks awarded for these questions indicate the level of detail required in the answers. In the examination, the number of marks awarded to questions like these may be different.*

1. For each of the following reactions, say whether the compound formed is ionic or not:

    **a)** hydrogen and chlorine (1 mark)

    **b)** carbon and hydrogen (1 mark)

    **c)** sodium and oxygen (1 mark)

    **d)** chlorine and oxygen (1 mark)

    **e)** calcium and bromine. (1 mark)

2. Write down the formulae of the ions formed by the following elements:

    **a)** potassium (1 mark)

    **b)** aluminium (1 mark)

    **c)** sulfur (1 mark)

    **d)** fluorine. (1 mark)

3. The table below shows the electronic arrangement of three atoms, X, Y and Z. Copy and complete the table to show the electronic arrangements and charges of the ions these atoms will form. **(3 marks)**

| Atom | Electronic arrangement of the atom | Electronic arrangement of the ion | Charge on the ion |
|------|------------------------------------|-----------------------------------|-------------------|
| X | 2,6 | | |
| Y | 2,8,8,2 | | |
| Z | 2,1 | | |

4. **EXTENDED** Draw dot and cross diagrams to show how the following atoms combine to form ionic compounds. (You must show the electronic arrangements of the starting atoms and the finishing ions.)

    **a)** potassium and oxygen (proton numbers: K 19; O 8) (2 marks)

    **b)** magnesium and chlorine (proton numbers: Mg 12; Cl 17) (2 marks)

5. **EXTENDED** Explain why an ionic substance such as potassium chloride:

    **a)** has a high melting point (2 marks)

    **b)** can conduct electricity. (2 marks)

6. **EXTENDED** Explain why magnesium oxide has a higher melting point and boiling point than sodium chloride. (2 marks)

# Molecules and covalent bonds

## INTRODUCTION

Unlike ionic compounds, covalent substances are formed when atoms of non-metals combine. Although covalent substances all contain the same type of bond, their properties can be quite different – some are gases, others are very hard solids with high melting points. Plastics are a common type of covalent substance. Because chemists now understand how the molecules form and link together, they can produce plastics with almost the perfect properties for a particular use, from soft and flexible (as in contact lenses) to hard and rigid (as in electrical sockets).

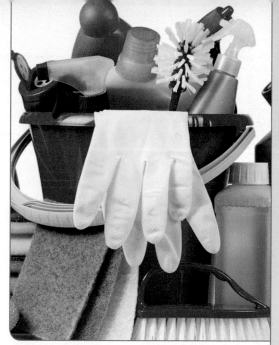

△ Fig. 1.51 All plastics are covalent substances.

## KNOWLEDGE CHECK

✓ Understand that molecules are made up of two or more atoms combined together.
✓ Know what is meant by proton number.
✓ Know that electrons are found in shells around the nucleus of an atom.
✓ Know that an element's group in the Periodic Table is governed by the number of electrons in the outer shell of the atom.

## LEARNING OBJECTIVES

✓ Be able to describe the formation of single covalent bonds in $NH_3$, $H_2$, $Cl_2$, $H_2O$, $CH_4$ and HCl as the sharing of pairs of electrons leading to the noble gas configuration.
✓ Be able to describe the differences in volatility, solubility and electrical conductivity between ionic and covalent compounds.
✓ **EXTENDED** Be able to describe the electron arrangement in more complex covalent molecules such as $N_2$, $C_2H_4$, $CH_3OH$ and $CO_2$.
✓ **EXTENDED** Be able to explain the differences in melting point and boiling point of ionic and covalent compounds in terms of intermolecular forces.
✓ Be able to describe the giant covalent structures of graphite and diamond.
✓ Be able to relate their structures to the use of graphite as a lubricant and of diamond in cutting.
✓ **EXTENDED** Be able to describe the macromolecular structure of silicon(IV) oxide (silicon dioxide).
✓ **EXTENDED** Be able to describe the similarity in properties between diamond and silicon(IV) oxide, related to their structures.

# HOW COVALENT BONDS ARE FORMED

Covalent bonding involves electron sharing and occurs between atoms of non-metals. It results in the formation of a **molecule**.

The non-metal atoms try to achieve complete outer electron shells or the electron arrangement of the nearest noble gas by sharing electrons.

A single **covalent bond** is formed when two atoms each contribute one electron to a shared pair of electrons. For example, hydrogen gas exists as $H_2$ molecules. Each hydrogen atom needs to fill its electron shell. They can do this by sharing electrons.

represented as

H—H

△ Fig. 1.52 The dot and cross diagram and displayed formula of $H_2$.

A covalent bond is the result of attraction between the bonding pair of electrons (negative charges) and the nuclei (positive charges) of the atoms involved in the bond. A single covalent bond can be represented by a single line. The formula of a hydrogen molecule can be written as a displayed formula, H—H. The hydrogen atoms and oxygen atoms in water are also held together by single covalent bonds.

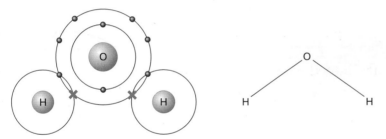

△ Fig. 1.53 Water contains single covalent bonds.

The hydrogen and carbon atoms in methane are held together by single covalent bonds.

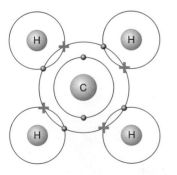

△ Fig. 1.54 Methane contains four single covalent bonds.

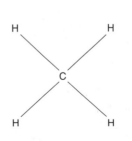

△ Fig. 1.55 The displayed formula for methane.

The hydrogen chloride molecule, HCl, is also held together by a single covalent bond.

H—Cl

△ Fig. 1.56 Hydrogen chloride has a single covalent bond.

Ethane has a slightly more complex electron arrangement.

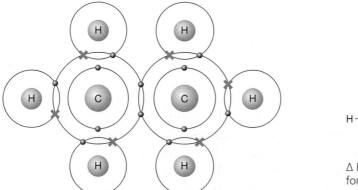

△ Fig. 1.57 Covalent bonds in ethane.

△ Fig. 1.58 Displayed formula for ethane.

The alcohol methanol is covalently bonded as shown in Fig. 1.59.

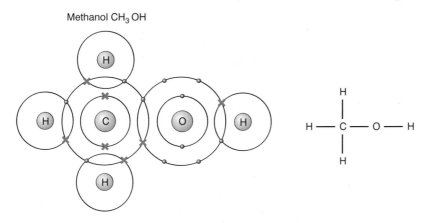

△ Fig. 1.59 Covalent bonds in methanol.

Some molecules contain double covalent bonds. In carbon dioxide, the carbon atom has an electron arrangement of 2,4 and needs an additional four electrons to complete its outer electron shell. It needs to share its four electrons with four electrons from oxygen atoms (electron arrangement 2,6). So two oxygen atoms are needed, each sharing two electrons with the carbon atom. $(C_2H_4)$

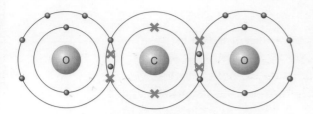

$$O = C = O$$

△ Fig. 1.60 Carbon dioxide contains double bonds.

△ Fig. 1.61 Ethene contains a double bond.

Some molecules contain triple covalent bonds. In the nitrogen molecule, each nitrogen atom has an electron arrangement of 2,5 and needs an additional three electrons to complete its outer electron shell. It needs to share three of its outer electrons with another nitrogen atom. This forms a triple bond, which is shown as N≡N.

◁ Fig. 1.62 A nitrogen molecule contains a triple bond.

**END OF EXTENDED**

## QUESTIONS

1. Draw a dot cross diagram and displayed formula to show how the covalent bonds are formed in chlorine gas ($Cl_2$). The proton number of chlorine is 17.

2. **EXTENDED** Draw a dot and cross diagram and displayed formula to show how the covalent bonds are formed in the gas ammonia ($NH_3$). The proton number of hydrogen is 1; the proton number of nitrogen is 7.

3. **EXTENDED** Draw a dot and cross diagram and displayed formula to show the double bond in an oxygen molecule ($O_2$). The proton number of oxygen is 8.

4. **EXTENDED** Draw a dot and cross diagram and displayed formula to show the covalent bonds in ethene ($C_2H_4$). The proton number of hydrogen is 1; the proton number of carbon is 6.

5. **EXTENDED** Draw a dot and cross diagram and displayed formula to show the covalent bonds in hydrazine ($N_2H_4$). The proton number of hydrogen is 1; the proton number of nitrogen is 7.

## HOW MANY COVALENT BONDS CAN AN ELEMENT FORM?

The number of covalent bonds a non-metal atom can form is linked to its position in the Periodic Table. Metals (Groups I, II, III) do not form covalent bonds. The noble gases in Group 0, for example helium, neon and argon, are unreactive and also do not usually form covalent bonds.

| Group in the Periodic Table | I | II | III | IV | V | VI | VII | O |
|---|---|---|---|---|---|---|---|---|
| Covalent bonds formed | – | – | – | 4 | 3 | 2 | 1 | – |

△ Table 1.10 Group number and number of covalent bonds formed.

## MOLECULAR CRYSTALS

Covalent compounds can form simple molecular crystals. Many covalent crystals exist only in the solid form at low temperatures. Some simple molecular crystals are ice, solid carbon dioxide and iodine.

EXTENDED

## PROPERTIES OF COVALENT COMPOUNDS

Substances with molecular structures are usually gases, liquids or solids with low melting points and boiling points.

Covalent bonds are strong bonds. They are **intramolecular** bonds – formed *within* each molecule. Much weaker **intermolecular** forces attract the individual molecules to each other.

The properties of covalent compounds can be explained using a simple model involving these two types of bond or forces.

| Properties of hydrogen | Explanation in terms of structure |
|---|---|
| Hydrogen is a gas with a very low melting point (−259 °C). | The intermolecular forces of attraction between the molecules are weak. |
| Hydrogen does not conduct electricity. | There are no ions or free electrons present. The covalent bond (intramolecular bond) is a strong bond and the electrons cannot be removed from it easily. |

△ Table 1.11 Properties of hydrogen.

△ Fig. 1.63 Force in and between hydrogen molecules.

END OF EXTENDED

## COMPARING THE PROPERTIES OF COVALENT AND IONIC COMPOUNDS

Simple covalent compounds typically have very different properties to ionic compounds. A comparison can be seen in Table 1.12. The volatility of a compound is a measure of how easily it forms a vapour. Compounds with low melting and boiling points are often described as being **volatile.**

| Property | Ionic compounds | Simple covalent compounds |
|---|---|---|
| Volatility | Non-volatile (high melting and boiling points) | Volatile (low melting and boiling points) |
| Solubility | Often soluble in water | Mostly insoluble in water |
| Electrical conductivity | Conduct electricity only when dissolved in water or molten (the ions separate and are free to move, carrying their electric charge) | Low electrical conductivity – are non-electrolytes (do not contain ions and so cannot carry an electrical current; however, some covalent compounds do form ions when dissolved in water) |

△ Table 1.12 Comparison of simple covalent compounds with ionic compounds.

**EXTENDED**

| Type of compound | Intermolecular force | Property |
|---|---|---|
| Ionic | Strong | High melting and boiling points |
| Simple covalent | Weak | Low melting and boiling points |

**END OF EXTENDED**

## QUESTIONS

1. EXTENDED Why does a covalently bonded compound such as carbon dioxide have a relatively low melting point?

2. Would you expect a covalently bonded compound such as ethanol to conduct electricity? Explain your answer.

# MACROMOLECULES

## Diamond and graphite

Some covalently bonded compounds do not exist as simple molecular structures in the way that hydrogen does. Diamond, for example, has a giant structure with each carbon atom covalently bonded to four others (Fig. 1.65). Another form of carbon is graphite. Graphite has a different giant structure, as seen in Fig. 1.66. Different forms of the same element, like these, are called **allotropes**. In diamond, each carbon atom forms four strong covalent bonds. In graphite, each carbon atom forms three strong covalent bonds. There are weak forces of attraction between the layers in graphite (Fig.1.66).

Δ Fig. 1.64 A cut diamond is one of the hardest substances in nature.

—— strong bond

Δ Fig. 1.65 Structure of diamond.

------ Structure of graphite

Δ Fig. 1.66 Graphite is made of the same atoms as diamond but with a different molecular structure.

In diamond, all the bonding is extremely strong, which makes diamond an extremely hard substance – one of the hardest natural substances known. This is why diamonds are used in cutting.

In graphite, carbon atoms form layers of hexagons in the plane of their strong covalent bonds. The weak forces of attraction are between the layers. Because the layers can slide over each other, graphite is flaky and can be used as a lubricant. Graphite can also conduct electricity, because the fourth unbonded electron from each carbon atom is **delocalised** and so can move along the layer.

The atoms in both diamond and graphite are held together by strong covalent bonds, which result in very high sublimation or melting points. Diamond has a melting point of about 3730 °C.

## DIAMONDS

Diamond is the hardest naturally occurring material in the world. It is formed by high pressures and high temperatures deep underground. Volcanic eruptions often bring the diamonds closer to the surface, where they can be mined. In some cases diamonds can be mined almost on the surface of the land, whereas in other cases tunnels need to be dug deep into the ground. Diamonds are mined throughout Africa. The ore is called kimberlite, and diamonds are found in kimberlite gravels and pipe formations.

After mining, the ore is crushed, washed and screened by X-rays to find the diamonds. Finally the diamonds are sorted by hand, then washed and classified for sale. Diamond mining and recovery is a very clean operation. Processing of the ore uses no toxic chemicals and produces no chemical pollutants. However, getting the diamonds from deep in the ground can be very dangerous for the miners.

△ Fig. 1.67 This saw has diamonds on its cutting edges.

The quality of diamonds used in jewellery is judged in terms of the four Cs: carat weight, colour, clarity (how transparent the diamond is and how well it reflects light) and cut (the shape of the diamond). One carat is 0.2 g. Although the carat weight is the most important, prices can vary widely depending on the other three factors. In 2009 the largest producers were Russia and Botswana, each producing about 32 million carats of uncut diamonds. In the same year the world demand for diamonds was estimated at 39 billion dollars. Diamonds are clearly big business!

△ Fig. 1.68 An open cast diamond mine in Yakutia, Russia.

## Silicon(IV) oxide

Silicon(IV) oxide (silicon dioxide, $SiO_2$) is another giant covalent molecule. It is the main component of sand.

△ Fig. 1.69 The structure of silicon(IV) oxide.

You can see from its structure that every silicon atom has four covalent bonds. The structure is similar to the diamond structure in Fig. 1.65, which is why silicon(IV) oxide has a high melting point and is hard like diamond.

Structures can usually be identified as being 'giant' or 'molecular' from their melting points.

| Structure | Atom | Molecule | Ion |
|---|---|---|---|
| Giant | Diamond, graphite and metals have high melting points | Sand (silicon(IV) oxide) have high melting points | All ionic compounds such as sodium chloride high melting points |
| Simple molecular | Noble gases such as helium low melting points | Carbon dioxide, water low melting points | None |

△ Table 1.13 Giant structures have higher melting points than simple molecular structures.

## QUESTIONS

**1.** Explain why diamond has a very high melting point.

**2.** How is the structure of graphite different from that of diamond?

# End of topic checklist

## Key terms

allotropes, covalent bond, delocalised electrons, molecule, intermolecular, intramolecular, volatile

## During your study of this topic you should have learned:

○ How to describe the formation of single covalent bonds in $NH_3$, $H_2$, $Cl_2$, $H_2O$, $CH_4$ and HCl as the sharing of pairs of electrons leading to the noble gas configuration.

○ How to describe the differences in volatility, solubility and electrical conductivity between ionic and covalent compounds.

○ **EXTENDED** How to describe the electron arrangements in more complex covalent molecules such as $N_2$, $C_2H_4$, $CH_3OH$ and $CO_2$.

○ **EXTENDED** How to explain the difference in melting point and boiling point of ionic and covalent compounds in terms of intermolecular forces.

○ How to describe the giant covalent structures of graphite and diamond.

○ How to relate their structures to the use of graphite as a lubricant and of diamond in cutting.

○ **EXTENDED** How to describe the macromolecular structure of silicon(IV) oxide (silicon dioxide).

○ **EXTENDED** How to describe the similarities in properties between diamond and silicon(IV) oxide, related to their structures.

# End of topic questions

*Note: The marks awarded for these questions indicate the level of detail required in the answers. In the examination, the number of marks awarded to questions like these may be different.*

1. Draw dot and cross diagrams to show the bonding in the following compounds:

   **a)** hydrogen fluoride, HF                                          **(2 marks)**

   **b)** carbon disulfide, $CS_2$                                       **(2 marks)**

   **c)** ethanol, $C_2H_5OH$.                                       **(2 marks)**

2. Candle wax is a covalently bonded compound. Explain why candle wax has a relatively low melting point.           **(2 marks)**

3. Ozone ($O_3$) is a gas found in the Earth's atmosphere. How do you know that ozone is covalently bonded and not ionically bonded?     **(2 marks)**

4. **EXTENDED** Explain why methane ($CH_4$), which has strong covalent bonds between the carbon atom and the hydrogen atoms, is a gas at room temperature and pressure and has a very low melting point.     **(2 marks)**

5. **EXTENDED** Substance X has a simple molecular structure.

   **a)** In which state(s) of matter might you expect it to exist in at room temperature and pressure? Explain your answer.     **(2 marks)**

   **b)** How would you expect the boiling point of X to compare with the boiling point of an ionic compound such as sodium chloride? Explain your answer.     **(2 marks)**

6. Use the structure of graphite to explain:

   **a)** how carbon fibres can add strength to tennis racquets.     **(2 marks)**

   **b)** how graphite conducts electricity.     **(2 marks)**

7. **a)** Diamond is probably the hardest naturally occurring material in the world. Explain this by referring to the structure of diamond.     **(2 marks)**

   **b)** Apart from jewellery, name another use of diamond.     **(1 mark)**

# Metallic bonding

## INTRODUCTION

The structure of a metal contains an orderly arrangement of atoms and can form crystals. The bonding in metals is different from that in ionic or covalent substances. As with ionic and covalent substances, the nature of the bonding in metals gives them their characteristic properties.

△ Fig. 1.70 Copper atoms are held together by strong metallic bonds and form a giant structure.

## KNOWLEDGE CHECK

✓ Understand the structure and arrangement of protons, neutrons and electrons in an atoms.
✓ Be familiar with some of the characteristic properties of metals.

## LEARNING OBJECTIVES

✓ **EXTENDED** Be able to describe metallic bonding as a lattice of positive ions in a 'sea of electrons' and use this to describe the electrical conductivity and malleability of metals.

## EXTENDED

### THE STRUCTURE OF METALS

Metals are giant structures with high melting and boiling points.

Metal atoms give up one or more of their electrons to form positive ions called **cations**. The electrons they give up form a 'sea of electrons' surrounding the positive metal ions, and the negative electrons are attracted to the positive ions holding the structure together.

The electrons are free to move through the whole structure. The electrons are **delocalised**, meaning they are not fixed in one position.

## The properties of metals

Metals are shiny, **malleable** (can be hammered into a sheet), **ductile** (can be drawn or pulled into a wire), good **conductors** of electricity and good conductors of heat.

Metals are good conductors because their delocalised electrons are free to move through the structure. When a metal is in an electric circuit, electrons can move toward the positive terminal and the negative terminal can supply electrons to the metal.

Metals are malleable and ductile because metallic bonds are not as rigid as the bonds in diamond, for example, although they are still very strong. So the ions in the metal can move around into different positions when the metal is hammered or worked.

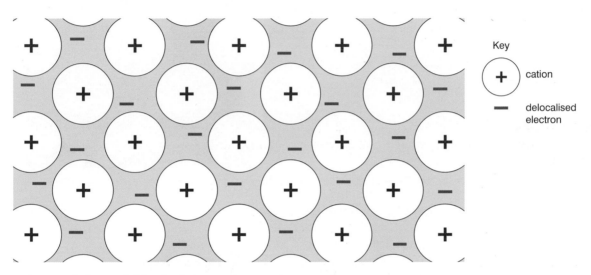

Key

+ cation

− delocalised electron

△ Fig. 1.71 Cations and delocalised electrons in a metal.

## QUESTIONS

1. What is a cation?

2. Why are metals good conductors of electricity?

3. What happens to a metal when you bend it?

**END OF EXTENDED**

## FACTS ABOUT METALS

1. The use of metals can be traced back to about 7000 years ago. An archaeological site in Serbia has evidence of the extraction of copper about that time, and gold artefacts dating to about 1000 years later have been found at a burial site at Varna in Bulgaria. In the period up to 2700 years ago, seven metals were known and used. These so-called 'metals of antiquity' were gold, copper, silver, lead, tin, iron and mercury. Of these gold, silver, copper, iron and mercury were found in their native state – that is, as pure elements. (Iron as a pure metal is found only in meteors.)

2. Mercury is the only liquid metal at normal room temperature and pressure.

3. The most reactive metals are found in Group I of the Periodic Table and include sodium and potassium.

4. Many of the metals used in construction are found in the middle of the Periodic Table and are called the transition metals.

△ Fig. 1.72 The Burj Khalifa building in Dubai.

5. Most of the metallic structures around us are not made from pure metals but from alloys. Alloys are mixtures of metals or occasionally mixtures of metals and non-metals: for example, steel is an alloy of iron and carbon. 39,000 tonnes of steel were used in building the Burj Khalifa building in Dubai (the world's tallest skyscraper at 828 metres). Alloys allow the properties of a metal to be modified for a particular purpose. For instance, aluminium is useful in building aircraft because it has a low density, but alloying it with other metals increases its strength. Bronze, an alloy of copper and tin, was the first alloy invented.

6. Some elements have the properties of both metals and non-metals. They are called **metalloids**. One of the most common metalloids is silicon.

# End of topic checklist

**Key terms**

cation, conductor, delocalised, ductile, malleable, metalloids

**During your study of this topic you should have learned:**

⭕ **EXTENDED** How to describe metallic bonding as a lattice of positive ions in a 'sea of electrons' and use this to describe the electrical conductivity and malleability of metals.

# End of topic questions

*Note: The marks awarded for these questions indicate the level of detail required in the answers. In the examination, the number of marks awarded to questions like these may be different.*

1. **EXTENDED** Describe the structure of a metal. **(2 marks)**

2. **EXTENDED** Use your knowledge of the structure of a metal to explain why metals:

   **a)** conduct electricity **(2 marks)**

   **b)** can be beaten into sheets (they are malleable). **(2 marks)**

3. **EXTENDED** Graphite can conduct electricity in only one plane, but metals can conduct in all planes. Explain why this is so. **(3 marks)**

4. Use the information in the table to answer the questions that follow.

| Substance | Melting point (°C) | Boiling point (°C) | Electrical conductivity | |
|-----------|--------------------|--------------------|-------------------------|---|
| | | | Solid | Molten |
| A | 751 | 1244 | Poor | Good |
| B | −50 | 148 | Poor | Poor |
| C | 630 | 1330 | Good | Good |
| D | 247 | 696 | Poor | Poor |

Which substance:

   **a)** is a metal? **(1 mark)**

   **b)** contains ionic bonds? **(1 mark)**

   **c)** has a giant covalent structure? **(1 mark)**

   **d)** has a simple molecular structure? **(1 mark)**

5. **a)** What is an *alloy*? **(1 mark)**

   **b)** What advantages do alloys often have over pure metals? **(2 marks)**

# Stoichiometry

## INTRODUCTION

Stoichiometry is the branch of chemistry concerned with the relative quantities of reactants and products in a chemical reaction. A study of stoichiometry depends on balanced chemical equations which, in turn, depend on knowledge of the chemical symbols for the elements and the formulae of chemical compounds. This topic starts by considering how simple chemical formulae are written and then looks in detail at chemical equations. The topic then focuses on how chemical equations can be used to work out how much reactant is needed to make a certain amount of product.

△ Fig. 1.73 When this reaction is described as $S(s) + O_2(g) \rightarrow SO_2(g)$, it is understood by chemists all over the world.

## KNOWLEDGE CHECK

✓ Know that elements are made up of atoms.
✓ Know that compounds are formed when atoms combine together.
✓ Know that molecules are formed in covalent bonding and that ions are formed in ionic bonding.

## LEARNING OBJECTIVES

✓ Be able to use the symbols of the elements and write the formulae of simple compounds.
✓ Be able to deduce the formula of a simple compound from the relative number of atoms present.
✓ Be able to deduce the formula of a simple compound from a model or a diagrammatic representation.
✓ Be able to construct word equations and simple balanced chemical equations.
✓ Be able to define relative atomic mass ($A_r$) as the average mass of naturally occurring atoms of an element on a scale where the $^{12}C$ atom has a mass of exactly 12 units.
✓ Be able to define relative molecular mass ($M_r$) as the sum of the relative atomic masses.
✓ Know that relative formula mass ($M_r$) is used for ionic compounds.
✓ Be able to use simple proportion to work out reacting masses.
✓ **EXTENDED** Be able to determine the formula of an ionic compound from the charges on the ions present.
✓ **EXTENDED** Be able to construct equations with state symbols, including ionic equations.
✓ **EXTENDED** Be able to deduce the balanced equation for a chemical reaction, given relevant information.

✓ **EXTENDED** Be able to define the mole and the Avogadro constant.

✓ **EXTENDED** Be able to use the molar gas volume (24 dm³ at room temperature and pressure).

✓ **EXTENDED** Be able to calculate stoichiometric reacting masses, and volumes of gases and solutions.

✓ **EXTENDED** Know that solution concentrations are expressed in g/dm³ and mol/dm³.

✓ **EXTENDED** Be able to calculate empirical formulae and molecular formulae.

✓ **EXTENDED** Be able to calculate percentage yield and percentage purity.

## HOW ARE CHEMICAL FORMULAE WRITTEN?

When elements chemically combine, they form compounds. A compound can be represented by a **chemical formula**.

All substances are made up from simple building blocks called elements. Each element has a unique **chemical symbol**, containing one or two letters. Elements discovered a long time ago often have symbols that don't seem to match their name. For example, silver has the chemical symbol Ag. This is derived from *argentum*, the Latin name for silver.

## 'COMBINING POWERS' OF ELEMENTS

There are a number of ways of working out chemical formulae. In this topic you will start with the idea of a 'combining power' for each element and then look at how the charges on ions can be used for ionic compounds. Later in the course you will be introduced to oxidation states and how these can be used to work out chemical formulae.

There is a simple relationship between an element's *group number* in the Periodic Table and its combining power. Groups are the vertical columns in the Periodic Table. The combining power is linked to the *number of electrons* in the outer shell of atoms of the element.

| Group number | I | II | III | IV | V | VI | VII | VIII |
|---|---|---|---|---|---|---|---|---|
| Combining power | 1 | 2 | 3 | 4 | 3 | 2 | 1 | 0 |

Δ Table 1.14 Combining powers of elements.

Groups I–IV: combining power = group number

Groups V–VII: combining power = 8 − (group number)

If an element is not in one of the main groups, its combining power is included in the name of the compound containing it. For example, copper is a transition metal and is in the middle block of the Periodic Table. In copper(II) oxide, copper has a combining power of 2.

Sometimes an element does not have the combining power you would predict from its position in the Periodic Table. The combining power of these elements is also included in the name of the compound containing it. For example, phosphorus is in Group V, so you would expect it to have a combining power of 3, but in phosphorus(V) oxide its combining power is 5.

*The only exception is hydrogen.* Hydrogen is not included in a group, nor is its combining power given in the name of compounds containing hydrogen. It has a combining power of 1.

## SIMPLE COMPOUNDS

Many compounds contain just two elements. For example, when magnesium burns in oxygen, a white ash of magnesium oxide is formed. To work out the chemical formula of magnesium oxide:

**1.** Write down the name of the compound.

**2.** Write down the chemical symbols for the elements in the compound.

**3.** Use the Periodic Table to find the 'combining power' of each element. Write the combining power of each element under its symbol.

**4.** If the numbers can be cancelled down, do so.

**5.** Swap the combining powers. Write them after the symbol, slightly below the line (as a 'subscript').

**6.** If any of the numbers are 1, you do not need to write them.

Magnesium oxide has the chemical formula you would have probably guessed: MgO.

The chemical formula of a compound is not always immediately obvious, but if you follow these rules you will have no problems.

| magnesium | oxide |
|---|---|
| Mg | O |
| 2 | 2 |
| 1 | 1 |
| $Mg_1$ | $O_1$ |

MgO

| calcium | chloride |
|---|---|
| Ca | Cl |
| 2 | 1 |

(They don't cancel)

| $Ca_1$ | $Cl_2$ |
|---|---|

$CaCl_2$

△ Fig. 1.74 Working out the chemical formulae for magnesium oxide and calcium chloride.

## Compounds containing more than two elements

Some elements exist bonded together in what is called a **radical**. For example, in copper(II) sulfate, the sulfate part of the compound is a radical.

There are a number of common radicals, each having its own combining power. You cannot work out these combining powers easily from the Periodic Table – you have to learn them. Notice that all the radicals exist as ions.

| Combining power = 1 | Combining power = 2 | Combining power = 3 |
|---|---|---|
| Hydroxide $OH^-$ | Carbonate $CO_3^{2-}$ | Phosphate $PO_4^{3-}$ |
| Hydrogencarbonate $HCO_3^-$ | Sulfate $SO_4^{2-}$ | |
| Nitrate $NO_3^-$ | | |
| Ammonium $NH_4^+$ | | |

△ Table 1.15 Combining compounds for common radicals.

The same rules for working out formulae apply to radicals as to elements. For example:

| Copper(II) sulfate | | Potassium nitrate | |
|---|---|---|---|
| Cu | $SO_4$ | K | $NO_3$ |
| 2 | 2 | 1 | 1 |
| $CuSO_4$ | | $KNO_3$ | |

△ Table 1.16 Combining elements and radicals.

If the formula contains more than one radical unit, the radical must be put in brackets. For example:

| calcium hydroxide | |
|---|---|
| Ca | OH |
| 2 | 1 |
| $Ca(OH)_2$ | |

△ Fig. 1.75 Working out the chemical formula for calcium hydroxide.

The brackets are used just as they are used in mathematics: the number outside a bracket multiplies everything inside it. Be careful how you use the brackets – for example, do not be tempted to write calcium hydroxide as $CaOH_2$ rather than $Ca(OH)_2$. This is wrong.

$CaOH_2$      contains one Ca, one O, two H ✗

$Ca(OH)_2$      contains one Ca, two O, two H ✓

**EXTENDED**

The formula of an ionic compound can be worked out from the ions present. For example, sodium chloride is an ionic compound.

Sodium is in Group I and forms an ion with a charge of 1+, $Na^+$

Chlorine is in Group VII and forms an ion with a charge of 1−, $Cl^-$

When these ions combine, the charges must cancel each other out:

NaCl (the 1+ and 1− charges cancel)

What is the formula of lead(II) bromide, which contains $Pb^{2+}$ and $Br^-$ ions?

To cancel the 2+ charge, two 1− charges are needed, so the formula is $PbBr_2$.

**END OF EXTENDED**

## QUESTIONS

**1.** Work out the chemical formulae of the following compounds:

**a)** potassium bromide

**b)** calcium oxide

**c)** aluminium chloride

**d)** carbon hydride (methane).

**2.** Work out the chemical formulae of the following compounds:

**a)** copper(II) nitrate

**b)** aluminium hydroxide

**c)** ammonium sulfate

**d)** iron(III) carbonate.

**3.** EXTENDED Work out the chemical formulae of the following compounds:

**a)** a compound containing $Zn^{2+}$ ions and $Cl^-$ ions

**b)** a compound containing $Cr^{3+}$ ions and $O^{2-}$ ions

**c)** a compound containing $Fe^{2+}$ and $OH^-$ ions.

## WRITING CHEMICAL EQUATIONS

In a chemical equation the starting chemicals are called the **reactants** and the finishing chemicals are called the **products**.

Follow these rules to write a chemical equation.

**1.** Write down the word equation.

**2.** Write down the symbols (for elements) and formulae (for compounds).

**3.** Balance the equation, to make sure there are the same number of each type of atom on each side of the equation.

**4.** EXTENDED Include the **state symbols** solid (s); liquid (l); gas (g); solution in water (aq).

| State | State symbol |
|---|---|
| Solid | (s) |
| Liquid | (l) |
| Gas | (g) |
| Solution | (aq) |

△ Table 1.17 States and their symbols.

Remember that some elements are **diatomic**. They exist as molecules containing two atoms.

| Element | Formula |
|---------|---------|
| Hydrogen | $H_2$ |
| Oxygen | $O_2$ |
| Nitrogen | $N_2$ |
| Chlorine | $Cl_2$ |
| Bromine | $Br_2$ |
| Iodine | $I_2$ |

Δ Table 1.18 Some diatomic elements.

## WORKED EXAMPLES

**1.** When a lighted splint is put into a test tube of hydrogen, the hydrogen burns with a 'pop'. In fact the hydrogen reacts with oxygen in the air (the reactants) to form water (the product). Write the chemical equation for this reaction.

Word equation:        hydrogen  +  oxygen  →  water

Symbols and formulae:     $H_2$   +   $O_2$   →   $H_2O$

Balance the equation:     $2H_2$   +   $O_2$   →   $2H_2O$

For every two molecules of hydrogen that react, one molecule of oxygen is needed and two molecules of water are formed.

**EXTENDED**

Add the state symbols:     $2H_2(g)$  +  $O_2(g)$   →   $2H_2O(l)$

**END OF EXTENDED**

**2.** What is the equation when sulfur burns in air?

Word equation:        sulfur  +  oxygen   →  sulfur dioxide

Symbols and formulae:     S  +  $O_2$   →   $SO_2$

Balance the equation:     S  +  $O_2$   →   $SO_2$

**EXTENDED**

Add the state symbols:     $S(s)$  +  $O_2(g)$   →   $SO_2(g)$

**END OF EXTENDED**

PRINCIPLES OF CHEMISTRY

◁ Fig. 1.76 Methane is burning in the oxygen in the air to form carbon dioxide and water.

## BALANCING EQUATIONS

Balancing equations can be quite tricky. It is essentially done by trial and error. However, the golden rule is that *balancing numbers can only be put in front of the formulae*.

For example, to balance the equation for the reaction between methane and oxygen:

| | Reactants | Products |
|---|---|---|
| Start with the unbalanced equation | $CH_4 + O_2$ | $CO_2 + H_2O$ |
| Count the number of atoms on each side of the equation | 1C ✓, 4H, 2O | 1C ✓, 2H, 3O |
| There is a need to increase the number of H atoms on the products side of the equation. Put a '2' in front of the $H_2O$ | $CH_4 + O_2$ | $CO_2 + 2H_2O$ |
| Count the number of atoms on each side of the equation again | 1C ✓, 4H ✓, 2O | 1C ✓, 4H ✓, 4O |
| There is a need to increase the number of O atoms on the reactant side of the equation. Put a '2' in front of the $O_2$ | $CH_4 + 2O_2$ | $CO_2 + 2H_2O$ |
| Count the atoms on each side of the equation again | 1C ✓, 4H ✓, 4O ✓ | 1C ✓, 4H ✓, 4O ✓ |

△ Table 1.19 Steps in balancing the equation for the reaction between methane and oxygen.

No atoms have been created or destroyed in the reaction. The equation is balanced.

$$CH_4(g) \quad + \quad 2O_2(g) \quad \rightarrow \quad CO_2(g) \quad + \quad 2H_2O(l)$$

△ Fig. 1.77 The number of each type of atom is the same on the left and right sides of the equation.

In balancing equations involving radicals such as sulfate, hydroxide and nitrate, you can use the same procedure. For example, when lead(II) nitrate solution is mixed with potassium iodide solution, lead(II) iodide and potassium nitrate are produced (Fig. 1.78).

**1.** Words:

| lead(II) | + | potassium | → | lead(II) | + | potassium |
|---|---|---|---|---|---|---|
| nitrate | | iodide | | iodide | | nitrate |

**2.** Symbols:

$$Pb(NO_3)_2 \quad + \quad KI \quad \rightarrow \quad PbI_2 \quad + \quad KNO_3$$

**3.** Balance the nitrates:

$$Pb(NO_3)_2 \quad + \quad KI \quad \rightarrow \quad PbI_2 \quad + \quad 2KNO_3$$

**4.** Balance the iodides:

$$Pb(NO_3)_2(aq) \quad + \quad 2KI(aq) \quad \rightarrow PbI_2(s) \quad + \quad 2KNO_3(aq)$$

◁ Fig. 1.78 This reaction occurs simply on mixing the solutions of lead(II) nitrate and potassium iodide. Lead iodide is an insoluble yellow solid.

## QUESTIONS

**1.** Balance the following chemical equations:

    **a)** $Ca(s) + O_2(g) \rightarrow CaO(s)$

    **b)** $H_2S(g) + O_2(g) \rightarrow SO_2(g) + H_2O(l)$

    **c)** $Pb(NO_3)_2(s) \rightarrow PbO(s) + NO_2(g) + O_2(g)$

**2.** Write balanced equations for the following word equations:

    **a)** sulfur + oxygen $\rightarrow$ sulfur dioxide

    **b)** magnesium + oxygen $\rightarrow$ magnesium oxide

    **c)** copper(II) oxide + hydrogen $\rightarrow$ copper + water

## EXTENDED

As mentioned earlier, the general method for balancing equations is by trial and error, but it helps if you are systematic – always start on the left-hand side with the reactants. Sometimes you can balance an equation using fractions. In more advanced study such balanced equations are perfectly acceptable. Getting rid of the fractions is not difficult though. Look at this example:

## WORKED EXAMPLE

Ethane $(C_2H_6)$ is a hydrocarbon fuel and burns in air to form carbon dioxide and water.

Unbalanced equation: $C_2H_6(g) + O_2(g) \rightarrow CO_2(g) + H_2O(l)$

Balancing the carbon and hydrogen atoms gives:

$$C_2H_6(g) \quad + \quad O_2(g) \quad \rightarrow \quad 2CO_2(g) \quad + \quad 3H_2O(l)$$

The equation can then be balanced by putting 3½ in front of the $O_2$. By doubling every balancing number, the equation is then balanced using whole numbers.

$$2C_2H_6(g) \quad + \quad 7O_2(g) \quad \rightarrow \quad 4CO_2(g) \quad + \quad 6H_2O(l)$$

During your course you will become familiar with balancing equations and become much quicker at doing it. Try balancing the equations below. The third is the chemical reaction often used for making chlorine gas in the laboratory.

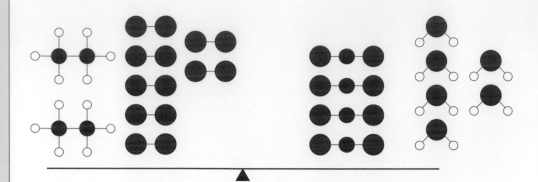

△ Fig. 1.79 Balancing the equation for burning ethane in air.

## QUESTIONS

**1.** Balance the following equations:

　　**a)** $C_5H_{10}(g) + O_2(g) \rightarrow CO_2(g) + H_2O(l)$

　　**b)** $Fe_2O_3(s) + CO(g) \rightarrow Fe(s) + CO_2(g)$

　　**c)** $KMnO_4(s) + HCl(aq) \rightarrow KCl(aq) + MnCl_2(aq) + H_2O(l) + Cl_2(g)$

### Ionic equations

**Ionic equations** show reactions involving ions (atoms or radicals that have lost or gained electrons). The size of the charge on an ion is the same as its combining power – whether it is positive or negative depends on which part of the Periodic Table the element is placed in.

In many ionic reactions some of the ions play no part in the reaction. These ions are called **spectator ions**. A simplified ionic equation can then be written, using only the important, reacting ions. In these equations, state symbols are often used and appear in brackets.

The equation must balance in terms of chemical symbols and charges.

### WORKED EXAMPLES

**1.** In the reaction to produce lead(II) iodide, the potassium ions and nitrate ions are spectators – the important ions are the lead(II) ions and the iodide ions.

The simplified ionic equation is:

$Pb^{2+}(aq) + 2I^-(aq) \rightarrow PbI_2(s)$

|  | **Reactants** | **Products** |
|---|---|---|
|  | $Pb^{2+}(aq) + 2I^-(aq)$ | $PbI_2(s)$ |
| Symbols | 1Pb ✓, 2I ✓ | 1Pb ✓, 2I ✓ |
| Charges | 2+ and 2– = 0 ✓ | 0 ✓ |

The equation shows that *any* solution containing lead(II) ions will react with *any* solution containing iodide ions to form lead(II) iodide.

**2.** Any solution containing copper(II) ions and any solution containing hydroxide ions can be used to make copper(II) hydroxide, which appears as a solid:

$$Cu^{2+}(aq) + 2OH^-(aq) \rightarrow Cu(OH)_2(s)$$

|  | **Reactants** | **Products** |
|---|---|---|
|  | $Cu^{2+}(aq) + 2OH^-(aq)$ | $Cu(OH)_2(s)$ |
| Symbols | 1Cu ✓, 2O ✓, 2H ✓ | 1Cu ✓, 2O ✓, 2H ✓ |
| Charges | 2+ and 2− = 0 ✓ | 0 ✓ |

△ Fig. 1.80 Copper(II) hydroxide.

**END OF EXTENDED**

## REACTING QUANTITIES

Observing chemical reactions can be fun. Some can be quite dramatic, producing sparks or flames; others might produce unexpected colour changes. However, many of the reactions you might see in the laboratory are used on an industrial scale to make chemicals for manufacturing other products or in everyday living. So it is not enough to know *what* can be made in a reaction; scientists also need to know *how much* can be made from the quantities of starting materials available. To do this we need to be able to weigh atoms or do we?

△ Fig. 1.81 What volume of chlorine was needed to make this bottle of bleach?

## RELATIVE ATOMIC MASS

Atoms are far too light to be weighed. Instead, scientists have developed a **relative atomic mass** scale. The lightest atom, hydrogen, was chosen at first as the unit that all other atoms were weighed against.

On this scale, a carbon atom weighs the same as 12 hydrogen atoms, so carbon's relative atomic mass was given as 12.

Using this relative mass scale you can see, for example, that:

• 1 atom of magnesium is 24 × the mass of 1 atom of hydrogen.
• 1 atom of magnesium is 2 × the mass of 1 atom of carbon.
• 1 atom of copper is 2 × the mass of 1 atom of sulfur.

|  | Hydrogen | Carbon | Oxygen | Magnesium | Sulfur | Calcium | Copper |
|---|---|---|---|---|---|---|---|
| Symbol | H | C | O | Mg | S | Ca | Cu |
| Relative atomic mass | 1 | 12 | 16 | 24 | 32 | 40 | 64 |
| Relative size of atom | | | | | | | |

Δ Table 1.20 Relative atomic masses and sizes of atoms.

Since 1961 the reference point of the relative atomic scale has been carbon-12.

The relative atomic mass, $A_r$, is the average mass of naturally occurring atoms of an element on a scale where the $^{12}C$ atom has a mass of exactly 12 units. This takes into account the abundance of all existing isotopes of that element.

## RELATIVE FORMULA MASSES, $M_r$

A **relative formula mass** ($M_r$) can be worked out from the relative atomic masses of the atoms in the formula.

The relative formula mass of a molecule (or the relative molecular mass) can be worked out by simply adding up the relative atomic masses of the atoms in the molecule. For example:

Water, $H_2O$ (H = 1, O = 16)

The relative formula mass ($M_r$) = 1 + 1 + 16 = 18

Note: The subscript $_2$ only applies to the hydrogen atom.

Carbon dioxide, $CO_2$ (C = 12, O = 16)

$M_r$ = 12 + 16 + 16 = 44

Note: The subscript $_2$ only applies to the oxygen atom.

A similar approach can be used for any formula, including ionic formulae.

The relative atomic mass of an element expressed in grams represents what is called a **mole** of atoms. The mole represents a number of atoms which is approximately $6 \times 10^{23}$. This number is called the **Avogadro constant**. Similarly, the **relative molecular mass** of a molecule expressed in grams represents 1 mole of molecules – that is $6 \times 10^{23}$ molecules.

**END OF EXTENDED**

## WORKED EXAMPLES

**1.** Sodium chloride, NaCl ($A_r$: Na = 23, Cl = 35.5)
The relative formula mass ($M_r$) = 23 + 35.5 = 58.5

**2.** Potassium nitrate, $KNO_3$ ($A_r$: K = 39, N = 14, O = 16)

$M_r = 39 + 14 + 16 + 16 + 16 = 101$

(Note: The subscript $_3$ only applies to the oxygen atoms.)

**3.** Calcium hydroxide, $Ca(OH)_2$ ($A_r$: Ca = 40, O = 16, H = 1)

$M_r = 40 + (16 + 1) \, 2 = 40 + 34 = 74$

(Note: The subscript $_2$ applies to everything inside the bracket.)

**4.** Magnesium nitrate, $Mg(NO_3)_2$ ($A_r$: Mg = 24, N = 14, O = 16)

$M_r = 24 + (14 + 16 + 16 + 16) \, 2 = 24 + (62)2 = 24 + 124 = 148$

## QUESTIONS

**1.** What is the formula mass of methane, $CH_4$? ($A_r$: H = 1, C = 12)

**2.** What is the formula mass of ethanol, $C_2H_5OH$? ($A_r$: H = 1, C = 12, O = 16)

**3.** What is the formula mass of ozone, $O_3$? ($A_r$: O = 16)

## EXPERIMENTS TO FIND THE FORMULAE OF SIMPLE COMPOUNDS

### Finding the formula of magnesium oxide

Magnesium ribbon can be heated in a crucible to make a white powder called magnesium oxide. The magnesium reacts with oxygen from the air. The reaction is called oxidation because the magnesium combines with oxygen.

If you measure the masses of the magnesium used and the magnesium oxide formed in this reaction, you can use the relative atomic masses of magnesium and oxygen to work out the formula of the compound made.

| Measurement | Mass in grams (g) |
|---|---|
| Mass of crucible + lid | 30.00 |
| Mass of crucible + lid + magnesium | 30.24 |
| Mass of crucible + lid + magnesium oxide | 30.40 |
| Mass of magnesium | 30.24 − 30.00 = 0.24 |
| Mass of magnesium oxide | 30.40 − 30.0 = 0.40 |
| Mass of oxygen | 30.40 − 30.24 = 0.16 |

△ Table 1.21 Typical results when 0.24 g of magnesium is oxidised.

The result is that 0.24 g of magnesium joins with 0.16 g of oxygen. Therefore 24 g of magnesium would join with 16 g of oxygen. The relative atomic mass of magnesium is 24 and that of oxygen is 16. So 1 magnesium atom combines with 1 oxygen atom, or 1 mole of magnesium atoms joins with 1 mole of oxygen atoms. This means that the formula of magnesium oxide is MgO.

△ Fig. 1.82 Magnesium ribbon is put in a crucible with a lid on it. The crucible is heated until the magnesium is red hot. The lid is lifted very slightly (to allow oxygen in) and put back down. This lets the magnesium burn but prevents loss of magnesium oxide.

## WORKED EXAMPLE

Copper(II) oxide can be heated in hydrogen to produce copper and water. This reaction can be used to find the formula of copper(II) oxide.

In an experiment 12.8 g of copper was produced from 16.0 g of copper(II) oxide.

Relative atomic masses: H = 1, O = 16, Cu = 64

Word equation: copper(II) oxide + hydrogen → copper + water

Masses                  16.0 g                  12.8 g

So the mass of oxygen that was combined with the copper = 16.0 − 12.8 = 3.2 g.

Therefore 32 g of oxygen would combine with 128 g of copper.

Therefore $\frac{32}{16}$ = 2 moles of oxygen would combine with $\frac{128}{64}$ = 2 moles of copper.

Therefore 1 mole of oxygen would combine with 1 mole of copper.

Therefore the formula for copper(II) oxide is CuO.

## Developing investigative skills

△ Fig. 1.83 Apparatus to find the chemical formula of a sample of copper(II) oxide.

Two students set out to find the chemical formula of a sample of copper(II) oxide. First they weighed an empty combustion tube, then used a spatula to put a full measure of copper(II) oxide near the centre of the tube, being careful not to spill any of the powder near the opening of the tube. They then reweighed the tube and set up the apparatus as shown in Fig.1.83. (Note: copper(II) oxide is harmful if swallowed.)

The gas was turned on very slowly and after about 10 seconds a lighted splint was held over the jet. The gas flow was adjusted until a flame about 1 cm high was burning at the jet. The copper(II) oxide was then heated strongly in a Bunsen flame for about 15 minutes until all the copper(II) oxide had been turned into copper. At this point the tube was allowed to cool, but with the gas still flowing through the tube and being burned at the jet.

When the the tube was cold, the gas was turned off and the tube and contents reweighed. The results are shown in the table:

| | |
|---|---|
| Mass of tube + copper(II) oxide | = 24.15 g |
| Mass of tube + copper | = 23.92 g |
| Mass of tube | = 23.15 g |
| Mass of copper(II) oxide | = |
| Mass of copper | = |
| Mass of oxygen combined with the copper | = |

### Using and organising techniques, apparatus and materials

❶ Why was it important not to spill any of the copper(II) oxide near the opening of the tube?

❷ Why was the gas supply turned on very slowly?

❸ Why was the tube allowed to cool before turning the gas supply off?

### Observing, measuring and recording

❹ What colour change would you expect to see as the copper(II) oxide changes into copper?

❺ Use the results to work out the masses of copper(II) oxide, copper and oxygen.

### Handling experimental observations and data

❻ Use your results to calculate the number of moles of copper and the number of moles of oxygen ($A_r$: O = 16; Cu = 64)

❼ What is the ratio of moles of copper: moles of oxygen? (Write this as Cu:O 1:?)

### Evaluating methods

❽ What do your calculations suggest is the most likely formula of copper(II) oxide?

❾ List the main sources of error in the experiment.

**END OF EXTENDED**

## QUESTIONS

1. In the experiment used to find the formula of magnesium oxide:

   a) Why is the lid of the crucible lifted whilst the magnesium is being heated?

   b) Why is the crucible lid lifted only very slightly during the heating of the magnesium?

   c) What is the colour of magnesium oxide?

## USING MOLES OF ATOMS TO FIND CHEMICAL FORMULAE

A chemical formula shows the number of atoms of each element that combine together. For example:

$H_2O$: a water molecule contains two hydrogen atoms and one oxygen atom.

Alternatively:

$H_2O$: 1 mole of water molecules is made from two moles of hydrogen atoms and 1 mole of oxygen atoms.

The formula of a compound can be calculated if the numbers of moles of the combining elements are known.

## WORKED EXAMPLES

**1.** What is the simplest formula of a hydrocarbon that contains 60 g of carbon combined with 20 g of hydrogen? ($A_r$: H = 1, C = 12)

|  | **C** | **H** |
|---|---|---|
| Write down the mass of each element: | 60 | 20 |
| Work out the number of moles of each element: | $\dfrac{60}{12} = 5$ | $\dfrac{20}{1} = 20$ |
| Find the simplest ratio (divide by the smaller number): | $\dfrac{5}{5} = 1$ | $\dfrac{20}{5} = 4$ |
| Write the formula showing the ratio of atoms: | $CH_4$ | |

**2.** What is the simplest formula of calcium carbonate if it contains 40% calcium, 12% carbon and 48% oxygen? ($A_r$: C = 12, O = 16, Ca = 40)

|  | **Ca** | **C** | **O** |
|---|---|---|---|
| Write down the mass of each element: (in 100 g of calcium carbonate) | 40 | 12 | 48 |
| Work out the number of moles of each element: | $\dfrac{40}{40} = 1$ | $\dfrac{12}{12} = 1$ | $\dfrac{48}{16} = 3$ |
| Find the simplest ratio: | Already in the simplest ratio | | |
| Write the formula showing the ratio of atoms: | $CaCO_3$ | | |

## REMEMBER

When calculating moles of elements, you must be careful to make sure you know what the question refers to. For example, you may be asked for the mass of 1 mole of nitrogen gas. N = 14, but nitrogen gas is diatomic, that is $N_2$, so the mass of 1 mole of $N_2$ = 28 g. This applies to other diatomic elements, such as $Cl_2$, $Br_2$, $I_2$, $O_2$ and $H_2$.

Formulae such as $CH_4$ and $CaCO_3$ are called **empirical formulae**. This means that the formula shows the simplest ratio of the atoms present.

Now consider the substance ethane. The formula for ethane is $C_2H_6$. The simplest ratio of the atoms in ethane would be $CH_3$ – but this substance cannot exist. The formula $C_2H_6$ shows the actual number of atoms of each element in one molecule of ethane.

This is called the **molecular formula**.

**END OF EXTENDED**

## QUESTIONS

1. EXTENDED In an experiment, 5.6 g of iron reacts to form 8.0 g of iron oxide. What is the formula of the iron oxide? ($A_r$: O = 16; Fe = 56)

2. 16.2 g of zinc oxide is reduced by carbon to form 13.0 g of zinc. What is the formula of zinc oxide? ($A_r$: O = 16; Zn = 65)

3. Butane has an empirical formula of $C_2H_5$. Its relative formula mass is 58. What is the molecular formula of butane? ($A_r$: H = 1; C = 12)

4. Hydrogen peroxide has an empirical formula of HO. Its relative formula mass is 34. What is the molecular formula of hydrogen peroxide? ($A_r$: H= 1; O = 16)

**EXTENDED**

### MOLES

A mole is an amount of substance. It is a very large number, approximately $6 \times 10^{23}$. This number is called the Avogadro number or Avogadro constant.

For example, you can have a mole of atoms, a mole of molecules or a mole of electrons. A mole of atoms is about $6 \times 10^{23}$ atoms.

The relative atomic mass of an element tells you the mass of a mole of atoms of that element. So, for example, a mole of carbon atoms has a mass of 12 grams.

The relative formula mass ($M_r$) tells you the mass of a mole of that substance. For example, a mole of sodium chloride, NaCl, has a relative formula mass of 58.5, so one mole has a mass of 58.5 g.

## WORKED EXAMPLES

1. How many moles of atoms are there in 72 g of magnesium?
   ($A_r$ of magnesium = 24)

   Write down the formula: $\quad\quad$ moles $= \dfrac{\text{mass}}{A_r}$

   Rearrange if necessary: $\quad\quad$ (None needed)

   Substitute the numbers: $\quad\quad$ moles $= \dfrac{72}{24}$

   Write the answer and units: $\quad\quad$ moles = 3 moles

2. What is the mass of 0.1 mole of carbon atoms? ($A_r$ of carbon = 12)

Write down the formula: $\qquad$ $moles = \dfrac{mass}{A_r}$

Rearrange if necessary: $\qquad$ $mass = moles \times A_r$

Substitute the numbers: $\qquad$ $mass = 0.1 \times 12$

Write the answer and units: $\qquad$ $mass = 1.2 \text{ g}$

**END OF EXTENDED**

## LINKING REACTANTS AND PRODUCTS

Chemical equations allow quantities of reactants and products to be linked together. They tell you how much of the products you can expect to make from a fixed amount of reactants.

In a balanced equation, the numbers in front of each symbol or formula indicate the numbers of moles represented. The numbers of moles can then be converted into masses in grams.

For example, when magnesium ($A_r$ = 24) reacts with oxygen ($A_r$ = 16):

Write down the balanced equation: $2Mg(s) \; + \; O_2(g) \; \rightarrow \; 2MgO(s)$

Write down the number of moles: $\quad 2 \qquad\qquad + \quad 1 \qquad \rightarrow \quad 2$

Convert moles to masses: $\qquad\qquad 48 \text{ g} \quad + \quad 32 \text{ g} \; \rightarrow \; 80 \text{ g}$

So when 48 g of magnesium reacts with 32 g of oxygen, 80 g of magnesium oxide is produced. From this you should be able to work out the mass of magnesium oxide produced from any mass of magnesium.

◁ Fig. 1.84 In an oxidation reaction, magnesium reacts with oxygen – the reaction can be used in fireworks and flares producing a brilliant white colour.

## WORKED EXAMPLES

**1.** What mass of magnesium oxide can be made from 6 g of magnesium? ($A_r$: O = 16, Mg = 24)

| | | | | |
|---|---|---|---|---|
| Equation: | $2Mg(s)$ | $+$ | $O_2(g)$ | $\rightarrow$ | $2MgO(s)$ |
| Moles: | 2 | | 1 | | 2 |
| Masses: | 48 g | | 32 g | | 80 g |
| ÷ 8 | 6 g | | | | 10 g |

Therefore 6 g of Mg will form 10 g of MgO.

Note: In this example, there was no need to work out the mass of oxygen needed. It was assumed that there would be as much as was necessary to convert all the magnesium to magnesium oxide.

**2.** What mass of ammonia can be made from 56 g of nitrogen?
($A_r$: H = 1, N = 14)

| Equation: | $N_2(g)$ | + | $3H_2(g)$ | $\rightarrow$ | $2NH_3(g)$ |
|---|---|---|---|---|---|
| Moles: | 1 | | 3 | | 2 |
| Masses: | 28 g | | 6 g | | 34 g |
| ×2 | 56 g | | | | 68 g |

Mass of ammonia = 68 g

## MOLES OF SOLUTIONS

A **solution** is made when a **solute** dissolves in a **solvent**. The **concentration** of a solution depends on how much solute is dissolved in how much solvent. Fig.1.84 shows how to make up a solution of 1 mol/dm³ copper(II) sulpate.

zero the balance or the mass of the container

spatula

large beaker

find the mass of container

add 160 g copper(II) sulfate:
Cu + S + O₄
64 + 32 + (4 × 16)
160 g =1 mole

add copper(II) sulfate to 250 cm³ water and stir until dissolved

1 dm³ volumetric flask

make volume up to 1 dm³ with water and shake flask a few times

add solution to a 1 dm³ volumetric flask

△ Fig. 1.85 Making a 1 mol/dm³ solution of copper(II) sulfate.

The concentration of a solution can be expressed in terms of g/dm³ of copper(II) sulfate.

## WORKED EXAMPLE

**1.** A solution is made by dissolving 1 g of sodium hydroxide in distilled water to make 250 cm³ of solution. What is the concentration of the sodium hydroxide solution?

1 g in 250 cm³ is the same concentration as 4 g in 1 dm³ (remember 1 dm³ is 1000 cm³).

So, the concentration of the solution = 4 g/dm³

The concentration of a solution can also be expressed in terms of moles per dm³ (1000 cm³), or mol/dm³ 1 mole can be written 1 M.

1 mole of solute dissolved to make 1000 cm³ of solution produces a 1 mol/dm³ solution.

2 moles dissolved to make a 1000 cm³ solution produces a 2 mol/dm³ solution.

0.5 moles dissolved to make a 1000 cm³ solution produces a 0.5 mol/dm³ solution.

1 mole dissolved to make a 500 cm³ solution produces a 2 mol/dm³ solution.

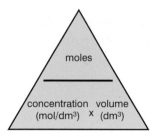

1 mole dissolved to make a 250 cm³ solution produces a 4 mol/dm³ solution.

△ Fig. 1.86 This triangle will help you to calculate concentrations of solutions.

If the same amount of solute is dissolved to make a smaller volume of solution, the solution will be more concentrated.

**2.** How much sodium chloride can be made by reacting 100 cm³ of 1.0 mol/dm³ hydrochloric acid with excess sodium hydroxide solution? (Na = 23, Cl = 35.5)

| Equation: | HCl(aq) + NaOH(aq) → NaCl(aq) + H₂O(l) | | | |
|---|---|---|---|---|
| Moles: | 1 | 1 | 1 | 1 |
| Masses/volumes: | 1000 cm³ of 1 mol/dm³ | 58.5 g | | |
| Therefore | 100 cm³ of 1 mol/dm³ | 5.85 g | | |

(the quantities are scaled down by 10 times.)

# EXTENDING THE MOLE CONCEPT

The mole is the amount of substance that contains $6.023 \times 10^{23}$ particles. The particles can be atoms, molecules or ions.

| | | | | |
|---|---|---|---|---|
| Atoms | Elements only | all metals / some non-metals / noble gases | **Aluminium** — one mole of aluminium **atoms** (mass 27.0g) / **Carbon** — one mole of carbon **atoms** (mass 12.0g) / **Helium** airship — one mole of helium **atoms** (mass 4.0g) | one mole of **atoms** contains $6.023 \times 10^{23}$ atoms |
| Molecules | Elements or Compounds | | **Oxygen** — one mole of oxygen **molecules** (mass 32.0g) / **Bromine** — one mole of bromine **molecules** (mass 160g) / **Iodine** — one mole of iodine **molecules** (mass 254g) / **Ammonia** — one mole of ammonia **molecules** (mass 17.0g) / **Water** — one mole of water **molecules** (mass 18.0g) | one mole of **molecules** contains $6.023 \times 10^{23}$ molecules |
| Ions | Compounds only | | **Sodium chloride** — one mole of sodium chloride. 1 mole of sodium chloride contains: $6.023 \times 10^{23}$ sodium **ions** and $6.023 \times 10^{23}$ chloride **ions** | |

Δ Fig. 1.87 Moles of atoms, molecules and ions.

# Developing investigative skills

A student wanted to find the concentration of a solution of potassium hydroxide. She decided to use a titration method using a 0.10 M ('M' is short for 'moles per cubic decimetre') solution of sulfuric acid. (Note: dilute sulfuric acid may cause harm to eyes or a cut. Potassium hydroxide can be corrosive and can cause severe burns and damage to the eyes. Methyl orange indicator is toxic if swallowed.)

$$2KOH(aq) + H_2SO_4(aq) \rightarrow K_2SO_4(aq) + 2H_2O(l)$$

The method she used is described below:

❶ Wearing eye protection, she washed a pipette and a burette carefully making sure they were drained after washing.

❷ She used the pipette to transfer 25.00 cm³ of the potassium hydroxide solution into a clean conical flask and added 3 drops of methyl orange indicator.

❸ She filled the burette with sulfuric acid solution, making sure that there were no air bubbles in the jet of the burette. Finally she took the first reading of the volume of acid in the burette.

❹ She ran the acid into the alkali in the conical flask, swirling the flask all the time. When she thought the indicator colour was close to changing, she added the acid more slowly until the colour changed. She then took the second reading on the burette.

She repeated the procedure steps 2 to 4 twice, making sure that between each titration she washed the conical flask carefully. Her results are shown in the table.

Volume of potassium hydroxide solution = 25.00 cm³

| Burette reading | 1st titration | 2nd titration | 3rd titration |
|---|---|---|---|
| 2nd reading (cm³) | 17.50 | 19.50 | 20.50 |
| 1st reading (cm³) | 0.00 | 2.50 | 3.50 |
| Difference (cm³) | 17.50 | 17.00 | 17.00 |

## Using and organising techniques, apparatus and materials

❺ Describe precisely how the student should have washed a) the pipette and b) the burette at the beginning of the experiment.

❻ How could the pipette be used most safely to measure out the 25.00 cm³ of potassium hydroxide solution?

❼ How can a burette be filled most easily without spilling acid?

❽ What could the student have done to make the colour change easier to observe? What colour change was she looking for?

❾ How should she have washed out the conical flask between titrations to prevent contamination?

⑩ Why are the second and third titrations likely to be more accurate than the first?

⑪ What volume of sulfuric acid would you use in your calculation? Explain your answer.

⑫ Use the results and the balanced equation to work out the concentration of the potassium hydroxide solution. (Hint: start by writing down the number of moles of $H_2SO_4$ used.)

**END OF EXTENDED**

## QUESTIONS

1. What mass of calcium oxide can be made from the **decomposition** of 50 g of calcium carbonate? ($A_r$: C = 12; O = 16; Ca = 40)

   Equation: $CaCO_3(s) \rightarrow CaO(s) + CO_2(g)$

2. **EXTENDED** How many moles of solute are there in the following solutions?

   **a)** 2000 cm³ of 1 M sodium chloride solution

   **b)** 100 cm³ of 0.1 M copper(II) sulfate solution

   **c)** 500 cm³ of 0.5 M sodium hydroxide solution.

**EXTENDED**

### MOLES OF GASES

In reactions involving gases it is often more convenient to measure the *volume* of a gas rather than its mass.

There are many gases and they are crucially important in science. In experiments or industrial processes it's often necessary to know the amount of a gas – but a gas is difficult to weigh. Molar volumes make it possible to find out the amount of a gas by using volume rather than mass.

△ Fig. 1.88 Each of these contains 1 mole of molecules.

One mole of any gas occupies the same volume under the same conditions of temperature and pressure. The conditions chosen are usually room temperature (25 °C) and normal atmospheric pressure (1 atmosphere).

The volume of one mole of any gas contains the Avogadro number of molecules (particles) of that gas. This means that equal volumes of all gases at the same temperature and pressure must contain the same number of molecules. This is sometimes called **Avogadro's law**.

One mole of any gas occupies 24 000 cm³ (24 dm³) at room temperature and pressure (rtp). The following equation can be used to convert gas volumes into moles and vice versa:

$$\text{moles} = \frac{\text{volume in cm}^3}{24\ 000}$$

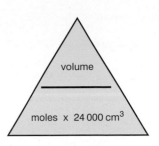

△ Fig. 1.89 The triangle can be used to decide whether to multiply or divide the quantities.

## QUESTIONS

1. **EXTENDED** How many moles of molecules are there in the following:

   a) 88 g of carbon dioxide, $CO_2$? ($A_r$: C = 12; O = 16)

   b) 9 g of water, $H_2O$? ($A_r$: H = 1; O = 16)

   c) 2.8 g of ethene, $C_2H_4$? ($A_r$ : H = 1; C = 12)

2. How many moles of molecules are there in the following:

   a) 12 000 cm³ of sulfur dioxide, $SO_2$, at room temperature and pressure?

   b) 2 400 cm³ of methane, $CH_4$, at room temperature and pressure?

   c) 48 000 cm³ of oxygen, $O_2$, at room temperature and pressure?

## WORKED EXAMPLES

1. What volume of hydrogen is formed at room temperature and pressure when 4 g of magnesium is added to excess dilute hydrochloric acid? ($A_r$: H = 1, Mg = 24, molar volume at room temperature and pressure = 24 000 cm³)

   Balanced equation:   $Mg(s) + 2HCl(aq) \rightarrow MgCl_2(aq) + H_2(g)$

   Moles:                    1          2              1            1

   Masses/volumes:      24 g                                  24 000 cm³

   Number of moles of magnesium $= \dfrac{4}{24} = 0.167$

   Therefore 0.167 moles hydrogen gas will be produced.

   Therefore volume of hydrogen gas = 0.167× 24 000

   $\qquad\qquad\qquad\qquad\qquad\qquad = 4000$ cm³

   Note: The hydrochloric acid is in excess. This means that there is enough to react with all the magnesium.

2. What volume of carbon dioxide will be produced when 124 g of copper carbonate is broken down by heating?

$(A_r = C = 12, O = 16, Cu = 64$, molar volume at room temperature and pressure $= 24\ 000\ cm^3)$

| Words: | copper carbonate | $\rightarrow$ | copper oxide | + | carbon dioxide |
| --- | --- | --- | --- | --- | --- |
| Balanced equation: | $CuCO_3(s)$ | $\rightarrow$ | $CuO(s)$ | + | $CO_2(g)$ |
| Moles: | 1 | | 1 | | 1 |
| Masses/vols: | 124 g | | | | 24 000 cm³ |

The relative formula mass of $CuCO_3$ is $64 + 12 + 16 + 16 + 16 = 124$ g

As there is exactly one mole of reactant, there must be one mole of each of the products. So, one mole of $CO_2$ is produced or 24 000 cm³.

**END OF EXTENDED**

## AMEDEO AVOGADRO

Amedeo Avogadro was born in Italy in 1776. At age 20 he graduated from university with a degree in religious law. However, his real interests were science and mathematics, and this was where he started to devote his university research. At the beginning of the 19th century, scientists across the world were trying to work out the relative masses of different atoms. There was much confusion and disagreement about the existence of other particles, which we now call molecules. Against this background of confusion, in 1811 Avogadro published a research paper on 'determining the relative masses of elementary molecules'. It was in this paper that he proposed his hypothesis:

**'All gases under the same conditions of temperature and pressure contain the same number of molecules.'**

Δ Fig. 1.90 Amedeo Avogadro.

The scientific community paid little attention to his work at the time. There were doubts about the existence of molecules and conflicting evidence coming from the research of more well-known and respected scientists. In fact, it was not until four years after his death in 1856 that his idea was accepted, following work done by a highly respected scientist called Cannizzaro. So Avogadro died without ever knowing the importance of his contribution to the development of science. It was only in 1911 that Avogadro's contribution to chemistry was formally recognised when, in honour of his work, the number of molecules in one mole of a substance was called the Avogadro number, equal to approximately $6 \times 10^{23}$.

How many other great advances or discoveries in science have not been recognised during the lifetime of the scientist concerned?

### PERCENTAGE YIELD

When you prepare chemicals using chemical reactions, the substances that are formed are called the products. The amount of product you get is called the **yield**.

Sometimes the yield is lower than you would expect. There may be some product left behind at different stages in the preparation.

A useful way of comparing the yields from different processes is to find the **percentage yield**. To do this, the chemist measures the actual yield (how much was actually made), works out the predicted yield for the reaction using the balanced equation and then uses this formula:

$$\text{percentage yield} = \frac{\text{actual yield}}{\text{predicted yield}} \times 100$$

## WORKED EXAMPLE

$25 \text{ cm}^3$ of ammonium hydroxide solution is reacted to form the fertiliser ammonium sulfate and the predicted yield is 3.30 g.

However, when chemists actually made this they found that 2.64 g was the mass produced.

What is the percentage yield?

$$\text{percentage yield} = \frac{\text{actual yield}}{\text{predicted yield}} \times 100$$

$$= \frac{2.64}{3.30} \times 100$$

$$= 80\%$$

### PERCENTAGE PURITY

In a similar way, **percentage purity** can be calculated.

The equation is:

$$\text{percentage purity} = \frac{\text{mass of pure substance}}{\text{mass of impure product}} \times 100$$

The following example shows how this works.

## WORKED EXAMPLE

A sample of impure common salt had a mass of 5.6 g. When purified, the mass of sodium chloride produced was 4.2 g. What is the percentage purity of the impure sample?

$$\text{Percentage purity} = \frac{\text{pure}}{\text{impure}} \times 100$$

$$= \frac{4.2}{5.6} \times 100 = 75.0\%$$

# End of topic checklist

## Key terms

Avogadro constant, Avogadro's law, chemical formula, chemical symbol, concentration, decomposition, diatomic, empirical formula, ionic equation, mole, molecular formula, percentage yield, percentage purity, product, radical, reactant, relative atomic mass ($A_r$), relative formula mass ($M_r$), relative molecular mass ($M_r$), spectator ions, yield

## During your study of this topic you should have learned:

○ How to use the symbols of the elements to write the formulae of simple compounds.

○ How to deduce the formula of a simple compound from the numbers of atoms present.

○ How to deduce the formula of a simple compound from a model or a diagrammatic representation.

○ How to construct word equations and simple balanced chemical equations.

○ The definition of relative atomic mass ($A_r$).

○ The definition of relative molecular mass ($M_r$) as the sum of the relative atomic masses.

○ That relative formula mass ($M_r$) is used for compounds.

○ How to use simple proportion to work out reacting masses.

○ EXTENDED How to determine the formula of an ionic compound from the charges on the ions present.

○ EXTENDED How to construct equations with state symbols, including ionic equations.

○ EXTENDED How to deduce the balanced equation for a chemical reaction, given relevant information.

○ EXTENDED The definition of the mole and the Avogadro constant.

○ EXTENDED How to use the molar gas volume (24 dm³ at room temperature and pressure).

○ EXTENDED How to calculate stoichiometric reacting masses and volumes of gases and solutions.

○ EXTENDED That solution concentrations are expressed in g/dm³ and mol/dm³(M).

○ EXTENDED How to calculate empirical formulae and molecular formulae.

○ EXTENDED How to calculate percentage yield and percentage purity.

# End of topic questions

*Note: The marks awarded for these questions indicate the level of detail required in the answers. In the examination, the number of marks awarded to questions like these may be different.*

1. Work out the chemical formulae of the following compounds:

   **a)** sodium chloride (1 mark)

   **b)** magnesium fluoride (1 mark)

   **c)** aluminium nitride (1 mark)

   **d)** lithium oxide (1 mark)

   **e)** carbon (IV) oxide (carbon dioxide). (1 mark)

2. Work out the chemical formulae of the following compounds:

   **a)** iron(III) oxide (1 mark)

   **b)** phosphorus(V) chloride (1 mark)

   **c)** chromium(III) bromide (1 mark)

   **d)** sulfur(VI) oxide (sulfur trioxide) (1 mark)

   **e)** sulfur(IV) oxide (sulfur dioxide). (1 mark)

3. Work out the chemical formulae of the following compounds:

   **a)** potassium carbonate (1 mark)

   **b)** ammonium chloride (1 mark)

   **c)** sulfuric acid (1 mark)

   **d)** magnesium hydroxide (1 mark)

   **e)** ammonium sulfate. (1 mark)

4. Write symbol equations from the following word equations:

   **a)** carbon + oxygen → carbon dioxide (1 mark)

   **b)** iron + oxygen → iron(III) oxide (1 mark)

   **c)** iron(III) oxide + carbon → iron + carbon dioxide (1 mark)

   **d)** calcium carbonate + hydrochloric acid → calcium chloride + carbon dioxide + water. (1 mark)

5. What is the formula mass of:

   **a)** ethene, $C_2H_4$ (1 mark)

   **b)** sulfur dioxide, $SO_2$ (1 mark)

   **c)** methanol, $CH_3OH$? (1 mark)

   ($A_r$: H = 1; C = 12; O = 16: S = 32)

**6.** Magnesium burns in oxygen to form magnesium oxide:

$2Mg(s) + O_2(g) \rightarrow 2MgO(s)$

($A_r$: O = 16; Mg = 24)

Calculate:

**a)** the mass of magnesium required to make 8 g of magnesium oxide    **(3 marks)**

**b)** the mass of oxygen required to make 8 g of magnesium oxide.    **(1 mark)**

**7.** What mass of sodium hydroxide can be made by reacting 2.3 g of sodium with water?    **(3 marks)**

$2Na(s) + 2H_2O(l) \rightarrow 2NaOH(aq) + H_2(g)$

($A_r$: H = 1, O = 16, Na = 23)

**8.** **EXTENDED** How many moles are in the following?

**a)** 64 g of $S_8$    **(1 mark)**

**b)** 9.8 g of $H_2SO_4$    **(1 mark)**

**c)** 21 g of Li    **(1 mark)**

($A_r$: S = 32; H = 1; O = 16; Li = 7)

**9.** **EXTENDED** What is the mass of the following?

**a)** 2.5 moles of Sr    **(1 mark)**

**b)** 0.25 moles of MgO    **(1 mark)**

**c)** 0.1 moles of $C_2H_5Br$    **(1 mark)**

(Sr = 88; Mg = 24; O = 16; C = 12; H = 1; Br = 80)

**10.** **EXTENDED** How many moles are in the following?

**a)** 24 000 cm³ of hydrogen gas, measured at room temperature and pressure.    **(1 mark)**

**b)** 1200 cm³ of nitrogen gas measured at room temperature and pressure.    **(1 mark)**

**11.** **EXTENDED** 0.64 g of copper when heated in air forms 0.80 g of copper oxide. What is the simplest formula of copper oxide?    **(2 marks)**

($A_r$: O = 16; Cu = 64)

**12. EXTENDED** Calculate the simplest formulae of the compounds formed in the following reactions:

**a)** 2.3 g of sodium reacting with 8.0 g of bromine **(2 marks)**

**b)** 0.6 g of carbon reacting with oxygen to make 2.2 g of a compound **(2 marks)**

**c)** 11.12 g of iron reacting with chlorine to make 32.20 g of a compound. **(2 marks)**

($A_r$: C = 12; O = 16; Na = 23; Cl = 35.5; Fe = 56; Br = 80)

**13. EXTENDED** Titanium chloride contains 25% titanium and 75% chlorine by mass. Work out the simplest formula of titanium chloride. ($A_r$: Ti = 48, Cl = 35.5) **(3 marks)**

**14. EXTENDED** Ethene has an empirical formula of $CH_2$ and a relative formula mass of 28. What is the molecular formula of ethene? **(3 marks)**

**15. EXTENDED** A hydrocarbon contains 92.3% carbon and 7.7% hydrogen.

**a)** What is its empirical formula? **(2 marks)**

**b)** Its relative formula mass is 26. What is its molecular formula? **(2 marks)**

**16. EXTENDED** What mass of barium sulfate can be produced from 50 cm³ of 0.2 mol/dm³ barium chloride solution and excess sodium sulfate solution?

**(3 marks)**

($A_r$: O = 16, S = 32, Ba = 137)

$BaCl_2(aq) + Na_2SO_4(aq) \rightarrow BaSO_4(s) + 2NaCl(aq)$

**17. EXTENDED** Iron(III) oxide is reduced to iron by carbon monoxide.

($A_r$: C = 12, O = 16, Fe = 56)

$Fe_2O_3(s) + 3CO(g) \rightarrow 2Fe(s) + 3CO_2(g)$

**a)** Calculate the mass of iron that could be obtained by the reduction of 800 tonnes of iron(III) oxide. **(3 marks)**

**b)** What volume of carbon dioxide, measured at room temperature and pressure, would be obtained by the reduction of 320 g of iron(III) oxide? **(3 marks)**

**18. EXTENDED** In an experiment to make calcium oxide, the predicted yield was 2.8 g. The actual yield was 2.1 g. Calculate the percentage yield achieved.

**(2 marks)**

**19. EXTENDED** An impure sample of solid X has a mass of 1.20 g. After purification the mass of pure X was 0.80 g. What was the percentage purity of the original sample? **(2 marks)**

**20. EXTENDED** Write ionic equations for the following reactions:

**a)** calcium ions and carbonate ions form calcium carbonate **(2 marks)**

**b)** iron(III) ions and hydroxide ions form iron(III) hydroxide **(2 marks)**

**c)** silver(I) ions and bromide ions form silver(I) bromide **(2 marks)**

# Exam-style questions
## Sample student answer

*Note: The questions, sample answers and marks in this section have been written by the authors as a guide only. The marks awarded for these questions indicate the level of detail required in the answers. In the examination, the number of marks awarded to questions like these may be different.*

## Question 1

**a)** The diagrams show the arrangement of particles in the three states of matter.

Each circle represents a particle.

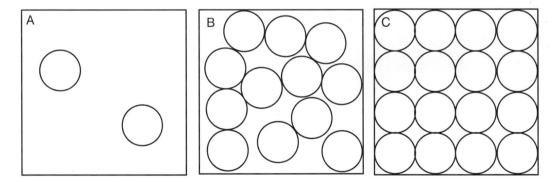

Use the letters A, B, and C to give the starting and finishing states of matter for each of the changes in the table. For the mark, both the starting state and the finishing state need to be correct.

| Change | Starting state | Finishing state | |
|---|---|---|---|
| **i)** The formation of water vapour from a puddle of water on a hot day | *B* | *A* | ✓ ① |
| **ii)** The formation of solid iron from molten iron | *B* | *C* | ✓ ① |
| **iii)** The manufacture of poly(ethene) from ethene | *B* | *A* | ✗ |
| **iv)** The reaction whose equation is ammonium hydrogen chloride(s) → ammonia(g) + hydrogen chloride(g) | *B* | *A* | ✓ ① |

(4)

**a)** It is important to identify the states of matter:

A = gas,  B = liquid, C = solid.

  **i)** Correct – evaporation process.

 **ii)** Correct – solidifying.

**iii)** Incorrect – should be 'AC' order because ethene is a gas, poly(ethene) a solid.

**iv)** Correct – equation shows solid → gases (sublimation).

**b)** Answer is 'liquid'. In the Periodic Table, at room temperature the majority of elements are solids, a few are gases but only two are liquids – mercury and bromine.

**c)** **i)** Correct – sulfur.

**ii)** Incorrect – this is a 'mixture' of two elements.

**iii)** Correct – a mixture of an element ($O_2$) and a compound ($H_2O$).

**iv)** Correct – sulfuric acid.

The answers rely on using the state symbols for the equation and a thorough knowledge of the terms elements, mixtures and compounds.

**b)** Which state of matter is the *least* common for the elements of the Periodic Table at room temperature?

*gases* ✗                                                                 (1)

**c)** The manufacture of sulfuric acid can be summarised by the equation:

$$2S(s) + 3O_2(g) + 2H_2O(l) \rightarrow 2H_2SO_4(l)$$

Tick one box in each line to show whether the formulae in the table represents a compound, an element or a mixture.

| | Compound | Element | Mixture | |
|---|---|---|---|---|
| i) $2S(s)$ | | ✓ | | ✓ ① |
| ii) $2S(s) + 3O_2(g)$ | | ✓ | | ✗ |
| iii) $3O_2(g) + 2H_2O(l)$ | | | ✓ | ✓ ① |
| iv) $2H_2SO_4(l)$ | ✓ | | | ✓ ① |

(4)

**(Total 9 marks)**

⑥/⑨

## Exam-style questions continued

### Question 2

This question is about atoms.

**a)** **i)** Choose words from the box to label the diagram of an atom. (3)

| proton | neutron | electron | ion |
|--------|---------|----------|-----|

    **ii)** What is the proton number of this atom? (1)

    **iii)** What is the nucleon number of this atom? (1)

**b)** Carbon has three isotopes. State one way in which the atoms of the three isotopes are:

   **i)** the same (1)

   **ii)** different. (1)

**(Total 7 marks)**

### Question 3

**a)** Some elements combine together to form ionic compounds. Use words from the box to complete the sentences.

Each word may be used once, more than once or not at all.

| gained | high | lost | low |
|--------|------|------|-----|
| medium | metals | non-metals | shared |

Ionic compounds are formed between ............................ and ............................ .

Electrons are ............................ by atoms of one element and ............................ by atoms of the other element.

The ionic compound formed has a ............................ melting point and a ............................ boiling point. (6)

**b)** Two elements react to form an ionic compound with the formula $MgCl_2$. (proton number of Mg = 12; proton number of Cl = 17)

   **i)** Give the electronic configurations of the two elements in this compound *before* the reaction. (2)

   **ii)** Give the electronic configurations of the two elements in this compound *after* the reaction. (2)

**(Total 10 marks)**

## Question 4

9.12 g of iron(II) sulfate was heated. It decomposes to sulfur dioxide ($SO_2(g)$) and sulfur trioxide ($SO_3(g)$) and iron (III)oxide. Calculate the mass of iron(III) oxide formed and the volume of sulfur trioxide produced (measured at room temperature and pressure).

$$2FeSO_4(s) \rightarrow Fe_2O_3(s) + SO_2(g) + SO_3(g)$$

($A_r$: O = 16, S = 32, Fe = 56; 1 mole of gas at room temperature and pressure occupies 24 000 $cm^3$)

**(Total 6 marks)**

## Question 5

The following equation shows the reaction between potassium hydroxide solution and dilute sulfuric acid:

$$2KOH\,(aq) + H_2SO_4\,(aq) \rightarrow K_2SO_4\,(aq) + 2H_2O\,(l)$$

**a)** A 25.0 $cm^3$ sample of 0.15 mol/$dm^3$ potassium hydroxide solution was titrated with dilute sulfuric acid. It was found that 15.0 $cm^3$ of dilute sulfuric acid was needed to neutralise the potassium hydroxide solution.

**b)** Describe how you would carry out the titration experiment. You should include details of the apparatus you would use and how you would know when the potassium hydroxide had been neutralised. (4)

**c)** Use the equation and the experimental results to calculate the concentration of the sulfuric acid. (4)

**(Total 8 marks)**

## Question 6

The structures of some substances are shown here:

**A**

**B**

**C**

H — Br

**D**

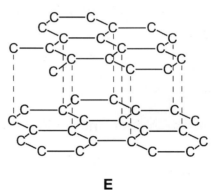

**E**

**a)** Answer these questions using the letters **A**, **B**, **C**, **D** or **E**.

**i)** Which structure is methane? (1)

**ii)** Which two structures are giant structures? (1)

**iii)** Which two structures are hydrocarbons? (1)

**iv)** Which structure contains ions? (1)

**v)** Which two structures have very high melting points? (1)

**b)** Structure **E** is a form of carbon.

**i)** What is the name of this structure? Put a ring around the correct answer.

carbide        graphite        lead        poly(hexene) (1)

**ii)** Name another form of carbon. (1)

**c)** Write the simplest formula for substance **B**. (1)

**d)** Is substance **D** an element or a compound? Explain your answer. (3)

**(Total 11 marks)**

## Question 7

Strontium and sulfur chlorides both have a formula of the type $XCl_2$ but they have different properties.

| Property | Strontium chloride | Sulfur chloride |
|---|---|---|
| Appearance | White crystalline solid | Red liquid |
| Melting point /°C | 873 | −80 |
| Particles present | Ions | Molecules |
| Electrical conductivity of solid | Poor | Poor |
| Electrical conductivity of liquid | Good | Poor |

a) The formulae of the chlorides are similar because both elements have a valency of 2.

Explain why Group II and Group VI elements both have a valency of 2. **(2)**

b) Draw a dot and cross diagram of one covalent molecule of sulfur chloride. Use x to represent an electron from a sulfur atom. Use o to represent an electron from a chlorine atom. **(3)**

c) Explain the difference in electrical conductivity between the following.

  i) solid and liquid strontium chloride **(1)**

  ii) liquid strontium chloride and liquid sulfur chloride. **(1)**

**(Total 7 marks)**

Modern physical chemistry originated in the 19th century. It is not as clearly defined a category as organic chemistry, but it is still a useful description of this branch of science. Physical chemistry focuses on chemical processes at the 'macro level' (where properties can be observed) more than at the 'micro level' (too small to see) of individual atoms, molecules and ions. However, observed physical properties can still be explained in terms of what the atoms, molecules or ions are doing.

In this section you will explore the chemical reactions that can be caused by using electricity, a process known as electrolysis. You will then investigate some chemical reactions that produce significant amounts of heat energy, as well as some strange ones that seem to absorb energy and make everything cooler. The speed or rate of chemical reactions will also be explored, together with chemists' strategies to try to control them. You will learn about reactions that go from reactants to products and then back again. These are a particular challenge when chemists want to make a product that could turn back into the reactants that made it! You will learn about redox reactions, which are reactions involving reduction and oxidation, as well as about acids, bases and salts. Finally, you will look at some of the simple analytical techniques that can be used to identify ions and gases.

## STARTING POINTS

1. How many non-renewable fuels can you name? What products do they form when they burn?

2. Give an example of a very rapid, almost instantaneous, chemical reaction. Now give an example of a very slow one.

3. Explain how you can easily distinguish between an acid and an alkali.

4. What is a catalyst? Name two examples where catalysts are used in everyday life.

5. Name a process that can be reversed easily.

6. Acids react with alkalis in neutralisation reactions. What is meant by neutralisation?

## SECTION CONTENTS

a) Electricity and chemistry

b) Chemical energetics

c) Rate of reaction

d) Reversible reactions

e) Redox reactions

f) Acids, bases and salts

g) Identification of ions and gases

h) Exam-style questions

# 2
# Physical chemistry

Δ Physical chemistry deals with properties that can be observed.

# Electricity and chemistry

## INTRODUCTION

Most elements in nature are found combined with other elements as compounds. These compounds must be broken down to obtain the elements that they contain. One of the most efficient and economical ways to break down some compounds is using electricity in a process called electrolysis. Simple electrolysis experiments can be performed in the laboratory, and electrolysis is also used

△ Fig. 2.1 Industrial electroplating is a form of electrolysis.

in large-scale industrial processes to produce important chemicals like aluminium and chlorine.

This topic deals with the underlying principles of electrolysis as well as some of the experiments that can be performed in the laboratory and some of the important industrial processes involving electrolysis.

## KNOWLEDGE CHECK

✓ Know the different arrangements of the particles in solids, liquids and gases.
✓ Understand the terms 'conductor' and 'insulator'.
✓ Understand the differences between ionic and covalent bonding.

## LEARNING OBJECTIVES

✓ Be able to define electrolysis as the breakdown of an ionic compound, either molten or in aqueous solution, by the passage of electricity.
✓ Be able to describe the electrode products in the electrolysis of:
  – molten lead (II) bromide
  – concentrated hydrochloric acid
  – concentrated aqueous sodium chloride
  – dilute sulfuric acid
  – between inert electrodes (platinum or carbon).
✓ Be able to state that metals or hydrogen are formed at the negative electrode (cathode) and that non-metals (other than hydrogen) are formed at the positive electrode (anode).
✓ Be able to predict the products of the electrolysis of a binary (two-element) compound in the molten state.
✓ Be able to describe the electroplating of metals.
✓ Be able to name some of the uses of electroplating.
✓ Be able to describe the reasons for the use of copper and (steel-cored) aluminium in cables.

✓ Be able to describe why plastics and ceramics are used as insulators.

✓ **EXTENDED** Be able to relate the products of electrolysis to the electrolyte and electrodes in specific examples (including copper (II) sulfate using carbon or copper electrodes).

✓ **EXTENDED** Be able to describe electrolysis in terms of the ions present and reactions at the electrodes in specific examples.

✓ **EXTENDED** Be able to predict the products of electrolysis of a specified halide in dilute or concentrated aqueous solution.

✓ **EXTENDED** Be able to construct ionic half-equations for reactions at a cathode.

✓ **EXTENDED** Be able to describe the transfer of charge during electrolysis to include:
  – the movement of electrons in the metallic conductor
  – the removal or addition of electrons from the external circuit at the electrodes
  – the movement of ions in the electrolyte.

✓ **EXTENDED** Be able to describe the production of electrical energy from simple cells – i.e. two electrodes in an electrolyte.

✓ **EXTENDED** Be able to describe in outline the manufacture of aluminium from pure aluminium oxide in molten cryolite.

✓ **EXTENDED** Be able to describe in outline the manufacture of chlorine, hydrogen and sodium hydroxide from concentrated aqueous sodium chloride.

## ELECTROLYTES AND NON-ELECTROLYTES

Compounds that can conduct electricity are called **electrolytes** – they undergo a reaction called **electrolysis**. Experiments can be carried out using a simple electrical cell, as shown in Fig. 2.2.

Δ Fig. 2.2 A simple electrolysis cell.

When the solution in the beaker is an electrolyte, a complete circuit will form and the bulb will light. The electric current that flows is caused by electrons moving in the electrodes and wires of the circuit, and by ions moving in the solution. If a current does not flow then the beaker must contain a non-electrolyte. Because of this, a simple circuit like this can be used to distinguish between electrolytes and non-electrolytes.

## CONDITIONS FOR ELECTROLYSIS

The substance being electrolysed (the electrolyte) must contain ions, and these ions must be free to move. In other words, the substance must either be molten or dissolved in water.

A direct current (d.c.) voltage must be used. The **electrode** connected to the positive terminal of the power supply is known as the **anode**. The electrode connected to the negative terminal is known as the **cathode**. The electrical circuit can be drawn as shown in Fig. 2.3.

◁ Fig. 2.3 A typical electrical circuit used in electrolysis.

---

### EXTENDED

During electrolysis electrical charge is transferred as follows:
- negative ions move to the anode and give up electrons
- the electrons travel through the anode and round the circuit in the connecting wires to the cathode
- the electrons reaching the cathode are taken up by positive ions.

### END OF EXTENDED

---

## QUESTIONS

**1.** What is meant by the term *electrolysis*?

**2.** What is the name given to the positive electrode?

**3.** What two conditions must exist for a substance to be an electrolyte and allow an electric current to pass through it?

---

### ELECTROLYSIS OF MOLTEN LEAD(II) BROMIDE

When an electric current passes through an electrolyte, new substances are formed. The examples below show how you can work out what products will form.

Lead(II) bromide ($PbBr_2$) is ionically bonded and contains $Pb^{2+}$ ions and $Br^-$ ions. When the solid is melted and a voltage is applied, the ions are able to move. The positive lead ions move to the negative electrode (the cathode), and the negative bromide ions move to the positive electrode (the anode). The electrodes are usually made of carbon, which is inert. This means they do not undergo any **chemical change** during the electrolysis. The products of the electrolysis are lead and bromine. Silvery deposits of lead form near the bottom of the dish, and brown bromine vapour near the anode.

## EXTENDED

At the cathode (negative electrode), the lead ions accept electrons to form lead atoms:

$$Pb^{2+}(l) + 2e^- \rightarrow Pb(l)$$

At the anode (positive electrode), the bromide ions give up electrons to form bromine atoms, and then bromine molecules:

$$2Br^-(l) \rightarrow Br_2(g) + 2e^-$$

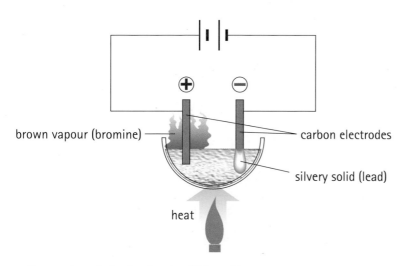

△ Fig. 2.4 Electrolysis of molten lead(II) bromide.

Note: the two equations above are known as half-equations. Unlike normal chemical equations, they do not show the whole chemical change – just the change occurring at an electrode. In the half-equations above, you will see that the numbers of electrons accepted and released are the same. The electric current is produced by this flow of electrons around the external circuit.

## END OF EXTENDED

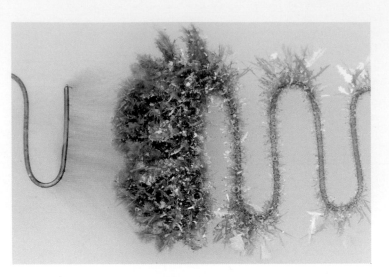

△ Fig. 2.5 Electrolysis of tin bromide solution – tin ions go to the cathode; bromide ions go to the anode.

## THE ELECTROLYSIS OF CONCENTRATED HYDROCHLORIC ACID

When concentrated hydrochloric acid is electrolysed, hydrogen forms as a colourless gas at the cathode and chlorine as a pale green gas at the anode.

The hydrochloric acid is a strong acid and fully ionises, or breaks down into ions, in solution:

$HCl(aq) \rightarrow H^+(aq) + Cl^-(aq)$

When concentrated hydrochloric acid is electrolysed using inert (graphite) electrodes the following reactions occur at the electrodes.

• At the cathode (negative electrode):

$H^+(aq)$ ions will be discharged and accept electrons to form hydrogen atoms and then hydrogen molecules

$2H^+(aq) + 2e^- \rightarrow H_2(g)$

• At the anode (positive electrode):

as the solution is concentrated, chloride ions ($Cl^-$) will be discharged. The $Cl^-$ ions lose electrons to form chlorine atoms and then chlorine molecules.

$2Cl^-(aq) \rightarrow Cl_2(g) + 2e^-$

## ELECTROLYSIS OF SODIUM CHLORIDE SOLUTION

When concentrated sodium chloride solution is electrolysed, hydrogen ions (from the water solvent) form hydrogen molecules at the cathode and chloride ions form chlorine molecules at the anode.

This experiment can be performed using a cell as shown in Fig. 2.2. Again, inert carbon electrodes are used.

**EXTENDED**

When the ionic compound sodium chloride dissolves in water, the sodium and chloride ions separate and are free to move independently. In addition, the water provides a small quantity of hydrogen ($H^+$) and hydroxide ($OH^-$) ions:

$NaCl(aq) \rightarrow Na^+(aq) + Cl^-(aq)$

$H_2O(l) \rightleftharpoons H^+(aq) + OH^-(aq)$

This process is known as **dissociation**. The water breaks up and forms ions. In fact, the ions also combine to form water – the reaction goes both ways: it is a **reversible** reaction. Although there are very few ions present, if they are removed they will be immediately replaced. Therefore, whenever you consider the electrolysis of an aqueous solution you must always include the $H^+$ and $OH^-$ ions.

- At the cathode (negative electrode):

two ions, $Na^+$ and $H^+$, move to the cathode but only $H^+$ ions are discharged. The sodium ions remain as ions, but the solution turns alkaline because the loss of hydrogen ions leaves a surplus of hydroxide ions.

$2H^+(aq) + 2e^- \rightarrow H_2(g)$

△ Fig. 2.6 The electrolysis of sodium chloride solution (brine).

The hydrogen ions accept electrons and form hydrogen molecules.

- At the anode (positive electrode):

two ions, $Cl^-$ and $OH^-$, move to the anode. Either ion could be discharged depending on the concentration of the solution. If the solution is very dilute, $OH^-$ ions are discharged; if the solution is concentrated, $Cl^-$ ions are discharged. At intermediate concentrations both ions are likely to be discharged, giving a mixture of products.

$4OH^-(aq) \rightarrow 2H_2O(l) + O_2(g) + 4e^-$

The hydroxide ions give up electrons and form oxygen molecules.

$2Cl^-(aq) \rightarrow Cl_2(g) + 2e^-$

The chloride ions give up electrons and form chlorine molecules.

Bubbling or effervescence is seen at each of the two electrodes, and the products of the electrolysis are hydrogen and oxygen and/or chlorine.

**END OF EXTENDED**

## REMEMBER

When the sodium chloride solution is concentrated, the main product at the anode is chlorine, which forms as a pale green gas.

When the sodium chloride solution is dilute, the main product at the anode is oxygen, which forms as a colourless gas.

Whatever the concentration of the sodium chloride solution, hydrogen forms as a colourless gas at the cathode.

When dilute sodium chloride solution is electrolysed, the solution becomes increasingly alkaline as sodium hydroxide is formed.

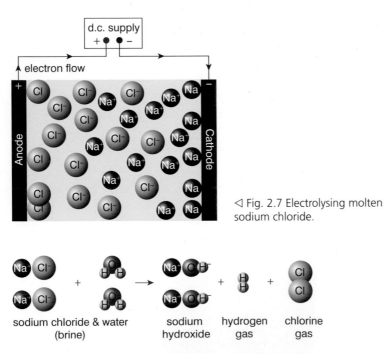

◁ Fig. 2.7 Electrolysing molten sodium chloride.

sodium chloride & water (brine) + → sodium hydroxide + hydrogen gas + chlorine gas

△ Fig. 2.8 Electrolysing brine. At which electrode is hydrogen formed?

## ELECTROLYSIS OF COPPER(II) SULFATE SOLUTION
### Using carbon electrodes

When copper(II) sulfate solution is electrolysed using inert carbon electrodes, the products of the electrolysis are copper and oxygen. The copper forms as a red-brown coating on the carbon cathode and bubbles of a colourless gas, oxygen, are seen next to the anode. The solution will become paler blue as the copper ions are discharged.

The following changes occur.

• At the cathode (negative electrode):

two ions, $Cu^{2+}$ and $H^+$, move to the cathode and $Cu^{2+}$ ions are discharged.

$Cu^{2+}(aq) + 2e^- \rightarrow Cu(s)$

The copper ions accept electrons and form copper atoms.

• At the anode (positive electrode):

two ions, $SO_4^{2-}$ and $OH^-$, move to the anode and $OH^-$ ions are discharged.

$4OH^-(aq) \rightarrow 2H_2O(l) + O_2(g) + 4e^-$

The hydroxide ions give up electrons and form oxygen molecules.

As the ions are discharged the electrolyte will increasingly contain sulfuric acid ($H^+$ ions and $SO_4^{2-}$ ions).

### Using copper electrodes

When the electrolysis is repeated with copper electrodes, copper is deposited as a red/brown coating at the cathode but there is a difference in the reaction that takes place at the anode.

• At the cathode (negative electrode):

$Cu^{2+}$ ions gain two electrons and are discharged. Copper atoms are formed and the mass of the electrode increases.

$Cu^{2+}(aq) + 2e^- \rightarrow Cu(s)$

• At the anode (positive electrode):

copper atoms lose two electrons and $Cu^{2+}$ ions are formed. The anode slowly dissolves and loses mass.

The concentration of the $Cu^{2+}$ ions in the solution remains constant because the rate of production of $Cu^{2+}$ ions at the anode is *exactly balanced* by the rate of removal of $Cu^{2+}$ ions at the cathode. This reaction is important in the refining of copper. Copper is extracted from its ore by reduction with carbon, but the copper produced is not pure enough for many of its uses, such as in electrical cables. It can be purified using electrolysis.

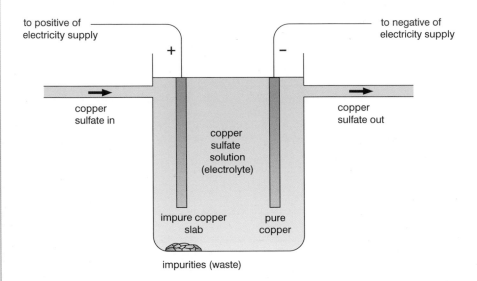

Δ Fig. 2.9 Copper is purified by electrolysis.

The impure copper is made the anode in a cell with copper(II) sulfate solution as the electrolyte. The cathode is made of a thin piece of pure copper. At the anode the copper atoms form copper ions and impurities fall to the bottom of the tank. The copper ions are then deposited as pure copper on the cathode. The cathode can be replaced by another thin piece of copper once sufficient copper has been deposited.

**END OF EXTENDED**

## PREDICTING THE PRODUCTS OF ELECTROLYSIS

Predicting the products of the electrolysis of simple molten ionic compounds is relatively straightforward. The metal forms at the cathode and the non-metal forms at the anode. For example, the electrolysis of molten aluminium oxide forms aluminium (at the cathode) and oxygen (at the anode).

In the case of aqueous solutions, there is potentially a number of different products. At the cathode, the product is either the metal or hydrogen. From the **reactivity series** of metals shown in Fig. 2.10, the rule is: only metals below hydrogen in the series are deposited as the metal on the cathode; metals above hydrogen produce hydrogen gas instead.

For example, if magnesium chloride solution is electrolysed, hydrogen, not magnesium, is formed at the cathode.

At the anode, the main product often depends on the concentration of the solution. For example, if concentrated hydrochloric acid is electrolysed, chlorine is the main product at the anode; if a dilute hydrochloric acid is electrolysed instead, oxygen is likely to be the main product.

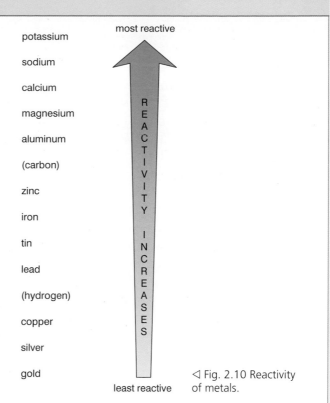

◁ Fig. 2.10 Reactivity of metals.

## REMEMBER

In electrolysis, negative ions give up electrons and usually form molecules (such as $Cl_2$, $Br_2$). Positive ions accept electrons and usually form metallic atoms (such as Cu, Al) or hydrogen gas.

The loss of electrons is **oxidation** (of the non-metal ions), the gain of electrons is **reduction** (of the metal ions).

## END OF EXTENDED

## QUESTIONS

1. **a)** What is an *inert* electrode?

   **b)** Give an example of a substance that is often used as an inert electrode.

2. What products are formed when the following molten solids are electrolysed?

   **a)** lead(II) chloride

   **b)** magnesium oxide

   **c)** aluminium oxide.

3. **EXTENDED** What are the products at the cathode when the following solutions are electrolysed?

   **a)** sodium bromide solution

   **b)** zinc chloride solution

   **c)** silver nitrate solution.

4. **EXTENDED** **a)** Write a half-equation showing how oxide ions ($O^{2-}$) are discharged as oxygen gas.

   **b)** At which electrode would this change take place?

## ELECTROPLATING

Electroplating involves using electrolysis to coat an object with a thin film of metal. Often this is done for economic reasons, with a fairly cheap metal like steel or nickel being coated with more expensive metals like silver, gold or chromium. Expensive-looking 'silver' knives and forks sometimes have the letters EPNS stamped on them. EPNS stands for **E**lectro-**P**lated **N**ickel **S**ilver. The item is made from nickel with a thin coating of silver added by electrolysis.

Electroplating can also be used to modify the chemical reactivity of the object plated. One example of this is steel cans for food containers plated inside with a thin layer of tin. Tin itself is too soft and expensive to use for the whole can, but it is fairly unreactive and prevents the food from causing the steel to rust.

To summarise: electroplating is a good way of improving the appearance of metals and preventing their corrosion.

silver nitrate solution

the object to be electroplated is used as the cathode – in this case a teaspoon

silver anode

△ Fig. 2.11 Electroplating.

## Developing investigative skills

Fig. 2.12 shows the apparatus that can be used to electrolyse dilute sulfuric acid. (Note: dilute sulfuric acid may cause harm in eyes or a cut.)

### Using and organising techniques, apparatus and materials

❶ Inert electrodes were used. Suggest what the electrodes were made of.

❷ Was the hydrogen formed at the anode or the cathode?

❸ What name is given to solutions, such as sulfuric acid, that allow an electric current to flow through them?

### Observing, measuring and recording

❹ Oxygen was collected at the left-hand electrode. How would you expect the volume of oxygen collected to compare with the volume of hydrogen collected at the right-hand electrode?

△ Fig. 2.12 Electrolysis of dilute sulfuric acid.

### Interpreting observations and data

❺ **EXTENDED** What ions are present in a solution of sulfuric acid?

❻ **EXTENDED** Write a half-equation showing the formation of the hydrogen at the right- hand electrode.

In this example of silver plating, the following reactions occur.

• At the anode (positive electrode):

each silver atom loses an electron and forms a silver ion

$$Ag(s) \rightarrow Ag^+(aq) + e^-$$

• At the cathode (negative electrode):

each silver ion accepts an electron and forms a silver atom

$$Ag^+(aq) + e^- \rightarrow Ag(s)$$

The increase in mass at the cathode is equal to the decrease in mass at the anode. Therefore the concentration of the silver ions in the silver nitrate electrolyte remains constant.

## QUESTIONS

1. **EXTENDED** Electrolysis of aqueous solutions can be used in electroplating. The metal to be plated needs to made as the negative electrode (cathode) made in a solution containing ions of the plating metal. The positive electrode (anode) is made of the pure plating metal. Electroplating can be set up on a small scale in a school laboratory.

   A student wanted to copper plate a ring. She was provided with a beaker (100 cm³), the ring, copper(II) sulfate solution, a copper strip, a set of leads with crocodile clips and a battery.

   a) Draw a labelled diagram to show how this could be done.

   b) Write the ionic half-equations to show what occurs at each electrode.

**END OF EXTENDED**

## MAKING USE OF CONDUCTORS AND INSULATORS

Metals like copper and aluminium are very good conductors of electricity. They possess delocalised (free to move) valence electrons within their structure allowing electricity to flow through them easily. Copper is used in electrical wiring because it is ductile (can be drawn into wires) and is a very good conductor of electricity. For overhead power lines or electrical cables, aluminium is often used rather than copper because it has a lower density. However, aluminium is not particularly strong and so it is strengthened for its use in overhead cables by wrapping it round a central core of steel.

△ Fig. 2.13 Electricity cables. The ceramic discs are insulators and isolate the power lines from the rest of the pylon.

△ Fig. 2.14 Copper wiring behind a domestic socket, exposed to show the flexible plastic insulators surrounding the wires.

Insulators are non-conductors of electricity because they have no mobile electrons. **Ceramic** discs are used as insulators to prevent the electric current passing from the cables to the pylons themselves. Ceramics are made from clay and are excellent insulators. They have very high melting points and do not react with water. The electrical wiring in houses usually contains copper as the conductor and a flexible **plastic** material is used as an insulator to surround the copper. The plastic is flexible, does not deteriorate quickly but does melt easily if overheating occurs.

EXTENDED

## EXTRACTING ALUMINIUM

Aluminium is extracted from the ore bauxite. Aluminium oxide is extracted from bauxite by purification. It is insoluble in water and has an extremely high melting point (2045 °C), therefore it is dissolved in molten cryolite at about 950 °C (this saves considerably on energy costs). This allows the ions to move when an electric current is passed through it. The anodes are made from carbon and the cathode is the carbon-lined steel case.

• At the cathode aluminium is formed:

$$Al^{3+}(l) + 3e^- \rightarrow Al(l)$$

• At the anode oxygen is formed:

$2O^{2-}(l) \rightarrow O_2(g) + 4e^-$

The overall equation is:

$2Al_2O_3(l) \rightarrow 4Al(l) + 3O_2(g)$

The oxygen reacts with the carbon anodes to form carbon dioxide, which escapes. Because of this the rods need to be replaced constantly.

$C(s) + O_2(g) \rightarrow CO_2(g)$

The process uses a great deal of electricity and is not cost-efficient unless the electricity is cheap. Aluminium is often extracted in countries with well-developed hydroelectric power.

carbon anodes

pure aluminium oxide is added continually

carbon lining of the cell is the cathode

the electrolyte is molten cryolite and aluminium oxide

molten aluminium tapped off

molten aluminium

+

Δ Fig. 2.15 Extracting aluminium is expensive. Molten cryolite is used to produce an electrolyte that has a lower melting point than that of pure aluminium oxide.

## REMEMBER

Remember that the aluminium ions are reduced by the addition of electrons to form aluminium atoms. The oxide ions are oxidised because they lose electrons to form oxygen molecules.

## THE USES OF ALUMINIUM

The uses of aluminium are linked directly to its properties.

| Uses of aluminium | Properties making aluminium suitable for the use |
|---|---|
| Packaging – drinks cans, foil wrapping, foil containers | Non-toxic<br>Impermeable – no aroma or loss of flavour<br>Resistant to corrosion |
| Transport – aeroplanes | High strength-to-weight ratio<br>Low density<br>Resistant to corrosion<br>(Note: alloys are often used because they are stronger than pure aluminium) |
| Overhead electrical cables | High electrical conductivity; low density |
| As a building material | Easily shaped<br>Low corrosion<br>High strength-to-weight ratio |
| For kitchen utensils | Shiny appearance; non-corrosive |

Δ Table 2.1 Uses of aluminium.

## QUESTIONS

**1.** In the extraction of aluminium using electrolysis:

   **a)** Why is cryolite used?

   **b)** At which electrode do the aluminium ions form aluminium atoms?

   **c)** Write a half-equation for the formation of aluminium atoms from aluminium ions.

   **d)** Are the aluminium ions oxidised or reduced as they form aluminium atoms? Explain your answer.

   **e)** Why is it necessary to replace the carbon electrodes regularly?

**2.** What properties of aluminium make it a suitable material for constructing an aeroplane?

**END OF EXTENDED**

## FACTS ABOUT ALUMINIUM

**1.** Aluminum is the most abundant metal in the Earth's crust, and the third most abundant element overall, after oxygen and silicon. It makes up about 8% by weight of the Earth's solid surface. Aluminum metal is too reactive to occur in nature. Instead, it is found combined in over 270 different minerals. The main ore of aluminum is bauxite. Bauxite is mined extensively to meet the demand for aluminum: Australia produced 62 million tonnes of bauxite in 2005.

**2.** The gemstones ruby and sapphire are crystals of aluminium oxide coloured by chromium or iron compounds.

△ Fig. 2.16 Worldwide we use 6 billion aluminium cans each year, about 200 000 tonnes of aluminium.

**3.** The cost of electricity represents about 20% to 40% of the total cost of producing aluminium, depending on the location of the smelter. Smelters tend to be situated where electric power is both plentiful and inexpensive, such as in the United Arab Emirates where there are excess natural gas supplies, and Iceland and Norway with energy generated from renewable sources such as hydroelectric power. Aluminium production consumes roughly 5% of the electricity generated in the USA.

**4.** The corrosion resistance of aluminum is due to a thin surface layer of aluminum oxide that forms when the metal is exposed to air, effectively preventing further oxidation.

**5.** Aluminum is 100% recyclable without any loss of its natural qualities. Recycling involves melting the scrap, which requires only 5% of the energy used to produce aluminum from its ore, although a significant part (up to 15% of the input material) is lost as dross (an ash-like oxide). However, the dross can undergo a further process to extract more aluminum.

## MANUFACTURING SODIUM HYDROXIDE AND CHLORINE

Sodium hydroxide and chlorine are manufactured by the electrolysis of concentrated sodium chloride solution (brine) in a diaphragm cell. This process is the basis of what is known as the chlor-alkali industry.

During the electrolysis three products are made – chlorine, sodium hydroxide and hydrogen. It is very important to keep these products separate, and this is why the diaphragm cell is used.

### REMEMBER

The fact that there are four ions involved in sodium chloride solution, yet in electrolysis only two ions are converted to atoms or molecules, is called *preferential discharge*.

You will need to remember the two ions that are discharged, and that oxidation and reduction are involved:

$2Cl^-(aq) \rightarrow Cl_2(g) + 2e^-$ = oxidation of $Cl^-$

$2H^+(aq) + 2e^- \rightarrow H_2(g)$ = reduction of $H^+$

When sodium chloride dissolves in water, its ions separate:

$NaCl(aq) \rightarrow Na^+(aq) + Cl^-(aq)$

There are also two ions from the water:

$H_2O(l) \rightleftharpoons H^+(aq) + OH^-(aq)$

In the process of electrolysis, ions are converted to atoms or molecules. In the case of brine:

- $Na^+(aq)$ and $H^+(aq)$ are attracted to the cathode
- $Cl^-(aq)$ and $OH^-(aq)$ are attracted to the anode.

| At the cathode (−) | At the anode (+) |
|---|---|
| Sodium is more reactive than hydrogen, so only the hydrogen ions are changed to form a molecule: | Both $OH^-$ and $Cl^-$ are attracted to the anode, but only the chloride ions are changed to form a molecule: |
| $2H^+(aq) + 2e^- \rightarrow H_2(g)$ | $2Cl^-(aq) \rightarrow Cl_2(g) + 2e^-$ |

△ Table 2.2 What happens when brine is electrolysed.

The remaining solution contains the ions $Na^+(aq)$ and $OH^-(aq)$, so it is sodium hydroxide solution, $NaOH(aq)$.

Summary

At the cathode: hydrogen gas

At the anode: chlorine gas

The solution: sodium hydroxide.

Both chlorine and sodium
hydroxide are vitally important
chemicals in the manufacture of
other industrial products and
millions of tonnes of them are
used every year.

△ Fig. 2.17 The diaphragm cell.

## REMEMBER

You should know that the reason for keeping the chlorine and sodium
hydroxide apart in the diaphragm cell is because they react together to
form sodium chlorate(I), NaOCl (used as a bleach).

△ Fig. 2.18 Uses of sodium hydroxide.

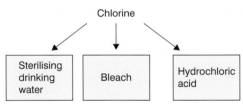

△ Fig. 2.19 Uses of chlorine.

## QUESTIONS

1. **a)** What ions are present in an aqueous solution of sodium
   chloride?

   **b)** Which two of these ions will be attracted to the cathode?
   What factor determines which of these ions will be
   discharged?

   **c)** Write a half-equation to show the discharge of this ion at the
   cathode.

2. List the major uses of sodium hydroxide.

## SIMPLE CELLS

Metals and solutions of their salts can be used to generate electricity.

If the apparatus in Fig. 2.20 is set up, the lamp glows, showing that electricity has been produced by the **cell**. A cell is a device that converts chemical energy into electrical energy.

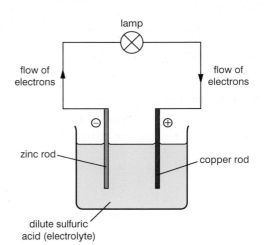

△ Fig. 2.20 A simple cell.

Zinc is higher than copper in the reactivity series, so zinc is the producer of electrons (the cathode) and the copper takes the electrons (the anode).

• At the cathode (negative electrode):

each zinc atom loses 2 electrons and forms a zinc ion, $Zn^{2+}$, which is released into the solution. The zinc rod loses mass and eventually dissolves. The electrons flow through the external circuit to the copper.

$Zn(s) \rightarrow Zn^{2+}(aq) + 2e^-$

Although a zinc/copper pair is used here as the example, you can generate electricity from any pair of different metals set up as shown in Fig. 2.20.

The voltage produced depends on the position of the metals in the reactivity series. The rule is:

the further apart the metals are in the reactivity series, the higher the potential difference or voltage will be.

## QUESTION

1. A student replaced the zinc rod in the cell in Fig. 2.20 with an aluminium rod.

   **a)** How would you expect the cell voltage to change? Explain your answer.

   **b)** Which combination of the four metals aluminium, copper, iron and zinc would produce the largest voltage in a simple cell? Explain your answer.

**END OF EXTENDED**

# End of topic checklist

**Key terms**

anode, cathode, cell, ceramic, chemical change, dissociation, electrode, electrolysis, electrolyte, oxidation, plastic, reactivity series, reduction, reversible reaction

## During your study of this topic you should have learned:

○ That electrolysis is the breakdown of an ionic compound, molten or in aqueous solution, by the passage of electricity.

○ How to describe the electrode products in the electrolysis, using inert electrodes of platinum or carbon, of:

- molten lead(II) bromide
- concentrated hydrochloric acid
- concentrated aqueous sodium chloride
- dilute sulfuric acid.

○ That metals or hydrogen are formed at the negative electrode (cathode) and that non-metals (other than hydrogen) are formed at the positive electrode (anode).

○ How to predict the product of the electrolysis of a binary (two element) compound in the molten state.

○ How to describe the electroplating of metals.

○ About some of the uses of electroplating.

○ How to describe the reasons for the use of copper and (steel-cored) aluminium in cables.

○ How to describe why plastics and ceramics are used as insulators.

○ **EXTENDED** How to relate the products of electrolysis to the electrolyte and electrodes used in the following examples:

- molten lead(II) bromide
- concentrated hydrochloric acid
- concentrated aqueous sodium chloride
- dilute sulfuric acid
- aqueous copper(II) sulfate using carbon and copper electrodes.

○ **EXTENDED** How to describe electrolysis in terms of the ions present and reactions at the electrodes in the above examples.

○ **EXTENDED** How to predict the products of electrolysis of a specified halide in dilute or concentrated aqueous solution.

○ **EXTENDED** How to describe, in outline, the manufacture of:

- aluminium from pure aluminium oxide in molten cryolite
- chlorine, hydrogen and sodium hydroxide from concentrated aqueous sodium chloride.

○ **EXTENDED** How to construct ionic half-equations for reactions at the cathode.

○ **EXTENDED** How to describe the transfer of charge during electrolysis to include:

- the movement of electrons in the metallic conductor
- the removal or addition of electrons from the external circuit at the electrodes
- the movement of ions in the electrolyte.

○ **EXTENDED** How to describe the production of electrical energy from simple cells i.e. two electrodes in an electrolyte.

# End of topic questions

*Note: The marks awarded for these questions indicate the level of detail required in the answers. In the examination, the number of marks awarded to questions like these may be different.*

1. Explain the following terms:

   **a)** *electrolysis*                                                           (1 mark)

   **b)** *electrolyte*                                                            (1 mark)

   **c)** *electrode*                                                             (1 mark)

   **d)** *anode*                                                               (1 mark)

   **e)** *cathode.*                                                             (1 mark)

2. Zinc bromide, $ZnBr_2$, is an ionic solid. Why does the solid not conduct electricity?                                                                        (2 marks)

3. Copy and complete the following table which shows the products formed when molten electrolytes undergo electrolysis.                      (4 marks)

| Electrolyte | Product at the anode | Product at the cathode |
|---|---|---|
| Silver bromide | | |
| Lead(II) chloride | | |
| Aluminium oxide | | |
| | Iodine | Magnesium |

4. Sodium chloride, NaCl, is ionic. What are the products at the anode and cathode in the electrolysis of:

   **a)** molten sodium chloride                                                 (2 marks)

   **b)** concentrated aqueous sodium chloride?                                  (2 marks)

5. An iron fork is to be silver plated.

   **a)** Which electrode would be the iron fork?                               (1 mark)

   **b)** What would be used as the other electrode?                            (1 mark)

6. Suggest reasons for the following:

   **a)** Aluminium is often used instead of copper in overhead electrical cables.  (2 marks)

   **b)** Ceramic discs are used to support overhead electrical cables or pylons.  (2 marks)

**7. EXTENDED** Write half-equations for the following reactions:

**a)** the formation of aluminium atoms from aluminium ions                    **(2 marks)**

**b)** the formation of sodium atoms from sodium ions                          **(2 marks)**

**c)** the formation of oxygen gas from oxide ions                             **(2 marks)**

**d)** the formation of bromine gas from bromide ions                          **(2 marks)**

**e)** the formation of oxygen gas and water from hydroxide ions.              **(2 marks)**

**8. EXTENDED** Aluminium is extracted from aluminium oxide ($Al_2O_3$) by electrolysis. Aluminium oxide contains $Al^{3+}$ and $O^{2-}$ ions. The aluminium oxide is dissolved in molten cryolite.

**a)** Why is the electrolysis carried out in a solution of aluminium oxide rather than solid aluminium oxide?                                               **(2 marks)**

**b)** Write a half-equation to show how $O^{2-}$ ions are converted into oxygen gas.   **(2 marks)**

**c)** The carbon electrodes used in the electrolysis need to be constantly replaced. Explain why this is necessary.                                         **(2 marks)**

**d)** Write a half-equation to show the formation of aluminium at the cathode.   **(2 marks)**

**e)** The extraction of aluminium often takes place in areas with easy access to hydroelectric power. Suggest a reason for this.                             **(2 marks)**

**9. EXTENDED** Sodium hydroxide and chlorine are manufactured by the electrolysis of concentrated sodium chloride solution.

**a)  i)** At which electrode is the chlorine gas formed?                       **(1 mark)**

**ii)** Write a half-equation, including state symbols, for the formation of chlorine.                                                                 **(2 marks)**

**b)  i)** What gas is formed at the other electrode?                           **(1 mark)**

**ii)** Write a half-equation, including state symbols, for the formation of this gas.                                                                 **(2 marks)**

**c)** Where does the sodium hydroxide form?                                    **(2 marks)**

10. **EXTENDED** The table shows the results of an experiment to measure the voltages produced in a series of simple cells made with different combinations of metals. The metals are labelled A, B, C and D.

| Metal 1 | Metal 2 | Voltage (V) |
| --- | --- | --- |
| A | B | 0.1 |
| A | C | 2.2 |
| A | D | 1.6 |
| B | C | 1.9 |

a) Draw and label a diagram showing how a simple cell can be made using two metals. Show where the voltmeter would be connected. **(2 marks)**

b) Metal A is the least reactive metal. Which metal, B, C or D, must be the most reactive? Explain your answer. **(2 marks)**

c) Write down the complete order of reactivity of the metals, starting with the most reactive metal. **(2 marks)**

# Chemical energetics

## INTRODUCTION

When chemicals react together, the reactions cause energy changes. This is obvious when a fuel is burned and heat energy is released into the surroundings. Heat changes in other reactions may be less dramatic but they still take place. A knowledge of chemical bonding can really help to understand how these energy changes occur. As well as from fuels, energy can also be obtained from radioactive substances and increasingly from fuel cells.

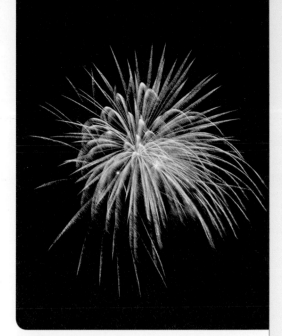

△ Fig. 2.21 Fireworks are carefully controlled chemical reactions.

## ENERGY CHANGES IN CHEMICAL REACTIONS

In most reactions, energy is transferred to the surroundings and the temperature goes up. These reactions are **exothermic**. Some examples of exothermic reactions are combustion, respiration and neutralisation. In a minority of cases, energy is absorbed from the surroundings as a reaction takes place and the temperature goes down. These reactions are **endothermic**. Some examples of endothermic reactions are photosynthesis and thermal decomposition.

For example, when magnesium ribbon is added to dilute hydrochloric acid, the temperature of the acid increases – the reaction is exothermic. In contrast, when sodium hydrogencarbonate is added to hydrochloric acid, the temperature of the acid decreases – the reaction is endothermic.

△ Fig. 2.22 Measuring energy changes in reactions.

Energy changes in reactions like these can be measured using a polystyrene cup (an insulator) as a calorimeter. If a lid is added to the cup, very little energy is transferred to the air and reasonably accurate results can be obtained.

## QUESTIONS

**1.** What is an *exothermic* reaction?

**2.** What is an *endothermic* reaction?

**3.** Why do polystyrene cups make good calorimeters for measuring energy changes in some chemical reactions?

All reactions involving the **combustion** of fuels are exothermic. The energy transferred when a fuel burns can be measured using **calorimetry**, as shown in the diagram.

◁ Fig. 2.23. Measuring the energy produced by burning a liquid fuel.

The rise in temperature of the water is a measure of the energy transferred to the water. This technique will not give a very accurate answer because much of the energy will be transferred to the surrounding air. Nevertheless, it can be used to compare the energy released by **burning** the same amounts of different fuels.

## ENTHALPY CHANGE

The heat energy in chemical reactions is called enthalpy. An **enthalpy change** is given the symbol $\Delta H$. The enthalpy change for a particular reaction is shown at the end of the balanced equation. The units are kJ/mol.

## QUESTIONS

**1.** Measuring energy changes when burning fuels in a liquid burner does not give very accurate results. Why do you think this is?

**2.** A group of students was comparing the energy released on burning different liquid fuels in spirit burners using apparatus similar to that shown in Fig. 2.23. The results obtained are shown here:

| Name of fuel | Amount of fuel burned (g) | Rise in temperature of 200 cm³ of water in a metal can (° C) | Temperature rise of the water per g of fuel burned (° C/g) |
|---|---|---|---|
| Ethanol | 1.1 | 32 | |
| Paraffin | 0.9 | 30 | |
| Pentane | 1.5 | 38 | |
| Octane | 0.5 | 20 | |

**a)** How do you think the students worked out how much fuel was burned in each experiment?

**b)** Complete the last column of the table by working out the temperature rise in each experiment per gram of fuel burned. (Give your answers to the nearest whole number)

**i)** Which fuel produced the greatest temperature rise per gram burned?

**ii)** If the octane experiment were repeated using 400 cm³ of water in the metal can, approximately what temperature rise would you expect? Explain how you worked out your answer.

**3.** Another group of students used a glass beaker rather than a metal can in their experiments. Which group of students would you expect to get more accurate results? Explain your answer.

## ENERGY PROFILES AND Δ*H*

Energy level diagrams show the enthalpy difference between the reactants and the products.

| In an exothermic reaction, the energy content of the reactants is greater than the energy content of the products. Energy is being lost to the surroundings. ΔH is negative. | In an endothermic reaction, the energy content of the products is greater than the energy content of the reactants. Energy is being absorbed from the surroundings. ΔH is positive. |
|---|---|

All ΔH values should have a + or − sign in front of them to show if they are endothermic or exothermic.

**Activation energy** is the *minimum* amount of energy required for a reaction to occur. Fig. 2.25 shows the activation energy of a reaction.

The energy profile can now be completed as shown. The reaction for this profile is exothermic, with ΔH negative.

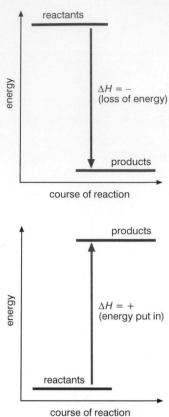

△ Fig. 2.24 Energy level diagrams for exothermic and endothermic reactions.

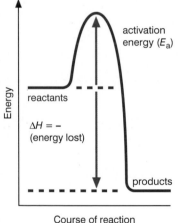

◁ Fig. 2.25 Energy profile.

## QUESTIONS

**1.** The enthalpy change for a particular reaction is positive. Is the reaction endothermic or exothermic?

**2.** On an energy profile, what is the name given to the minimum amount of energy required for a reaction to occur?

**3.** **EXTENDED** Methane burns in excess oxygen to form carbon dioxide and water. When 1 mole of methane is burnt 882kJ of energy is released. Draw an energy level diagram for this reaction.

**4.** **EXTENDED** Draw and label energy level diagrams for each of the reactions shown in the table below:

| Reaction | Activation Energy (kJ/mol) | Enthalpy Change (kJ/mol) |
|---|---|---|
| A | 120 | −90 |
| B | 80 | +10 |

# Developing investigative skills

Two students used a polystyrene cup to compare the energy changes in two reactions:

- magnesium with hydrochloric acid
- sodium hydrogencarbonate with hydrochloric acid.

They added 50 cm$^3$ of 0.5 M hydrochloric acid to a polystyrene cup and measured its temperature. They then added a known mass of magnesium ribbon to the acid. They stirred the reaction mixture with a glass stirring rod until the reaction was complete and then took the final temperature. They then repeated the procedure using sodium hydrogencarbonate. Their results are shown in the table.

| Reaction | Mass of solid used (g) | Initial temperature of the acid (° C) | Final temperature of the acid (° C) | Temperature change (° C) |
|---|---|---|---|---|
| Magnesium + hydrochloric acid | 0.1 | 22 | 35 | |
| Sodium hydrogencarbonate + hydrochloric acid | 2.5 | 22 | 18 | |

## Using and organising techniques, apparatus and materials

❶ What apparatus do you think was used to measure the volumes of hydrochloric acid?

❷ Why did the students stir the reaction mixtures until the reaction was complete and the final temperature was taken?

## Observing, measuring and recording

❸ What would you expect to observe when magnesium ribbon is added to dilute hydrochloric acid?

## Interpreting observations and data

❹ Work out the temperature change in each reaction.

❺ Work out the temperature change per gram of solid in each reaction.

❻ In each case is the reaction exothermic or endothermic?

❼ Draw a simple energy level diagram to represent the reaction between magnesium and hydrochloric acid.

## Evaluating methods

❽ Energy is often lost from the polystyrene cup, making the temperature change lower than it should be. Suggest one way this error could be reduced.

## WHERE DOES THE ENERGY COME FROM?

The reaction that occurs when a fuel is burning can be considered to take place in two stages. In the first stage the covalent bonds between the atoms in the fuel molecules and the oxygen molecules are broken. In the second stage the atoms combine and new covalent bonds are formed. For example, in the combustion of propane:

| propane | + | oxygen | → | carbon dioxide | + | water |
|---------|---|--------|---|----------------|---|-------|
| $C_3H_8(g)$ | + | $5O_2(g)$ | → | $3CO_2(g)$ | + | $4H_2O(l)$ |

$\Delta H = -2202$ kJ/mol

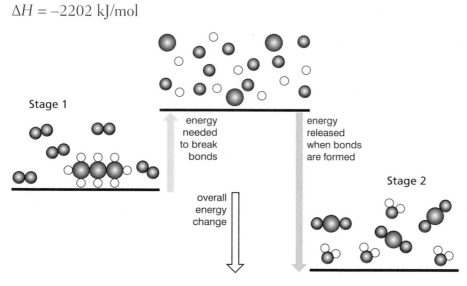

△ Fig. 2.26 Energy changes in an exothermic reaction.

Stage 1: Energy is needed (absorbed from the surroundings) to break the bonds. This process is endothermic.

Stage 2: Energy is released (transferred to the surroundings) as the new bonds form. This process is exothermic.

The overall reaction is exothermic because forming the new bonds releases more energy than is needed initially to break the old bonds. Fig. 2.27 is a simplified energy level diagram showing the exothermic nature of the reaction.

◁ Fig. 2.27 A simplified energy level diagram for the reaction.

The larger the alkane molecule, the more the energy is released on combustion. This is because although more bonds must be broken in the first stage of the reaction, more bonds are formed in the second stage.

| Alkane | | Molar enthalpy of combustion (kJ/mol) |
|---|---|---|
| Methane | $CH_4$ | −882 |
| Ethane | $C_2H_6$ | −1542 |
| Propane | $C_3H_8$ | −2202 |
| Butane | $C_4H_{10}$ | −2877 |
| Pentane | $C_5H_{12}$ | −3487 |
| Hexane | $C_6H_{14}$ | −4141 |

△ Table 2.3 Molar enthalpy of combustion of alkanes.

## REMEMBER

In an exothermic reaction, the energy released on forming new bonds is greater than that needed to break the old bonds.

In an endothermic reaction, more energy is needed to break the old bonds than is released when new bonds are formed. The energy changes in endothermic reactions are usually relatively small.

The enthalpy figures given in Table 2.3 for the alkanes are calculated when 1 mole of each alkane is completely burned in a plentiful supply of oxygen to form carbon dioxide and water. The increase in energy from one alkane to the next is almost constant due to the extra $CH_2$ unit in the molecule.

## BOND ENERGY CALCULATIONS

Every covalent bond has a particular amount of energy needed to break it. This is the same as the amount of energy given out when it is made. This is the **bond energy** and its units are kJ/mol.

Table 2.4 shows some values of average bond energies.

| Bond | C–C | C–H | O=O | H–H | H–O | C=O | Cl–Cl | H–Cl |
|---|---|---|---|---|---|---|---|---|
| Average bond energy (kJ/mol) | 348 | 413 | 498 | 436 | 464 | 745 | 242 | 431 |

△ Table 2.4  Some average bond energies.

## WORKED EXAMPLE

Calculate the energy change for the reaction between hydrogen and chlorine:

$$H_2 + Cl_2 \rightarrow 2HCl \qquad \text{i.e. } H\text{–}H + Cl\text{–}Cl \rightarrow 2 \times H\text{–}Cl$$

What does the sign of the energy change tell you about the reaction?

| H–H | + | Cl–Cl | → | 2 | × | H–Cl |
|-----|---|-------|---|---|---|------|
| 436 kJ/mol | | 242 kJ/mol | | 2 | × | 431 kJ/mol |

total for breaking bonds = +678 kJ/mol (endothermic because bond breaking)

total for making bonds = −862 kJ/mol (exothermic because bond making)

Overall difference =   −862 kJ/mol

+678 kJ/mol

−184 kJ/mol

Answer:      $\Delta H = -184$ kJ/mol

It is an exothermic reaction ($\Delta H$ negative).

Summary:

**1.** Total all the bonds on the left and allocate a + sign.

**2.** Total all the bonds on the right and allocate a − sign.

**3.** Find the difference between the two values. Remember to include the sign (+ or −).

**4.** State if exothermic (−) or endothermic (+).

## REMEMBER

In bond energy calculation questions you must identify the sign of the answer and link it to exothermic (−) or endothermic (+). You will gain extra credit for linking 'exothermic' to more energy being released by bond making than used in bond breaking, and the opposite for 'endothermic'.

## END OF EXTENDED

## QUESTIONS

1. What does the sign of $\Delta H$ indicate about a reaction?

2. **EXTENDED** Is energy needed or released when bonds are broken?

3. **EXTENDED** In an endothermic reaction is more or less energy needed to break the old bonds than is recovered when new bonds are formed?

4. **EXTENDED** What units are used for bond energy values?

5. **EXTENDED** Calculate the energy change when 2 moles of hydrogen molecules react with 1 mole of oxygen molecules to make 2 moles of water molecules. Use the bond energy values in Table 2.4.

## HOW COMMON ARE ENDOTHERMIC REACTIONS?

Almost all chemical reactions in which simple compounds or elements react to make new compounds are exothermic. One exception is the formation of nitrogen oxide (NO) from nitrogen and oxygen. Overall, energy is needed to create this compound, with less energy being released on forming bonds than was needed to break the bonds of the reactants. Nitrogen oxide is often formed in lightning storms. The lightning provides enough energy to split the nitrogen and oxygen molecules before the atoms combine to form nitrogen oxide:

$$N_2(g) + O_2(g) \rightarrow 2NO(g) \quad \Delta H \text{ positive}$$

△ Fig. 2.28 These plants are making food by photosynthesis, an endothermic reaction.

Another exception is **photosynthesis**. Plants use energy from sunlight to convert carbon dioxide and water into glucose and oxygen:

$$6CO_2(g) + 6H_2O(l) \rightarrow C_6H_{12}O_6(aq) + 6O_2(g) \quad \Delta H \text{ positive}$$

'Cold packs', which you can buy in some countries, can be used to help you keep cool. Usually you have to bend a pack to break a partition inside and allow two substances to mix. The pack will then stay cold for an hour or longer. However, it may not be an endothermic reaction that is working in the cold pack. Dissolving chemicals like urea or ammonium nitrate in water also cause the temperature of water to fall, but dissolving is a **physical change**, not a chemical change. Whether it is an endothermic reaction or not is the manufacturer's secret.

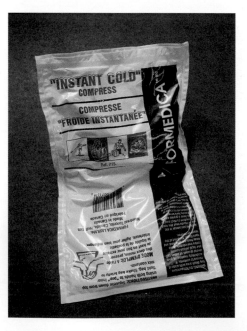

△ Fig. 2.29 A cold pack.

## HYDROGEN AS A FUEL

The reaction between hydrogen and oxygen is very exothermic and produces a lot of heat energy:

$$2H_2(g) + O_2(g) \rightarrow 2H_2O(l)$$

Burning 2 g of hydrogen releases 286 J of energy.

The reaction is used for powering space rockets.

Table 2.5 compares the amount of energy produced per gram when several substances are burned. You will see that hydrogen releases much more energy per gram than the other substances.

| Fuel | Energy produced per g of fuel (kJ) |
|---|---|
| Hydrogen | 143 |
| Methane | 55 |
| Octane (main component in petrol) | 44 |
| Glucose | 16 |

△ Table 2.5 Energy per gram produced by burning.

The advantages and disadvantages of using hydrogen as a combustion fuel in motor vehicles are summarised in Table 2.6.

| Advantages of using hydrogen | Disadvantages of using hydrogen |
|---|---|
| Compared to other fuels it produces a large amount of energy per gram | Liquid hydrogen has one-tenth the density of petrol, so vehicles using hydrogen need much larger fuel tanks than those using petrol or diesel |
| No carbon dioxide or sulfur dioxide emissions | The hydrogen has to be compressed and stored safely in the fuel tank |
| | Currently there are very few fuel stations that serve hydrogen fuel |

△ Table 2.6 Comparison of advantages and disadvantages of hydrogen fuel in motor vehicles.

△ Fig. 2.30 This car is fuelled by hydrogen gas. Why is hydrogen called 'clean energy'?

## ENERGY AND RADIOACTIVE ISOTOPES

Nuclear power stations use the heat produced by the decay of radioactive isotopes.

The heat generated is used to boil water to make steam, which then turns turbines and generators, producing electricity.

Uranium–235 ($^{235}$U) is the radioactive isotope used in nuclear reactions as a source of energy.

The process is known as nuclear fission. A slow-moving neutron is absorbed by the nucleus and then the nucleus splits into two almost equal parts releasing a large amount of energy.

▷ Fig. 2.31 Loading fuel rods into a nuclear reactor. The reactor is immersed in the blue water.

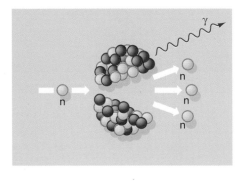

◁ Fig. 2.32 Splitting a single atom.

**EXTENDED**

## FUEL CELLS

Hydrogen and oxygen can be used to produce electricity in a fuel cell. The hydrogen gas is pumped onto the anode and oxygen gas onto the cathode. The platinum catalyst removes an electron from each hydrogen atom (forming hydrogen ions, $H^+$) and the electrons pass through the external circuit to the anode, producing an electric current. The chemical reactions are complicated but overall the hydrogen and oxygen combine to form water.

◁ Fig. 2.33 Hydrogen fuel cell. The platinum, used as the catalyst, is expensive and rare.

**END OF EXTENDED**

## QUESTIONS

**1.** What is the most common radioactive isotope used in nuclear power stations?

**2.** Another radioactive isotope that is used is plutonium-239. What does the number '239' represent?

# End of topic checklist

**Key terms**

activation energy, bond energy, burning, calorimetry, combustion, endothermic, enthalpy change, exothermic, photosynthesis, physical change

## During your study of this topic you should have learned:

○ How to describe the meaning of exothermic and endothermic reactions.

○ How to interpret energy level diagrams showing exothermic and endothermic reactions.

○ **EXTENDED** How to describe bond breaking as endothermic and bond forming as exothermic.

○ **EXTENDED** How to calculate the energy of a reaction using bond energies.

○ How to describe the release of heat energy by burning fuels.

○ How to describe hydrogen as a fuel.

○ How to describe radioactive isotopes, such as $^{235}U$, as a source of energy.

○ **EXTENDED** How to describe the use of hydrogen as a potential fuel reacting with oxygen to generate electricity in a fuel cell.

○ **EXTENDED** Be able to draw and label energy level diagrams for exothermic and endothermic reactions using data provided.

# End of topic questions

*Note: The marks awarded for these questions indicate the level of detail required in the answers. In the examination, the number of marks awarded to questions like these may be different.*

1. Explain each of the following:

   **a)** A polystyrene cup is used when measuring energy changes in simple reactions, such as adding magnesium ribbon to an acid. **(2 marks)**

   **b)** When sodium hydrogencarbonate is added to a solution of an acid the temperature of the acid falls. **(1 mark)**

   **c)** Hydrogen gas is a 'clean' fuel for use in motor vehicles. **(2 marks)**

   **d)** Uranium-235 is used as a source of energy. **(2 marks)**

2. An estimate of the energy produced when a fuel burns can be made by burning the fuel under a container holding water and measuring the temperature rise of the water.

   **a)** What type of material should the container be made of? Explain your answer. **(2 marks)**

   **b)** Why does this method give an estimate rather than an accurate value? **(2 marks)**

   **c)** How can the accuracy of this method be improved? **(2 marks)**

3. Calcium oxide reacts with water as shown in the equation:

   $$CaO(s) + H_2O(l) \rightarrow Ca(OH)_2(s)$$

   An energy level diagram for this reaction is shown below.

   **a)** What does the energy level diagram tell us about the type of energy change that takes place in this reaction? **(1 mark)**

   **b)** **EXTENDED** What does the energy level diagram indicate about the amounts of energy required to break original bonds and form new bonds in this reaction? **(1 mark)**

4. **EXTENDED** Chlorine ($Cl_2$) and hydrogen ($H_2$) react together to make hydrogen chloride (HCl). The equation can be written as:

   $H–H + Cl–Cl \rightarrow H–Cl + H–Cl$

   When this reaction occurs, energy is transferred to the surroundings. Explain this in terms of the energy transfer processes taking place when bonds are broken and when bonds are made. **(2 marks)**

5. **EXTENDED a)** Calculate the energy change for the combustion of methane ($CH_4$) in oxygen ($O_2$). **(3 marks)**

   $$\begin{array}{c} H \quad H \\ \diagdown \diagup \\ C \\ \diagup \diagdown \\ H \quad H \end{array} + 2 \times O{=}O \rightarrow O{=}C{=}O + 2 \times H–O–H$$

   Use the bond energy values in Table 2.4.

   **b)** What does the sign of the energy change tell you about the reaction? **(1 mark)**

# Rate of reaction

## INTRODUCTION

Some chemical reactions take place extremely quickly. For example, when petrol is ignited it combines with oxygen almost instantaneously. Reactions like these have a *high rate*. Other reactions are much slower, for example when an iron bar rusts in the air; reactions like these have a *low rate*. Chemical reactions can be controlled and made to be quicker or slower. This can be very important in situations like food production, either by slowing down or increasing the rate at which food ripens, or in the chemical industry where the rate of a reaction can be adjusted to an optimum level.

△ Fig. 2.34 Petrol igniting.

## KNOWLEDGE CHECK

✓ Know the arrangement, movement and energy of the particles in the three states of matter: solid, liquid and gas.

✓ Understand how the course of a reaction can be shown in an energy level diagram.

✓ Be able to write and interpret balanced chemical equations.

## LEARNING OBJECTIVES

✓ Be able to identify physical change and chemical change and understand the differences between them.

✓ Be able to describe the effects of concentration, particle size, catalysts (including enzymes) and temperature on the rates of reactions.

✓ Be able to describe a practical method for investigating the rate of a reaction involving the evolution of a gas.

✓ Be able to describe the application of the above factors to the dangers of explosive combustion with fine powders (such as in flour mills) and gases (such as in mines).

✓ **EXTENDED** Be able to describe a suitable method for investigating the effect of a given variable on the rate of a reaction.

✓ **EXTENDED** Be able to interpret data obtained from experiments concerned with rate of reaction.

✓ **EXTENDED** Be able to describe and explain the effects of temperature and concentration in terms of collisions between reacting particles.

✓ **EXTENDED** Be able to explain that an increase in temperature causes an increase in collision rate *and* more of the colliding particles have sufficient energy (activation energy) to react, whereas an increase in concentration only causes an increase in collision rate.

✓ **EXTENDED** Be able to describe the role of light in photochemical reactions and the effect of light on these reactions.

## PHYSICAL AND CHEMICAL CHANGES

A chemical change, or chemical reaction, is quite different from physical changes that occur, for example, when sugar dissolves in water.

In a chemical change, one or more new substances are produced. In many cases an observable change is apparent, for example, the colour changes or a gas is produced.

An apparent change in mass can occur. This change is often quite small and difficult to detect unless accurate balances are used. Mass is conserved in *all* chemical reactions – the apparent change in mass usually occurs because one of the reactants or products is a gas (whose mass may not have been measured).

An energy change is almost always involved. In most cases energy is released and the surroundings become warmer. In some cases energy is absorbed from the surroundings, and so the surroundings become colder. Note: Some physical changes, such as evaporation, also have energy changes.

**EXTENDED**

## COLLISION THEORY

For a chemical reaction to occur, the reacting particles (atoms, molecules or ions) must collide. The energy involved in the collision must be enough to break the chemical bonds in the reacting particles – or the particles will just bounce off one another.

A collision that has enough energy to result in a chemical reaction is an **effective collision**.

unsuccessful          successful

Δ Fig. 2.35 Particles must collide with sufficient energy to make an effective collision.

Some chemical reactions occur extremely quickly (for example, the explosive reaction between petrol and oxygen in a car engine) and some more slowly (for example, iron rusts over days or weeks). This is because they have different **activation energies**. Activation energy acts as a barrier to a reaction. It is the minimum amount of energy required in a collision for a reaction to occur. As a general rule, the bigger the activation energy, the slower the reaction will be at a particular temperature.

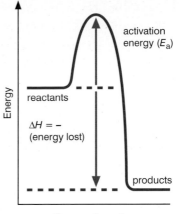

△ Fig. 2.36 Reaction profile.

The 'barrier' preventing a reaction from occurring is called the activation energy. If the activation energy of a reaction is low, more of the collisions will be effective and the reaction will proceed quickly. If the activation energy is high, a smaller proportion of collisions will be effective and the reaction will be slow.

**END OF EXTENDED**

## RATE OF A REACTION

A quick reaction takes place in a short time. It has a high **rate of reaction**. As the time taken for a reaction to be completed increases, the rate of the reaction decreases. In other words:

| Speed | Rate | Completion time |
|---|---|---|
| Quick or fast | High | Short |
| Slow | Low | Long |

△ Table 2.7 Speed, rate and time.

## QUESTIONS

1. What is the main difference between a physical change and a chemical change?

2. In a chemical change there is often an apparent change in mass even though mass cannot be created nor destroyed in a chemical reaction. What is a possible cause of this apparent change in mass?

3. EXTENDED In the collision theory, what two things must happen for two particles to react?

4. EXTENDED What is an *effective* collision?

5. EXTENDED Describe, using a diagram, what is meant by the term *activation energy*.

## MONITORING THE RATE OF A REACTION

The rate of a reaction changes as the reaction proceeds. There are some easy ways of monitoring this change.

When marble (calcium carbonate) reacts with hydrochloric acid, the following reaction starts straight away:

calcium carbonate + hydrochloric acid → calcium chloride + carbon dioxide + water

$CaCO_3(s)$       + 2HCl(aq)       → $CaCl_2(aq)$       + $CO_2(g)$       + $H_2O(l)$

The reaction can be monitored as it proceeds either by measuring the volume of gas being formed or by measuring the change in mass of the reaction flask.

The volume of gas produced in this reaction can be measured using the apparatus shown in Fig. 2.37. The hydrochloric acid is put into the conical flask, the marble chips are added, the bung is quickly fixed into the neck of the flask and the stopclock is started.

gas syringe

dilute hydrochloric acid

calcium carbonate (marble chips)

◁ Fig. 2.37 Monitoring the rate of a reaction.

The reaction will start immediately, effervescence (bubbling) will occur in the flask as the carbon dioxide gas is produced and the plunger on the syringe will start to move. Measuring the volume of gas in the syringe every 10 seconds will indicate how the total amount of gas produced changes as the reaction proceeds. The change in the rate of the reaction with time can be shown on a graph of the results (see Fig. 2.39).

### EXTENDED

To measure the change in mass in the same reaction, the apparatus shown in Fig. 2.38 can be used. The hydrochloric acid is put into the conical flask, the marble chips are added, the cotton wool plug is put in the neck of the flask and the stopclock is started. The mass of the flask and contents is measured as soon as the plug is inserted and then every 10 seconds as the reaction occurs. The mass will decrease as carbon dioxide gas escapes from the flask.

- loose cotton wool plug to stop spray escaping

- dilute hydrochloric acid

stopclock

- marble chips

balance

◁ Fig. 2.38  Measuring the change in mass.

As before, drawing a graph of the results shows the change in the rate of the reaction over time.

Graphs of the results from both experiments have almost identical shapes. The rate of the reaction decreases as the reaction proceeds.

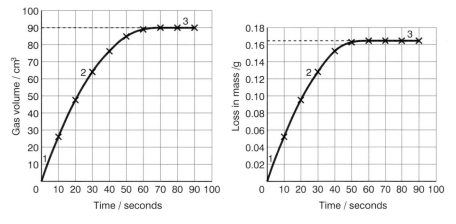

△ Fig. 2.39 Volume of carbon dioxide produced or loss in mass.

## Loss in mass during the reaction

The rate of the reaction at any point can be calculated from the gradient of the curve. The shapes of the graphs can be divided into three regions.

**1.** At this point, the curve is the steepest (has the highest gradient) and the reaction has its highest rate. The maximum number of reacting particles are present and the number of effective collisions per second is at its greatest.

**2.** The curve is not as steep (has a lower gradient) at this point and the rate of the reaction is lower. Fewer reacting particles are present and so the number of effective collisions per second is less.

**3.** The curve is horizontal (gradient is zero) and the reaction is complete. At least one of the reactants has been completely used up and so no further collisions can occur between the two reactants.

**END OF EXTENDED**

In experiments like these it is helpful to have a good understanding of the types of **variables** involved. The factor you are investigating is called the **independent variable** – when investigating how the reaction between marble and hydrochloric acid changes over time, time is the independent variable. A **dependent variable** is changed by the independent variable – in the marble and hydrochloric acid reaction, the volume of carbon dioxide produced is the dependent variable. Other variables involved are **control variables** and are not allowed to change to ensure a 'fair test'. So temperature could be a control variable in the reaction between marble and hydrochloric acid.

In chemical reactions it is very rare that exact (as predicted by the equation) quantities of reactants are used. In the marble and hydrochloric acid reaction all the marble may be used up (it is called the *limiting reactant*) but not all the hydrochloric acid; some is left when the reaction has stopped (it is *in excess*).

## QUESTIONS

1. What piece of apparatus can accurately measure the volume of gas produced in a reaction?

2. EXTENDED On a volume versus time graph, what does a horizontal line show?

3. EXTENDED When comparing two reactions, will the slower or quicker reaction have a steeper volume/ time gradient at the beginning?

## WHAT CAN CHANGE THE RATE OF A REACTION?

There are five key factors that can change the rate of a reaction:

- concentration (of a solution)
- temperature
- particle size (of a solid)
- a catalyst
- EXTENDED light.

### EXTENDED

A simple **collision theory** can be used to explain how these factors affect the rate of a reaction. Two important parts of the theory are:

- The reacting particles must collide with each other.
- There must be sufficient energy in the collision to overcome the activation energy.

### END OF EXTENDED

## Concentration

Increasing the concentration of a reactant will increase the rate of reaction. When a piece of magnesium ribbon is added to a solution of hydrochloric acid, the following reaction occurs:

| magnesium | + | hydrochloric acid | → | magnesium chloride | + | hydrogen |
|---|---|---|---|---|---|---|
| $Mg(s)$ | + | $2HCl(aq)$ | → | $MgCl_2(aq)$ | + | $H_2(g)$ |

As the magnesium and acid come into contact, there is effervescence ('bubbling') and hydrogen gas is given off. Two experiments were performed using the same length of magnesium ribbon, but different concentrations of acid. In experiment 1 the hydrochloric acid used was 2.0 mol/dm³, in experiment 2 the acid was 0.5 mol/dm³. The graph in Fig. 2.40 shows the results of the two experiments.

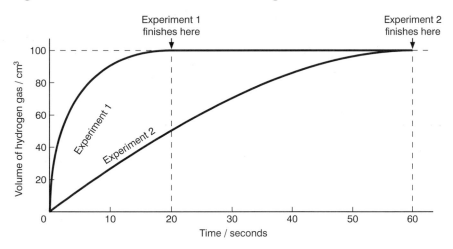

△ Fig. 2.40 Volume of hydrogen produced in the reaction between magnesium and hydrochloric acid.

In experiment 1 the curve is steeper (has a higher gradient) than in experiment 2. In experiment 1 the reaction is complete after 20 seconds, whereas in experiment 2 it takes 60 seconds. The initial rate of the reaction is higher with 2.0 mol/dm³ hydrochloric acid than with 0.5 mol/dm³ hydrochloric acid.

## EXTENDED

In the 2.0 mol/dm³ hydrochloric acid solution there are more hydrogen ions in a given volume, a higher concentration of hydrogen ions, and so there will be a lot more effective collisions per second with the surface of the magnesium ribbon than in the 0.5 mol/dm³ hydrochloric acid.

△ Fig. 2.41 Using dilute and concentrated solutions in a reaction.

# Developing investigative skills

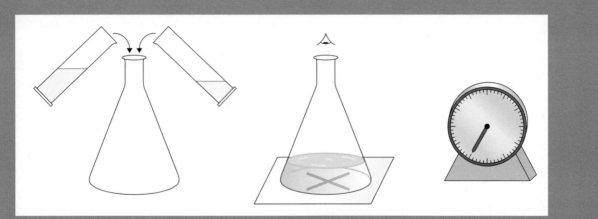

△ Fig. 2.42 Experiment with sodium thiosulfate solution and hydrochloric acid.

A student was investigating the reaction between sodium thiosulfate solution and hydrochloric acid. As the reaction takes place, a precipitate of sulfur forms in the solution and makes it change from colourless (and clear) to pale yellow (and opaque). The time it takes for a certain amount of sulfur to form can be used as a measure of the rate of the reaction.

The student used 1.0 mol/dm³ sodium thiosulfate solution and made up different concentrations of the solution by using the volumes of the solution and water shown in the table that follows.

She then drew a cross in pencil on a piece of paper.

She then added 5 cm³ of dilute hydrochloric acid to the solution in one of the flasks, the stopclock was started, the mixture was quickly stirred or swirled and then the conical flask was put on top of the pencilled cross.

The student looked through the conical flask to the cross and stopped the stopclock as soon as the cross could no longer be seen.

She then repeated the process with the other four solutions. Her results are shown in the table:

| Volume of sodium thiosulfate solution (cm³) | 50 | 40 | 30 | 20 | 10 |
| Volume of water (cm³) | 0 | 10 | 20 | 30 | 40 |
| Volume of hydrochloric acid (cm³) | 5 | 5 | 5 | 5 | 5 |
| Time for the cross to be obscured (s) | 14 | 18 | 23 | 36 | 67 |

## Using and organising techniques apparatus and materials

❶ Why was the total volume in the flask always 55 cm³?

❷ Why was the stopclock started when the acid was added and not when the flask was put on the pencilled cross?

❸ What apparatus would you use to measure the volume of sodium thiosulfate solution?

## Interpreting observations and data

Draw a graph of volume of sodium thiosulfate solution against time. Draw a smooth curve through the points.

❹ What does the overall shape of the curve tell you about the effect of changing the concentration of sodium thiosulfate on the rate of the reaction?

❺ Use your results to predict what the time would have been if 15 cm³ of sodium thiosulfate and 35 cm³ of water had been used.

## Evaluating methods

❻ What do you think are the main sources of error in this experiment? (Pick the two you think would have the most effect on the accuracy of the results.)

**END OF EXTENDED**

## TEMPERATURE

Increasing the temperature of the reactants will increase the rate of a reaction.

**EXTENDED**

Warming a substance transfers kinetic energy to its particles. More kinetic energy means that the particles move faster. Because they are moving faster there will be more collisions each second. The increased energy of the collisions also means that the proportion of collisions that are effective will increase. A reaction was carried out at two different temperatures – first at 20 °C and then at 30 °C.

△ Fig. 2.43 Effect of increasing temperature on particles.

Increasing the temperature of the reaction between some marble chips and hydrochloric acid will not increase the final amount of carbon dioxide produced. The same amount of gas will be produced in a shorter time. The rates of the two reactions are different but the final loss in mass is the same.

△ Fig. 2.44 The effect of temperature on the reaction between hydrochloric acid and marble chips.

### END OF EXTENDED

## QUESTIONS

1. What units are used to measure the concentration of solutions?

2. **EXTENDED** In terms of particles colliding, why does increasing the concentration of a solution increase the rate of reaction?

3. **EXTENDED** Give two reasons why increasing temperature increases the rate of reaction.

## SCIENCE IN CONTEXT

## THE EXPLOSIVE TRUTH ABOUT FLOUR MILLS

The surface area of particles really does affect the rate of some reactions!

Baking bread is a common and important activity, but making the flour that goes into the bread can be a dangerous business. Ever since a serious explosion at a flour mill near Minneapolis in the USA in 1878 killed 18 people, the milling industry has tried to reduce the risk of flour particles igniting into 'flour bombs'. In fact flour dust is thought to be more explosive than coal dust! Similar explosions have occurred in other factories when dust has exploded.

The key components to a flour or dust explosion are very small particles suspended in a plentiful supply of air, in a confined space and with a source of ignition. In factories the source of ignition doesn't have to be something

△ Fig. 2.45 Dropping milk powder on a flame.

obvious such as a discarded cigarette or match; it could be a spark from an electric motor or other electrical device, or even a light switch. In the case of the 1878 flour mill explosion, the cause of the explosion was thought to be a spark from an ageing electric motor.

In the laboratory or at home, if you put a match to some flour you might be able to get it to burn, but it certainly won't explode – the flour needs to be suspended in the air as very small particles that are close enough together so that if one flour particle ignites it starts a rapid chain reaction with other particles and then an explosion. So don't underestimate the importance of particle size on the rate of some reactions.

## PARTICLE SIZE

Decreasing the particle size (or increasing the **surface area**) of a solid reactant will increase the rate of a reaction.

### EXTENDED

A reaction can only take place if the reacting particles collide. This means that the reaction takes place at the surface of a solid. The particles within the solid cannot react until those on the surface have reacted and moved away.

### END OF EXTENDED

Powdered calcium carbonate has a smaller particle size (or much larger surface area) than the same mass of marble chips. A lump of coal will burn slowly in the air, whereas coal dust can react explosively. This is a hazard in coal mines where coal dust can react explosively with air. In addition, as well as the danger of explosive mixtures of coal dust and air, the build-up of methane gas can also form an explosive mixture with the air.

△ Fig. 2.46 Powdered carbon has a much larger surface area than the same mass in larger lumps.

## CATALYSTS

A **catalyst** is a substance that alters the rate of a chemical reaction and is chemically unchanged at the end of the reaction. An **enzyme** is a biological catalyst, for example amylase, which is found in saliva.

Note: Enzymes are involved in the fermentation of glucose. Enzymes are present in yeast and these increase the rate at which glucose is converted into ethanol and carbon dioxide. The reaction rate increases as the yeast multiplies – but as the concentration of ethanol increases, the rate decreases because the ethanol begins to kill or denature the enzymes.

### EXTENDED

Most catalysts work by providing an alternative 'pathway' for the reaction – one that has a lower activation energy. The lower activation energy means that more of the collisions between particles will be effective.

△ Fig. 2.47 The catalyst provides a lower energy route from reactants to products.

One example of the effect of a catalyst on a reaction is the use of manganese(IV) oxide in the decomposition of hydrogen peroxide. Hydrogen peroxide decomposes at room temperature into water and oxygen. The rate of this reaction is considerably increased by adding manganese(IV) oxide. As a gas is produced, the rate of the reaction can be monitored by collecting the gas in a gas syringe.

$$2H_2O_2(aq) \rightarrow 2H_2O(l) + O_2(g)$$

Catalysts are often used in industry to manufacture important chemicals. Table 2.8 shows some important industrial catalysts.

△ Fig. 2.48 The effect of manganese dioxide catalyst on the decomposition of hydrogen peroxide.

| Industrial process | Catalyst used |
|---|---|
| Manufacture of ethanol | Phosphoric acid |
| Cracking long-chain alkanes | Silica or alumina |
| Manufacture of ammonia | Iron |
| Manufacture of sulfuric acid | Vanadium(V) oxide |

△ Table 2.8 Uses of catalysts.

## REMEMBER

Enzymes are often very specific to a particular reaction. They have an 'active site' which is just the right shape for the reacting particles to fit into. Molecules with other structures and shapes cannot do this. Metals, such as iron used in the manufacture of ammonia, work in the same sort of way that enzymes do. The surface of the iron allows molecules of nitrogen and hydrogen to get 'trapped'. They then collide more frequently in the confined space and effective collisions become more likely.

## LIGHT

Light energy (visible or ultraviolet radiation) can start or speed up some chemical reactions.

In photography, the film in a camera is coated in a film consisting of silver salts. These salts are silver chloride (AgCl), silver bromide (AgBr) and silver iodide (AgI). All three are sensitive to light but have different sensitivities.

When light hits the film, the silver ions in the salts are reduced by gaining electrons:

$$Ag^+(s) + e^- \rightarrow Ag(s)$$

Light energy speeds up this reduction process.

The film is developed to produce negatives, which show dark and light patches. The darker areas have received most light and contain most silver; the lighter areas have received least light and have the least silver.

The film with its silver salts needs to be kept in the dark but even then they very slowly change to silver. This is why photographic film has to be used by a certain date. Of course, the arrival of digital photography has changed how photographs are now taken, stored and viewed.

Photosynthesis in plants is initiated by the light absorbed by chlorophyll molecules (the green pigment in plants):

$6CO_2(g) + 6H_2O(l) \rightarrow C_6H_{12}O_6(aq) + 6O_2(g)$

Carbon dioxide + water $\rightarrow$ glucose + oxygen

## END OF EXTENDED

## QUESTIONS

1. What is a *catalyst*?

2. What is a biological catalyst usually called?

3. **EXTENDED** Name a silver compound that is used in the manufacture of photographic film.

# End of topic checklist

## Key terms

activation energy, catalyst, collision theory, control variable, dependent variable, effective collision, enzyme, independent variable, rate of reaction, surface area, variable

## During your study of this topic you should have learned:

○ How to identify physical and chemical changes and understand the differences between them.

○ How to describe the effect of concentration, particle size, catalysts (including enzymes) and temperature on the rate of reactions.

○ How to describe a practical method for investigating the rate of a reaction involving the evolution of a gas.

○ How to describe the application of the above factors to the dangers of explosive combustion with fine powders (such as in flour mills) and gases (such as in mines).

○ **EXTENDED** How to describe a suitable method for investigating the effect of a given variable on the rate of a reaction.

○ **EXTENDED** How to interpret data obtained from experiments concerned with rate of reaction.

○ **EXTENDED** How to describe and explain the effects of temperature and concentration on reaction rate in terms of collisions between reacting particles.

○ **EXTENDED** That an increase in temperature causes an increase in collision rate and more of the colliding particles have sufficient energy (the activation energy) to react, whereas an increase in concentration only causes an increase in collision rate.

○ **EXTENDED** How to describe the role of light in photochemical reactions and the effect of light on these reactions.

○ **EXTENDED** How to describe the use of silver salts in photography as a process of reduction of silver ions to silver atoms.

○ **EXTENDED** How to describe photosynthesis as the reaction between carbon dioxide and water in the presence of chlorophyll and sunlight (energy) to produce glucose and oxygen.

# End of topic questions

*Note: The marks awarded for these questions indicate the level of detail required in the answers. In the examination, the number of marks awarded to questions like these may be different.*

**1.** This question is about the reaction between magnesium and hydrochloric acid.

    **a)** Draw and label a diagram of the apparatus that could be used to monitor the rate of the reaction by measuring the volume of hydrogen produced. **(2 marks)**

    **b)** How will the following changes affect the rate of the reaction?

        **i)** Using powdered magnesium rather than magnesium ribbon **(1 mark)**

        **ii)** Using a less concentrated solution of hydrochloric acid **(1 mark)**

        **iii)** Lowering the temperature of the hydrochloric acid. **(1 mark)**

**2.** Explain why there is a risk of an explosion in a flour mill. **(2 marks)**

**3.** **EXTENDED** For a chemical reaction to occur, the reacting particles must collide. Why don't all collisions between the particles of the reactants lead to a chemical reaction? **(2 marks)**

**4.** The diagrams below show the activation energies of two different reactions A and B.

    **a)** What is the *activation energy* of a reaction? **(1 mark)**

    **b)** Which reaction is likely to have the higher rate of reaction at a particular temperature? Explain your answer. **(2 marks)**

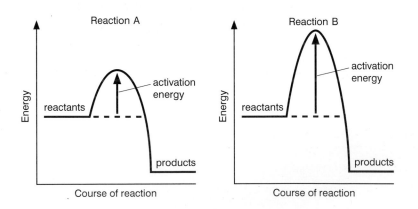

**5. EXTENDED** Look at the table of results obtained when dilute hydrochloric acid is added to marble chips.

| Time (seconds) | 0 | 10 | 20 | 30 | 40 | 50 | 60 | 70 | 80 | 90 |
|---|---|---|---|---|---|---|---|---|---|---|
| Volume of gas (cm³) | 0 | 20 | 36 | 49 | 58 | 65 | 69 | 70 | 70 | 70 |

**a)** What is the name of the gas produced in this reaction? **(1 mark)**

**b)** Write a balanced equation, including state symbols, for the reaction. **(2 marks)**

**c)** Draw a graph of volume of gas (*y*-axis) against time (*x*-axis).

Label it 'Graph 1'. **(3 marks)**

**d)** Use the results to calculate the volume of gas produced:

   **i)** in the first 10 seconds **(1 mark)**

   **ii)** between 10 and 20 seconds **(1 mark)**

   **iii)** between 20 and 30 seconds **(1 mark)**

   **iv)** between 80 and 90 seconds. **(1 mark)**

**e)** Explain why the rate of the reaction changes as the reaction takes place.
**(2 marks)**

**f)** Use the collision theory to explain the change in the rate of reaction.
**(2 marks)**

**g)** The reaction was repeated using the same volume and concentration of hydrochloric acid with the same mass of marble, but as a powder instead of chips. Draw another curve on your graph paper, using the same axes as before (label as Graph 2), to show how the original results will change. **(3 marks)**

**h)** The reaction was repeated, but this time using the original mass of new marble chips and the same volume of hydrochloric acid, but with the acid only half as concentrated as originally. Draw another curve on your graph paper, using the same axes as before (label as Graph 3), to show how the original results will change. **(3 marks)**

# Reversible reactions

## INTRODUCTION

Many of the reactions used in the manufacture of important chemicals 'go both ways'. In other words, the reactants form the products, but the products, sometimes at the same time, revert to the reactants. These reversible reactions came as something of a shock to the early chemists but today's chemists have found ways to maximise the direction of the reaction and so produce as much product as is possible.

△ Fig. 2.49 When hydrated copper(II) sulfate crystals are heated they turn from blue to white. The reaction can then be reversed by adding water.

If all the products and reactants are kept in a closed system (that is, nothing is allowed to escape or enter) all reversible reactions reach a 'balance point' or equilibrium. This balance point may be at a point where the concentrations of reactants and products are the same, but this is rarely the case – the balance point often favours the reactants or the products. For industrial chemists, altering the balance point or equilibrium is a key part of their work.

## KNOWLEDGE CHECK

✓ Understand what is meant by the rate of a reaction.
✓ Know what enthalpy changes are associated with exothermic and endothermic reactions.
✓ Be able to interpret chemical equations and associated state symbols.

## LEARNING OBJECTIVES

✓ Be able to describe the idea that some chemical reactions can be reversed by changing the reaction conditions, including the action of heat on hydrated copper(II) sulfate and the action of heat on hydrated cobalt(II) chloride.
✓ **EXTENDED** Be able to predict the effects of changing the concentration, temperature and pressure on a reversible reaction.
✓ **EXTENDED** Understand the concept of equilibrium.

## TYPES OF REVERSIBLE REACTION

Carbon burns in oxygen to form carbon dioxide:

carbon + oxygen → carbon dioxide

$C(s)$ + $O_2(g)$ → $CO_2(g)$

Carbon dioxide cannot be changed back into carbon and oxygen. The reaction cannot be reversed.

When **hydrated** blue copper(II) sulfate crystals are heated, a white powder is formed (anhydrous copper(II) sulfate) and water is lost as steam. If water is added to this white powder, hydrated blue copper(II) sulfate is formed again. The reaction is **reversible**:

hydrated copper(II) sulfate crystals $\rightleftharpoons$ anhydrous copper(II) sulfate + water

$CuSO_4.5H_2O(s)$ $\rightleftharpoons$ $CuSO_4(s)$ + $5H_2O(l)$

A reversible reaction can go from left to right or from right to left – notice the double-headed $\rightleftharpoons$ arrow used when writing these equations.

A similar reaction occurs when hydrated cobalt(II) chloride crystals are heated.

hydrated cobalt(II) chloride $\rightleftharpoons$ anhydrous cobalt(II) chloride + water

$CoCl_2.6H_2O(s)$ $\rightleftharpoons$ $CoCl_2(s)$ + $6H_2O(l)$

The pink hydrated cobalt(II) chloride crystals turn to blue anhydrous cobalt(II) chloride on strong heating. If water is added to the blue anhydrous cobalt(II) chloride, the pink hydrated cobalt(II) chloride is reformed.

## EXTENDED

Another example of a reversible reaction is the decomposition of ammonium chloride. If ammonium chloride is heated in a long tube, the solid produces 'white fumes' of a mixture of gases. The volume of the solid decreases. In the cooler parts of the tube the fumes reform the white solid. The equation is:

ammonium chloride $\rightleftharpoons$ ammonia + hydrogen chloride

$NH_4Cl(s)$ $\rightleftharpoons$ $NH_3(g)$ + $HCl(g)$

The reaction between ethene and water to make ethanol is also a reversible reaction. This is one of the reactions used industrially to make ethanol:

ethene + water $\rightleftharpoons$ ethanol

$C_2H_4(g)$ + $H_2O(g)$ $\rightleftharpoons$ $C_2H_5OH(g)$

When ethene and water are heated in the presence of a catalyst in a sealed container, ethanol is produced.

As the ethene and water are used up, the rate of the forward reaction decreases. As the amount of ethanol increases, the rate of the backward reaction (the decomposition of ethanol) increases. Eventually the rate of formation of ethanol will exactly equal the rate of decomposition of ethanol. The amounts of ethene, water and ethanol will be constant. The reaction is said to be in **equilibrium**.

## EQUILIBRIUM REACTIONS

A chemical equilibrium is an example of a **dynamic equilibrium** (a moving equilibrium). Reactants are constantly forming products, and products are constantly reforming the reactants. Equilibrium is reached when the rates of the forward and backward reactions are the same.

△ Fig. 2.50 On heating, ammonium chloride forms ammonia and hydrogen chloride. In the cooler parts of the tube these recombine to form ammonium chloride.

To get an idea of a dynamic equilibrium, imagine you are walking up an escalator as the escalator is moving down. You are still moving forward and the escalator is moving towards you. If your rate of movement is the same as the escalator's rate of movement, but in the opposite direction, you will appear not to be moving. This 'moving balance point' is called a dynamic equilibrium. If you imagine a situation where you walk up the escalator when it is moving only slowly in the opposite direction, but gradually speeds up to the speed you are walking, you might get almost to the top of the escalator before your rates of movement are balanced. Alternatively, if the escalator starts slowly but then very quickly reaches your rate of movement, the balance point may be near the bottom of the escalator. In the same sort of way, different chemical reactions can have very different balance points (nearer to the reactants or nearer to the products).

△ Fig. 2.51 At equilibrium, the rate of the forward reaction equals the rate of the backward reaction.

### REMEMBER

In a dynamic equilibrium, the rates of the forward and backward reactions are the same. Therefore once a reaction has reached equilibrium, the concentrations of the reactants and products don't change.

### END OF EXTENDED

## QUESTIONS

1. Use the example of copper(II) sulfate to explain what a reversible reaction is.

2. **EXTENDED** What does it mean if a reaction is in equilibrium?

3. **EXTENDED** An equilibrium in a chemical reaction is dynamic. What does this mean?

## Changing the position of equilibrium

Reversible reactions can be a nuisance to an industrial chemist. You want to make a particular product, but as soon as it forms it starts to change back into the reactants! Fortunately scientists have found ways of increasing the amount of product that can be obtained (the **yield**) in a reversible reaction by moving the position of balance to favour the products rather than the reactants.

The position of equilibrium can be changed in the following ways:

- changing concentrations
- changing pressure
- changing temperature.

To be able to predict how the position of an equilibrium will change, it is useful to remember that whatever change is applied to the reaction, the reaction will oppose the change and try to nullify it. Reactions are awkward!

In the following example:

$$A(g) + 2B(g) \rightleftharpoons 2C(g) \qquad \Delta H \text{ positive}$$

| Change made | Effect on the equilibrium position | Method of predicting the effect |
|---|---|---|
| Increasing the concentration of A or B | Moves to the right-hand side | The equilibrium moves in the direction that reduces the concentration of A or B. It does this by converting A and B into C |
| Decreasing the concentration of C | Moves to the right-hand side | The equilibrium moves in a direction that increases the concentration of C. It does this by converting A and B into C |
| Increasing the pressure acting on the reaction | Moves to the right-hand side | The equilibrium moves in the direction that produces fewer molecules of gas. There are fewer molecules of gas on the right-hand side. It does this by converting A and B into C |
| Increasing the temperature of the reaction | Moves to the right-hand side | The equilibrium moves in the direction that absorbs heat energy, i.e. the endothermic reaction. The forward reaction is endothermic ($\Delta H$ is positive) so A and B are converted into C |

△ Table 2.9 Effects of changes on the equilibrium position.

Note: If the forward reaction is endothermic ($\Delta H$ positive), then the backward reaction will be exothermic ($\Delta H$ negative).

A catalyst increases the rate at which an equilibrium is achieved. Because it changes the rates of both the forward and reverse reactions it does not change the position of the equilibrium. It does not change the yield either.

Getting the best balance between rate and equilibrium position is important in industrial processes, such as in the **Haber process** for making ammonia.

**END OF EXTENDED**

## QUESTIONS

1. **EXTENDED** This question is about the reaction of ethene and steam:

$C_2H_4(g) + H_2O(g) \rightleftharpoons C_2H_5OH(g)$   $\Delta H$ = negative

Which conditions would maximise the amount of ethanol in the equilibrium mixture?

a) high or low temperature

b) high or low pressure

c) catalyst or no catalyst.

2. **EXTENDED** In the manufacture of ammonia referred to above:

a) Why is a catalyst used?

b) What would be the disadvantage of using a temperature below 350 °C?

# End of topic checklist

## Key terms

dynamic equilibrium, equilibrium, Haber process, hydrated, reversible reaction, yield

## During your study of this topic you should have learned:

◯ How to describe the idea that some chemical reactions can be reversed by changing the reaction conditions, including the action of heat on hydrated copper(II) sulfate and the action of heat on hydrated cobalt(II) chloride.

◯ **EXTENDED** How to predict the effects of the following changes on a reversible reaction:

- changing the concentration of reactants or products
- changing the temperature
- changing the pressure.

◯ **EXTENDED** About the concept of equilibrium.

# End of topic questions

*Note: The marks awarded for these questions indicate the level of detail required in the answers. In the examination, the number of marks awarded to questions like these may be different.*

1. What is a *reversible reaction*? **(1 mark)**

2. Describe what you would observe in the following reactions:

   **a)** Hydrated copper(II) sulfate is heated strongly until there is no further change. **(3 marks)**

   **b)** After cooling, water is added to the product formed in reaction a). **(2 marks)**

3. Write a balanced equation, including state symbols, for the reaction in question 2a. **(3 marks)**

4. Some hydrated cobalt(II) chloride is heated strongly in a boiling tube. Describe what you would expect to observe. **(3 marks)**

5. **EXTENDED** What does it mean when a chemical reaction is in *dynamic equilibrium*? **(2 marks)**

6. **EXTENDED** The reaction between sulfur dioxide and oxygen is reversible as shown by the equation:

   $$2SO_2(g) + O_2(g) \rightleftharpoons 2SO_3(g) \; \Delta H = \text{negative}$$

   What effect will the following changes have on the yield of sulfur trioxide ($SO_3$)?

   **a)** Increasing the volume of oxygen. Explain your answer. **(2 marks)**

   **b)** Increasing the pressure on the reaction. Explain your answer. **(2 marks)**

   **c)** Increasing the temperature of the reaction. Explain your answer. **(2 marks)**

7. **EXTENDED** The equation for the reaction between nitrogen and oxygen to form nitrogen oxide is shown below:

   $$N_2(g) + O_2(g) \rightleftharpoons 2NO(g) \; \Delta H \text{ positive}$$

   What effect will the following changes have on the amount of nitrogen oxide in the equilibrium mixture?

   **a)** Increasing the concentration of oxygen. Explain your answer. **(2 marks)**

   **b)** Increasing the pressure on the reaction. Explain your answer. **(2 marks)**

   **c)** Increasing the temperature of the reaction. Explain your answer. **(2 marks)**

# Redox reactions

## INTRODUCTION

Oxidation reactions are very familiar in everyday life – like the rusting of iron and bleaching, which is effective because bleach is a powerful oxidising agent. Whenever anything burns, an oxidation reaction takes place between the fuel and oxygen in the air. Reduction reactions may seem less familiar, but oxidation and reduction go hand in hand – if an element or compound in a chemical reaction is oxidised, then another element or compound in the same reaction must be reduced. So even when a bonfire is burning furiously and using oxygen from the air, reduction is taking place at the same time!

△ Fig. 2.52 Oxidation and reduction are both taking place in this bonfire.

## KNOWLEDGE CHECK

✓ Know about ions and ion charges.
✓ Be able to interpret chemical equations and associated state symbols.
✓ **EXTENDED** Know about half-equations.

## LEARNING OBJECTIVES

✓ Know the definitions of oxidation and reduction in terms of oxygen loss or gain.
✓ Know that oxidation states are used to name ions – e.g. iron(II), iron(III), copper(II), manganate(VII).
✓ **EXTENDED** Know the definition of redox in terms of electron transfer.
✓ **EXTENDED** Be able to identify redox reactions by changes in oxidation state and by the colour changes involved when using acidified potassium manganate(VII) and potassium iodide.
✓ **EXTENDED** Know that an oxidising agent is a substance that oxidises another substance during a redox reaction.
✓ **EXTENDED** Know that a reducing agent is a substance that reduces another substance during a redox reaction.
✓ **EXTENDED** Be able to identify oxidising agents and reducing agents from simple equations.

## OXIDATION, REDUCTION AND REDOX

When oxygen is added to an element or a compound, the process is called **oxidation**:

$2Cu(s) + O_2(g) \rightarrow 2CuO(s)$

The copper has been oxidised.

Removing oxygen from a compound is called **reduction**:

$CuO(s) + Zn(s) \rightarrow ZnO(s) + Cu(s)$

The copper(II) oxide has been *reduced*.

If we look more carefully at this last reaction, we see the zinc has changed to zinc oxide: that is, it has been oxidised at the same time as the copper(II) oxide has been reduced.

This is one example of reduction and oxidation taking place at the same time, in the same reaction. These are called **redox** reactions.

**EXTENDED**

There is another way to look at redox reactions if we consider the reaction in a different way:

| $CuO(s)$ | + | $Zn(s)$ | $\rightarrow$ | $ZnO(s)$ | + | $Cu(s)$ |
|---|---|---|---|---|---|---|
| ionic compound | | element | | ionic compound | | element |

Rewrite it:

$Cu^{2+} + O^{2-} + Zn \rightarrow Zn^{2+} + O^{2-} + Cu$

Remove the oxygen ions because they are on both sides of the equation (the $O^{2-}$ ion is unchanged and so is a spectator ion):

$Cu^{2+}(s) + Zn(s) \rightarrow Zn^{2+}(s) + Cu(s)$

Split the equation into two half-equations and add electrons to balance them:

$Cu^{2+} + 2e^- \rightarrow Cu$

that is: CuO to Cu = reduction

$$Zn \rightarrow Zn^{2+} + 2e^-$$

that is: Zn to ZnO = oxidation

In this reaction the copper(II) oxide has been reduced by the zinc. The zinc is a **reducing agent**.

The zinc itself has been oxidised by the copper(II) oxide. The copper(II) oxide is an **oxidising agent**.

You now have a new definition using electrons instead of oxygen:

- Oxidation is loss of electrons.
- Reduction is gain of electrons.

Remember this as OIL-RIG: Oxidation *Is Loss* – *Reduction Is* Gain.

**END OF EXTENDED**

## OXIDATION STATES

When you learned to write chemical formulae, you were introduced to the use of Roman numerals for metals that had more than one ion – for example, iron as $Fe^{2+}$ or $Fe^{3+}$:

- iron(II) oxide = FeO
- iron(III)oxide = $Fe_2O_3$

The II and III are called **oxidation states**.

- $Fe^{2+}$ has an oxidation state of +2
- $Fe^{3+}$ has an oxidation state of +3
- oxygen has an oxidation state of –2.

You take the ion charge and reverse it, so an ion of 3– has oxidation number –3.

The oxidation state of elements is always 0 (zero).

An oxidation state describes how many electrons an atom loses or gains when it forms a chemical bond.

**EXTENDED**

If you look at the equation for the reaction between $Cu^{2+}$ and Zn again, you will see that we can use oxidation states:

$$Cu^{2+} + 2e^- \rightarrow Cu \quad \text{reduction}$$
$$+2 \qquad\qquad 0$$

$$Zn \rightarrow Zn^{2+} + 2e^- \quad \text{oxidation}$$
$$0 \quad +2$$

This gives another definition for oxidation/reduction:

- Oxidation happens when oxidation states increase
- Reduction happens when oxidation states decrease

## Changes in oxidation state

Solid potassium manganate(VII) comes in the form of dark purple crystals.

Manganese is in the oxidation state +7 (the 'VII' in the name) and is the cause of the purple colour.

Potassium manganate(VII) crystals dissolve in water to produce a dark purple solution, which is a powerful oxidising agent. When potassium manganate(VII) is used , the manganate(VII) ion is reduced to the manganese(II) ion, which is almost colourless:

◁ Fig. 2.53 When manganate (VII) ions are reduced colourless $Mn^{2+}$ ions are formed.

$MnO_4^-(aq) \quad \rightarrow \quad Mn^{2+}(aq)$

+7                 +2

   purple           colourless

When the manganate(VII) ions are reduced, the colour changes from purple to colourless.

Another example of colour changes linked to changes in oxidation states is given by potassium iodide, KI, which is a white solid dissolving in water to form a colourless solution.

In some reactions the iodide ion, $I^-$, is oxidised to iodine (there is an increase in oxidation state), which has a dark orange colour in solution:

$2I^-(aq) \quad \rightarrow \quad I_2(aq) + 2e^-$

2(–1)             2(0)

colourless       orange

Fumes of iodine are produced when potassium iodide is oxidised by concentrated sulfuric acid.

**END OF EXTENDED**

# PHOTOCHROMIC GLASS

Some people who wear glasses prefer those with photochromic lenses, which darken when exposed to bright light. These glasses eliminate the need for sunglasses,—they can reduce up to 80% of the light transmitted through the lenses to the eyes. The basis of this change in colour in response to light can be explained in terms of oxidation reduction or redox reactions.

△ Fig. 2.54 A photochromic reaction was produced when the right lens of these glasses was exposed to bright light.

Glass is ordinarily transparent to visible light. In photochromic lenses, silver chloride (AgCl) and copper(I) chloride (CuCl) crystals are added during the manufacturing of the glass. These crystals become uniformly embedded in the glass.

One characteristic of silver chloride is that it is affected by light. The following reactions occur:

$Cl^- \rightarrow Cl + e^-$ = oxidation

$Ag^+ + e^- \rightarrow Ag$ = reduction

The chloride ions are oxidised to produce chlorine atoms and the silver ions are reduced to silver atoms. The silver atoms cluster together and block the transmission of light, causing the lenses to darken. This process occurs almost instantaneously.

The photochromic process would not be useful unless it were reversible. The presence of copper(I) chloride reverses the darkening process in the following way. When the lenses are removed from bright light, the following reactions occur:

$Cl + Cu^+ \rightarrow Cu^{2+} + Cl^-$

The chlorine atoms formed by the exposure to light are reduced by the copper(I) ions forming chloride ions ($Cl^-$). The copper(I) ions are oxidised to copper(II) ions. The copper(II) ions then oxidise the silver atoms:

$Cu^{2+} + Ag \rightarrow Cu^+ + Ag^+$

The result of these reactions is that the lenses become transparent again as the silver atoms are converted back to silver ions.

## QUESTIONS

1. Define the term *reduction*.

2. What is the oxidation state of the metal ion in each of the following compounds?

   a) copper(II) oxide

   b) iron(III) chloride

   c) potassium manganate(VII).

3. **EXTENDED** In the following half-equation, has the $Cu^{2+}$ ion been oxidised or reduced? Explain your answer.

$Cu^{2+}(aq) + e^- \rightarrow Cu^+(aq)$

4. **EXTENDED** In the following half-equation, has the chromium (Cr) atom been oxidised or reduced? Explain your answer.

$Cr(s) \rightarrow Cr^{3+}(aq) + 3e^-$

# End of topic checklist

## Key terms

oxidation, oxidising agent, redox, reducing agent, reduction

## During your study of this topic you should have learned:

○ The definitions of oxidation and reduction in terms of oxygen loss or gain.

○ That oxidation states are used to name ions – e.g. iron(II), iron(III), copper(II), manganate(VII).

○ **EXTENDED** The definition of redox in terms of electron transfer.

○ **EXTENDED** How to identify redox reactions by changes in oxidation state and by the colour changes involved when using acidified potassium manganate(VII) and potassium iodide.

○ **EXTENDED** That an oxidising agent is a substance that oxidises another substance during a redox reaction.

○ **EXTENDED** That a reducing agent is a substance that reduces another substance during a redox reaction.

○ **EXTENDED** How to identify oxidising agents and reducing agents from simple equations.

# End of topic questions

*Note: The marks awarded for these questions indicate the level of detail required in the answers. In the examination, the number of marks awarded to questions like these may be different.*

1. The following equation shows a redox reaction:

   $$Mg(s) + ZnO(s) \rightarrow MgO(s) + Zn(s)$$

   **a)** What has been oxidised in the reaction?     (1 mark)

   **b)** What has been reduced in the reaction?     (1 mark)

   **c)** <u>EXTENDED</u> What is the oxidising agent?     (1 mark)

   **d)** <u>EXTENDED</u> What is the reducing agent?     (1 mark)

2. <u>EXTENDED</u> The relationship between lead atoms and lead ions is shown in the following half-equation:

   $$Pb(s) \rightarrow Pb^{2+}(s) + 2e^-$$

   In this reaction, has the lead atom been oxidised or reduced?
   Explain your answer.     (2 marks)

3. <u>EXTENDED</u> The reaction between copper and chlorine produces copper(II) chloride.

   $$Cu(s) + Cl_2(g) \rightarrow CuCl_2(s)$$

   **a)** What is the oxidation state of copper as an element?     (1 mark)

   **b)** What is the oxidation state of the copper in copper(II) chloride?     (1 mark)

   **c)** Is this reaction a redox reaction? Explain your answer.     (2 marks)

# Acids, bases and salts

## INTRODUCTION

Acids are commonly used in everyday life. Many of them, such as hydrochloric and sulfuric acids, are extremely toxic and corrosive. About 20 million tonnes of hydrochloric acid are manufactured worldwide each year. Some of this is used to make important chemicals such as PVC (polyvinyl chloride) plastic. Alkalis and bases are less common in everyday use, yet about 60 million tonnes of sodium hydroxide are

△ Fig. 2.55 Sodium hydroxide.

produced worldwide each year and used in the manufacture of paper and **soap**. Sodium hydroxide is harmful and corrosive. Common salt, sodium chloride, is an example of a salt.

## KNOWLEDGE CHECK

✓ Know the names of some common acids, including hydrochloric acid and sulfuric acid.
✓ Know that vegetable dyes can be used as indicators to identify acids and alkalis.
✓ Be able to use state symbols such as (s), (l), (g) and (aq).

## LEARNING OBJECTIVES

✓ Be able to describe the characteristic properties of acids as reactions with metals, bases, carbonates and the effect on litmus and methyl orange.
✓ Be able to describe the characteristic properties of bases as reactions with acids and with ammonium salts and the effect on litmus and methyl orange.
✓ Be able to describe neutrality and relative acidity and alkalinity in terms of pH measured using universal indicator paper.
✓ Be able to describe and explain the importance of controlling acidity in soil.
✓ **EXTENDED** Know the definitions of acids and bases in terms of proton transfer in aqueous solutions.
✓ **EXTENDED** Be able to describe the meaning of weak and strong acids and bases.
✓ Be able to classify oxides as either acidic or basic, related to metallic and non-metallic character.
✓ **EXTENDED** Be able to classify other oxides as neutral or amphoteric.
✓ Be able to describe the preparation, separation and purification of soluble salts.
✓ Be able to demonstrate knowledge and understanding of preparation, separation and purification of salts.
✓ **EXTENDED** Be able to describe the preparation of insoluble salts by precipitation.
✓ **EXTENDED** Be able to suggest a method of making a given salt from a suitable starting material, given appropriate information.

## AQUEOUS SOLUTIONS

When any substance dissolves in water, it forms an aqueous solution, shown by the state symbol (aq). Aqueous solutions can be acidic, alkaline or neutral. A neutral solution is neither acidic or alkaline.

**Indicators** are used to tell if a solution is acidic, alkaline or neutral. They can be used either as liquids or in paper form, and they turn different colours with different solutions. There are different indicators that can be used.

The most common indicator is **litmus**. Its colours are shown in the table:

| Colour of litmus | Type of solution |
|---|---|
| Red | Acidic |
| Blue | Alkaline |

△ Table 2.10 Litmus.

**Universal indicator** can show how strongly acidic or how strongly alkaline a solution is because it has more colours than litmus. Each colour is linked to a number ranging from 0 (most strongly acidic solution) to 14 (most strongly alkaline solution). A neutral substance has a pH of 7. This range is called the **pH scale** and is related to the concentration of hydrogen ions ($H^+(aq)$).

| Concentration of hydrogen ions compared to distilled water | pH | Examples of solutions and their respective pH |
|---|---|---|
| 1/10 000 000 | 14 | Liquid drain cleaner, caustic soda |
| 1/1 000 000 | 13 | Bleaches, oven cleaner |
| 1/100 000 | 12 | Soapy water |
| 1/10 000 | 11 | Household ammonia (11.9) |
| 1/1 000 | 10 | Milk of magnesia (10.5) |
| 1/100 | 9 | Toothpaste (9.9) |
| 1/10 | 8 | Baking soda (8.4), seawater, eggs |
| 0 | 7 | Pure water (7) |
| 10 | 6 | Urine (6) milk (6.6) |
| 100 | 5 | Acid rain (5.6) black coffee (5) |
| 1000 | 4 | Tomato juice (4.1) |
| 10 000 | 3 | Grapefruit and orange juice, soft drink |
| 100 000 | 2 | Lemon juice (2.3) vinegar (2.9) |
| 1 000 000 | 1 | Hydrochloric acid secreted from the stomach lining (1) |
| 10 000 000 | 0 | Battery acid |

△ Fig. 2.56 The pH scale.

*Phenolphthalein* indicator is colourless in acid solution but turns pink in alkaline solution.

*Methyl orange* indicator is pink in acid solution and yellow in alkaline solution.

## WHAT ARE ACIDS?

**Acids** are substances that contain replaceable hydrogen atoms. These hydrogen atoms are replaced in chemical reactions by metal atoms, forming a compound known as a salt. Acids have pHs in the range 0–7.

| Acid name | Acid formula |
|---|---|
| Hydrochloric acid | HCl |
| Nitric acid | $HNO_3$ |
| Sulfuric acid | $H_2SO_4$ |
| Phosphoric acid | $H_3PO_4$ |

△ Table 2.11 Common acids.

### EXTENDED

Acids only show their acidic properties when water is present. This is because in water acids form hydrogen ions, $H^+(aq)$ (which are also protons) and it is these ions that create acidic properties. An acid is therefore a proton donor. For example:

$$HCl(aq) \rightarrow H^+(aq) + Cl^-(aq)$$

### END OF EXTENDED

The typical reactions of acids include:

- Acid + metal makes a salt and hydrogen gas.
- Acid + carbonate makes a salt, carbon dioxide and water.
- Acid + base makes a salt and water.

## WHAT ARE BASES AND ALKALIS?

The oxides and hydroxides of metals are called **bases**.

If the oxide or hydroxide of a metal dissolves in water, it is also called an **alkali**. For example:

sodium + oxygen → sodium oxide

$$4Na(s) + O_2(g) \rightarrow 2Na_2O(s)$$

sodium oxide + water → sodium hydroxide

$$Na_2O(s) + H_2O(l) \rightarrow 2NaOH(aq)$$

Sodium oxide is a base because it is the oxide of the metal sodium. In addition, it reacts with water to make the alkali sodium hydroxide. Alkalis have pHs in the range 7–14 (but not 7.0).

The typical reactions of bases include:

• Base + acids make a salt and water.
• Base + an ammonium compound makes ammonia gas.

## EXTENDED

In their reactions with acids, in the presence of water, bases and alkalis accept protons ($H^+$ ions). Alkalis only show their alkaline properties when water is present. This is because in water the alkali forms hydroxide ions, $OH^-(aq)$, which can then react with $H^+(aq)$ ions from an acid to make water.

## REMEMBER

Acids are proton ($H^+$) donors in water.

Bases are proton ($H^+$) acceptors in water.

## THE STRENGTH OF ACIDS AND BASES

Acids and bases can be described as being 'strong' or 'weak' depending on the 'degree of ionisation' in water (that is, how many HCl molecules split to become $H^+$ and $Cl^-$ ions, for example).

'Strong' acids and bases are completely ionised in water – for example:

$$HCl(aq) \rightarrow H^+(aq) + Cl^-(aq)$$

$$NaOH(aq) \rightarrow Na^+(aq) + OH^-(aq)$$

This is why the one-way arrow sign is used in these chemical equations.

'Weak' acids and bases are only partially ionised in water – for example, ethanoic acid ($CH_3COOH$):

$$CH_3COOH(aq) \rightleftharpoons CH_3COO^-(aq) + H^+(aq)$$

and ammonia solution (ammonium hydroxide):

$$NH_3(g) + H_2O(l) \rightleftharpoons NH_4^+(aq) + OH^-(aq)$$

The partial ionisation is the reason why the equilibrium sign is used in these chemical equations.

'Weak' acids (pH 4 to 6) and weak bases (pH 8 to 10) produce fewer ions in solution than strong acids and bases at the same concentration. This is why their electrical conductivity is lower than that of strong acids and bases, and also explains their slower rates of reactions.

**END OF EXTENDED**

## QUESTIONS

1. Two solutions are tested with universal indicator paper. Solution A has a pH of 8 and solution B has a pH of 14. What does this tell you about the two solutions?

2. Methyl orange is added to a solution and the solution turns pink. What does this tell you about the solution?

3. Calcium oxide is an example of a base. How do we know this?

4. **EXTENDED** Hydrochloric acid is a strong acid, whereas ethanoic acid is a weak acid. Explain the differences between these two acids.

## THE IMPORTANCE OF CONTROLLING ACIDITY IN SOIL

If soil is too acidic, then it can be neutralised using quicklime. Quicklime is made from limestone, which is quarried from limestone rocks. It is heated in lime kilns at 1200 °C to make calcium oxide or quicklime:

1200 °C ↑

limestone $\rightarrow$ quicklime + carbon dioxide

$CaCO_3(s) \rightarrow CaO(s) + CO_2(g)$

When quicklime is added to water, it makes calcium hydroxide, which is an alkali and so can neutralise the acidic soil:

quicklime + water $\rightarrow$ slaked lime

$CaO(s) + H_2O(l) \rightarrow Ca(OH)_2(s)$

Different plants grow better in different types of soil. The pH of a soil is an important factor in the growth of different plants – some plants prefer slightly acidic conditions and others slightly alkaline conditions.

Adding fertilisers to soil can also affect the pH and so the soil may have to be treated by adding acids or alkalis. The pH of soil can be measured by taking a small sample, putting it in a test tube with distilled water and adding indicator solution or using indicator paper. The pH can be found from a pH chart.

## TYPES OF OXIDES

The **oxides** of elements can often be made by heating the element in air or oxygen. For example, the metal magnesium burns in oxygen to form magnesium oxide:

magnesium   +   oxygen   →   magnesium oxide

$$2Mg(s) \quad + \quad O_2(g) \quad → \quad 2MgO(s)$$

Magnesium oxide forms as a white solid. When distilled water is added to the ash and the mixture is tested with universal indicator, the pH is greater than 7 – the oxide has formed an alkaline solution.

△ Fig. 2.57 Magnesium burning in oxygen.

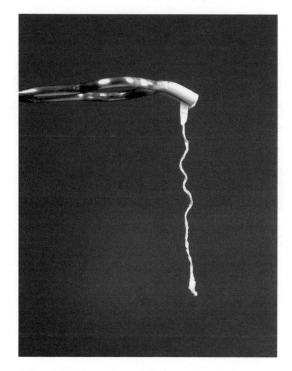

△ Fig. 2.58 Magnesium oxide is a white solid.

When sulfur is burned in oxygen, sulfur dioxide gas is formed:

sulfur   +   oxygen   →   sulfur dioxide

$$S(s) \quad + \quad O_2(g) \quad → \quad SO_2(g)$$

When sulfur dioxide is dissolved in water and then tested with universal indicator solution, the pH is less than 7 – the oxide has formed an acidic solution.

The oxides of most elements can be classified as **basic oxides** or **acidic oxides**. Some elements form neutral oxides. For example, water is a neutral oxide. Basic oxides that dissolve in water are called alkalis.

Oxides that do not dissolve in water cannot be identified using the pH of their solutions. For insoluble oxides, the test is seeing if they will react with hydrochloric acid, HCl (these would be basic oxides) or sodium hydroxide solution, NaOH (these would be acidic oxides). Oxides that do not react with hydrochloric acid or sodium hydroxide are neutral oxides.

Most metal oxides are basic oxides, such as CaO, MgO, BaO, Na$_2$O.

Basic oxides react with acids (neutralisation):

| acid | + | base | → | a salt | + | water |
|------|---|------|---|--------|---|-------|
| $2HCl(aq)$ | + | $MgO(s)$ | → | $MgCl_2(aq)$ | + | $H_2O(l)$ |

Most non-metal oxides are acidic, for example:

$NO_2$, $SO_2$, $SO_3$, $CO_2$, $P_2O_5$

Acidic oxides react with bases (neutralisation) and dissolve in water to form acids, for example sulfuric acid ($H_2SO_4$):

$$SO_3(g) + H_2O(l) \rightarrow H_2SO_4(aq)$$

| Oxide | Type of oxide | pH of solution | Other reactions of the oxide |
|-------|---------------|----------------|------------------------------|
| Metal oxide | Basic | More than 7 (alkaline) | Reacts with an acid to make a salt + water |
| Non-metal oxide | Acidic | Less than 7 (acidic) | Reacts with a base to make a salt + water |

△ Table 2.12 Acidic and basic oxides.

## EXTENDED

**Amphoteric oxides** are the oxides of less reactive metals, e.g. Al$_2$O$_3$, ZnO and PbO. They can behave as both acidic oxides *and* basic oxides, so react with both bases and acids.

Neutral oxides do not react with acids or alkalis. Examples of neutral oxides are water, H$_2$O, nitrogen monoxide, NO, nitrous oxide, N$_2$O, and carbon monoxide, CO.

## END OF EXTENDED

1. Is potassium oxide a basic oxide or acidic oxide? Explain your answer.

2. **EXTENDED** What is the difference between a basic oxide and an amphoteric oxide?

## WHAT ARE SALTS?

Acids contain replaceable hydrogen atoms. When metal atoms take their place, a compound called a **salt** is formed. The names of salts have two parts, as shown in Fig. 2.59.

sodium chloride (NaCl)

the name of the metal that replaced the hydrogen

the part of the salt name showing which acid was used

△ Fig. 2.59 Salt – sodium chloride.

Table 2.13 shows the four most common acids and their salt names.

| Acid | Salt name |
|------|-----------|
| Hydrochloric (HCl) | Chloride ($Cl^-$) |
| Nitric ($HNO_3$) | Nitrate ($NO_3^-$) |
| Sulfuric ($H_2SO_4$) | Sulfate ($SO_4^{2-}$) |
| Phosphoric ($H_3PO_4$) | Phosphate ($PO_4^{3-}$) |

△ Table 2.13 Common acids and their salt names.

△ Fig. 2.60. Sodium chloride crystals.

△ Fig. 2.61 Copper(II) sulfate crystals.

Salts are ionic compounds. The names of these compounds are created by taking the first part of the name from the metal ion, which is a positive ion (cation), and the second part of the name from the acid, which is a negative ion (anion). For example:

copper(II) sulfate: $Cu^{2+}$ and $SO_4^{2-} \rightarrow CuSO_4$

           cation   anion   salt

Salts are often found in the form of crystals. Crystals of many salts contain **water of crystallisation**, which is responsible for their crystal shape. Water of crystallisation is shown in the chemical formula of a salt. For example:

copper(II) sulfate crystals: $CuSO_4.5H_2O$

iron(II) sulfate crystals: $FeSO_4.7H_2O$

Salts that do not contain water of crystallisation are **anhydrous**.


## MAKING SALTS

There are five common methods for making salts. Four of these make soluble salts and one makes insoluble salts.


### The solubility of salts in water

Here are the general rules that describe the solubility of common types of salts in water:

- All common sodium, potassium and ammonium salts are soluble.
- All nitrates are soluble.
- Common chlorides, bromides and iodides are soluble – except those of silver chloride, silver bromide and silver iodide.
- Common sulfates are soluble – except those of barium, lead and calcium.
- Common carbonates are insoluble – except those of sodium, potassium and ammonium.


### Making soluble salts

**1.**

| | | | | | | |
|---|---|---|---|---|---|---|
| acid | + | alkali | → | a salt | + | water |

For example:

| | | | | | | |
|---|---|---|---|---|---|---|
| HCl(aq) | + | NaOH(aq) | → | NaCl(aq) | + | $H_2O(l)$ |

**2.**

| | | | | | | |
|---|---|---|---|---|---|---|
| acid | + | base | → | a salt | + | water |

For example:

| | | | | | | |
|---|---|---|---|---|---|---|
| $H_2SO_4$(aq) | + | CuO(s) | → | $CuSO_4$(aq) | + | $H_2O(l)$ |

**3.**

acid      + carbonate  →  a salt    + water + carbon dioxide

For example:

$$2HNO_3(aq) + CuCO_3(s) \rightarrow Cu(NO_3)_2(aq) + H_2O(l) + CO_2(g)$$

**4.**

acid     + metal  → a salt    + hydrogen

For example:

$$2HCl(aq) + Mg(s) \rightarrow MgCl_2(aq) + H_2(g)$$

Here is a shortcut for remembering the four general equations above. Remember the initials of the reactants:

A (acid) + A (alkali)

A (acid) + B (base)

A (acid) + C (carbonate)

A (acid) + M (metal)

The symbol '(aq)' after the formula of the salt shows that it is a soluble salt.

**Neutralisation** describes the reactions of acids with alkalis and bases. When acids react with alkalis, the reaction is between $H^+$ ions and $OH^-$ ions to make water, as in:

$$H^+(aq) + OH^-(aq) \rightarrow H_2O(l)$$

Reactions of acids with alkalis are used in the experimental procedure of **titration**, in which solutions react together to give the end-point shown by an indicator. Calculations can then be performed to find the concentration of the acid or the alkali.

### In the laboratory

Of the four methods for making soluble salts, shown by the symbol (aq), only one uses two solutions:

**1.** acid(aq) + alkali(aq) → a salt(aq) + water(l)

The other three methods involve adding a solid(s) to a solution(aq):

**2.** acid(aq) + base(s) → a salt(aq) + water(l)

**3.** acid(aq) + carbonate(s) → a salt(aq) + water(l) + carbon dioxide(g)

**4.** acid(aq) + metal(s) → a salt(aq) + hydrogen(g)

Method 1 involves the titration method. An indicator is used to show when exact quantities of acid and alkali have been mixed. The procedure is then repeated using the same exact volumes of acid and alkali, but without the indicator. The resulting solution is evaporated to the point of crystallisation, then left to cool and the salt to crystallise.

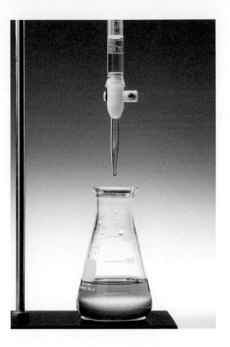

▷ Fig. 2.62 Using the neutralisation method for a titration.

**REMEMBER**

You should know that because acids in water form $H^+$ (aq) ions and alkalis form $OH^-$(aq) ions, the neutralisation reaction of acids with alkalis can be summarised as:

$$H^+(aq) \quad + \quad OH^-(aq) \quad \rightarrow \quad H_2O(l)$$

All neutralisation reactions can be represented by this equation, whatever the acid or alkali used.

The general procedure used for each of the methods 2, 3 and 4 is the same:

• The solid (base, carbonate or metal) is added to the acid with stirring until no more solid will react. Heating may be necessary.
• The mixture is filtered to remove unreacted solid and the solution is collected as the **filtrate** in an evaporating dish.
• The solution is evaporated to the point of crystallisation and is then left to cool and the salt to crystallise.

ACIDS, BASES AND SALTS

The process is summarised in Fig. 2.63:

△ Fig. 2.63 Making soluble salts from solids.

## QUESTIONS

**1.** What is a *salt*?

**2.** Which acid would you use to make a sample of sodium sulfate?

**3.** Would you expect potassium chloride to be soluble or insoluble in water? Explain your answer.

**4.** What is the name of the salt formed when calcium carbonate reacts with nitric acid?

**5.** What does the word *neutralisation* mean?

**6.** Which ion do all acids form in solution?

**7.** Which ion do all alkalis form in solution?

## EXTENDED

### Making insoluble salts

If two solutions of **soluble** salts are mixed together to form two new salts, and one of the products is **insoluble**, the insoluble salt forms a precipitate – a solid made in solution. This process is called **precipitation**. The general equation is:

soluble salt　+　soluble salt　→　insoluble salt　+　soluble salt
(precipitate)

For example:

$$Na_2CO_3(aq) \quad + \quad CuSO_4(aq) \quad \rightarrow \quad CuCO_3(s) \quad + \quad Na_2SO_4(aq)$$

The state symbols show the salts in solution as (aq) and the precipitate – the insoluble salt – as (s).

### In the laboratory

The practical method involves making a precipitate of an insoluble salt by mixing solutions of two soluble salts.

The procedure is as follows:

**1.** The two solutions of soluble salts are mixed together and a precipitate forms.

**2.** The precipitate is separated by filtration.

**3.** The precipitate is then washed with a little cold water and allowed to dry.

The process is summarised in Fig. 2.64.

△ Fig. 2.64 Making an insoluble salt.

## QUESTIONS

**1.** What is a *precipitation* reaction?

**2.** When preparing an insoluble salt what process is used to separate the insoluble salt from any soluble salts?

**3.** Why is the insoluble salt washed with a little cold water before it is left to dry?

**4.** Lead(II) chloride is an insoluble salt and can be prepared by mixing solutions of lead(II) nitrate and sodium chloride.

   **a)** Write a word equation for the reaction.

   **b)** Write a balanced equation for the reaction.

**END OF EXTENDED**

## SOME INTERESTING FACTS ABOUT ACIDS AND ALKALIS

1. Pure sulfuric acid is a clear, oily, highly corrosive liquid. It was well known to Islamic, Greek and Roman scholars in the ancient world, when it was called 'oil of vitriol'. Although pure sulfuric acid does not occur naturally on Earth because of its attraction for water, dilute sulfuric acid is found in acid rain and in the upper atmosphere of the planet Venus. It has a wide range of industrial uses from making fertilisers, dyes, paper and

△ Fig. 2.65 A wasp.

pharmaceuticals to batteries, steel and iron. Sulfuric acid is not toxic but it is highly reactive with water, in a strongly exothermic reaction. It can cause severe burns. The acid must be stored in glass containers (never plastic or metal) and handled with extreme care.

2. Hydrochloric acid, although classified as toxic and corrosive, is part of the gastric acid in the stomach and is involved in digestion. Excess acid in the stomach can cause indigestion but 'anti-acid' (alkali) medications can be taken to neutralise this.

3. Perhaps the strongest acid is a mixture of nitric acid and hydrochloric acid, known as 'aqua regia' because it reacts with the 'royal' metals. Unlike other acids, it reacts with very unreactive metals such as gold and platinum. However, some metals like titanium and silver are not affected.

4. Formic acid (now called methanoic acid) is in the venom of ant and bee stings. Such stings can be relieved by (or neutralised) with an alkali such as sodium bicarbonate (sodium hydrogencarbonate). Wasp stings, however, contain an alkali and so need to be neutralised by a weak acid such as vinegar.

The differences can be remembered using:

**B**ee – **B**icarb

Wasp (W looks like two **V**s) – **V**inegar

## Developing investigative skills

A student wanted to make a sample of copper(II) sulfate crystals, $CuSO_4.5H_2O$. She used the following steps in her method.

She put on eye protection and warmed 50 $cm^3$ of dilute sulfuric acid in a 250 $cm^3$ beaker and then copper(II) oxide is added a spatula at a time, stirring the reaction mixture with a glass rod.

When no more copper(II) oxide would react, she filtered the mixture and collected the copper(II) sulfate solution in an evaporating basin.

She then heated the solution in the evaporating basin until she could see crystals starting to form and then allowed it to cool.

After several hours, blue crystals of copper(II) sulfate had formed. She drained off any remaining liquid and dried the crystals between filter papers.

### Using and organising techniques, apparatus and materials

❶ Copper(II) sulfate crystals are 'hydrated'. Explain what this means.

❷ Draw a diagram showing the apparatus the student could have used to filter the mixture in step 2.

❸ What is the general name given to a liquid that passes through a filter paper?

❹ How could the student have tested for the crystallisation point while heating the filtrate?

### Observing, measuring and recording

❺ What is the colour of copper(II) oxide?

❻ What would be the colour of the solution the student evaporated?

### Evaluating methods

❼ While heating the solution in the evaporting dish the student noticed some very pale blue powder around the edges of the evaporating basin. What do you think this powder was and how do you think it had formed?

❽ Write a fully balanced equation for the reaction.

# End of topic checklist

## Key terms

acid, alkali, amphoteric oxide, anhydrous, base, filtrate, hydrated, indicator, insoluble, litmus, neutralisation, oxide, pH scale precipitation, salt, soap, soluble, titration, universal indicator, water of crystallisation

## During your study of this topic you should have learned:

○ How to describe the characteristic properties of acids as reactions with metals, bases, carbonates and the effect on litmus and methyl orange.

○ How to describe the characteristic properties of bases as reactions with acids and with ammonium salts and the effect on litmus and methyl orange.

○ How to describe neutrality and relative acidity and alkalinity in terms of pH measured using universal indicator paper.

○ How to describe and explain the importance of controlling acidity in soil.

○ **EXTENDED** The definitions of acids and bases in terms of proton transfer in aqueous solutions.

○ **EXTENDED** How to describe the meaning of weak and strong acids and bases.

○ How to classify oxides as either acidic or basic, related to metallic and non-metallic character.

○ **EXTENDED** How to classify other oxides as neutral or amphoteric.

○ How to describe the preparation, separation and purification of salts as prepared by the following reactions:
  - acid + metal
  - acid + base
  - acid + carbonate
  - acid + alkali.

○ **EXTENDED** How to describe the preparation of insoluble salts by precipitation.

○ **EXTENDED** How to suggest a method of making a given salt from a suitable starting material, given appropriate information.

# End of topic questions

*Note: The marks awarded for these questions indicate the level of detail required in the answers. In the examination, the number of marks awarded to questions like these may be different.*

1. **a)** What is an *indicator*? (1 mark)

   **b)** What is the *pH scale*? (1 mark)

   **c)** What do the following pH numbers indicate about a solution that has been tested?

      **i)** pH 6 (1 mark)

      **ii)** pH 8 (1 mark)

      **iii)** pH 14. (1 mark)

2. **a)** What is an *acid*? (1 mark)

   **b)** What is an *alkali*? (1 mark)

   **c)** What is the name of the process when an acid reacts with an alkali to form water? (1 mark)

3. Calcium chloride can be made from calcium oxide and dilute hydrochloric acid.

   **a)** What type of chemical is calcium oxide? (1 mark)

   **b)** What type of chemical is calcium chloride? (1 mark)

   **c)** Is calcium chloride soluble or insoluble in water? (1 mark)

   **d)** Describe the different stages in the preparation of calcium chloride crystals. (4 marks)

   **e)** Write a fully balanced equation, including symbols, for the reaction. (2 marks)

4. **EXTENDED** Barium sulfate is an insoluble salt and can be made using a precipitation reaction.

   **a)** What acid can be used to make barium sulfate? (1 mark)

   **b)** What other chemical could be used to make barium sulfate? (1 mark)

   **c)** Describe the different stages in the preparation of a dry sample of barium sulfate. (3 marks)

   **d)** Write a fully balanced equation, including state symbols, for the reaction. (2 marks)

5. **EXTENDED** Copy and complete the following equations and include state symbols:

   **a)** $2KOH(aq) + H_2SO_4(aq) \rightarrow$ _____ + _____ (2 marks)

   **b)** $2HCl(aq) + MgO(s) \rightarrow$ _____ + _____ (2 marks)

   **c)** $2HNO_3(aq) + BaCO_3(s) \rightarrow$ _____ + _____ + _____ (2 marks)

   **d)** $2HCl(aq) + Zn(s) \rightarrow$ _____ + _____ (2 marks)

   **e)** $ZnCl_2(aq) + K_2CO_3(aq) \rightarrow$ _____ + _____ (2 marks)

# Identification of ions and gases

## INTRODUCTION

It is important to be able to analyse different substances and identify the different elements or components. The techniques used today are fairly sophisticated but many of them are based on simple laboratory tests. With improved understanding of the beneficial and harmful properties of chemical substances, it has become more and more important to identify metals and non-metals in chemical processes and in the environment.

△ Fig. 2.66 A chemist performs a chemical test on a substance in her pharmaceutical laboratory.

### KNOWLEDGE CHECK

✓ Understand the nature of the chemical bonding in ionic compounds.
✓ Be familiar with the terms anion and cation.
✓ Know some of the characteristics of Group I and Group VII elements.
✓ Know the order of the common metals that are included in the reactivity series.

### LEARNING OBJECTIVES

✓ Be able to describe the tests for the aqueous cations of aluminium, ammonium, calcium, chromium(III), copper(II), iron(II), iron(III) and zinc using aqueous sodium hydroxide and aqueous ammonia.
✓ Be able to use a flame test to identify lithium, sodium, potassium and copper(II) cations.
✓ Be able to describe the tests for the anions carbonate, chloride, bromide, iodide, nitrate, sulfate and sulfite.
✓ Be able to describe the tests for the gases ammonia, carbon dioxide, chlorine, hydrogen, oxygen and sulfur dioxide.

## IDENTIFYING METAL IONS (CATIONS)

Ions of metals are **cations** – positive ions – and are found in ionic compounds. There are two ways of identifying metal cations:

• *either* from solids of the compound
• *or* from solutions of the compound.

### Flame tests

In a flame test, a piece of nichrome wire is dipped into concentrated hydrochloric acid, then into the solid compound, and then into a blue Bunsen flame. The colour seen in the flame identifies the metal ion in the compound.

| Name of ion | Formula of ion | Colour seen in flame |
|---|---|---|
| lithium | $Li^+$ | bright red |
| sodium | $Na^+$ | golden yellow/orange |
| potassium | $K^+$ | lilac (light purple) |
| copper | $Cu^{2+}$ | green |

△ Table 2.14 Colours of ions in a flame.

## Tests on solutions in water

Metal ions are found in ionic compounds, so most of them will dissolve in water to form solutions. These solutions can be tested with sodium hydroxide solution to identify the aqueous cation.

△ Fig. 2.67 The colour of the flame can be used to identify the metal ions present.

| Name of ion in solution | Formula | Result |
|---|---|---|
| Aluminium | $Al^{3+}(aq)$ | White precipitate formed; dissolves in excess sodium hydroxide solution |
| Calcium | $Ca^{2+}(aq)$ | White precipitate formed; remains, even when excess sodium hydroxide solution added |
| Chromium(III) | $Cr^{3+}(aq)$ | Green precipitate formed; dissolves in excess sodium hydroxide solution |
| Copper(II) | $Cu^{2+}(aq)$ | Light blue precipitate formed; insoluble in excess sodium hydroxide solution |
| Iron(II) | $Fe^{2+}(aq)$ | Green precipitate formed; insoluble in excess sodium hydroxide solution; after a few minutes starts to change to reddish-brown colour |
| Iron(III) | $Fe^{3+}(aq)$ | Reddish-brown precipitate formed; insoluble in excess sodium hydroxide solution |
| Zinc | $Zn^{2+}(aq)$ | White precipitate formed; dissolves in excess sodium hydroxide solution |

△ Table 2.15 Tests for identifying cations by adding sodium hydroxide solution to excess.

△ Fig. 2.68 Colourful hydroxide precipitates.

**Note:**

Similar results can be obtained if these reactions are performed using ammonia solution instead of sodium hydroxide solution. However, there is a noticeable difference in the case of copper(II) ions. At first, as with sodium hydroxide solution, a pale blue precipitate is formed, but then as excess ammonia solution is added the precipitate dissolves to form a royal blue solution.

## EXTENDED

The reactions in the table can be represented by ionic equations. For example:

$$Al^{3+}(aq) \quad + \quad 3OH^-(aq) \quad \rightarrow \quad Al(OH)_3(s)$$

white precipitate

$$Ca^{2+}(aq) \quad + \quad 2OH^-(aq) \quad \rightarrow \quad Ca(OH)_2(s)$$

white precipitate

$$Cu^{2+}(aq) \quad + \quad 2OH^-(aq) \quad \rightarrow \quad Cu(OH)_2(s)$$

light blue precipitate

$$Fe^{3+}(aq) \quad + \quad 3OH^-(aq) \quad \rightarrow \quad Fe(OH)_3(s)$$

reddish-brown precipitate

## END OF EXTENDED

## QUESTIONS

1. a) What would you observe if you added sodium hydroxide solution to a solution of calcium chloride?

   b) In what way would the observations be different if zinc chloride solution were used instead of calcium chloride solution?

2. What test can be used to distinguish between $Fe^{2+}$ and $Fe^{3+}$ ions? What is the result of the test with each ion?

## IDENTIFYING AMMONIUM IONS, $NH_4^+$

The test for the ammonium ion is shown in Fig. 2.69.

△ Fig. 2.69 Test for the ammonium ion $NH_4^+$.

The suspected ammonium compound is dissolved in water in a test tube and a few drops of dilute sodium hydroxide are added. The mixture is then warmed over a Bunsen burner and some damp red litmus paper (or universal indicator paper) is placed in the mouth of the test tube. A colour change in the indicator to blue (alkaline) shows that an ammonium compound is present.

## IDENTIFYING ANIONS

Negative ions (**anions**) can be tested as solids or in solution.

### Testing for anions in solids or solutions

The following test for anions in solids applies only to **carbonates**.

Dilute hydrochloric acid is added to the solid, and any gas produced is passed through limewater. If the limewater goes cloudy/milky, the solid contains a carbonate.

△ Fig. 2.70 Testing for anions in solids.

This reaction is as follows:

acid      + carbonate    → a salt      + water    + carbon dioxide

$2HCl(aq) + Na_2CO_3(s) \rightarrow 2NaCl(aq) + H_2O(l) + CO_2(g)$

$2HCl(aq) + ZnCO_3(s) \rightarrow ZnCl_2(aq) + H_2O(l) + CO_2(g)$

The reaction between an acid and a carbonate can be represented by the following ionic equation:

$$CO_3^{2-}(s) \quad + \quad 2H^+(aq) \quad \rightarrow \quad CO_2(g) \quad + \quad H_2O(l)$$

Many ionic compounds are soluble in water, and so they form solutions that contain anions.

The tests and results used to identify some other common anions are shown in the table.

| Name of ion | Formula | Test | Result |
|---|---|---|---|
| Chloride | $Cl^-(aq)$ | To a solution of the halide ions add: | White precipitate (of AgCl) |
| Bromide | $Br^-(aq)$ | 1. Dilute nitric acid<br>2. Silver nitrate solution | Cream precipitate (of AgBr) |
| Iodide | $I^-(aq)$ | | Yellow precipitate (of AgI) |
| Sulfate | $SO_4^{2-}(aq)$ | Add:<br>1. Dilute hydrochloric acid<br>2. Barium chloride solution | White precipitate (of BaSO$_4$) |
| Nitrate | $NO_3^-(s)$ | 1. Add sodium hydroxide solution and warm<br>2. Add aluminium powder<br>3. Test any gas produced with damp red litmus paper | Red litmus paper goes blue (ammonia gas is produced) |
| Sulfite | $SO_3^{2-}(aq)$ | 1. Add dilute hydrochloric acid.<br>2. Warm the mixture. | Filter paper soaked in potassium manganate(VII) turns from purple to colourless |

Δ Table 2.16 Tests for anions.

◁ Fig. 2.71 Test for the halide ions. Left: chloride, white precipitate. Centre: bromide, pale cream precipitate. Right: iodide, pale yellow precipitate.

These reactions can be represented by ionic equations:

$Ag^+(aq)$ + $Cl^-(aq)$ → $AgCl(s)$

white precipitate

$Ag^+(aq)$ + $Br^-(aq)$ → $AgBr(s)$

cream precipitate

$Ag^+(aq)$ + $I^-(aq)$ → $AgI(s)$

yellow precipitate

$Ba^{2+}(aq)$ + $SO_4^{2-}(aq)$ → $BaSO_4(s)$

white precipitate

1. Describe how you would test for an ammonium compound. Give the result of the test.

2. When a carbonate is reacted with dilute hydrochloric acid, a gas is given off.

   a) What is the name of the gas?

   b) What is the test for the gas? Give the result of the test.

3. Sodium hydroxide solution is added to solution X and a reddish-brown precipitate is formed. What metal ion was present in solution X?

4. A mixture of dilute nitric acid and silver nitrate solution is added to solution Y in a test tube. A white precipitate forms. What anion is present in solution Y?

5. EXTENDED Metallic ions in solution can be identified using sodium hydroxide solution.

   Sodium hydroxide is useful because it forms coloured precipitates with many metallic ions although it will form white precipitates with others.

   a) Copy and complete the table with the names of two cations that form white precipitates and three cations that give coloured precipitates.

| Name of cation | Colour of precipitate |
|---|---|
|  |  |
|  |  |
|  |  |
|  |  |
|  |  |

   b) Halide ions can be identified using nitric acid and silver nitrate. Give a general ionic equation to show the formation of the precipitate of the halide ion.

   c) When testing for sulfate ions, why is it important to add dilute hydrochloric acid before adding barium chloride?

6. A forensic scientist has been provided with a small sample of a blue compound which is suspected to be copper(II) sulfate, and a white compound that is suspected to be sodium carbonate. Devise a series of tests that could be followed to identify the ions. Indicate in your plan the expected results if the samples are to be positively identified.

## IDENTIFYING GASES

Many chemical reactions produce a gas as one of the products. Identifying the gas is often a step towards identifying the compound that produced it in the reaction.

| Gas | Formula | Test | Result of test |
|---|---|---|---|
| Hydrogen | $H_2$ | Put in a lighted splint (a flame) | 'Pop' or 'squeaky pop' heard (flame usually goes out) |
| Oxygen | $O_2$ | Put in a glowing splint | Splint relights, producing a flame |
| Carbon dioxide | $CO_2$ | Pass gas through limewater | Limewater goes cloudy/milky |
| Chlorine | $Cl_2$ | Put in a piece of damp blue litmus paper or universal indicator paper | Paper goes red then white (bleached) |
| Ammonia | $NH_3$ | Put in a piece of damp red litmus or universal indicator paper | A strong smell is produced and the indicator paper goes blue |
| Sulfur dioxide | $SO_2$ | Put in a piece of filter paper soaked in potassium manganate (VII) solution | Filter paper changes from purple to colourless |

△ Table 2.17 Tests for gases.

### REMEMBER

Carbon dioxide: cloudiness with limewater is caused by insoluble calcium carbonate. If carbon dioxide continues to be passed through, the cloudiness disappears: $CaCO_3(s)$ is changed to soluble calcium hydrogencarbonate, $Ca(HCO_3)_2(aq)$.

Chlorine: the gas is acidic, but also a bleaching agent.

Ammonia: the only basic gas.

### QUESTIONS

1. What is the name of a gas that is alkaline?
2. What is the name of a gas that supports combustion?
3. What is the name of a gas that acts as a bleach?

# End of topic checklist

## Key terms

anion, carbonate, cation, halide

## During your study of this topic you should have learned:

○ How to carry out tests for the aqueous cations aluminium, ammonium, calcium, chromium(III), copper(II), iron(II), iron(III) and zinc using aqueous sodium hydroxide and aqueous ammonia.

○ How to use a flame test to identify lithium, sodium, potassium and copper (II).

○ How to carry out tests for the anions:

- carbonate by reaction with dilute acid and then limewater
- chloride, bromide and iodide by reaction under acidic conditions with aqueous silver nitrate
- nitrate by reduction with aluminium
- sulfate by reaction under acidic conditions with aqueous barium ions
- sulfite by reaction with dilute hydrochloric acid and then aqueous potassium manganate(VII).

○ How to carry out tests for gases:

- ammonia using damp red litmus paper
- carbon dioxide using limewater
- chlorine using damp litmus paper
- hydrogen using a lighted splint
- oxygen using a glowing splint
- sulfur dioxide using aqueous potassium manganate(VII).

# End of topic questions

*Note: The marks awarded for these questions indicate the level of detail required in the answers. In the examination, the number of marks awarded to questions like these may be different.*

1. What ions are likely to be present in the compounds X, Y, and Z?

   a) Solution X forms a pale blue precipitate when sodium hydroxide solution is added. **(1 mark)**

   b) Solution Y forms no precipitate when sodium hydroxide solution is added, but produces a strong-smelling, alkaline gas when the mixture is heated. **(1 mark)**

   c) Solution Z forms an orange-brown precipitate when sodium hydroxide solution is added. **(1 mark)**

2. Copy and complete the table about the identification of gases. **(3 marks)**

| Gas | Test | Observations |
|---|---|---|
| Chlorine | Damp universal indicator paper | |
| | Bubble through limewater | White precipitate or suspension forms |
| Hydrogen | | Burns with a 'pop' |

3. A white powder is labelled 'lithium carbonate'. What test could you do to prove it was a carbonate? **(2 marks)**

4. How would you test a solid to identify the presence of each of the ions shown below?

   a) the sulfate ion, $SO_4^{2-}$ **(3 marks)**

   b) the iodide ion, $I^-$ **(3 marks)**

   c) the nitrate ion, $NO_3^-$ **(3 marks)**

5. **EXTENDED** Write ionic equations for the following reactions:

   a) between copper(II) sulfate and sodium hydroxide solution **(2 marks)**

   b) between sodium carbonate and dilute hydrochloric acid. **(2 marks)**

# Exam-style questions
## Sample student answer

*The questions, sample answers and marks in this section have been written by the authors as a guide only. The marks awarded for these questions indicate the level of detail required in the answers. In the examination, the number of marks awarded to questions like these may be different.*

## Question 1

Solutions of lead(II) nitrate and potassium iodide react together to make the insoluble substance lead(II) iodide.

The equation for the reaction is

$$Pb(NO_3)_2(aq) + 2KI(aq) \rightarrow 2KNO_3(aq) + PbI_2(s)$$

An investigation was carried out to find how much precipitate formed with different volumes of lead(II) nitrate solution.

A student measured out 15 cm$^3$ of potassium iodide solution using a measuring cylinder.

He poured this solution in to a clean boiling tube.

Using a clean measuring cylinder, he measured out 2 cm$^3$ of lead(II) nitrate solution (of the same concentration as the potassium iodide solution). He added this to the potassium iodide solution.

A cloudy yellow mixture formed and the precipitate was left to settle.

The student then measured the height (in cm) of the precipitate using a ruler.

The student repeated the experiment using different volumes of lead(II) nitrate solution. The graph shows the results obtained.

PHYSICAL CHEMISTRY

**a)** **i)** On the graph, circle the point that seems to be anomalous. (1)

   **ii)** Explain two things that the student may have done in the experiment to give this anomalous result.

*Precipitate not settled* ✓ ①   *Because not left long enough* ✓ ① (2)

   **iii)** Why must the graph line go through (0, 0)?

*Cannot have a precipitate if no lead nitrate added yet.* ✓ ① (1)

**b)** Suggest a reason why the height of the precipitate stops increasing.

*No more potassium iodide left to react.* ✓ ① (1)

**c)** **i)** How much precipitate has been made in the tube drawn on the right?

*1.5 cm* ✓ ① (1)

   **ii)** Use the graph to find the volume of lead(II) nitrate solution needed to make this amount of precipitate.

*2.9 cm* ✗ (1)

solution of soluble salts

precipitate of solid lead(II) iodide

**d)** After he had plotted the graph, the student decided he should obtain some more results.

   **i)** Suggest what volumes of lead(II) nitrate solution he should use.

*Between 6 cm³ and 10 cm³* ✓ ① (1)

   **ii)** Explain why he should use these volumes.

*Need to know exactly where the graph levels off* ✓ ① (1)

**e)** Suggest a different method for measuring the amount of precipitate formed.

*Filter* ✓ ①   *off each precipitate and weigh it* ✓ ① (4)

(Total 13 marks)

⑩⁄₁₃

## Question 2

Dilute nitric acid reacts with marble chips to produce carbon dioxide. The equation is given below:

$$2HNO_3(aq) + CaCO_3(s) \rightarrow Ca(NO_3)_2(aq) + H_2O(l) + CO_2(g)$$

Some students investigated the effect of changing the temperature of the nitric acid on the rate of the reaction. The method is:

- Use a measuring cylinder to pour 50 cm³ of dilute nitric acid into a conical flask.
- Heat the acid to the required temperature.
- Put the flask on the balance.
- Add 15 g (an excess) of marble chips to the flask.
- Time how long it takes for the mass to decrease by 1.00 g.
- Repeat the experiment at different temperatures.

The students' results are shown in the table.

| Temperature of acid (°C) | Time to lose 1.00 g (s) |
|---|---|
| 20 | 93 |
| 33 | 68 |
| 44 | 66 |
| 55 | 40 |
| 67 | 30 |
| 76 | 25 |

**a)** **i)** Draw a graph of the results. (3)

   **ii)** One of the points is inaccurate. Circle this point on your graph. (1)

   **iii)** Suggest a possible cause for this inaccurate result. (1)

**b)** Use the graph to find the times taken to lose 1.00 g at 40 °C and 60 °C. (2)

**c)** The rate of the reaction can be found using the equation:

$$\text{rate of reaction} = \frac{\text{mass lost}}{\text{time taken to lose mass}}$$

   **i)** Use this equation and your results from **b)** to calculate the rates of reaction at 40 °C and 60 °C. (2)

**ii)** What will be the unit for these rates? (1)

**iii)** State how the rate of reaction changes when the temperature increases. (1)

**iv)** Explain in terms of particles and collisions why the rate changes when the temperature increases. (1)

**d)** Describe how the method could be changed to obtain a result at 5 °C. (1)

**(Total 13 marks)**

## Question 3

Sulfuric acid is manufactured in the Contact process. Part of the process involves a reaction that produces sulfur trioxide. The equation for this reaction is shown below.

$$2SO_2(g) + O_2(g) \rightleftharpoons 2SO_2(g) \; \Delta H = \text{negative}$$

**a)** What type of reaction is represented by the sign $\rightleftharpoons$? (1)

**b)** What information about the reaction can you work out from the information that $\Delta H$ is negative? (1)

**c)** A temperature of 450 °C is used in this reaction. Explain why this temperature has been chosen. (3)

**d) i)** A catalyst is used to increase the rate of the reaction. How does a catalyst do this? (2)

**ii)** Name the catalyst used in this reaction. (1)

**(Total 8 marks)**

## Question 4

The diagram shows the apparatus used to electrolyse lead(II) bromide.

**a)** The wires connected to the electrodes are made of copper.

Explain why copper conducts electricity. (1)

# Exam-style questions continued

**b)** Explain why electrolysis does not occur unless the lead(II) bromide is molten. **(2)**

**c)** The reactions occurring at the electrodes can be represented by the equations shown in the table.

Copy and complete the table to show the electrode (A or B) at which each reaction occurs, and the type of reaction occurring (oxidation or reduction). **(2)**

| Electrode reaction | Electrode | Type of reaction |
|---|---|---|
| $Pb^{2+} + 2e^- \rightarrow Pb$ | | |
| $2Br^- \rightarrow Br_2 + 2e^-$ | | |

**(Total 5 marks)**

## Question 5

Read the following instructions for the preparation of hydrated nickel(II) sulfate ($NiSO_4.7H_2O$), then answer the questions that follow.

**1.** Put 25 cm³ of dilute sulfuric acid in a beaker.

**2.** Heat the sulfuric acid until it is just boiling and then add a small amount of nickel(II) carbonate.

**3.** When the nickel carbonate has dissolved, stop heating, then add a little more nickel carbonate. Continue in this way until nickel carbonate is in excess.

**4.** Filter the hot mixture into a clean beaker.

**5.** Make the hydrated nickel(II) sulfate crystals from the nickel(II) sulfate solution.

The equation for the reaction is

$$NiCO_3(s) + H_2SO_4(aq) \rightarrow NiSO_4(aq) + CO_2(g) + H_2O(l)$$

**a)** What piece of apparatus would you use to measure out 25 cm³ of sulfuric acid? **(1)**

**b)** Why is the nickel(II) carbonate added in excess? **(1)**

**c)** When nickel(II) carbonate is added to sulfuric acid, there is fizzing. Explain why. **(1)**

**d)** Draw a diagram to describe step 4. You must label your diagram. (3)

**e)** After filtration, which one of the following describes the nickel(II) sulfate in the beaker?

Select the correct answer.

crystals          filtrate          precipitate          water          (1)

**f)** Explain how you would obtain pure dry crystals of hydrated nickel(II) sulfate from the solution of nickel(II) sulfate. (2)

**g)** When hydrated nickel(II) sulfate is heated gently in a test tube, it changes colour from green to white.

**i)** Complete the symbol equation for this reaction.

$NiSO_4.7H_2O(s) \rightleftharpoons NiSO_4(s) +$ (1)

**ii)** What does the sign $\rightleftharpoons$ mean? (1)

**h)** How can you obtain a sample of green nickel(II) sulfate starting with white nickel(II) sulfate? (1)

**(Total 12 marks)**

## Question 6

Electroplating iron with chromium involves four stages.

**1.** Iron object is cleaned with sulfuric acid, then washed with water.

**2.** The iron is plated with copper.

**3.** It is then plated with nickel to prevent corrosion.

**4.** It is then plated with chromium.

**a)** The equation for Stage 1 is:

$Fe + H_2SO_4 \rightarrow FeSO_4 + H_2$

**i)** Write a word equation for this reaction. (2)

**ii)** Describe a test for the gas given off in this reaction. (2)

# Exam-style questions continued

**b)** The diagram shows how iron is electroplated with copper.

rod of
pure
copper

iron object

copper(II) sulfate
solution

> **i)** Choose a word from the list below that describes the iron object. Draw a ring
> around the correct answer.
>
> anion        anode        cathode        cation        (1)
>
> **ii)** What is the purpose of the copper(II) sulfate solution?        (1)
>
> **iii)** Describe what happens during the electroplating to:
>
> the iron object        (2)
>
> the rod of pure copper.        (2)
>
> **iv)** Describe a test for copper(II) ions.        (2)

**c)** Suggest why chromium is used to electroplate articles.        (1)

**d)** The information below shows the reactivity of chromium, copper and iron with warm
hydrochloric acid.

chromium – a few bubbles of gas produced every second

copper – no bubbles of gas produced

iron – many bubbles of gas produced every second

Put these three metals in order of their reactivity with hydrochloric acid,
most reactive first.        (1)

**(Total 14 marks)**

## Question 7

The following diagram shows a simple cell.

**a)** Predict how the voltage of the cell would change if the tin electrode was replaced with a silver one. (1)

**b)** Which electrode would go into the solution as positive ions? Give a reason for your choice. (1)

**c)** State how you can predict the direction of the electron flow in cells of this type. (1)

**(Total 3 marks)**

This section concentrates on a 'branch' of chemistry known as inorganic chemistry. As the title suggests, it focuses on the chemical elements, of which there are over 100. This may seem rather a lot, but the good news is that you will not study all 100 elements! However, because the chemical elements are arranged in a particular pattern, known as the Periodic Table, learning about one element often provides a very good idea of how other elements may behave. So it should be possible to learn about the chemistry of about 45 elements from studying this section.

The section starts with the Periodic Table. You will learn about how the elements are arranged into groups and periods. You will then study a group of metals and a group of non-metals, followed by the transition metals and noble gases. The topic on metals highlights differences in the reactivity of metals and how this influences the methods used to extract them from their ores. A topic on air and water allows a consideration of the environmental impact of living in an industrial world. Finally, this study of the elements and some of their compounds provides an opportunity to look at sulfur and some important compounds, carbonates.

## STARTING POINTS

1. What is an element – how would you define the term?

2. What does the proton number of an atom tell you about its structure?

3. In terms of electronic structures, what is the difference between a metal and a non-metal?

4. You will be learning about the Periodic Table of elements. Look at the Periodic Table and make a list of the things that you notice about it.

5. You will be learning about the composition of gases in the air. What is the most abundant gas in the air?

6. Make a list of about six to eight metals that you have come across. Which metal in your list do you think is the most reactive? Which metal do you think is the least reactive? Explain your choices.

## SECTION CONTENTS

a) The Periodic Table

b) Group I elements

c) Group VII elements

d) Transition metals and noble gases

e) Metals

f) Air and water

g) Sulfur

h) Carbonates

i) Exam-style questions

# 3
# Inorganic chemistry

△ Many batteries contain lithium, which is a Group I metal.

# The Periodic Table

## INTRODUCTION

With over 100 different elements in existence, it's very important to have some way of ordering them. The Periodic Table puts elements with similar properties into columns, with a gradual change in properties moving from left to right along the rows. This topic looks at some of the basic features of the Periodic Table. Later topics will look in more detail at particular groups and arrangements of the elements.

△ Fig. 3.1 This ordering of elements was first published in 1871 by the Russian chemist Dmitri Mendeleev.

### KNOWLEDGE CHECK

✓ Understand that all matter is made up of elements.
✓ Know that the proton number of an element gives the number of protons (and electrons) in an atom of the element.
✓ Know that electrons are arranged in shells around the nucleus of the atom.

### LEARNING OBJECTIVES

✓ Be able to describe the Periodic Table as a method of classifying elements and recognise its use in predicting properties of elements.
✓ Be able to describe the change from metallic to non-metallic character across a period.

✓ **EXTENDED** Be able to describe the relationship between group number, number of valency electrons and metallic/non-metallic character.

## THE ARRANGEMENT OF THE PERIODIC TABLE

As new elements were discovered in the 19th century, chemists tried to organise them into patterns based on the similarities in their properties. The English chemist John Newlands was the first to classify elements according to their properties and produced his classification system before Mendeleev produced his. When the structure of the atom was better known, elements were arranged in order of increasing proton number, and then the patterns started to make more sense. (Proton number is the number of protons in an atom.)

# HOW ARE ELEMENTS CLASSIFIED IN THE MODERN PERIODIC TABLE?

More than 110 elements have now been identified, and each has its own properties and reactions. In the **Periodic Table**, elements with similar properties and reactions are shown close together.

The Periodic Table arranges the elements in order of increasing proton number. They are then arranged in periods and groups.

| Groups | I | II | | | | | | | | | | | III | IV | V | VI | VII | 0 |
|---|---|---|---|---|---|---|---|---|---|---|---|---|---|---|---|---|---|---|
| **Periods** | | | | | | | | | | | | | | | | | | |
| **1** | | | | | | H<br>hydrogen<br>1 | | | | | | | | | | | | He<br>helium<br>2 |
| **2** | Li<br>lithium<br>3 | Be<br>beryllium<br>4 | | | | | | | | | | | B<br>boron<br>5 | C<br>carbon<br>6 | N<br>nitrogen<br>7 | O<br>oxygen<br>8 | F<br>fluorine<br>9 | Ne<br>neon<br>10 |
| **3** | Na<br>sodium<br>11 | Mg<br>magnesium<br>12 | | | transition metals | | | | | | | | Al<br>aluminium<br>13 | Si<br>silicon<br>14 | P<br>phosphorus<br>15 | S<br>sulfur<br>16 | Cl<br>chlorine<br>17 | Ar<br>argon<br>18 |
| **4** | K<br>potassium<br>19 | Ca<br>calcium<br>20 | Sc<br>scandium<br>21 | Ti<br>titanium<br>22 | V<br>vanadium<br>23 | Cr<br>chromium<br>24 | Mn<br>manganese<br>25 | Fe<br>iron<br>26 | Co<br>cobalt<br>27 | Ni<br>nickel<br>28 | Cu<br>copper<br>29 | Zn<br>zinc<br>30 | Ga<br>gallium<br>31 | Ge<br>germanium<br>32 | As<br>arsenic<br>33 | Se<br>selenium<br>34 | Br<br>bromine<br>35 | Kr<br>krypton<br>36 |
| **5** | Rb<br>rubidium<br>37 | Sr<br>strontium<br>38 | Y<br>yttrium<br>39 | Zr<br>zirconium<br>40 | Nb<br>niobium<br>41 | Mo<br>molybdenum<br>42 | Tc<br>technetium<br>43 | Ru<br>ruthenium<br>44 | Rh<br>rhodium<br>45 | Pd<br>palladium<br>46 | Ag<br>silver<br>47 | Cd<br>cadmium<br>48 | In<br>indium<br>49 | Sn<br>tin<br>50 | Sb<br>antimony<br>51 | Te<br>tellurium<br>52 | I<br>iodine<br>53 | Xe<br>xenon<br>54 |
| **6** | Cs<br>caesium<br>55 | Ba<br>barium<br>56 | La<br>lanthanum<br>57 | Hf<br>hafnium<br>72 | Ta<br>tantalum<br>73 | W<br>tungsten<br>74 | Re<br>rhenium<br>75 | Os<br>osmium<br>76 | Ir<br>iridium<br>77 | Pt<br>platinum<br>78 | Au<br>gold<br>79 | Hg<br>mercury<br>80 | Tl<br>thallium<br>81 | Pb<br>lead<br>82 | Bi<br>bismuth<br>83 | Po<br>polonium<br>84 | At<br>astatine<br>85 | Rn<br>radon<br>86 |

metal | non metal | transition metal | metalloid

△ Fig. 3.2 The Periodic Table.

## Periods

Horizontal rows of elements are arranged in increasing proton number from left to right. Rows correspond to **periods,** which are numbered from 1 to 7.

Moving across a period, each successive atom of the elements gains one proton and one electron (in the same outer shell/orbit).

You can see how this works in Fig. 3.3.

| Group I | Group II | Group III | Group IV | Group V | Group VI | Group VII | Group 0 |
|---|---|---|---|---|---|---|---|
| sodium | magnesium | aluminium | silicon | phosphorus | sulfur | chlorine | argon |
| 2,8,1 | 2,8,2 | 2,8,3 | 2,8,4 | 2,8,5 | 2,8,6 | 2,8,7 | 2,8,8 |

△ Fig. 3.3 Moving across a period shows the atomic structure of each element.

Moving across a period like Period 3 (sodium to argon), the following trends take place:

- Metals on the left going to non-metals on the right.
- Group I elements are the most reactive metal group, and as you go to the right the reactivity of the groups decreases. Group IV elements are the least reactive.
- Continuing right from Group IV, the reactivity increases until Group VII, the most reactive of the non-metal groups.

## Groups

Vertical columns contain elements with the proton number increasing down the column – they are called **groups**. They are numbered from I to VII and 0 (Group 0 is sometimes referred to as Group VIII).

Groups are referred to as 'families' of elements because they have similar characteristics, just like families – the alkali metals (Group I), the alkaline earth metals (Group II) and the halogens (Group VII).

### REMEMBER

It is important to understand the relationship between group number, number of outer electrons, and metallic and non-metallic character across periods.

## QUESTIONS

1. Find the element calcium in the Periodic Table. Answer these questions about calcium:

   a) What is its proton number?

   b) What information does the proton number give about the structure of a calcium atom?

   c) Which group of the Periodic Table is calcium in?

   d) Which period of the Periodic Table is calcium in?

   e) Is calcium a metal or a non-metal?

2. What is the family name for the Group VII elements?

3. Are the Group VII elements metals or non-metals?

### EXTENDED

#### CHARGES ON IONS AND THE PERIODIC TABLE

We can explain why elements in the same group have similar reactions in terms of the electron structures of their atoms. Elements with the same number of electrons in their outer shells have similar chemical properties. The relationship between the group number and the number of electrons in the outer electron shell is shown in Table 3.1.

| Group number | I | II | III | IV | V | VI | VII | 0 (VIII) |
|---|---|---|---|---|---|---|---|---|
| Electrons in the outer electron shell | 1 | 2 | 3 | 4 | 5 | 6 | 7 | 2 or 8 |

△ Table 3.1 Relationship between group number and number of electrons in outer shell.

The ion formed by an element can be worked out from the element's position in the Periodic Table. The elements in Group IV and Group VIII (or 0) generally do not form ions.

| Group number | I | II | III | IV | V | VI | VII | VIII (or 0) |
|---|---|---|---|---|---|---|---|---|
| Ion charge | 1+ | 2+ | 3+ | Typically no ions | 3– | 2– | 1– | No ions |
| Metallic or non-metallic | Metallic | | | Non-metallic, metalloid and metallic | Non-metallic (except for some metalloids) | | | |

△ Table 3.2 Groups and their ions.

## REACTIVITIES OF ELEMENTS

Going from the top to the bottom of a group in the Periodic Table, metals become more reactive, but non-metals become less reactive. As the metal atom gets bigger, the outer electrons get further away from the nucleus and can be removed more easily to form positive ions. So the larger metal atoms can react more easily with other elements and form compounds.

The reverse is true for a group of non-metal atoms: the smaller the atom, the easier it is to accept electrons and form ions. So the smaller non-metal atoms react more easily with other elements to form compounds.

Group 0 elements, known as the noble gases, are very unreactive. They already have full outer electron shells (eight electrons in the outer shell) and so rarely react with other elements to form compounds.

△ Fig. 3.4 The Group VII elements (non-metal) become more reactive further up the group.

△ Fig. 3.5 Group I elements (metals) become more reactive further down the group.

**END OF EXTENDED**

1. How many electrons does an aluminium atom have in its outer shell?

2. What ion charge does oxygen have?

3. Which is the most reactive element in Group VII?

4. Which is the most reactive element in Group II?

 **SCIENCE IN CONTEXT** **THE FIRST PERIODIC TABLE**

In 1871 the Russian chemist Dmitri Mendeleev published his work on the Periodic Table. It included the 66 elements that were known at the time. Interestingly, Mendeleev left gaps in his arrangement when the next element in his order did not seem to fit. He predicted that there should be elements in the gaps but that they had yet to be discovered. One such element is gallium (discovered in 1875), which Mendeleev predicted would be between aluminium and indium.

By June 2011 there were 118 known elements, but only 91 of these occurred naturally – the others had been made artificially. Some of these artificial elements can now be detected in small quantities in the environment – for example the element americium (Am, proton number 95), which is used in smoke detectors.

# End of topic checklist

**Key terms**

group, period, Periodic Table

## During your study of this topic you should have learned:

○ How to describe the Periodic Table as a method of classifying elements and its use to predict properties of elements.

○ How to describe the change from metallic to non-metallic character across a period.

○ **EXTENDED** How to describe the relationship between group number, number of valency electrons and metallic/non-metallic character.

# End of topic questions

*Note: The marks awarded for these questions indicate the level of detail required in the answers. In the examination, the number of marks awarded to questions like these may be different.*

1. Look at the diagram representing the Periodic Table. The letters stand for elements.

    **a)** Which element is in Group IV? (1 mark)

    **b)** Which element is in the second period? (1 mark)

    **c)** Which element is a noble gas? (1 mark)

    **d)** Which element is a transition metal? (1 mark)

    **e)** Which elements are non- metals? (1 mark)

    **f)** Which element is most likely to be a gas? (1 mark)

2. What are the electron arrangements in the following atoms?

    **a)** sodium (proton number = 11) (1 mark)

    **b)** silicon (proton number = 14) (1 mark)

    **c)** fluorine (proton number = 9) (1 mark)

3. How does the metallic and non-metallic nature of the elements change across Period 3 of the Periodic Table? (1 mark)

4. Why do elements in the same group have similar chemical properties? (1 mark)

5. What ions would you expect the following atoms to form?

    **a)** sodium (1 mark)

    **b)** chlorine. (1 mark)

6. In the Periodic Table, what is the trend in reactivity:

    **a)** down a group of metals? (1 mark)

    **b)** down a group of non-metals? (1 mark)

7. Explain why the noble gases in Group 0 are very unreactive. (2 marks)

# Group I elements

## INTRODUCTION

Metals are positioned on the left-hand side and in the middle of the Periodic Table. Therefore the Group I elements are metals, but rather different from the metals in everyday use. In fact, when you see how the Group I metals react with air and water, it is hard to think how they could be used outside the laboratory. This very high reactivity makes them interesting to study. Our focus is on the first three elements in the group: lithium, sodium and potassium. Rubidium, caesium and francium are not available in schools because they are too reactive.

△ Fig. 3.6 Potassium reacting with water.

## KNOWLEDGE CHECK

✓ Understand that metals are positioned on the left-hand side and middle of the Periodic Table.
✓ Know that elements in a group have similar electron arrangements.
✓ Know that metal oxides are basic and those that dissolve in water form alkalis.

## LEARNING OBJECTIVES

✓ Be able to describe lithium, sodium and potassium in Group I as a collection of relatively soft metals showing trends in melting point, density and reaction with water.
✓ Be able to predict the properties of other elements in Group I, given data where appropriate.
✓ **EXTENDED** Be able to identify trends in other groups, given information about the elements concerned.

## REACTIVITY OF GROUP I ELEMENTS

All Group I elements react with water to produce an alkaline solution. This makes them recognisable as a 'family' of elements, often called the **alkali metals.**

These very reactive metals all have only one electron in their outer electron shell. This electron is easily given away when the metal reacts with non-metals. The more electrons a metal atom has to lose in a reaction, the more energy is needed to start the reaction. This is why the Group II elements are less reactive – they have to lose two electrons when they react.

Reactivity increases down the group because as the atom gets bigger the outer electron is further away from the nucleus and so can be removed more easily, as the atoms react to form positive ions.

## PROPERTIES OF GROUP I METALS

The properties of Group I metals are as follows:

- Soft to cut.
- Shiny when cut, but quickly tarnish in the air.
- Very low melting points compared with most metals – melting points decrease down the group.
- Very low densities compared with most metals. Lithium, sodium and potassium float on water. Densities increase down the group.
- React very easily with air, water and elements such as chlorine. The alkali metals are so reactive that they are stored in oil to prevent reaction with air and water. Reactivity increases down the group.

△ Fig. 3.7 The freshly cut surface of sodium.

| Li lithium 3 |
| Na sodium 11 |
| K potassium 19 |
| Rb rubidium 37 |
| Cs caesium 55 |

INCREASING REACTIVITY

△ Fig. 3.8 Group I elements become more reactive as you go down the group.

## QUESTIONS

1. Why are the Group I elements known as the *alkali metals*?

2. How many electrons do the Group I elements atoms have in their outer shell?

3. The Group I metals are unusual metals. Give one property they have that is different to most other metals.

4. Predict how the melting point of rubidium will compare to that of sodium. Explain your answer.

5. **EXTENDED** Why is potassium more reactive than lithium?

| Reaction | Observations | Equations |
|---|---|---|
| Air or oxygen | The metals burn easily and their compounds colour flames:<br><br>lithium – red<br>sodium – orange/yellow<br>potassium – lilac<br><br>A white solid oxide is formed | lithium + oxygen $\rightarrow$ lithium oxide<br><br>$4Li(s) + O_2(g) \rightarrow 2Li_2O(s)$<br><br>sodium + oxygen $\rightarrow$ sodium oxide<br><br>$4Na(s) + O_2(g) \rightarrow 2Na_2O(s)$<br><br>potassium + oxygen $\rightarrow$ potassium oxide<br><br>$4K(s) + O_2(g) \rightarrow 2K_2O(s)$ |
| Water | The metals react vigorously<br><br>They float on the surface, moving around rapidly<br><br>With both sodium and potassium, the heat of the reaction melts the metal so it forms a sphere; bubbles of gas are given off and the metal 'disappears'<br><br>With the more reactive metals (such as potassium) the hydrogen gas produced burns<br><br>The resulting solution is alkaline | lithium + water $\rightarrow$ lithium hydroxide + hydrogen<br><br>$2Li(s) + 2H_2O(l) \rightarrow 2LiOH(aq) + H_2(g)$<br><br>sodium + water $\rightarrow$ sodium hydroxide + hydrogen<br><br>$2Na(s) + 2H_2O(l) \rightarrow 2NaOH(aq) + H_2(g)$<br><br>potassium + water $\rightarrow$ potassium hydroxide + hydrogen<br><br>$2K(s) + 2H_2O(l) \rightarrow 2KOH(aq) + H_2(g)$ |
| Chlorine | The metals react easily, burning in the chlorine to form a white solid, the metal chloride | lithium + chlorine $\rightarrow$ lithium chloride<br><br>$2Li(s) + Cl_2(g) \rightarrow 2LiCl(s)$<br><br>sodium + chlorine $\rightarrow$ sodium chloride<br><br>$2Na(s) + Cl_2(g) \rightarrow 2NaCl(s)$<br><br>potassium + chlorine $\rightarrow$ potassium chloride<br><br>$2K(s) + Cl_2(g) \rightarrow 2KCl(s)$ |

△ Table 3.3 Reactions of Group I metals.

## COMPOUNDS OF THE GROUP I METALS

The compounds of Group I metals are usually colourless crystals or white solids and always have ionic bonding. Most of them are soluble in water. Some examples are sodium chloride (NaCl) and potassium nitrate ($KNO_3$).

The compounds of the alkali metals are widely used:

- lithium carbonate – as a hardener in glass and ceramics
- lithium hydroxide – removes carbon dioxide in air-conditioning systems
- sodium chloride – table salt
- sodium carbonate – a water softener
- sodium hydroxide – used in paper manufacture
- monosodium glutamate – a flavour enhancer
- sodium sulfite – a preservative
- potassium nitrate – a fertiliser; also used in explosives.

△ Fig. 3.9 Sodium burning in chlorine.

## QUESTIONS

1. Sodium burns in oxygen to make sodium oxide. What colour would you expect sodium oxide to be?

2. What gas is produced when potassium reacts with water? What is the name of the solution formed in this reaction?

3. Are the compounds of the Group I metals usually soluble or insoluble in water?

It is important to understand the structure of the Periodic Table and how it relates to the properties and reactions of the elements. These questions link electronic structure with the reactivity trends of the different elements in the Periodic Table.

4. Predict how the melting point of rubidium will compare to that of sodium. Explain your answer.

5. **EXTENDED** These questions are based on Group I of the Periodic Table.

   a) What do you understand by a *group* in the Periodic Table?

   b) Name the first three metals of Group I.

   c) Why do the elements in this group have similar chemical properties?

   d) Group I elements are very reactive. Suggest reasons for this.

## FACTS ABOUT THE GROUP I METALS

1. Lithium is found in large quantities (estimated at 230 billion tonnes) in compounds in seawater.

2. Sodium is found in many minerals and is the sixth most abundant element overall in the Earth's crust (amounting to 2.6% by weight).

3. Potassium is also found in many minerals and is the seventh most abundant element in the Earth's crust (amounting to 1.5% by weight).

4. Rubidium was discovered by Bunsen (of Bunsen burner fame) in 1861. It is more abundant than copper, about the same as zinc, and is found in very small quantities in a large number of minerals. Because of this low concentration in mineral deposits, only 2 to 4 tonnes of rubidium are produced each year worldwide.

5. Caesium is more abundant than tin, mercury and silver. However, its very high reactivity makes it very difficult to extract from mineral deposits.

6. Francium was discovered as recently as 1939 as a product of the radioactive decay of an isotope of actinium.

△ Fig. 3.10 Lithium is used in all of these batteries.

# End of topic checklist

## Key terms

alkali metal

## During your study of this topic you should have learned:

○ How to describe lithium, sodium and potassium in Group I as a collection of relatively soft metals showing trends in melting point, density and reaction with water.

○ How to predict the properties of other elements in Group I, given data where appropriate.

○ **EXTENDED** How to identify trends in other groups, given information about the elements concerned.

# End of topic questions

*Note: The marks awarded for these questions indicate the level of detail required in the answers. In the examination, the number of marks awarded to questions like these may be different.*

1. This question is about the Group I elements lithium, sodium and potassium.

   **a)** Which is the most reactive of these elements? (1 mark)

   **b)** Why are the elements stored in oil? (1 mark)

   **c)** Which element is the easiest to cut? (1 mark)

   **d)** Why do the elements tarnish quickly when they are cut? (1 mark)

   **e)** Why does sodium float when added to water? (1 mark)

2. Why are the Group I elements known as the 'alkali metals'? (2 marks)

3. Write word equations and balanced equations for the following reactions:

   **a)** lithium and oxygen (3 marks)

   **b)** potassium and water (3 marks)

   **c)** potassium and chlorine. (3 marks)

4. EXTENDED This question is about rubidium (symbol Rb), which is a less common Group I element.

   **a)** What state of matter would you expect rubidium to be in at room temperature and pressure? (1 mark)

   **b)** When rubidium is added to water:

   **i)** Which gas is formed? (1 mark)

   **ii)** What chemical compound would be formed in solution? What result would you predict if universal indicator was added to the solution? (2 marks)

   **c)** Would you expect rubidium to be more or less reactive than potassium? Explain your answer. (2 marks)

5. EXTENDED Explain why potassium is more reactive than sodium. (3 marks)

# Group VII elements

## INTRODUCTION

Group VII elements are located on the right-hand side of the Periodic Table with the other non-metals. They look very different from each other, so it may seem strange that they are in the same group. However, their chemical properties are very similar, and all of them are highly reactive. This topic focuses on chlorine, bromine and iodine. Fluorine is a highly reactive gas and astatine is a radioactive black solid with a very short half-life (so will exist in only very small quantities).

△ Fig. 3.11 At room temperature and atmospheric pressure, chlorine is a pale green gas, bromine a red-brown liquid and iodine is a black solid.

### KNOWLEDGE CHECK

✓ Understand that non-metals are positioned on the right-hand side of the Periodic Table.
✓ Know that the elements in a group have similar electron arrangements.
✓ Be familiar with the terms oxidation and reduction.

### LEARNING OBJECTIVES

✓ Be able to describe chlorine, bromine and iodine in Group VII as a collection of diatomic non-metals showing trends in colour and in their reactions with other halide ions.
✓ Be able to predict the properties of other elements in Group VII, given data where appropriate.
✓ **EXTENDED** Be able to identify trends in other groups, given information about the elements concerned.

## REACTIVITY OF GROUP VII ELEMENTS

The Group VII elements are sometimes referred to as the **halogen** elements or halogens.

'Halogen' means 'salt-maker' – halogens react with most metals to make salts.

Halogen atoms have seven electrons in their outermost electron shell, so they need to gain only one electron to obtain a full outer shell. This is what makes them very reactive. They react with metals, gaining an electron and forming a singly charged negative ion.

The reactivity of the elements decreases down the group because as the atoms gets bigger, an eighth electron will be further from the attractive force of the nucleus. This makes it harder for the atom to gain this electron.

**END OF EXTENDED**

Δ Fig. 3.12 Increasing reactivity goes up Group VII.

## PROPERTIES OF GROUP VII ELEMENTS

The properties of the Group VII elements are as follows.

- Fluorine is a pale yellow gas; chlorine is a pale green gas; bromine is a red-brown liquid; iodine is a black shiny solid.
- All the atoms have seven electrons in their outermost electron shell.
- All exist as diatomic molecules–each molecule contains two atoms. For example–$F_2$, $Cl_2$, $Br_2$, $I_2$.
- Halogens react with water and react with metals to form salts. Iodine has very low solubility and little reaction with water.
- They undergo **displacement reactions.**

| Reaction | Observations | Equations |
|---|---|---|
| Water<br><br>chlorine gas<br><br>water | The halogens dissolve in water and also react with it, forming solutions that behave as bleaches<br><br>Chlorine solution is pale yellow<br><br>Bromine solution is orange<br><br>Iodine solution is yellow/brown. | chlorine + water → hydrochloric acid + chloric(I) acid<br><br>$Cl_2(g) + H_2O(l) \rightarrow HCl(aq) + HClO(aq)$ |
| Metals<br><br>chlorine<br><br>sodium | The halogens form salts with all metals. For example, gold leaf will catch fire in chlorine without heating<br><br>With a metal such as iron, brown fumes of iron(III) chloride form. | iron + chlorine → iron(III) chloride<br><br>$2Fe(s) + 3Cl_2(g) \rightarrow 2FeCl_3(s)$<br><br>Fluor*ine* forms salts called fluor*ides*<br>Chlor*ine* forms salts called chlor*ides*<br>Brom*ine* forms salts called brom*ides*<br>Iod*ine* forms salts called iod*ides* |
| Displacement<br><br>chlorine gas<br><br>potassium iodide solution<br><br>iodine being formed | A more reactive halogen will displace a less reactive halogen from a solution of a salt<br><br>Chlorine displaces bromine from sodium bromide solution. The colourless solution (sodium bromide) turns orange when chlorine is added due to the formation of bromine<br><br>Chlorine displaces iodine from sodium iodide solution. The colourless solution (sodium iodide) turns brown when chlorine is added due to the formation of iodine | chlorine + sodium bromide → sodium chloride + bromine<br>$Cl_2(g) + 2NaBr(aq) \rightarrow 2NaCl(aq) + Br_2(aq)$<br><br>chlorine + sodium iodide → sodium chloride + iodine<br>$Cl_2(g) + 2NaI(aq) \rightarrow 2NaCl(aq) + I_2(aq)$ |

△ Table 3.4 Properties of the Group VII elements.

The displacement reactions between halogens and solutions of halide ions (shown above) are examples of redox reactions – that is, oxidation and reduction reactions. The $Na^+$ ions are 'spectator' ions and play no part in the reaction, so if the reaction between chlorine and sodium bromide solution is written with them removed, the equation becomes:

$$Cl_2(aq) + 2Br^-(aq) \rightarrow 2Cl^-(aq) + Br_2(aq)$$

This reaction can be written as two half-equations showing how electrons are involved:

$$Cl_2(aq) + 2e^- \rightarrow 2Cl^-(aq)$$

The chlorine has gained electrons – it has been reduced.

$$2Br^-(aq) \rightarrow Br_2(aq) + 2e^-$$

The bromide ions have lost electrons – they have been oxidised.

In this reaction the chlorine is an oxidising agent – it oxidises the bromide ions and is itself reduced. The bromide ions are reducing agents – they reduce the chlorine and are themselves oxidised.

**END OF EXTENDED**

## QUESTIONS

1. How many electrons do the Group VII element atoms have in their outer shell?

2. Why are the Group VII elements particularly reactive when compared to other non-metals?

3. Chlorine exists as diatomic molecules. Explain what this means.

4. Astatine is an element in Group VII. Predict whether you would expect it to be a solid, liquid or gas at room temperature. Explain your answer.

5. What is meant by a 'displacement reaction' involving the Group VII elements?

6. EXTENDED Why are displacement reactions also redox reactions?

# Developing investigative skills

A student was provided with three aqueous solutions containing chlorine, bromine and iodine. She added a few drops of cyclohexane to each solution in separate test tubes and then stirred each with a clean glass rod. Cyclohexane does not mix with water, it floats on top of aqueous solutions. When each cyclohexane layer separated from the solution, she recorded the colours of the cyclohexane layers in the table:

| Solution in water | Colour of the cyclohexane layer |
| --- | --- |
| chlorine | colourless |
| bromine | orange |
| iodine | violet |

She cleaned out the tubes and then performed a series of test tube reactions as indicated in the table below. In each case she mixed small quantities of solution A with twice the volume of solution B, added 10 drops of cyclohexane and then stirred the mixture with a clean glass rod. Once the cyclohexane layer had separated, she recorded her results.

| Solution A | Solution B | Colour of cyclohexane layer |
| --- | --- | --- |
| aqueous chlorine | sodium bromide | orange |
| aqueous chlorine | sodium iodide | violet |
| aqueous bromine | sodium chloride | orange |
| aqueous bromine | sodium iodide | violet |
| aqueous iodine | sodium chloride | violet |
| aqueous iodine | sodium bromide | orange |

## Using and organising techniques, apparatus and materials

❶ Cyclohexane is highly flammable and the chlorine and bromine solutions are both irritants. What precautions should the student have taken when doing this experiment?

## Interpreting observations and data

❷ What can you deduce about the relative reactivity of chlorine, bromine and iodine from the *first two* results in the second table?

❸ Write an equation for the reaction indicated by result 4 in the second table.

## Evaluating methods

❹ The student made a mistake in recording one of her results. Which one? Explain how you know.

## USES OF HALOGENS

Halogens and their compounds have a wide range of uses:

- fluorides – in toothpaste help prevent tooth decay
- fluorine compounds – making plastics like Teflon (the non-stick surface on pans)
- chlorofluorocarbons – propellants in aerosols and refrigerants (now being replaced because of their damaging effect on the ozone layer)
- chlorine – purifying water
- chlorine compounds – household bleaches
- hydrochloric acid – widely used in industry
- bromine compounds – making pesticides
- silver bromide – the light-sensitive film coating on photographic film
- iodine solution – an antiseptic.

---

**SCIENCE IN CONTEXT**

### FLUORINE

Fluorine is the most reactive non-metal in the Periodic Table. It reacts with most other elements except helium, neon and argon. These reactions are often sudden or explosive. Even radon, a very unreactive noble gas, burns with a bright flame in a jet of fluorine gas. All metals react with fluorine to form fluorides. The reactions of fluorine with Group I metals are explosive.

Early scientists tried to make fluorine from hydrofluoric acid (HF(aq)) but this proved to be highly dangerous, killing or blinding several scientists who attempted it. They became known as the 'fluorine martyrs'. Today fluorine is manufactured by the electrolysis of the mineral fluorite, which is calcium fluoride.

Fluorine is not an element to play with. You will certainly not see it in your laboratory!

---

## QUESTIONS

**1.** Why is chlorine used in the treatment of drinking water in many countries?

**2.** Which halogen element has medical uses as an antiseptic?

**3.** Fluorine is used to make a plastic material with the common name of 'Teflon'. What is Teflon used for?

You should be familiar with the elements of Group VII, the halogens. These are coloured non-metallic elements of varying reactivity. Although they are potentially harmful, their properties make them very useful. Use your knowledge of atomic structure, bonding and reaction types to answer the questions below.

4. **EXTENDED** Chlorine is a pale green gas which can obtained by the electrolysis of an aqueous solution of sodium chloride. Chlorine can be used to kill bacteria and is used in the manufacture of bleach.

   a) The electronic structure of a chlorine atom is 2,8,7. Draw simple diagrams to show the arrangement of the outer electrons in a diatomic molecule of $Cl_2$ and a chloride ion, $Cl^-$.

   b) In the electrolysis of an aqueous solution of sodium chloride., the positive anode attracts the $OH^-$ ions and $Cl^-$ ions to form chlorine molecules. Copy and complete the equation below and explain why this is oxidation.

   _____$Cl^-(aq) \rightarrow$ _____$(g) + 2e^-$

   c) Sodium hydroxide and chlorine react at room temperature to form bleach, sodium chlorate (I), which is used in domestic cleaning agents. Copy and complete and balance the equation shown.

   sodium hydroxide + chlorine → sodium chloride + sodium chlorate(I) + water

   _____ + $Cl_2(aq)$ → _____ + $NaClO(aq)$ + $H_2O(l)$

   d) Chlorine will displace bromine from a solution of potassium bromide to form bromine and potassium chloride. Explain why this reaction takes place and describe what you would observe if chlorine water was added to a solution of potassium bromide in a test tube.

5. **EXTENDED** Fluorine is a pale yellow gas and is the most reactive of the chemical elements. It is so reactive that glass, metals and even water burn with a bright flame in a jet of fluorine gas. Fluorides, however, are often added to toothpaste and, controversially, to some water supplies to prevent dental decay.

   a) Give a reason why fluorine is so reactive.

   b) Write an ionic half-equation that shows the conversion of fluorine to fluoride ions.

   c) Potassium fluoride is a compound that may be found in toothpaste. Explain why fluorine cannot be displaced from this compound using either chlorine or iodine.

# End of topic checklist

## Key terms

displacement reaction, halogens

## During your study of this topic you should have learned:

○ How to describe chlorine, bromine and iodine in Group VII as a collection of diatomic non-metals showing trends in colour and in their reactions with other halide ions.

○ How to predict the properties of other elements in Group VII, given data, where appropriate.

○ **EXTENDED** How to identify trends in other groups, given information about the elements concerned.

# End of topic questions

*Note: The marks awarded for these questions indicate the level of detail required in the answers. In the examination, the number of marks awarded to questions like these may be different.*

1. This question is about the Group VII elements: chlorine, bromine and iodine.

   a) Which is the most reactive of these elements? **(1 mark)**

   b) Which of the elements exists as a liquid at room temperature and pressure? **(1 mark)**

   c) Which of the elements exists as a solid at room temperature and pressure? **(1 mark)**

   d) What is the appearance of bromine? **(1 mark)**

2. Explain the following statements:

   a) The Group VII elements are the most reactive non-metals. **(2 marks)**

   b) The most reactive halogen is at the top of its group. **(2 marks)**

3. Write word and balanced equations for the following reactions:

   a) sodium and chlorine **(3 marks)**

   b) magnesium and bromine **(3 marks)**

   c) hydrogen and fluorine. **(3 marks)**

4. **EXTENDED** Aqueous bromine reacts with sodium iodide solution.

   a) What type of chemical reaction is this? **(1 mark)**

   b) Write a balanced equation for the reaction. **(2 marks)**

   c) The reaction involves oxidation and reduction.

   i) What is *oxidation*? What has been oxidised in this reaction? **(2 marks)**

   ii) What is *reduction*? What has been reduced in this reaction? **(2 marks)**

# Transition metals and noble gases

## INTRODUCTION

There are two other important families of elements. The first are the transition elements, a 'block' of metals – including more 'everyday' metals than Group I.
The second is the noble gases (Group 0 or VIII), a group of elements of interest because of their uses rather than their chemical reactions.

△ Fig. 3.13 This incandescent light bulb contains unreactive argon instead of air.

## TRANSITION ELEMENTS

The **transition metals** are grouped in the centre of the Periodic Table and include iron, copper, zinc and chromium.

All the transition metals have more than one electron in their outer electron shell. They are much less reactive than Group I and Group II metals and so are more 'everyday' metals. They have much higher melting points and densities. They react much more slowly with water and with oxygen.

They are widely used as construction metals (particularly iron through steel).

One of the typical properties of transition metals and their compounds is their ability to act as **catalysts** and speed up the rate of a chemical reaction by providing an alternative pathway with a lower activation energy – for example vanadium(V) oxide in the Contact process and iron in the Haber process.

| Property | Group I metal | Transition metal |
|---|---|---|
| Melting point | Low | High |
| Density | Low | High |
| Colour of compounds | White | Mainly coloured |
| Reactions with water/air | Vigorous | Slow or no reaction |
| Reactions with an acid | Violent (dangerous) | Slow or no reaction |

△ Table 3.5 Properties of the Group I metals and the transition metals.

## EXTENDED

Many transition metals have more than one oxidation state. For example, copper forms $Cu^+$ ions and $Cu^{2+}$ ions as shown in its compounds – for example copper(I) oxide, $Cu_2O$, and copper(II) oxide, $CuO$.

Also, iron forms $Fe^{2+}$ ions and $Fe^{3+}$ ions as shown in iron(II) hydroxide, $Fe(OH)_2$, and iron(III) hydroxide, $Fe(OH)_3$.

## END OF EXTENDED

The compounds of the transition metals are usually coloured. Copper compounds are usually blue or green; iron compounds tend to be either green or brown. When sodium hydroxide solution is added to a solution of a transition metal compound, a precipitate of the metal hydroxide is formed. The colour of the precipitate helps to identify the metal. For example:

copper(II) sulfate+ sodium hydroxide → copper(II) hydroxide + sodium sulfate

$CuSO_4(aq)$     +    $2NaOH(aq)$     →    $Cu(OH)_2(s)$     +    $Na_2SO_4(aq)$

## EXTENDED

This can be written as an ionic equation:

$Cu^{2+}(aq) + 2OH^-(aq) \rightarrow Cu(OH)_2(s)$

## END OF EXTENDED

| Colour of metal hydroxide | Likely metal present |
|---|---|
| Blue | Copper(II) $Cu^{2+}$ |
| Green | Nickel(II) $Ni^{2+}$ |
| Green turning to brown | Iron(II) $Fe^{2+}$ |
| Orange/brown | Iron(III) $Fe^{3+}$ |

△ Table 3.6 Transition metal hydroxides and their colours.

1. Would you expect a reaction to happen between copper and water?

2. Chromium forms a compound called chromium(III) oxide. What does the number in the name indicate?

3. a) Write a fully balanced equation for the reaction between iron(II) sulfate solution and sodium hydroxide solution.

   b) What will be the colour of the precipitate formed?

## THE NOBLE GASES

This is actually a group of *very* unreactive non-metals. They used to be called the inert gases as it was thought that they didn't react with anything. But scientists later managed to produce fluorine compounds of some of the **noble gases.** As far as your school laboratory work is concerned, however, they are completely unreactive.

| Name | Symbol |
|------|--------|
| Helium | He |
| Neon | Ne |
| Argon | Ar |
| Krypton | Kr |
| Xenon | Xe |
| Radon | Rn |

△ Table 3.7 The noble gases.

The unreactivity of the noble gases can be explained in terms of their electronic structures. The atoms all have complete outer electron shells or eight electrons in their outer shell. They don't need to lose electrons (as metals do), or gain electrons (as most non-metals do).

### Similarities of the noble gases
- Full outer electron shells
- Very unreactive
- Gases
- Exist as single atoms – they are **monatomic** (He, Ne, Ar, Kr, Xe, Rn).

How are the noble gases used?
- Helium – in balloons
- Neon – in red tube lights
- Argon – in lamps and light bulbs.

# End of topic checklist

**Key terms**

catalyst, monatomic, noble gas, transition metal

## During your study of this topic you should have learned:

○ How to describe the transition elements as a collection of metals with high densities, high melting points and forming coloured compounds.

○ That transition elements and their compounds are often used as catalysts.

○ **EXTENDED** That transition elements have variable oxidation states.

○ How to describe the noble gases as being unreactive.

○ How to describe the uses of the noble gases in providing an inert atmosphere, such as argon in lamps and helium in balloons.

# End of topic questions

*Note: The marks awarded for these questions indicate the level of detail required in the answers. In the examination, the number of marks awarded to questions like these may be different.*

**1.** This question is about the transition metals.

   **a)** Give two differences in the physical properties of the transition metals compared with the alkali metals. **(2 marks)**

   **b)** Transition metals are used as catalysts. What is a *catalyst*? **(1 mark)**

   **c)** Suggest why the alkali metals are more reactive than the transition metals. **(2 marks)**

**2.** Look at the table of observations.

| Compound tested | Colour of compound | Effect of adding sodium hydroxide solution to a solution of the compound |
|---|---|---|
| A | White | No change |
| B | Blue | Blue precipitate formed |
| C | White | White precipitate formed |

   **a)** Which of the compounds, A, B or C, contains a transition metal? Explain your answer. **(1 mark)**

   **b)** Which transition metal do you think it is? **(1 mark)**

   **c)** Compound B is a metal sulfate. Write a balanced equation for the reaction between a solution of this transition metal compound and sodium hydroxide solution. **(2 marks)**

**3.** Explain why the noble gases are so unreactive. **(2 marks)**

**4.** The noble gases are *monatomic*. What does this mean? **(1 mark)**

**5.** Although the noble gases are generally very unreactive, reactions do occur with very reactive elements such as fluorine. Which of the noble gases are more likely to react – helium at the top of the group or xenon near the bottom of the group? **(1 mark)**

# Metals

## INTRODUCTION

Metals are very important in our everyday lives and many have very similar physical properties. Some metals are highly reactive, like the Group I metals on the left-hand side of the Periodic Table. Other metals are much less reactive, such as the transition metals in the middle of the Periodic Table. Knowing the order of the reactivity of metals can help chemists make very accurate predictions about how the metals will react with different substances and also what individual metals can be used for.

△ Fig. 3.14 What sort of properties should the metals used in the construction of this helicopter have?

✓ **EXTENDED** Be able to describe the extraction of zinc from zinc blende.

✓ Know that aluminium is used in the manufacture of aircraft because of its strength and low density.

✓ Know that aluminium is used to make food containers because of its resistance to corrosion.

✓ Know that copper can be used for electrical wiring and for cooking utensils because of its properties.

✓ Know that mild steel is used to make car bodies and machinery and that stainless steel is used to make chemical plant and cutlery.

✓ **EXTENDED** Know that zinc can be used for galvanising and for making brass.

✓ **EXTENDED** Be able to describe the idea of changing the properties of iron by the controlled use of additives to form steel alloys.

## PROPERTIES OF METALS

Most metals have similar physical properties.

*Exceptions:*
• The alkali metals have low melting points and are not sonorous.
• Mercury has a low melting point.

△ Fig. 3.15 Properties of metals.

### Alloys

An **alloy** is a mixture of a metal with one or more other elements.

The reason for producing alloys is to 'improve' the properties of a metal. Table 3.8 shows some examples.

| Alloy | Property improved |
|---|---|
| Steel | Hardness/tensile strength |
| Bronze | Hardness |
| Solder | Lower melting point |
| Cupronickel | Cheaper than silver (used for coins) |
| Stainless steel | Resistance to corrosion |
| Brass | Easier to shape and stamp into shape |

△ Table 3.8 Alloys and their properties.

△ Fig. 3.16 Alloys are used to make coins.

## The structure of alloys

The structure of pure metallic elements is usually shown as in Fig. 3.17.

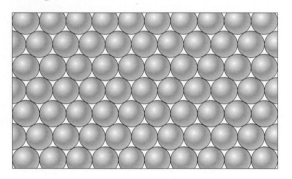

△ Fig. 3.17 Particles in a solid.

This is a simplified picture but, surprisingly, such a structure is very weak. If there is the slightest difference between the planes of atoms, the metal will break at that point.

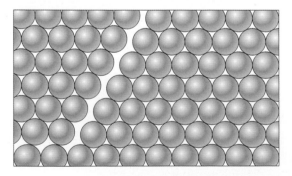

△ Fig. 3.18 The gaps show a weak point of a metal.

The more irregular (jumbled-up) the metal atoms are, the stronger the metal is. This is why alloy structures are stronger: because of the elements added.

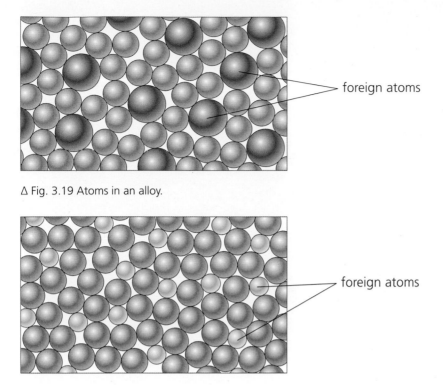

△ Fig. 3.19 Atoms in an alloy.

△ Fig. 3.20 Even smaller atoms make the metal stronger.

Steel that is heated to red heat and then plunged into cold water is made harder by the process of 'jumbling up' the metal atoms. Further heat treatment is used to increase the strength and toughness of the alloy.

## QUESTIONS

1. Metals are often *ductile.* What does this mean?

2. Metals are usually *malleable.* What does this mean?

3. What is an alloy?

4. Which alloy is used to make many coins?

5. Explain why an alloy of aluminium is likely to be stronger than pure aluminium.

### REACTIVITY SERIES

The Periodic Table is a way of ordering the chemical elements that highlights their similar and their different properties. The reactivity series is another way of classifying elements, this time in order of their reactivity to help explain or predict their reactions. This has many practical applications, such as being able to predict how metals can be extracted from their ores and how the negative effects of the chemical process of rusting can be reduced.

The more reactive metals react with oxygen to form oxides:

| calcium | + | oxygen | → | calcium oxide |
|---------|---|--------|---|---------------|
| 2Ca(s) | + | $O_2$(g) | → | 2CaO(s) |

Less reactive metals, such as gold, do not react with oxygen.

△ Fig. 3.21 Sodium, magnesium, gold – these are all metals, but they have very different reactivities.

Elements can be arranged in order of their reactivity. The more reactive a metal is, the easier it is to form compounds and the harder it is to break those compounds down. We can predict how metals might react by looking at the reactivity series (Fig. 3.22).

The most reactive metals react with water at room temperature. For example, potassium, sodium and lithium in Group I and calcium in Group II react rapidly with water:

| sodium | + | water | → | sodium hydroxide | + | hydrogen |
|--------|---|-------|---|------------------|---|----------|
| 2Na(s) | + | $2H_2O$(l) | → | 2NaOH(aq) | + | $H_2$(g) |

The less reactive metals such as magnesium and iron react with steam:

| magnesium | + | steam | → | magnesium oxide | + | hydrogen |
|-----------|---|-------|---|-----------------|---|----------|
| Mg(s) | + | $H_2O$(g) | → | MgO(s) | + | $H_2$(g) |

Some of the mid-reactivity series metals produce hydrogen when they react with dilute acids. So, for example, magnesium, aluminium, zinc and iron all release hydrogen when they react with dilute hydrochloric acid:

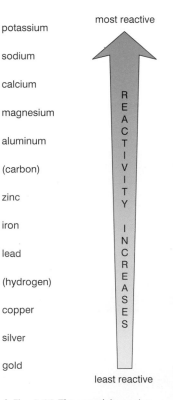

most reactive

potassium

sodium

calcium

magnesium

aluminum

(carbon)

zinc

iron

lead

(hydrogen)

copper

silver

gold

REACTIVITY INCREASES

least reactive

△ Fig. 3.22 The reactivity series shows elements, mainly metals, in order of decreasing reactivity.

| zinc | + | hydrochloric acid | $\rightarrow$ | zinc chloride | + | hydrogen |
|------|---|------|------|------|---|------|
| $Zn(s)$ | + | $2HCl(aq)$ | $\rightarrow$ | $ZnCl_2(aq)$ | + | $H_2(g)$ |

The metals below hydrogen in the reactivity series do not react to form hydrogen with water or dilute acids.

Another use of the reactivity series is to predict how metals can be extracted from their ores. The elements below carbon in the reactivity series can be obtained by heating their oxides with carbon:

| zinc oxide | + | carbon | $\rightarrow$ | zinc | + | carbon dioxide |
|------|---|------|------|------|---|------|
| $2ZnO(s)$ | + | $C(s)$ | $\rightarrow$ | $2Zn(s)$ | + | $CO_2(g)$ |

| copper(II) oxide | + | carbon | $\rightarrow$ | copper | + | carbon dioxide |
|------|---|------|------|------|---|------|
| $2CuO(s)$ | + | $C(s)$ | $\rightarrow$ | $2Cu(s)$ | + | $CO_2(g)$ |

This type of reaction is called a **displacement reaction**. A more reactive element, such as carbon, 'pushes' (or displaces) a less reactive metal, such as copper, out of its compound. In this reaction the copper(II) oxide has lost oxygen and been reduced. The carbon has gained oxygen and been oxidised.

## EXTENDED

The position of a metal in the reactivity series depends on how easily it forms ions. More reactive metals will form ions more readily than less reactive metals.

Any element higher up the reactivity series can displace an element lower down the series.

For example, magnesium is higher up the reactivity series than copper. So if magnesium powder is heated with copper(II) oxide, then copper and magnesium oxide are produced:

| magnesium | + | copper(II) oxide | $\rightarrow$ | magnesium oxide | + | copper |
|------|---|------|------|------|---|------|
| $Mg(s)$ | + | $CuO(s)$ | $\rightarrow$ | $MgO(s)$ | + | $Cu(s)$ |

This reaction is an example of a redox reaction. The magnesium has been oxidised to magnesium oxide and the copper(II) oxide has been reduced to copper. Because the magnesium is responsible for the reduction of the copper(II) oxide, it is acting as a reducing agent. Similarly, the copper(II) oxide is responsible for the **oxidation** of the magnesium, so it is acting as an oxidising agent. In a redox reaction, the reducing agent is always oxidised and the oxidising agent is always reduced.

What will happen if copper is heated with magnesium oxide? Nothing happens, because copper is lower in the reactivity series than magnesium.

## Using displacement reactions to establish a reactivity series

Displacement reactions of metals and their compounds in aqueous solution can be used to work out the order in the reactivity series.

In the same way that a more reactive element can push a less reactive element out of a compound, a more reactive metal ion in aqueous solution can displace a less reactive one.

For example, if you add zinc to copper(II) sulfate solution, the zinc displaces the copper because zinc is more reactive than copper. When the experiment is carried out, the blue colour of the copper(II) ion will fade as copper is produced and zinc ions are made:

zinc + copper(II) sulfate solution → zinc sulfate solution + copper

$Zn(s) + Cu^{2+}(aq) + SO_4^{2-}(aq) \rightarrow Zn^{2+}(aq) + SO_4^{2-}(aq) + Cu(s)$

To build up a whole reactivity series, a set of reactions can be tried to see if metals can displace other metal ions. By following the general rule that a more reactive metal can displace a less reactive metal it is possible to establish the reactivity series.

For example, you may have seen the reaction of copper wire with silver nitrate solution. As the reaction proceeds, a shiny grey precipitate appears (this is silver) and the solution begins to turn blue as Cu(II) ions are produced from the copper.

copper + silver nitrate → copper(II) nitrate + silver

$Cu(s) + 2AgNO_3(aq) \rightarrow Cu(NO_3)_2(aq) + 2Ag(s)$

This shows that silver can be displaced by copper, and so silver is below copper in the reactivity series.

**END OF EXTENDED**

## QUESTIONS

1. Will copper react with dilute hydrochloric acid to produce hydrogen? Explain your answer.

2. Write a balanced equation for the reaction of potassium with water.

3. Can carbon displace magnesium from magnesium oxide? Explain your answer.

4. **EXTENDED** Write the balanced equation for the reaction between magnesium and lead(II) oxide.

## Developing investigative skills

A student was asked to carry out some possible displacement reactions. She was given samples of four metals A, B, C and D and a solution of each of their metal nitrates. She set up a series of test tube reactions as summarised in the table:

| Solution | Metal A | Metal B | Metal C | Metal D |
|---|---|---|---|---|
| Metal A nitrate, $A(NO_3)_2$ (aq) | | Yes | Yes | No |
| Metal B nitrate, $B(NO_3)_2$ (aq) | No | | No | No |
| Metal C nitrate, $C(NO_3)_2$ (aq) | No | Yes | | No |
| Metal D nitrate, $D(NO_3)_2$ (aq) | 10 | 11 | 12 | |

She decided that she would need 12 test tubes. In each test tube she put a 1 cm depth of one of the solutions and then added a small piece of one of the metals. She left the tubes for 10 minutes and then examined the solution and the piece of metal to see if any reaction was evident. She then recorded a 'yes' if a displacement reaction had taken place and a 'no' where no reaction was evident. She didn't have time to record her results for the metal D nitrate solution (tubes 10, 11 and 12).

### Using and organising techniques, apparatus and materials

❶ Why didn't the student set up the tubes represented by the white rectangles?

❷ Even though the student didn't record her results for metal D nitrate solution, explain why she would still be able to put the metals in order of reactivity.

### Interpreting observations and data

❸ Use the results to put the four metals in order of reactivity. Start with the most reactive metal.

❹ Complete the results you would expect for the three reactions 10, 11 and 12.

❺ Write a balanced equation for the displacement reaction between metal B and metal C nitrate solution. (Use the symbols B and C for the two metals).

❻ Metal D nitrate solution was blue and metal D was a shiny orange colour. Suggest a name for metal D.

## Heating hydroxides

Sodium hydroxide, NaOH, and potassium hydroxide, KOH, are not changed by heating. Calcium hydroxide, $Ca(OH)_2$, and magnesium hydroxide, $Mg(OH)_2$, behave differently:

$$
\begin{array}{lcccc}
 & \text{heat} & & & \\
\text{hydroxide} & \uparrow & \rightarrow & \text{oxide} & + \quad \text{water} \\
Ca(OH)_2(s) & & \rightarrow & CaO(s) & + \quad H_2O(l) \\
Mg(OH)_2(s) & & \rightarrow & MgO(s) & + \quad H_2O(l)
\end{array}
$$

Zinc hydroxide, $Zn(OH)_2$, iron(III) hydroxide, $Fe(OH)_3$, and copper(II) hydroxide, $Cu(OH)_2$, decompose to the oxide and water:

$$
\begin{array}{lcccl}
Zn(OH)_2(s) & \rightarrow & ZnO(s) & + & H_2O(l) \\
2Fe(OH)_3(s) & \rightarrow & Fe_2O_3(s) & + & 3H_2O(l) \\
Cu(OH)_2(s) & \rightarrow & CuO(s) & + & H_2O(l)
\end{array}
$$

## Heating carbonates

Sodium carbonate ($Na_2CO_3$) and potassium carbonates ($K_2CO_3$) are not decomposed by heat. In contrast, other carbonates are broken down by heat to form the metal oxide and carbon dioxide. For example:

$$
\begin{array}{lcll}
\text{metal carbonate} & \text{metal oxide} & + & \text{carbon dioxide} \\
CaCO_3(s) & CaO(s) & + & CO_2(g) \\
MgCO_3(s) & MgO(s) & + & CO_2(g) \\
ZnCO_3(s) & ZnO(s) & + & CO_2(g) \\
FeCO_3(s) & FeO(s) & + & CO_2(g) \\
CuCO_3(s) & CuO(s) & + & CO_2(g)
\end{array}
$$

## Heating nitrates

Sodium nitrate, $NaNO_3$, and potassium nitrate, $KNO_3$, behave in the same way when heated:

$$
\begin{array}{lclll}
\text{metal nitrate} & \rightarrow & \text{metal nitrite} & + & \text{oxygen} \\
2NaNO_3(s) & \rightarrow & 2NaNO_2(s) & + & O_2(g) \\
2KNO_3(s) & \rightarrow & 2KNO_2(s) & + & O_2(g)
\end{array}
$$

All other metal nitrates produce the metal oxide, nitrogen dioxide (a brown gas) and oxygen when heated:

| metal nitrate | $\rightarrow$ | metal oxide | + | nitrogen dioxide | + | oxygen |
|---|---|---|---|---|---|---|
| $2Ca(NO_3)_2(s)$ | $\rightarrow$ | $2CaO(s)$ | + | $4NO_2(g)$ | + | $O_2(g)$ |
| $2Mg(NO_3)_2(s)$ | $\rightarrow$ | $2MgO(s)$ | + | $4NO_2(g)$ | + | $O_2(g)$ |
| $2Fe(NO_3)_2(s)$ | $\rightarrow$ | $2FeO(s)$ | + | $4NO_2(g)$ | + | $O_2(g)$ |
| $2Cu(NO_3)_2(s)$ | $\rightarrow$ | $2CuO(s)$ | + | $4NO_2(g)$ | + | $O_2(g)$ |
| $2Zn(NO_3)_2(s)$ | $\rightarrow$ | $2ZnO(s)$ | + | $4NO_2(g)$ | + | $O_2(g)$ |

## The unreactivity of aluminium

Aluminium's position in the reactivity series suggests that it should be quite reactive. However, it does not react with acids and is resistant to corrosion. This is because, although it may look shiny, it has a thin coating of aluminium oxide, $Al_2O_3$, all over its surface. Aluminium oxide is very unreactive and protects the aluminium below its surface.

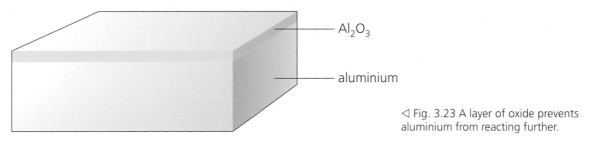

$Al_2O_3$

aluminium

◁ Fig. 3.23 A layer of oxide prevents aluminium from reacting further.

## QUESTIONS

**1.** Which metal hydroxides do not decompose on heating to form the metal oxide and water? Where are these metals in the reactivity series?

**2.** Some blue crystals of copper(II) nitrate are heated in a test tube.

**a)** What would you observe?

**b)** How could you show that oxygen gas was produced?

**c)** Write a balanced equation for the reaction.

**3.** Explain why aluminium, although a reactive metal, can be used to make window frames in houses and greenhouses.

**END OF EXTENDED**

## EXTRACTION OF METALS

Metals are found in the form of **ores** containing **minerals** mixed with unwanted rock. In almost all cases, the mineral is a compound of the metal, not the pure metal. One exception is gold, which can exist naturally in a pure state.

Extracting a metal from its ore usually involves two steps:

**1.** The mineral is physically separated from unwanted rock.

**2.** The mineral is broken down chemically to obtain the metal.

## Reactivity of metals

The chemical method chosen to break down a mineral depends on the reactivity of the metal. The more reactive a metal is, the harder it is to break down its compounds. The more reactive metals are obtained from their minerals by the process of electrolysis. For example, aluminium is obtained from its ore, bauxite, by electrolysis. For more detail on this process look at the Electricity and Chemistry topic.

The less reactive metals can be obtained by heating their oxides with carbon. This method will only work for metals below carbon in the reactivity series. It involves the **reduction** of a metal oxide to the metal.

| Metal | | Extraction method |
|---|---|---|
| Potassium | | The most reactive metals are obtained using electrolysis |
| Sodium | | |
| Calcium | | |
| Magnesium | | |
| Aluminium | | |
| (Carbon) | | |
| Zinc | | These metals are below carbon in the reactivity series and so can be obtained by heating their oxides with carbon |
| Iron | | |
| Tin | | |
| Lead | | |
| Copper | | |
| Silver | | The least reactive metals are found as pure elements |
| Gold | | |

Δ Table 3.9 Methods for extracting different metals.

## Extracting iron

Iron is produced on a very large scale by reduction using carbon. The reaction takes place in a huge furnace called a blast furnace.

Three important raw materials are put in the top of the furnace: iron ore (iron(III) oxide), coke (the source of carbon for the reduction) and limestone, to remove the impurities as slag. Iron ore is also known as haematite.

Δ Fig. 3.24 Coke (nearly pure carbon).

△ Fig. 3.25 Iron ore (haematite).

△ Fig. 3.26 Limestone.

△ Fig. 3.27 Molten iron.

△ Fig. 3.28 Slag.

1  Crushed iron ore, coke and limestone are fed into the top of the blast furnace

2  Hot air is blasted up the furnace from the bottom

3  Oxygen from the air reacts with coke to form carbon dioxide:
$$C(s) + O_2(g) \longrightarrow CO_2(g)$$

4  Carbon dioxide reacts with more coke to form carbon monoxide:
$$CO_2(g) + C(s) \longrightarrow 2CO(g)$$

5  Carbon monoxide is a reducing agent. Iron(III) oxide is reduced to iron:

   ⌐reduction = loss of oxygen ⌐
$$Fe_2O_3(s) + 3CO(g) \longrightarrow 2Fe(l) + 3CO_2(g)$$

6  Dense molten iron runs to the bottom of the furnace and is run off. There are many impurities in iron ore. The limestone helps to remove these as shown in processes 7 and 8.

7  Limestone is broken down by heat to calcium oxide:
$$CaCO_3(s) \longrightarrow CaO(s) + CO_2(g)$$

8  Calcium oxide reacts with impurities like sand (silicon dioxide) to form a liquid called 'slag':
$$CaO(s) + SiO_2(s) \longrightarrow CaSiO_3(l)$$
             impurity       slag
The liquid slag runs to the bottom of the furnace and is tapped off.

**Diagram labels (Fig. 3.29):**

crushed iron ore
coke
limestone

hot gas used to heat incoming air

250 °C

700 °C

furnace gets hotter

800–1000 °C

1500 °C

hot air blast

hot air blast

molten slag run off

molten slag

molten iron

molten iron run off

△ Fig. 3.29 How iron is extracted in a blast furnace.

The overall reaction is:

iron(III) oxide + carbon → iron + carbon dioxide

$$2Fe_2O_3(s) + 3C(s) \rightarrow 4Fe(s) + 3CO_2(g)$$

The reduction happens in three stages.

Stage 1 – The coke (carbon) reacts with oxygen 'blasted' into the furnace:

carbon + oxygen → carbon dioxide

$$C(s) + O_2(g) \rightarrow CO_2(g)$$

Stage 2 – The carbon dioxide is reduced by unreacted coke to form carbon monoxide:

carbon dioxide + carbon → carbon monoxide

$$CO_2(g) + C(s) \rightarrow 2CO(g)$$

Stage 3 – The iron(III) oxide is reduced by the carbon monoxide to iron:

iron(III) oxide + carbon monoxide → iron + carbon dioxide

$$Fe_2O_3(s) + 3CO(g) \rightarrow 2Fe(s) + 3CO_2(g)$$

### REMEMBER

In a blast furnace the iron(III) oxide is reduced to iron by carbon monoxide, formed when the carbon reacts with the air blasted into the furnace. In the reduction of iron(III) oxide, the carbon monoxide is oxidised to carbon dioxide.

## Making steel from iron

Iron from the blast furnace is brittle because it contains a relatively large percentage (usually 4%) of carbon (from the coke). It also rusts very easily. Because of this, most iron is converted into steel, an alloy of iron. Mild steel is used for car bodies and machinery and stainless steel for chemical plant and cutlery.

In steel making, the molten iron straight from the blast furnace is heated and oxygen is passed through it to remove some of the carbon present:

$$C(s) + O_2(g) \rightarrow CO_2(g)$$

Limestone ($CaCO_3$) is also added and is changed into calcium oxide:

$$CaCO_3(s) \rightarrow CaO(s) + CO_2(g)$$

The calcium oxide reacts with oxide impurities to form a slag, which can be removed from the steel.

Steel is iron with 0.1–1.5% carbon content. Steel is more resistant to corrosion and is less brittle than iron. It has a wide range of uses, depending on its carbon content. For example:

- low carbon (<0.3%): car bodies
- medium carbon (0.3–0.9%): railway tracks
- high carbon (0.9–1.5%): knives.

Stainless steels are made by adding a wide range of metals, such as chromium, nickel, vanadium and cobalt, to the steel. Each gives the steel particular properties for specific uses. For example, vanadium steel is used to make high-precision, hard-wearing industrial tools.

## Extracting zinc

Zinc is extracted from its ore zinc blende using a similar process to iron(III) oxide and the blast furnace. Zinc blende is the original name for zinc sulfide, ZnS.

The zinc blende is first heated in air to convert it to the oxide:

$$2ZnS(s) \; + \; 3O_2(g) \; \rightarrow \; 2SO_2(g) \; + \; 2ZnO(s)$$

The oxide is then reduced using carbon monoxide:

$$ZnO(s) \; + \; CO(g) \; \rightarrow \; Zn(s) \; + \; CO_2(g)$$

and zinc metal is produced.

**END OF EXTENDED**

## QUESTIONS

1. What solid raw materials are used in the blast furnace?

2. The iron ore used in the blast furnace is usually *haematite*. What is the name of the main compound present in the ore?

3. What gases will escape from the top of the blast furnace?

4. Write a balanced equation to show the reduction of iron(III) oxide by carbon.

5. This question is about steel.

   a) Steel is an *alloy*. What is an 'alloy'?

   b) The iron produced in the blast furnace contains a relatively high proportion of carbon. How is this proportion reduced when iron is converted into steel?

   c) Why is steel often used instead of the iron produced in the blast furnace?

The reactivity series of metals is useful to scientists in determining methods for metal extraction, ways of preventing corrosion and ensuring safe storage for reactive metals. Use the reactivity series to help answer the questions below.

**6.** The thermit process can be used to extract iron from iron(III) oxide using aluminium metal.

    **a)** Write a balanced equation for the extraction of iron using this process.

    **b)** Using the reactivity series, explain why this reaction occurs.

    **c)** Name two other metals that could be used to extract iron from its oxide indicating whether the reactions would be more or less reactive than when using aluminium.

    **d)** This reaction could be described as either a displacement or a redox reaction. Explain why.

**7.** Iron is a metal in common use, but unfortunately it rusts.

    **a)** Give the conditions needed for iron to rust.

    **b)** Chromium is used in chromium plating to prevent iron from rusting. Give a reason for this.

    **d)** Aluminium's position in the reactivity series indicates that it is a highly reactive metal. However, aluminium does not rust. Suggest a reason for this.

## RECYCLING

Extracting metals from their ores is an expensive process and so recycling metal objects can be economically worthwhile as well as environmentally more efficient. Recycling of metals essentially involves melting the metal and then using the molten metal to form a new object. Steel and aluminium are metals which are often recycled. One potential problem is separating the different types of metal. For example, a motor car as well as being made of steel may include some parts made of aluminium (as well as a range of other materials). Separating the two different metals needs to be done before they can be recycled. In some cases recycling could prove more expensive than extracting the metal form its ore. However, the supplies of metal ores are limited and will eventually be used up. Recycling metals such as steel and aluminium will therefore become increasingly essential.

## USES OF METALS

### Uses of aluminium

The uses of aluminium are based on its properties of having a low density but being quite a strong metal as well as being unreactive (because of its oxide coating). These properties make it useful in the manufacture of aircraft (because it is light and strong) and food containers (because it does not corrode).

## Uses of copper

Copper is an excellent conductor of electricity and this is why it is used for melting electrical cables.

Copper is also an excellent conductor of heat with a high melting point. These properties make it ideal for cooking utensils.

**EXTENDED**

## Uses of zinc

Zinc is used to make the alloy brass by mixing it with copper. Covering iron with zinc is called **galvanising**, and the zinc stops the iron from rusting (corroding).

---

**SCIENCE IN CONTEXT**

### THE EXTRACTION OF METALS

The reactivity of a metal determines how it can be extracted from ores from the Earth's crust. It also explains why some metals have been used for thousands of years while others have only been used much more recently.

The most unreactive metals can be found in their 'native' state, which is as the pure metal and not combined with other elements. Examples of such metals include gold and silver – metals that have been used for thousands of years. It is estimated that gold was first discovered in about 3000 BC.

△ Fig. 3.30 This gold shoulder cape from North Wales is nearly 4000 years old and still in good condition.

Metals below carbon in the reactivity series can be extracted by heating their ores with carbon. Examples include lead and iron. It is possible that lead was discovered by accident when the silvery element was seen in the ashes of a wood fire that had been made above a deposit of lead ore. It is estimated that lead was first discovered in about 2000 BC.

The most reactive metals, all those above carbon in the reactivity series, have to be extracted from their minerals by electrolysis. This process is a much more recent development and explains why these metals were not used until relatively recently. Aluminium was first extracted in 1825.

## THE SACRIFICIAL PROTECTION OF IRON AND MILD STEEL

Rusting is a chemical reaction between iron, water and oxygen. Water and oxygen must both be present for rusting to occur. The process is speeded up if there are also electrolytes, such as salt, in the water. This is why rusting takes place much faster in sea water.

The rusting of iron and steel can be prevented in a number of ways. The use of grease, oil or paint prevent water and oxygen from reaching the metal surface. Plastic coating does the same. However, these coatings can be damaged and then rusting will take place.

Iron can be prevented from rusting by using what we know about the reactivity series. Zinc is above iron in the reactivity series; that is, zinc reacts more readily than iron.

Galvanised iron is iron that is coated with a layer of zinc. To begin with, the coating will protect the iron. If the coating is damaged or scratched, the iron is still protected from rusting. This is because zinc is more reactive than iron and so it reacts and corrodes instead of the iron.

△ Fig. 3.31 Galvanised iron or steel resists corrosion by air and water.

If zinc blocks are attached to the hulls of ships, they will corrode instead of the hull. The zinc block is called a **sacrificial anode**.

## END OF EXTENDED

## QUESTIONS

1. What conditions are necessary for iron to rust?

2. What is the disadvantage of using grease to prevent the rusting of iron?

3. **EXTENDED** a) What is *galvanising*?

   b) Why is galvanised iron or steel still protected from corrosion when its surface has been scratched?

# End of topic checklist

## Key terms

alloy, displacement reaction, galvanising, mineral, ore, oxidation, reduction, sacrificial anode

## During your study of this topic you should have learned:

○ How to describe the general physical properties of metals.

○ How to describe the general chemical properties of metals (e.g. reactions with dilute acids and oxygen).

○ How to explain why metals are often used in the form of alloys.

○ How to identify representations of an alloy from a diagram of its structure.

○ About the order of reactivity of metals – potassium, sodium, calcium, magnesium, zinc, iron, (hydrogen) and copper – by reference to the reactions, if any, of the metals with water or steam, or dilute hydrochloric acid.

○ About which metal oxides can be reduced by carbon.

○ **EXTENDED** How to describe the reactivity series as being related to the tendency of a metal to form its positive ion, illustrated by its reaction, if any, with the aqueous ions or the oxides of the other listed metals.

○ **EXTENDED** How to describe the action of heat on metal hydroxides and metal nitrates.

○ **EXTENDED** How to account for the apparent unreactivity of aluminium in terms of the oxide layer that forms on the surface of the metal.

○ How to deduce an order of reactivity from a given set of experimental results.

○ How to describe the ease of obtaining metals from their ores by relating the metals to their positions in the reactivity series.

○ How to describe the essential reactions in the extraction of iron from haematite.

○ How to describe the conversion of iron into steel using basic oxides and oxygen.

○ That aluminium is extracted from the ore bauxite by electrolysis.

○ **EXTENDED** How to describe, in outline, the extraction of aluminium from bauxite including the role of cryolite and the reactions at the electrodes.

○ **EXTENDED** How to describe the extraction of zinc from zinc blende.

# End of topic checklist continued

○ That aluminium is used in the manufacture of aircraft because of its strength and low density.

○ That aluminium is used in food containers because of its resistance to corrosion.

○ That mild steel is used to make car bodies and machinery and that stainless steel is used to make chemical plant and cutlery.

○ That copper can be used for electrical wiring and for cooking utensils because of its properties.

○ **EXTENDED** That zinc can be used for galvanising and for making brass.

○ **EXTENDED** How to describe the idea of changing the properties of iron by the controlled use of additives to form steel alloys.

# End of topic questions

*Note: The marks awarded for these questions indicate the level of detail required in the answers. In the examination, the number of marks awarded to questions like these may be different.*

1. Arrange the following metals in order of reactivity, starting with the most reactive:

   calcium, copper, magnesium, sodium, zinc. **(2 marks)**

2. This question is about four metals represented by the letters Q, X, Y and Z. A series of displacement reactions was carried out and the results are shown below:

   Reaction 1: Q oxide + Y → Y oxide + Q

   Reaction 2: X oxide + Z → Z oxide + X

   Reaction 3: Q oxide + Z → no change

   a) Arrange the metals in order of reactivity starting with the most reactive. **(2 marks)**

   b) In reaction 1:

      i) Which substance has been oxidised? **(1 mark)**

      ii) Which substance has been reduced? **(1 mark)**

      iii) Which substance is the oxidising agent? **(1 mark)**

      iv) Which substance is the reducing agent? **(1 mark)**

3. The least reactive metals such as gold and silver are found in their native state. What do you understand by this? **(1 mark)**

4. Iron is extracted from iron ore (iron(III) oxide) in a blast furnace by heating with coke (carbon).

   a) Write a balanced equation including state symbols for the overall reaction. **(2 marks)**

   b) Is the iron(III) oxide oxidised or reduced in this reaction? Explain your answer. **(1 mark)**

   c) Why is limestone also added to the blast furnace? **(2 marks)**

5. Explain the following:

   a) Aluminium is used in the manufacture of aircraft. **(2 marks)**

   b) Aluminium is used in the manufacture of food containers. **(1 mark)**

6. a) Name one use of mild steel. **(1 mark)**

   b) Name one use of stainless steel. **(1 mark)**

**7.** **EXTENDED** This question is about the reaction between magnesium and lead(II) oxide.

   **a)** Write a balanced equation for the reaction.     **(2 marks)**

   **b)** Which is the more reactive metal, magnesium or lead?     **(1 mark)**

   **c)** This is an example of a redox reaction. Explain the term *redox*.     **(1 mark)**

**8.** **EXTENDED** Zinc can also be extracted from zinc oxide by heating with carbon.

   **a)** Write the balanced equation, including state symbols, for this reaction.

      **(2 marks)**

   **b)** Zinc could also be extracted by the electrolysis of molten zinc oxide. Suggest why heating with carbon is the preferred method of extraction.     **(2 marks)**

**9.** **EXTENDED** Copper(II) sulfate solution reacts with zinc as shown below:

$$CuSO_4(aq) + Zn(s) \rightarrow ZnSO_4(aq) + Cu(s)$$

   **a)** What type of chemical reaction is this?     **(1 mark)**

   **b)** What can be deduced about the relative reactivities of copper and zinc?     **(1 mark)**

**10.** **EXTENDED** Zinc prevents iron ship hulls from rusting (corroding).

   **a)** What is the name for this way of preventing rusting?     **(1 mark)**

   **b)** How does zinc protect iron from rusting?     **(2 marks)**

   **c)** Name three other methods of preventing iron from rusting.     **(3 marks)**

# Air and water

## INTRODUCTION

Clean air is precious. It provides the oxygen that all living things need to survive, and the carbon dioxide that plants need when they photosynthesise. Nitrogen in the air is also very important for healthy plant growth, but not all plants can make use of nitrogen in this form. Unfortunately not all the air we breathe is clean. It may contain a number of pollutants that can be harmful to living things and the environment. It is important to understand how these pollutants are produced and how they can be prevented from contaminating the air. Water vapour is also present in the air. With oxygen, this causes rusting, a process that can be very destructive.

△ Fig. 3.32 The smog over the Forbidden City in Beijing is so thick that it obscures the view from Feng Shui Hill.

## KNOWLEDGE CHECK

✓ Know that oxygen is present in the air and forms oxides when substances burn in it.
✓ Know that oxides of non-metals are acidic.
✓ Know that acids react with carbonates to make salts.
✓ Know that salts can be anhydrous or hydrated.

## LEARNING OBJECTIVES

✓ Be able to describe chemical tests for identifying the presence of water using cobalt(II) chloride and copper(II) sulfate.
✓ Be able to describe in outline the treatment of the water supply in terms of filtration and chlorination.
✓ **EXTENDED** Be able to discuss the implications of an inadequate supply of safe water for drinking and water for irrigating crops.
✓ Know some of the uses of water in industry and in the home.
✓ Know that clean air is approximately 78% nitrogen and 21% oxygen with the remainder made up of a mixture of noble gases, water vapour and carbon dioxide.
✓ Know that the common pollutants in the air are carbon monoxide, sulfur dioxide, oxides of nitrogen and lead compounds from leaded petrol.
✓ Know the sources of carbon monoxide, sulfur dioxide and the oxides of nitrogen.
✓ Know the adverse effects of the common pollutants on buildings and health.
✓ Be able to describe methods of rust protection including using paint and other coatings to exclude oxygen.
✓ Be able to describe the need for fertilisers containing nitrogen, phosphorus and potassium.
✓ Be able to describe the displacement of ammonia from its salts.
✓ Know that carbon dioxide and methane are greenhouse gases and may contribute to climate change.

✓ Be able to describe the formation of carbon dioxide from the complete combustion of carbon-containing substances, respiration, the reactions between and acid and a carbonate, and the thermal decomposition of a carbonate.

✓ Know the sources of methane, including the decomposition of vegetation and as a waste gas in digestion in animals.

✓ **EXTENDED** Be able to describe the separation of oxygen and nitrogen from liquid air by fractional distillation.

✓ **EXTENDED** Be able to describe and explain the presence of oxides of nitrogen in car exhausts and their catalytic removal.

✓ **EXTENDED** Be able to describe sacrificial protection in terms of the reactivity series of metals and galvanising as a method of rust prevention.

✓ **EXTENDED** Be able to describe the essential conditions for the manufacture of ammonia by the Haber process, including the sources of nitrogen (air) and hydrogen (hydrocarbons or steam).

✓ **EXTENDED** Be able to describe the carbon cycle, in simple terms, to include the processes of combustion, respiration and photosynthesis.

## A CHEMICAL TEST FOR WATER

The test for water is to add it to anhydrous copper(II) sulfate solid. If the liquid contains water, the powder will turn from white to blue as hydrated copper(II) sulfate forms.

◁ Fig. 3.33 Chemical test for water.

The equation for the reaction is:

anhydrous copper(II) sulfate + water → hydrated copper(II) sulfate

$CuSO_4(s) + 5H_2O(l) \rightarrow CuSO_4.5H_2O(s)$

The presence of water can also be detected using anhydrous cobalt(II) chloride. The pink anhydrous cobalt(II) chloride turns to blue hydrated cobalt(II) chloride. A convenient way of performing the test is to use cobalt(II) chloride paper:

anhydrous cobalt(II) chloride + water → hydrated cobalt(II) chloride

$CoCl_2(s) + 6H_2O(l) \rightarrow CoCl_2.6H_2O(s)$

Neither of these tests shows the water is pure—only that the liquid has water in it.

## THE WATER CYCLE

The recirculation of water that takes place all over the Earth is called the **water cycle**.

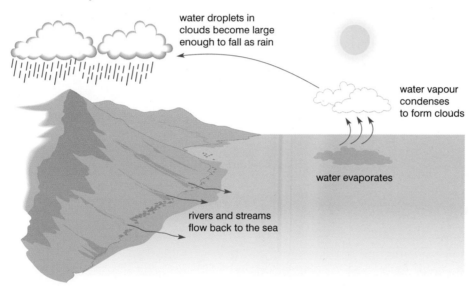

△ Fig. 3.34 The water cycle.

The pattern of rainfall over the planet determines where there are deserts, rainforests and areas of land that can or cannot be used for growing plants.

Some scientists think that **global warming** is responsible for climate changes that are affecting both where rain falls and how much there is of it. This could be causing both increased risks of flooding in some regions and droughts in others.

Water is essential for life on Earth, and the demand for drinking water is increasing as the world's population grows. Two-thirds of the water is used in homes for washing, cleaning, cooking and in toilets. The rest is used by industry. Most industrial processes use water either as a raw material or for cooling. For example, it takes 200 000 litres of water to make 1 tonne of steel.

Water stored in reservoirs must be purified to produce drinkable tap water.

Fig. 3.35 Water pipes discharging in Thailand.

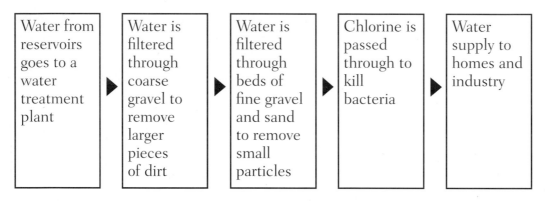

| Water from reservoirs goes to a water treatment plant | ▶ | Water is filtered through coarse gravel to remove larger pieces of dirt | ▶ | Water is filtered through beds of fine gravel and sand to remove small particles | ▶ | Chlorine is passed through to kill bacteria | ▶ | Water supply to homes and industry |

In addition, tap water in certain areas is treated with sodium fluoride ($NaF$) to combat tooth decay.

In certain parts of the world supplies of water are very limited. There is insufficient clean water to drink and not enough water to irrigate and support the growth of crops. Water that is not purified can often contain harmful bacteria and so is not safe to drink. In the absence of clean water people have little choice but to drink contaminated water and risk illness or death.

## THE COMPOSITION OF CLEAN AIR

Air is a mixture of gases that has remained fairly constant for the last 200 million years. The amount of water vapour varies around the world. For example, air above a desert area has a low proportion of water vapour.

△ Fig. 3.36 Components of air.

Nitrogen 78%

Oxygen 21%

Argon 0.9%

Carbon dioxide 0.04%

Trace amounts of other noble gases and water vapour 0.06%

The composition of the air is kept fairly constant by the **nitrogen cycle** and the **carbon cycle**.

## SCIENCE IN CONTEXT

## THE MANUFACTURE OF OXYGEN AND NITROGEN

Oxygen, nitrogen and the noble gases can all be manufactured from the air. The industrial process has several stages.

1. The air is cooled to about −80 °C so that carbon dioxide and water vapour solidify and can be removed.

2. The air is cooled further, compressed and then allowed to expand quickly. This causes further cooling, and at about −200 °C the air becomes a liquid.

3. The liquid air is fractionally distilled. This involves using a large fractionating column which separates liquids with different boiling points. Oxygen's boiling point is −183 °C and nitrogen's is −196 °C: so they can be separated.

Oxygen and nitrogen are stored in large metal cylinders under high pressure and remain as liquids until the pressure is released.

Oxygen is used in medicine to support patients with breathing difficulties. It is also mixed with hydrocarbons such as ethyne (acetylene) for use in cutting tools.

Nitrogen's uses depend on its very low reactivity. It is used in food packaging as a way of excluding air and stopping oxidation and decay. It is also used to reduce fire hazards, particularly in military aircraft fuel systems.

nitrogen gas out →

−190 °C

liquefied air in at -200 °C →

−185 °C

liquid oxygen out →

△ Fig. 3.37 Fractional distillation of liquid air.

## THE CARBON CYCLE

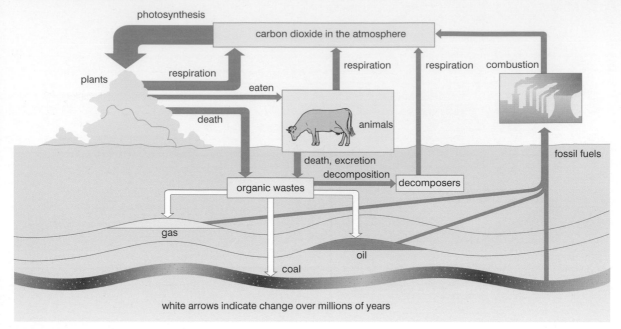

△ Fig. 3.38 The carbon cycle.

There are three key processes in the carbon cycle.

**1.** Combustion – burning fuels containing carbon react with oxygen and form carbon dioxide:

$C(s) + O_2(g) \rightarrow CO_2(g)$

**2.** Respiration – in living things carbohydrates (such as glucose) react with oxygen to form carbon dioxide:

$C_6H_{12}O_6(aq) + 6O_2(g) \rightarrow 6CO_2(g) + 6H_2O(l)$

**3.** Photosynthesis – in the presence of light, plants absorb carbon dioxide and produce oxygen:

$6CO_2(g) + 6H_2O(l) \rightarrow C_6H_{12}O_6(aq) + 6O_2(g)$

**END OF EXTENDED**

## THE NITROGEN CYCLE

Living things need nitrogen to make proteins, these are required, for example, to make new cells for growth.

The air is 78% nitrogen gas ($N_2$), but this gas is very unreactive and cannot be used by plants or animals. Instead, plants use nitrogen in the form of nitrates ($NO_3^-$ ions).

The process of getting nitrogen into this useful form is called **nitrogen fixation**.

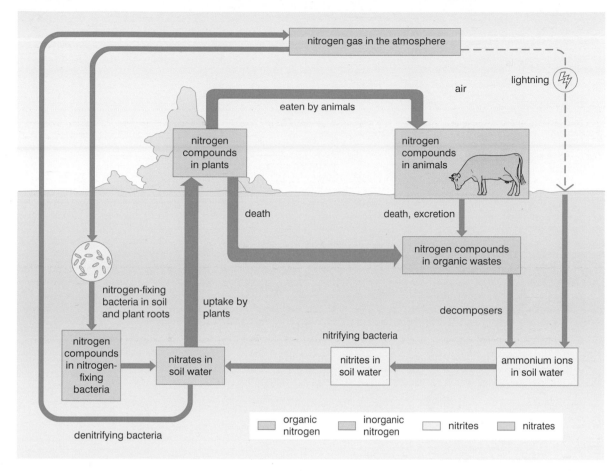

nitrogen gas in the atmosphere

air

lightning

eaten by animals

nitrogen compounds in plants

nitrogen compounds in animals

death

death, excretion

nitrogen compounds in organic wastes

nitrogen-fixing bacteria in soil and plant roots

uptake by plants

decomposers

nitrifying bacteria

nitrogen compounds in nitrogen-fixing bacteria

nitrates in soil water

nitrites in soil water

ammonium ions in soil water

denitrifying bacteria

| organic nitrogen | inorganic nitrogen | nitrites | nitrates |

△ Fig. 3.39 The nitrogen cycle.

The nitrogen in the soil can easily be used up by plants, for example when farmers are growing crops. Additional nitrogen can be added to the soil by using artificial fertilisers. Most of the nitrogen-containing artificial fertilisers are either nitrates or ammonium compounds. Other vital nutrients such as phosphorus (in the form of phosphates; it helps root growth) and potassium (in the form of potassium nitrate; it encourages flower and fruit formation) are often included with the nitrogen in what are called NPK fertilisers.

◁ Fig. 3.40 Ammonium nitrate fertiliser being sprayed onto a field. In some parts of the world, liquid ammonia is pumped directly into the ground as a fertiliser. This can be quite dangerous because liquid ammonia can cause chemical burns and irritate the respiratory tract.

◁ Fig. 3.41 Excess phosphate and nitrate nutrients in river water cause accelerated growth of green algae. The algae form a thick surface layer, which causes underwater plants and fish to die. Increased algal growth in the sea near river estuaries is also of concern.

Note: In the soil, ammonium compounds are converted first to ammonia and then to nitrates by bacteria. In the laboratory, ammonium compounds can be converted into ammonia by heating with an alkali such as sodium hydroxide.

## EXTENDED

Ammonia is used to make nitrogen-containing fertilisers. It is manufactured in the Haber process from nitrogen and hydrogen. This process requires an iron catalyst, a temperature of 450 °C and 200 times atmospheric pressure.

◁ Fig. 3.42 A fertiliser containing nitrogen.

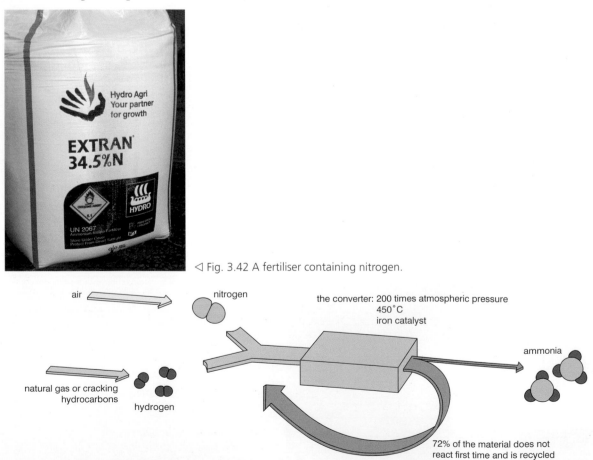

△ Fig. 3.43 The Haber process for making ammonia. The reactants must be recycled to increase the efficiency of the process.

The conditions in the Haber process are chosen carefully to give the highest possible yield of ammonia with a suitable rate of reaction.

nitrogen   +   hydrogen   →   ammonia

$N_2(g)$   +   $3H_2(g)$   $\rightleftharpoons$   $2NH_3(g)$ $\Delta H$   =   exothermic

The greatest yield of ammonia would be made using a low temperature (the reaction is exothermic), but it would be slow. The temperature of 450 °C is a compromise: less is made, but it is produced faster. The iron catalyst is also used to increase the rate; it does not increase the yield. High pressure increases the yield.

Fig. 3.44 shows the effect of temperature and pressure on the yield of ammonia.

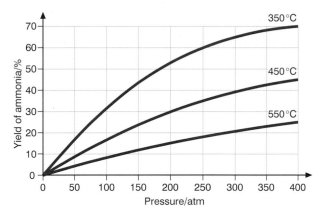

△ Fig. 3.44 Effect of temperature and pressure on yield of ammonia.

The ammonia is liquefied and removed from the reaction vessel and the unused nitrogen and hydrogen are recycled.

Ammonia is commonly used in domestic cleaning agents, in the manufacture of nitric acid and to make NPK fertilisers. 'NPK' means the fertiliser contains nitrogen (N), phosphorus (P) and potassium (K).

**END OF EXTENDED**

## QUESTIONS

**1.** What does *anhydrous* mean?

**2.** What colour change would you observe if water is added to anhydrous cobalt(II) chloride?

**3.** In the purification of water there are two important stages.

  **a)** In the first stage, the water is filtered twice. What is used as the filter in each case?

  **b)** In the second stage, bacteria are killed. What chemical is used to kill the bacteria?

4. This question is about the composition of the air.

   a) What is the percentage of nitrogen in clean air?

   b) What is the percentage of carbon dioxide in clean air?

5. **EXTENDED** Nitrogen and oxygen are manufactured from liquid air. What process is used to separate the two gases from the liquid mixture?

6. **EXTENDED** In the carbon cycle, name a process that removes carbon dioxide from the atmosphere.

7. **EXTENDED** What temperature and pressure are used in the Haber process?

## POLLUTANTS IN THE AIR

Pollutants in the air come from a variety of sources. Some come from burning waste and some from power stations burning coal or gas. Industry produces pollutants as well.

The most common pollutants in the air are:

- carbon monoxide–from the incomplete combustion of hydrocarbons (petrol/coal/gas/diesel)
- sulfur dioxide–from burning fossil fuels such as petrol and coal which contain sulfur compounds
- oxides of nitrogen–from burning fossil fuels (petrol/diesel/coal)
- lead compounds–from burning leaded petrol.

Δ Fig. 3.45 Cycling is encouraged in Amsterdam to reduce air pollution.

Under normal conditions nitrogen is a very unreactive gas. However, in a petrol engine temperatures of 1000 °C can be reached, and in these conditions nitrogen reacts with oxygen to make oxides of nitrogen. Nitrogen oxides are often represented by $NO_x$, but they are mainly nitrogen monoxide, NO. A catalytic converter in the car's exhaust system can reduce the nitrogen oxides back to nitrogen:

$$2NO(g) \rightarrow N_2(g) + O_2(g)$$

Rhodium is frequently used as a catalyst in catalytic convertors.

## HOW IS THE ATMOSPHERE CHANGING, AND WHY?

There are two major impacts caused by the burning of **fossil fuels** – the **greenhouse effect** and **acid rain**.

### The greenhouse effect

Carbon dioxide, methane and CFCs (chlorofluorocarbons) are known as **greenhouse gases**. The levels of these gases in the atmosphere are increasing due to the burning of fossil fuels, pollution from farm animals and the use of CFCs in aerosols and refrigerators.

Short-wave radiation from the Sun warms the ground, and the warm Earth gives off heat as long-wave radiation. Much of this radiation is stopped from escaping from the Earth by the greenhouse gases. This is known as the greenhouse effect.

The greenhouse effect is responsible for keeping the Earth warmer than it would otherwise be. This is normal – and important for life on Earth. However, most scientists think that increasing levels of greenhouse gases are stopping even more heat escaping and that the earth is slowly warming up. This is known as global warming. If global warming continues the Earth's climate may change, polar ice may melt and sea levels may rise flooding low-lying areas – some of them highly populated.

The Earth's average temperature is gradually increasing, but nobody knows for certain if the greenhouse effect is responsible. It may be that the recent rise in global temperatures is part of a natural cycle – there have been ice ages and intermediate warm periods all through history. Many people are concerned, however, that it is not part of a natural cycle and they say we should act now to reduce emissions of these greenhouse gases.

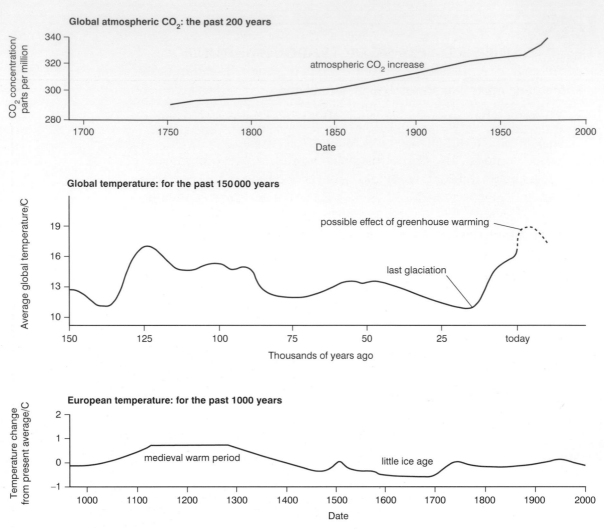

△ Fig. 3.46 How atmospheric carbon dioxide and temperature have varied.

## Acid rain

Burning fossil fuels gives off many gases, including sulfur dioxide and various nitrogen oxides:

sulfur + oxygen → sulfur dioxide

$S(s) + O_2(g) \rightarrow SO_2(g)$

Sulfur dioxide combines with water and oxygen to form sulfuric acid. Nitrogen oxide combines with water to form nitric acid. These substances can make the rain acidic (called acid rain).

sulfur dioxide + oxygen + water → sulfuric acid

$2SO_2(g) + O_2(g) + 2H_2O(l) \rightarrow 2H_2SO_4(aq)$

Buildings are damaged by acid rain, particularly those made of limestone and marble – both are forms of calcium carbonate, $CaCO_3$. Metal structures are also attacked by sulfuric acid.

**SCIENCE IN CONTEXT**

## SOME INTERESTING FACTS ABOUT METHANE

1. Methane makes up about 97% of natural gas.

2. It is formed by the decay of plant matter where there is no oxygen (anaerobic decay).

3. Biogas contains 40–70% methane. Biodigesters convert organic wastes into a nutrient-rich liquid fertiliser and biogas, a **renewable** source of electrical and heat energy. These are widely used in non-industrialised countries, particularly India, Nepal and Vietnam. Biodigesters can help families by providing a cheap source of fuel, reducing environmental pollution from the run-off from animal pens, and reducing diseases caused by the use of untreated manure as fertiliser. However, biodigesters only work efficiently in hot countries; they are not as effective at low temperatures.

△ Fig. 3.47 A commercial biodigester.

4. Methane is one of the greenhouse gases, thought by some scientists to be responsible for global warming. It has almost 25 times the effect of the same volume of carbon dioxide.

5. Ruminant animals such as cows and sheep produce methane. It has been estimated that a cow can produce as much as 200 litres of methane per day. So could cows be one of the causes of global warming?

Acid rain harms plants that take in the acidic water and the animals that live in the affected rivers and lakes. Acid rain also washes ions such as calcium and magnesium out of the soil, depleting the minerals available to plants. It also washes aluminium ions out of the soil and into rivers and lakes, where it poisons fish.

Nitrogen monoxide can be oxidised to a brown gas called nitrogen dioxide, $NO_2$. Under certain atmospheric conditions this can build up as a brown haze in large cities. Nitrogen dioxide is dangerous because it can cause respiratory diseases such as bronchitis.

Reducing emissions of the gases that cause acid rain is expensive. Part of the problem is that the acid rain usually falls a long way from the places where the gases were released.

Power stations are now being fitted with flue-gas desulfurisation plants (FGD) to reduce the amount of sulfur dioxide released into the atmosphere.

Catalytic converters are fitted to the exhaust systems of vehicles to reduce the level of pollutants released from burning petrol or diesel.

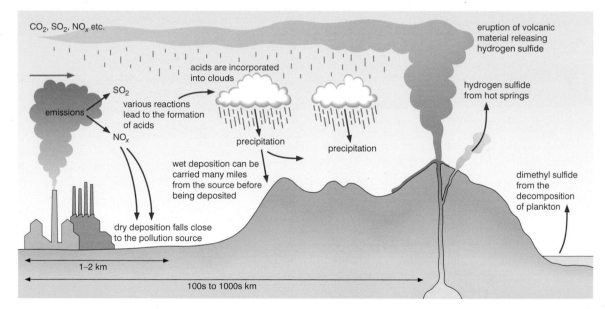

△ Fig. 3.48 The process of the formation of acid rain.

## QUESTIONS

1. Carbon monoxide is a common pollutant in the air. Name a major source of the carbon monoxide.

2. a) Methane is a greenhouse gas. Name two sources of methane.

   b) Name another greenhouse gas.

3. a) Name two gases that are responsible for causing acid rain.

   b) For each gas you named in part a) name the acid it forms.

   c) List three problems caused by acid rain in the environment.

**4. EXTENDED** Nitrogen monoxide (NO) is produced in the high temperature of a car engine.

**a)** Write a balanced equation to show how the nitrogen monoxide is formed.

**b)** What is the nitrogen monoxide converted to in a catalytic converter?

## CARBON DIOXIDE

Carbon dioxide is an important gas. It is formed as a product in the complete combustion of carbon-containing substances:

$$C(s) + O_2(g) \rightarrow CO_2(g)$$

Carbon dioxide is also formed in respiration. It can be made in the laboratory by the reaction of dilute hydrochloric acid and calcium carbonate in the form of marble chips.

▷ Fig. 3.49 Charcoal is mainly carbon. When it burns it gives off carbon dioxide.

calcium carbonate + hydrochloric acid → carbon dioxide + water + calcium chloride

$$CaCO_3(s) \qquad + 2HCl(aq) \qquad \rightarrow CO_2(g) \qquad + H_2O(l) + CaCl_2(aq)$$

HCl(aq) dilute hydrochloric acid

carbon dioxide collects here

CaCO₃ marble chips

water

△ Fig. 3.50 The laboratory preparation of carbon dioxide gas.

If the gas is bubbled through limewater (calcium hydroxide solution), a white precipitate forms. This is used as a laboratory test for carbon dioxide.

Carbon dioxide can also be prepared by the **thermal decomposition** of certain metal carbonates. Copper(II) carbonate and zinc carbonate are examples:

| copper(II) carbonate | $\rightarrow$ | copper(II) oxide | + | carbon dioxide |
|---|---|---|---|---|
| $CuCO_3(s)$ | $\rightarrow$ | $CuO(s)$ | + | $CO_2(g)$ |
| green | | black | | |

| zinc carbonate | $\rightarrow$ | zinc oxide | + | carbon dioxide |
|---|---|---|---|---|
| $ZnCO_3(s)$ | $\rightarrow$ | $ZnO(s)$ | + | $CO_2(g)$ |
| white | | white (yellow when hot) | | |

## METHODS OF PREVENTING RUSTING

Over time, the oxygen and water in the atmosphere affect metals. If they react together the metal is corroded. The corrosion of iron is called **rusting**.

In the presence of water, the following chemical reaction takes place:

$$4Fe(s) + 3O_2(g) \rightarrow 2Fe_2O_3(s)$$

In fact, rust is hydrated iron(III) oxide, $Fe_2O_3 . xH_2O$. The '$x$' can vary depending on the conditions.

Methods of preventing rusting fall into three main categories:

- Stopping oxygen and water reaching the iron – for example oiling/ greasing, as with bicycle chains; painting, as with car bodies.
- Alloying iron is mixed with other metals to produce alloys such as stainless steel that do not rust.

### EXTENDED

- **Sacrificial protection** – the iron is covered by, or put in contact with, another metal that is higher in the reactivity series, that is, more reactive than iron. The more reactive metal corrodes instead of the iron, so it is said to be 'sacrificed' to protect the iron.

Ship hulls made of iron have zinc bars attached to them. The zinc bars corrode, not the hull.

In **galvanising**, iron is covered with a coating of zinc. Even if the zinc surface is scratched exposing the iron, the zinc corrodes, not the iron.

### END OF EXTENDED

## Developing investigative skills

A student set up the apparatus as shown in Fig. 3.51 with the long tube turned upside-down in a trough of water. Previously some iron filings had been sprinkled into the tube, and many of these had stuck to the inside of the tube. With the same levels of water in the tube and the trough, the student recorded the volume of air in the tube (100 cm³).

After a few days he returned to the apparatus, equalised the water levels as before and took a second reading of the volume of air in the tube (85 cm³). He then worked out how much of the air had been replaced by water.

△ Fig. 3.51 Apparatus for experiment.

### Observing, measuring and recording

❶ What changes would you have expected to see in the iron filings that were put in the tube at the beginning of the experiment?

### Interpreting observations and data

❷ What chemical reaction was taking place in the tube? Write a balanced equation for the reaction.

❸ What do the results indicate about the composition of the air in the tube?

### Evaluating methods

❹ The results in this experiment are different to those obtained by other students. Suggest some possible reasons for this.

❺ Why did the student equalise the water levels in the trough and the tube before taking the reading of the volume of gas in the tube?

## QUESTIONS

1. Carbon dioxide is formed in the complete combustion of carbon. What product might form if carbon is burned in a limited supply of air?

2. In the laboratory, carbon dioxide can be prepared by the reaction of an acid with a metal carbonate.

    a) Write a word equation for the reaction between copper(II) carbonate and dilute hydrochloric acid.

    b) Write a balanced equation for the reaction in part a).

3. Carbon dioxide can also be prepared by the action of heat on a metal carbonate.

    a) Write a word equation for the action of heat on calcium carbonate.

    b) Write a balanced equation for the reaction in part a).

4. What is the name of the chemical compound present in rust?

5. Name two ways of preventing water and oxygen from getting into contact with the surface of an iron object.

6. **EXTENDED** What is *galvanising*?

7. **EXTENDED** Refer to the reactivity series to explain how zinc is able to offer sacrificial protection to iron.

# End of topic checklist

## Key terms

acid rain, carbon cycle, fossil fuel, galvanising, global warming, greenhouse effect, greenhouse gas, nitrogen cycle, nitrogen fixation, renewable energy, rusting, sacrificial protection, thermal decomposition, water cycle

## During your study of this topic you should have learned:

○ How to describe chemical tests for identifying the presence of water using cobalt(II) chloride and copper(II) sulfate.

○ How to describe in outline the treatment of the water supply in terms of filtration and chlorination.

○ About some of the uses of water in industry and in the home.

○ That clean air is approximately 78% nitrogen and 21% oxygen with the remainder made up of a mixture of noble gases, water vapour and carbon dioxide.

○ That the common pollutants in the air are carbon monoxide, sulfur dioxide, oxides of nitrogen and lead compounds from leaded petrol.

○ That the source of carbon monoxide is the incomplete combustion of carbon-containing substances.

○ That the source of sulfur dioxide is the combustion of fossil fuels that contain sulfur compounds.

○ That a source of the oxides of nitrogen is car exhausts.

○ About the adverse effects of the common pollutants on buildings and health.

○ How to describe methods of rust protection, including using paint and other coatings to exclude oxygen.

○ How to describe the need for fertilisers containing nitrogen, phosphorus and potassium.

○ How to describe the displacement of ammonia from its salts.

○ That carbon dioxide and methane are greenhouse gases and may contribute to climate change.

# End of topic checklist continued

○ How to describe the formation of carbon dioxide from:

- the complete combustion of carbon-containing substances
- the process of respiration
- the reactions between and acid and a carbonate
- the thermal decomposition of a carbonate.

○ About the sources of methane, including the decomposition of vegetation and as a waste gas in the digestion in animals.

○ **EXTENDED** How to describe the separation of oxygen and nitrogen from liquid air by fractional distillation.

○ **EXTENDED** How to describe and explain the presence of oxides of nitrogen in car exhausts and their catalytic removal.

○ **EXTENDED** How to describe sacrificial protection in terms of the reactivity series of metals and galvanising as a method of rust prevention.

○ **EXTENDED** How to describe the essential conditions for the manufacture of ammonia by the Haber process, including the sources of nitrogen (air) and hydrogen (hydrocarbons or steam).

○ **EXTENDED** How to describe the carbon cycle, including the processes of combustion, respiration and photosynthesis.

○ **EXTENDED** To discuss the implications of an inadequate supply of safe water for drinking and water for irrigating crops.

# End of topic questions

*Note: The marks awarded for these questions indicate the level of detail required in the answers. In the examination, the number of marks awarded to questions like these may be different.*

1. This question is about the composition of a sample of clean air.

   **a)** What is the proportion of oxygen? (1 mark)

   **b)** What is the proportion of carbon dioxide? (1 mark)

2. **a)** What could you use to detect the presence of water? (1 mark)

   **b)** What would you observe if water was present? (2 marks)

3. The table shows some of pollutants found in air. For each pollutant identify the source of the pollution and how it gets into the air. The first one has been done for you.

| Pollutant | What is the source of the pollutant? | How does the pollutant get into the air? |
|---|---|---|
| Lead compounds | Lead additives in petrol | Burning petrol in a car |
| Carbon monoxide | | |
| Sulfur dioxide | | |
| Oxides of nitrogen | | |

(6 marks)

4. This question is about the greenhouse effect.

   **a)** What is the *greenhouse effect*? (2 marks)

   **b)** Name two greenhouse gases. (2 marks)

   **c)** Apart from an increase in greenhouse gases, what else could be causing global warming? (1 mark)

5. Carbon dioxide can be prepared using the reaction between calcium carbonate and dilute hydrochloric acid.

   **a)** How can the gas be collected in this reaction? (1 mark)

   **b)** Write a balanced equation for the reaction. (2 marks)

6. Carbon dioxide can be made by the thermal decomposition of copper(II) carbonate.

   **a)** What does *thermal decomposition* mean? (2 marks)

   **b)** Write a balanced equation for this reaction. (2 marks)

**7.** **EXTENDED** Copy and complete the following table to explain some of the important processes in the carbon cycle.

| Process | What is removed from the air in the process? | What is put into the air in the process? |
|---|---|---|
| Combustion | | |
| Respiration | | |
| Photosynthesis | | |

(6 marks)

**8.** **EXTENDED** Describe how nitrogen and oxygen are extracted from the air.

(2 marks)

**9.** **EXTENDED** This question is about the manufacture of ammonia.

   **a)** What are the two reactants used in the reaction? (2 marks)

   **b)** What is the source of each reactant? (2 marks)

   **c)** Write a balanced equation for the reaction. (2 marks)

   **d)** What reaction conditions are needed? (3 marks)

# Sulfur

## INTRODUCTION

Sulfur is a non-metallic element in Group VI of the Periodic Table. It is the tenth most common element in the Universe and is found as the native (pure) element in certain parts of the world. Most often, though, it is found in the form of metal sulfides. Sulfur is often deposited in the craters of volcanoes and the characteristic smell close to active volcanoes is sulfur dioxide. Large quantities of sulfur are used to manufacture sulfuric acid. When converted into sulfur dioxide, it is used as a bleach to manufacture wood pulp, for making paper and as a food preservative because it kills bacteria.

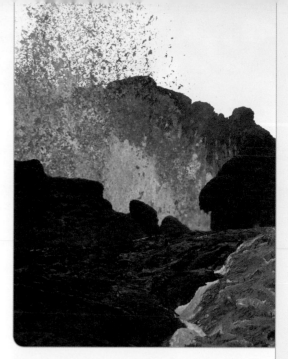

△ Fig. 3.52 About two-thirds of the sulfur found in the atmosphere comes from gases emitted by volcanoes.

## KNOWLEDGE CHECK

✓ Know that non-metals are positioned on the right side of the Periodic Table.
✓ Know that non-metals generally form acidic oxides.
✓ Know that dilute sulfuric acid will react with metals, bases and carbonates to form salts.

## LEARNING OBJECTIVES

✓ Be able to name some of the sources of sulfur.
✓ Be able to name the use of sulfur in the manufacture of sulfuric acid.
✓ Be able to name the uses of sulfur dioxide as a bleach in the manufacture of wood pulp for paper and as a food preservative.
✓ **EXTENDED** Be able to describe the manufacture of sulfuric acid by the Contact process, including the essential conditions.
✓ **EXTENDED** Be able to describe the properties of dilute and concentrated sulfuric acid.

## SULFURIC ACID

Sulfuric acid is made in industry from sulfur. The sulfur is mined in some parts of the world as the pure element. It is also found combined with metals as sulfides, e.g. lead(II) sulfide, PbS.

## EXTENDED

## THE CONTACT PROCESS

Sulfuric acid is a very important starting material in the chemical industry. It is used in the manufacture of many other chemicals including fertilisers, detergents and paints.

Sulfuric acid is manufactured in the **Contact process**, in which sulfur dioxide is oxidised to sulfur trioxide.

△ Fig. 3.53 The Contact process.

The equations for the steps in making sulfuric acid are shown below:

**1.**

| | | | |
|---|---|---|---|
| sulfur | + | oxygen | → | sulfur dioxide |
| $S(s)$ | + | $O_2(g)$ | → | $SO_2(g)$ |

**2.**

| | | | |
|---|---|---|---|
| sulfur dioxide | + | oxygen | ⇌ | sulfur trioxide |
| $2SO_2(g)$ | + | $O_2(g)$ | ⇌ | $2SO_3(g)$ | $\Delta H$ = exothermic |

**3.**

| | | | |
|---|---|---|---|
| sulfur trioxide | + | sulfuric acid | → | 'oleum' (concentrated) |
| $SO_3(g)$ | + | $H_2SO_4(l)$ | → | $H_2S_2O_7(l)$ |

**4.**

| | | | |
|---|---|---|---|
| 'oleum' | + | water | → | sulfuric acid |
| $H_2S_2O_7(l)$ | + | $H_2O(l)$ | → | $2H_2SO_4(l)$ |

Does it seem simpler to you to make sulfuric acid by adding sulfur trioxide straight to water and skipping steps 3 and 4?

$$H_2O(l) \quad + \quad SO_3(g) \quad \rightarrow \quad H_2SO_4(l)$$

This is dangerous because the reaction is very exothermic and an 'acid mist' is made.

Step 2 is the main reaction of the Contact process. The highest yield of sulfur trioxide would be made at a low temperature (the reaction is exothermic), but this would be slow. Using a compromise temperature of 450 °C makes less sulfur trioxide, but in a shorter time.

High pressure is not used because the yield is 98 per cent. Unconverted reactants are recycled. Vanadium(V) oxide is used as a catalyst to increase the rate, but it does not increase the yield.

## REMEMBER

A low temperature often gives a good conversion of reactant into product but a very slow rate of reaction.

The temperature chosen for an industrial process is often a compromise between one that favours the forward reaction (rather than the backward reaction) and one that gives a suitable rate of reaction.

△ Fig. 3.54 Uses of sulfuric acid.

## DILUTE SULFURIC ACID

Dilute sulfuric acid ($H_2SO_4$) is a typical acid.

**1.** It produces $H^+$ ions in aqueous solution:

$$H_2SO_4(aq) \rightarrow 2H^+(aq) + SO_4^{2-}(aq)$$

**2.** It reacts with metals to form a **salt** and hydrogen gas:

$$Mg(s) + H_2SO_4(aq) \rightarrow MgSO_4(aq) + H_2(g)$$

**3.** It reacts with alkalis to make salts (neutralisation):

$$2NaOH(aq) + H_2SO_4(aq) \rightarrow Na_2SO_4(aq) + 2H_2O(l)$$

**4.** It reacts with bases to make salts (neutralisation):

$$ZnO(s) + H_2SO_4(aq) \rightarrow ZnSO_4(aq) + H_2O(l)$$

**5.** It reacts with carbonates to make a salt, carbon dioxide and water:

$$K_2CO_3(s) + H_2SO_4(aq) \rightarrow K_2SO_4(aq) + CO_2(g) + H_2O(l)$$

△ Fig. 3.55 Nuggets of naturally occurring sulfur on a volcano in Indonesia.

### CONCENTRATED SULFURIC ACID

Concentrated sulfuric acid is highly corrosive. It often acts as a dehydrating agent and absorbs hydrogen and oxygen from compounds in the form of water. For example, when added to glucose carbon is formed.

$$C_6H_{12}O_6 \xrightarrow[\text{H}_2\text{SO}_4]{\text{concentrated}} 6C(s) + 6H_2O(g)$$

This reaction is highly exothermic and steam is produced. A honeycomb structure of black carbon is also formed.

## QUESTIONS

**1.** In the Contact process, a better yield of sulfur trioxide would be obtained at room temperature than at 450 °C. Why is a higher temperature used?

**2.** What catalyst is used in the Contact process?

**3.** The yield of sulfur trioxide could be increased if a higher pressure was used. Give a reason for not doing this.

**4.** Sulfuric acid is used to make ammonium sulfate, $(NH_4)_2SO_4$, fertiliser. What substance reacts with sulfuric acid to make ammonium sulfate? Write a balanced equation for the reaction.

**END OF EXTENDED**

# End of topic checklist

## Key terms

Contact process, salt

## During your study of this topic you should have learned:

○ About some sources of sulfur.

○ That sulfur is used in the manufacture of sulfuric acid.

○ That sulfur dioxide is used as a bleach in the manufacture of wood pulp for paper and as a food preservative (by killing bacteria).

○ **EXTENDED** How to describe the manufacture of sulfuric acid by the Contact process and about the essential conditions:

  ● a temperature of 450 °C

  ● a catalyst of vanadium(V) oxide

  ● atmospheric pressure.

○ **EXTENDED** How to describe the properties of dilute sulfuric acid as a typical acid:

  ● reaction with a metal to form a salt and hydrogen

  ● reaction with a base or alkali to form a salt and water

  ● reaction with a carbonate to form a salt, water and carbon dioxide.

○ **EXTENDED** That concentrated sulfuric acid is a very corrosive dehydrating agent.

# End of topic questions

*Note: The marks awarded for these questions indicate the level of detail required in the answers. In the examination, the number of marks awarded to questions like these may be different.*

**1. a)** Name one use of sulfur. **(1 mark)**

  **b)** Name two uses of sulfur dioxide. **(2 marks)**

**2. EXTENDED** This question is about the Contact process for making sulfuric acid.

  **a)** Write a balanced equation, including state symbols, for the reaction between sulfur dioxide and oxygen. **(3 marks)**

  **b)** Copy and complete the table, giving the reaction conditions for the contact process. **(3 marks)**

| Reaction factor | Conditions chosen |
|---|---|
| Temperature | |
| Pressure | |
| Catalyst | |

  **c)** Give two uses of sulfuric acid. **(2 marks)**

**3. EXTENDED** This question is about the properties of dilute sulfuric acid.

  **a)** What is the definition of an acid? **(1 mark)**

  **b)** What would you observe if magnesium ribbon were added to some dilute sulfuric acid? **(2 marks)**

  **c)** Warm dilute sulfuric acid reacts with copper(II) oxide.

   **i)** What type of oxide is copper(II) oxide? **(1 mark)**

   **ii)** What would you observe in this reaction? **(2 marks)**

   **iii)** Write a balanced equation for the reaction. **(2 marks)**

  **d)** Dilute sulfuric acid reacts with zinc carbonate.

   **i)** What would you observe in this reaction? **(2 marks)**

   **ii)** Write a balanced equation for this reaction. **(2 marks)**

**4. EXTENDED** What would you observe when concentrated sulfuric acid is added to some sugar? **(2 marks)**

# Carbonates

## INTRODUCTION

Carbonates are salts of **carbonic acid,** a weak acid that is made when carbon dioxide dissolves in water. They react with dilute hydrochloric acid and dilute sulfuric acid forming carbon dioxide. Many metals exist in nature as metal carbonates – the most important of these is calcium carbonate or limestone. Limestone is used for building but it has other important uses as well.

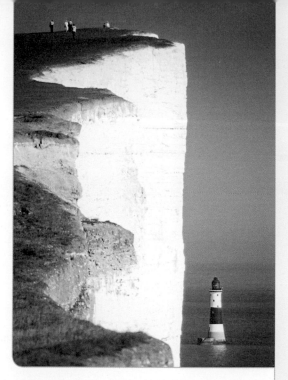

△ Fig. 3.56 The chalk cliffs of southern England are composed largely of calcium carbonate.

## KNOWLEDGE CHECK

✓ Know that dilute acids react with carbonates to form salts and carbon dioxide.
✓ Know how to detect the presence of carbon dioxide.

## LEARNING OBJECTIVES

✓ Be able to describe the manufacture of lime (calcium oxide) from calcium carbonate (limestone) in terms of thermal decomposition.
✓ Know some uses of lime and slaked lime, as in treating acidic soil and neutralising acidic industrial waste products, e.g. flue-gas desulfurisation.
✓ Know the uses of calcium carbonate in the manufacture of iron and of cement.

## HOW IS LIMESTONE USED?

For centuries limestone has been heated in lime kilns to make 'quicklime' (lime) or calcium oxide, CaO:

| $CaCO_3(s)$ | 1200 °C | $CaO(s) + CO_2(g)$ |
|---|---|---|
| limestone | $\longrightarrow$ | quicklime |

This is an example of **thermal decomposition**, the use of heat ('thermal') to break up a substance.

A modern rotary kiln is shown in Fig. 3.57.

△ Fig. 3.57 A modern rotary kiln.

When water is added to calcium oxide (quicklime), a vigorous exothermic (heat-producing) reaction takes place, and slaked lime – calcium hydroxide, $Ca(OH)_2$, is formed:

$$CaO(s) \quad + \quad H_2O(l) \quad \rightarrow \quad Ca(OH)_2(s)$$
quicklime                                        slaked lime

Slaked lime is an alkali, which is the basis of many of its uses.

The major uses of limestone, quicklime and slaked lime are listed below.

Limestone ($CaCO_3$):

• crushed and used as aggregate for road building
• added as a powder to lakes to **neutralise** acidity
• mixed and heated with clay to make cement
• used to extract iron in the blast furnace.

Quicklime (CaO):

• added to soil to neutralise acidity
• used as drying agent in industry
• used to neutralise acid gases, such as sulfur dioxide, $SO_2$, produced by power stations (flue-gas desulfurisation).

Slaked lime ($Ca(OH)_2$):

- added to soil to neutralise acidity
- used in mortar for building
- in solution it is called limewater used in testing for carbon dioxide, $CO_2(g)$
- used to neutralise acid gases such as $SO_2$ produced by power stations (flue-gas desulfurisation).

△ Fig. 3.58 Pouring concrete to form the foundation of a house.

# End of topic checklist

**Key terms**

carbonic acid, neutralisation, thermal decomposition

## During your study of this topic you should have learned:

○ How to describe the manufacture of lime (calcium oxide) from limestone (calcium carbonate) by thermal decomposition.

○ About some of the uses of lime and slaked lime:

- treating acidic soil
- neutralising acidic industrial waste products, such as flue-gas desulfurisation.

○ About the uses of calcium carbonate:

- in the manufacture of iron
- in the manufacture of cement.

# End of topic questions

*Note: The marks awarded for these questions indicate the level of detail required in the answers. In the examination, the number of marks awarded to questions like these may be different.*

1. Name two uses of calcium carbonate. **(2 marks)**

2. Write balanced equations, including state symbols, for the following:

   **a)** changing limestone into quicklime **(2 marks)**

   **b)** changing quicklime into slaked lime. **(2 marks)**

3. **a)** Describe the limewater test for carbon dioxide. **(2 marks)**

   **b)** Write the word equation and the balanced equation (including state symbols) for the reaction occurring in the limewater test. **(3 marks)**

4. Why is quicklime (CaO) used in power stations? **(3 marks)**

# Exam-style questions
## Sample student answer

*The questions, sample answers and marks in this section have been written by the authors as a guide only. The marks awarded for these questions indicate the level of detail required in the answers. In the examination, the number of marks awarded to questions like these may be different.*

## Question 1

Lithium (Li), sodium (Na) and potassium (K) are in Group I of the Periodic Table.

**a)** These elements have similar chemical properties

Explain why, using ideas about electronic structures.

*All the elements have one electron in their outer shell.* ✔ ① **(1)**

**b)** Lithium reacts with water to form a solution of lithium hydroxide and a colourless gas. During this reaction the temperature of the water increases.

**i)** What is the name of the colourless gas produced?

*hydrogen* ✔ ① **(1)**

**ii)** Why does the temperature of the water increase?

*The reaction between lithium and water is rapid.* ✗ **(1)**

**iii)** Describe what you would observe if a small piece of sodium is added to water.

*The sodium forms sodium hydroxide and hydrogen gas is given off.* ✗

*The reaction would be more rapid than the lithium reaction.* ✔ ① **(2)**

## TEACHER'S COMMENTS

**a)** The mark would have been given for stating that all the elements have the same number of electrons in their outer shell. The candidate has gone further and correctly stated that they all have one electron in the outer shell.

**b) i)** The correct answer has been given.

**ii)** This answer lacks precision. The mark would be awarded for either explaining that the reaction produced heat or that the reaction was exothermic.

**iii)** The candidate has not scored both marks. Apart from stating that the reaction would be more rapid than that with lithium, observations have not been given. The products have been correctly named but these are not what you would *observe*. Marks would be awarded for: fizzing/effervescence/bubbles (of gas), the sodium floats/moves around on the water, forms a ball/disappears.

**iv)** The correct answer and explanation have been given.

**iv)** Caesium (Cs) is another Group I metal.

Is caesium more or less reactive than lithium? Give a reason for your answer.

*More reactive, because reactivity in Group I increases down the group.*

✓ ① (1)

**(Total 6 marks)**

④/⑥

## Question 2

Use the Periodic Table to help you answer this question.

**a)** State the symbol of the element with proton number 14. (1)

**b)** State the symbol of the element that has a relative atomic mass of 32. (1)

**c)** State the number of the group that contains the alkali metals. (1)

**d)** Which group contains elements whose atoms form ions with a 2+ charge? (1)

**e)** Which group contains elements whose atoms form ions with a 1− charge? (1)

**(Total 5 marks)**

## Question 3

Three of the elements in Group VII of the Periodic Table are chlorine, bromine and iodine.

**a)** Chlorine has a proton number of 17. What is the electron configuration of chlorine? (1)

**b)** How many electrons will be in the outer shell of a bromine atom? (1)

**c)** Bromine reacts with hydrogen to form hydrogen bromide. The equation for the reaction is:

$Br_2(g) + H_2(g) \rightarrow 2HBr(g)$

What is the colour change during the reaction? (1)

**d)** Hydrogen iodide and hydrogen chloride have similar properties.

**i)** A sample of hydrogen iodide is dissolved in water. A piece of universal indicator paper is dipped into the solution. State, with a reason, the final colour of the universal indicator paper. (2)

**ii)** A sample of hydrogen iodide is dissolved in methylbenzene. A piece of universal indicator paper is dipped into the solution. State, with a reason, the final colour of the universal indicator paper. (2)

**(Total 7 marks)**

# Exam-style questions continued

## Question 4

The reactivity of metals can be compared by comparing their reactions with dilute sulfuric acid. Pieces of zinc, iron and magnesium of identical size are added to separate test tubes containing this acid.

**a)** What order of reactivity would you expect? Put the most reactive metal first. **(1)**

**b)** Write a word equation for the reaction between magnesium and dilute sulfuric acid. **(1)**

**c)** Write a balanced equation for the reaction in b). **(1)**

**d)** Name a metal that does not react with dilute sulfuric acid. **(1)**

**e)** What other reaction could be used to compare the reactivity of metals? **(1)**

**(Total 5 marks)**

## Question 5

Iron is extracted from iron ore in a blast furnace. Label the diagram of the blast furnace using only the words given below. Each word may be used once, more than once or not at all.

| | | | |
|---|---|---|---|
| bauxite | haematite | sodium hydroxide | cryolite |
| molten iron | sand | slag | |

**a)**

coke, limestone and
........................................

hot waste gases          hot waste gases

hot air          hot air

........................................

........................................

(3)

**b)** Coke (carbon) burns in the oxygen in the furnace.

**i)** Write a balanced equation for carbon burning in a plentiful supply of oxygen. (1)

**ii)** The product formed in reaction i) above then reacts with more carbon to form a gas. Write a balanced equation for this reaction. (1)

**c)** Why is limestone added to the furnace? (2)

**d)** Iron is produced in the furnace by the reduction of iron(III) oxide. An equation for the reaction is:

$$Fe_2O_3(s) + 3CO(g) \rightarrow 2Fe(s) + 3CO_2(g)$$

Explain how you know that the iron(III) oxide has been reduced. (1)

**e)** Aluminium is another important metal.

**i)** Unlike iron, aluminium cannot be obtained from aluminium ore by heating it with carbon. Explain why. (2)

**ii)** State one large scale use of aluminium and a property of aluminium that makes it suitable for this use. (2)

**(Total 12 marks)**

## Question 6

The table shows the composition of the mixture of gases in a typical car exhaust fumes.

| Gas | % of the gas in the exhaust fumes |
|---|---|
| Carbon dioxide | 9 |
| Carbon monoxide | 5 |
| Oxygen | 4 |
| Hydrogen | 2 |
| Hydrocarbons | 0.2 |
| Nitrogen oxides | 0.2 |
| Sulfur dioxide | less than 0.003 |
| Gas X | 79.6 |

**a)** State the name of the gas X. (1)

**b)** The carbon dioxide comes from the burning of hydrocarbons, such as octane, in the petrol.

**i)** Copy and complete the word equation for the complete combustion of octane.

octane + _____ → carbon dioxide + _____ (2)

**ii)** Which two elements are present in hydrocarbons? (1)

**iii)** To which homologous series of hydrocarbons does octane belong? (1)

**c)** Suggest a reason for the presence of carbon monoxide in exhaust fumes. (1)

**d)** Nitrogen oxides are present in small quantities in exhaust fumes.

  **i)** Copy and complete the following equation for the formation of nitrogen dioxide.

  $N_2(g) +$ _____ $O_2(g) \rightarrow$ _____ $NO_2(g)$ (1)

  **ii)** State one harmful effect of nitrogen dioxide on organisms. (1)

**e)** Sulfur dioxide is an atmospheric pollutant and is found in only small amounts in car exhaust fumes.

  **i)** What is the main source of sulfur dioxide pollution of the atmosphere? (1)

  **ii)** Sulfur dioxide is oxidised in the air to sulfur trioxide. The sulfur trioxide may dissolve in rainwater to form a dilute solution of sulfuric acid, $H_2SO_4$. State the meaning of the term *oxidation*. (1)

  **iii)** Sulfuric acid reacts with metals such as iron. Copy and complete the following word equation for the reaction of sulfuric acid with iron.

  sulfuric acid + iron $\rightarrow$ _____ + _____ (2)

  **iv)** What effect does acid rain have on buildings made of stone containing calcium carbonate? (1)

**(Total 13 marks)**

## Question 7

Look at the list of five elements below:

argon, bromine, chlorine, iodine, potassium

**a)** Put these five elements in order of increasing proton number. (1)

**b)** Put these five elements in order of increasing relative atomic mass. (1)

**c)** The orders of proton number and relative atomic mass for these five elements are different. Which one of the following is the most likely explanation for this?

A  The proton number of a particular element may vary.

B  The presence of neutrons

C  The atoms easily gain or lose electrons.

D  The number of protons must always equal the number of neutrons. (1)

**d)** Which of the five elements in the list are in the same group of the Periodic Table? (1)

**e) i)**  From the list, choose one element that has one electron in its outer shell. (1)

   **ii)** From the list, choose one element that has a full outer shell of electrons. (1)

**f)** Which two of the following statements about argon are correct?

A  Argon is a noble gas.

B  Argon reacts readily with potassium.

C  Argon is used to fill weather balloons.

D  Argon is used in light bulbs. (2)

**(Total 8 marks)**

## Question 8

The table gives some information about the elements in Group I of the Periodic Table.

| Element | Boiling point (°C) | Density (g/cm³) | Radius of atom in the metal (nm) | Reactivity with water |
|---------|---------|---------|---------|---------|
| Lithium | 1342 | 0.53 | 0.157 | |
| Sodium | 883 | 0.97 | 0.191 | Rapid |
| Potassium | 760 | 0.86 | 0.235 | Very rapid |
| Rubidium | | 1.53 | 0.250 | Extremely rapid |
| Caesium | 669 | 1.88 | | Explosive |

**a)** How does the density of the Group I elements change going down the group?  (2)

**b)** Suggest a value for the boiling point of rubidium.  (1)

**c)** Suggest a value for the radius of a caesium atom.  (1)

**d)** Use the information in the table to suggest how fast lithium reacts with water compared with the other Group I metals.  (1)

**e)** State three properties shown by all metals.  (3)

**f)** When sodium reacts with water, hydrogen is given off:

$2Na(s) + 2H_2O(l) \rightarrow 2NaOH(aq) + H_2(g)$

**i)** State the name of the other product formed in this reaction.  (1)

**ii)** Describe a test for hydrogen.  (2)

**g)** The diagrams show three types of hydrogen atom.

**i)** State the name of the positively charged particle in the nucleus.  (1)

**ii)** What is the name given to atoms with the same number of positive charges in the nucleus but different numbers of neutrons?  (1)

**iii)** State the number of nucleons in a single atom of tritium.  (1)

**iv)** Tritium is a radioactive form of hydrogen. State one medical use of radioactivity.  (1)

(Total 15 marks)

Organic chemistry is distinct from other branches of chemistry, such as inorganic and physical chemistry. It may be described as the chemistry of living processes (often referred to as biochemistry) but extends beyond that. Organic chemistry focuses almost entirely on the chemistry of covalently bonded carbon molecules. As well as life processes, it includes the chemistry of other types of compounds including plastics, petrochemicals, drugs and paint.

Early chemists never imagined that complex chemicals of living processes could ever be manufactured in a laboratory, but they were wrong. Today medical drugs can be made and then their structures modified to achieve improvements in their effectiveness.

An understanding of organic chemistry begins with knowledge of the structure of a carbon atom and how it can combine with other carbon atoms by forming covalent bonds. In this section you will be introduced to a few of the 'families' or series of organic compounds. This knowledge will provide a sound basis for further work in chemistry or biology.

## STARTING POINTS

1. Where is carbon in the Periodic Table of elements?

   What can you work out about carbon from its position?

2. What is the atomic structure of carbon? How are its electrons arranged?

3. How does carbon form covalent bonds? Show the bonding in methane ($CH_4$), the simplest of organic molecules?

4. You will be learning about a series of organic compounds which are hydrocarbons. What do you think a hydrocarbon is?

5. You will be learning about methane. Where can methane be found and what it is used for?

6. You will also be learning about ethanol, which belongs to a particular series of organic compounds. Do you know where you could find ethanol in everyday products?

## SECTION CONTENTS

a) Fuels

b) Alkanes

c) Alkenes

d) Alcohols

e) Acids

f) Macromolecules

g) Exam-style questions

# 4
# Organic chemistry

△ Oil rigs are used to extract hydrocarbons from the Earth.

# Fuels

## INTRODUCTION

The most common fuels used today are either fossil fuels or are made from fossil fuels. There are problems associated with using fossil fuels – burning them produces a number of polluting gases and releases carbon dioxide, a greenhouse gas. Nevertheless, fossil fuels are a very important source of energy.

Δ Fig. 4.1 Crude oil contains a mixture of hydrocarbons.

### KNOWLEDGE CHECK

✓ Know that the burning of fossil fuels produces carbon dioxide, a greenhouse gas.
✓ Know that burning some fossil fuels can also produce pollutant gases such as sulfur dioxide and nitrogen oxides.
✓ Know that there are alternative energy sources to fossil fuels.

### LEARNING OBJECTIVES

✓ Know the fuels coal, natural gas and petroleum (crude oil).
✓ Know that methane is the main constituent of natural gas.
✓ Be able to describe petroleum as a mixture of hydrocarbons and its separation into useful fractions by fractional distillation.
✓ Be able to describe the properties of molecules within a fraction.
✓ Know the uses of the fractions obtained from petroleum.

## WHAT ARE FOSSIL FUELS?

Petroleum (crude oil), natural gas (mainly methane) and coal are **fossil fuels**.

Crude oil was formed millions of years ago from the remains of animals and plants that were pressed together under layers of rock. It is usually found deep underground, trapped between layers of rock that it can't seep through (impermeable rock). Natural gas is often trapped in pockets above crude oil.

The supply of fossil fuels is limited – having taken millions of years to form, these fuels will eventually run out. They are called finite or **non-renewable** fuels. This makes them an extremely valuable resource that must be used efficiently.

Fossil fuels contain many useful chemicals (known as **fractions**) and these must be separated so that they are not wasted.

△ Fig. 4.2 Fractional distillation takes place in oil refineries, like this one in the Netherlands.

## FRACTIONAL DISTILLATION

The chemicals in petroleum are separated into useful fractions by a process known as **fractional distillation**.

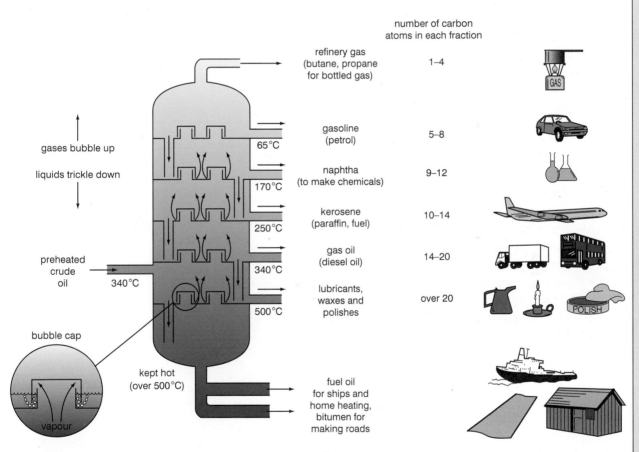

△ Fig. 4.3 A fractionating column converts crude oil into many useful fractions.

The crude oil is heated in a furnace and passed into the bottom of a fractionating column. It gives off a mixture of vapours that rise up the column, and the different fractions condense out at different heights. The fractions that come off near the top are light-coloured, runny liquids. Those removed near the bottom of the column are dark and sticky. Thick liquids that are not runny, such as these at the bottom of the fractionating column, are described as **viscous**.

## How does fractional distillation work?

The components of petroleum separate because they have different boiling points. A simple particle model explains why their boiling points differ. Petroleum is a mixture of **hydrocarbon** molecules, which contain only carbon and hydrogen. The molecules are chemically bonded in similar ways with strong covalent bonds but contain different numbers of carbon atoms.

△ Fig. 4.4 Octane has one more carbon atom and two more hydrogen atoms than heptane. Their formulae differ by $CH_2$.

### REMEMBER

The longer the molecule, the stronger the attractive force between the molecules.

The weak attractive forces between the molecules must be broken for the hydrocarbon to boil. The longer a hydrocarbon molecule is, the stronger the intermolecular forces between the molecules. The stronger these forces of attraction, the higher the boiling point because more energy is needed to overcome the forces.

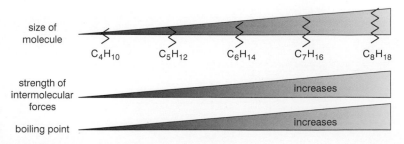

△ Fig. 4.5 How the properties of hydrocarbons change as molecules get longer.

The smaller-molecule hydrocarbons are more **volatile** – they form a vapour easily. For example, we can smell petrol (with molecules containing between 5 and 10 carbon atoms) much more easily than we can smell engine oil (with molecules containing between 14 and 20 carbon atoms) because petrol is more volatile.

Another difference between the fractions is how easily they burn and how smoky their flames are.

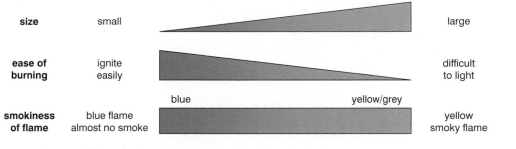

△ Fig. 4.6 How different hydrocarbons burn.

## QUESTIONS

1. Petroleum is a 'non-renewable' fuel. What does this mean?

2. When drilling for oil, there is often excess gas to be burned off. What is this gas? Where does it come from?

3. One of the oil fractions obtained from the fractional distillation of crude oil is light-coloured and runny.

   Is this fraction more likely to have a small chain of carbon atoms or a long chain?

4. Another of the oil fractions obtained from the fractional distillation of petroleum burns with a very sooty yellow flame.

   Is this fraction more likely to have a small chain of carbon atoms or a long chain?

5. Some fractions obtained from petroleum are very 'volatile'. What does this mean?

## CRACKING THE OIL FRACTIONS

The composition of petroleum varies in different parts of the world. Table 4.1 shows the composition of a sample of petroleum from the Middle East after fractional distillation.

| Fraction (in order of increasing boiling point) | Typical percentage produced by fractional distillation |
|---|---|
| Liquefied petroleum gases (LPG) | 3 |
| Gasoline | 13 |
| Naphtha | 9 |
| Kerosene | 12 |
| Diesel | 14 |
| Heavy oils and bitumen | 49 |

△ Table 4.1 Oil fractions.

Small molecules are much more useful than the larger molecules. Larger molecules can be broken down into smaller ones by **catalytic cracking**. This requires a high temperature of between 600 to 700 °C and a catalyst of silica or alumina.

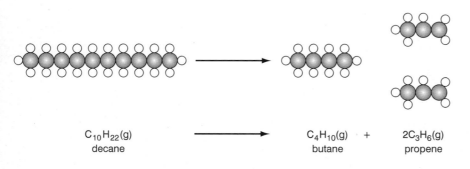

$$C_{10}H_{22}(g) \longrightarrow C_4H_{10}(g) \quad + \quad 2C_3H_6(g)$$
decane → butane + propene

△ Fig. 4.7 The decane molecule ($C_{10}H_{22}$) is converted into the smaller molecules butane ($C_4H_{10}$) and propene ($C_3H_6$) in cracking.

The butane and propene formed in this example have different types of structures.

### REMEMBER

Propene belongs to a family of hydrocarbons called **alkenes**.

Alkenes are much more reactive (and hence useful) than hydrocarbons like decane (an alkane).

# Developing Investigative Skills

A group of students set up an experiment to see if they could 'crack' some liquid paraffin. They soaked some mineral wool in liquid paraffin and assembled the apparatus as shown in Fig. 4.8. They then heated the pottery pieces very strongly, occasionally letting the flame heat the mineral wool. Bubbles of gas started to collect in the test tube. After a few minutes they had collected three test tubes full of gas and so they stopped heating. Almost immediately, water from the trough started to travel back up the delivery tube towards the boiling tube.

△ Fig. 4.8 Incorrectly set up apparatus for experiment.

## Evaluating methods

❶ The gas or gases produced in this reaction can be collected by displacement of water. What property of gas(es) does this demonstrate?

❷ Why did the water start to travel back up the delivery tube when heating was stopped?

## Using and organising techniques, apparatus and materials

❸ What are the hazards involved in this experiment? What safety precautions would minimise them?

❹ The first test tube of gas collected did not burn, but the second one did. Explain this difference.

❺ The third test tube of gas decolourised bromine water. What does this suggest about the gas present?

## Interpreting observations and data

❻ One of the students suggested that one of the two products was ethene ($C_2H_4$). Assuming that liquid paraffin has the formula $C_{14}H_{30}$, write an equation for the cracking of the liquid paraffin used in this experiment.

1. The cracking of hydrocarbons often produces ethene. To which homologous series does ethene belong?

2. Why is cracking needed in addition to the fractional distillation of crude oil?

3. What conditions are needed for the cracking of oil fractions?

---

**SCIENCE IN CONTEXT**

## THE FOSSIL FUEL DILEMMA

There is widespread agreement that supplies of the non- renewable fossil fuels – oil, gas and coal – will eventually run out. However, it is not easy to estimate exactly when they will run out. Many different factors need to be considered, including how much of each deposit is left in the Earth, how fast we are using each fossil fuel at the moment, whether or not countries that have supplies will sell to those that don't, and how this is likely to change in the future. If we start switching to alternative fuel sources that are renewable, the reserves that we currently have will last longer.

Current estimates suggest that crude oil (petroleum) will run out between 2025 and 2070. The estimate for natural gas is similar, with 2060 a possible date.

△ Fig. 4.9 A coal-fired power station.

The situation with coal is very different. Most coal deposits have not yet been tapped, and the decline of the coal mining industry in countries such as the UK means that many coal seams are lying undisturbed. If we carry on using coal at the same rate as we do today, there could be enough to last well over a thousand years. However, as other fossil fuels run out, particularly oil, the use of coal may increase, reducing that timespan considerably.

So should we increase our efforts to develop renewable forms of energy such as wind and solar energy; should we put greater emphasis on nuclear power; or should we plan to make much greater use of coal? Perhaps we should do all three? Solving this dilemma is likely to depend as much on political decisions as scientific ones. What would you recommend?

# End of topic checklist

## Key terms

alkene, catalytic cracking, fraction, fractional distillation, fossil fuel, hydrocarbon, non-renewable, viscous, volatile

## During your study of this topic you should have learned:

◯ About the fuels coal, natural gas and petroleum (crude oil).

◯ That methane is the main constituent of natural gas.

◯ How to describe petroleum as a mixture of hydrocarbons and its separation into useful fractions by fractional distillation.

◯ How to describe the properties of molecules within a fraction.

◯ About the uses of the following fractions obtained from petroleum:

- refinery gas for bottled gas for heating and cooking
- gasoline fraction for fuel (petrol) in cars
- naphtha fraction for making chemicals
- kerosene/paraffin fraction for jet fuel
- diesel/gas oil for fuel in diesel engines
- fuel oil fraction for fuel for ships and home heating systems
- lubricating fraction for lubricants, waxes and polishes
- bitumen for making roads.

# End of topic questions

*Note: The marks awarded for these questions indicate the level of detail required in the answers. In the examination, the number of marks awarded to questions like these may be different.*

**1. a)** How was crude oil (petroleum) formed? **(2 marks)**

  **b)** Why is crude oil called a 'non-renewable' fuel? **(1 mark)**

**2.** The diagram shows a column used to separate the components present in petroleum.

  **a)** Name the process used to separate petroleum into fractions. **(1 mark)**

  **b)** What happens to the boiling point of the mixture as it goes up the column? **(1 mark)**

  **c)** The mixture of vapours arrives at level X. What now happens to the various parts of the mixture? **(2 marks)**

**3.** The cracking of decane molecules is shown by the equation $C_{10}H_{22} \rightarrow Y + C_2H_4$.

  **a)** Decane is a *hydrocarbon*. What is a hydrocarbon? **(1 mark)**

  **b)** What reaction conditions are needed for cracking? **(2 marks)**

  **c)** Write down the molecular formula for hydrocarbon Y. **(1 mark)**

  **d)** What 'family' does hydrocarbon Y belong to? **(1 mark)**

  **e)** Why is the cracking of petroleum fractions so important? **(2 marks)**

**4.** Petrol is a hydrocarbon with a formula of $C_8H_{18}$.

**a)** What are the products formed when petrol burns in a plentiful supply of air? **(2 marks)**

**b)** Write a balanced equation, including state symbols, for the reaction when petrol burns in a plentiful supply of air. **(2 marks)**

**c)** When petrol is burned in a car engine, carbon monoxide may be formed. Explain why carbon monoxide is dangerous. **(2 marks)**

# Alkanes

## INTRODUCTION

Alkanes are the simplest family or homologous **series** of **organic molecules**. The first alkane, methane, is the major component of natural gas, a common fossil fuel. Other alkanes are obtained from petroleum and are widely used as fuels.

Δ Fig. 4.10 Natural gas is being extracted from beneath the ocean floor.

## WHAT ARE ALKANES?

**Alkanes** are **hydrocarbons**, which are molecules that contain only carbon and hydrogen atoms. They are made up of carbon atoms linked together by only single covalent bonds and are known as **saturated hydrocarbons**.

Many alkanes are obtained from crude oil by fractional distillation. The smallest alkanes are used extensively as fuels. Apart from burning, however, they are remarkably unreactive.

| Alkane | Molecular formula | Displayed formula | Boiling point (°C) | State at room temperature and pressure |
|--------|-------------------|-------------------|--------------------|-----------------------------------------|
| Methane | $CH_4$ | H<br>\|<br>H—C—H<br>\|<br>H | −162 | Gas |
| Ethane | $C_2H_6$ | H H<br>\| \|<br>H—C—C—H<br>\| \|<br>H H | −89 | Gas |
| Propane | $C_3H_8$ | H H H<br>\| \| \|<br>H—C—C—C—H<br>\| \| \|<br>H H H | −42 | Gas |
| Butane | $C_4H_{10}$ | H H H H<br>\| \| \| \|<br>H—C—C—C—C—H<br>\| \| \| \|<br>H H H H | 0 | Gas |
| Pentane | $C_5H_{12}$ | H H H H H<br>\| \| \| \| \|<br>H—C—C—C—C—C—H<br>\| \| \| \| \|<br>H H H H H | 36 | Liquid |

△ Table 4.2 Alkanes and their molecular structure.

## HOMOLOGOUS SERIES

Alkanes form a **homologous series**. Members of a homologous series have similar chemical properties.

They contain the same **functional group** (the part of the molecule that is responsible for the similar chemical properties) – in this case, the functional group is a C–H single bond.

EXTENDED

The general characteristics of an homologous series include:

- They have the same general formula. For alkanes this is $C_nH_{2n+2}$.
- They have similar chemical properties.
- They show a gradual change in physical properties, such as melting point and boiling point.
- They differ from the previous member of the series by $-CH_2-$.

△ Fig. 4.11 Formula 1 cars use specially blended mixtures of alkane hydrocarbons.

END OF EXTENDED

## THE PROPERTIES OF ALKANES

The properties of alkanes are given in Table 4.3.

|  | **Properties of Alkanes** |
| --- | --- |
| **General formula** | $C_nH_{2n+2}$ |
| **Description** | Saturated (no double C=C bond) |
| **Combustion** | Burn in oxygen to form $CO_2$ and $H_2O$ (CO if limited supply of oxygen) |
| **Reactivity** | Low |
| **Chemical test** | None |
| **Uses** | Fuels |

△ Table 4.3 Properties of alkanes.

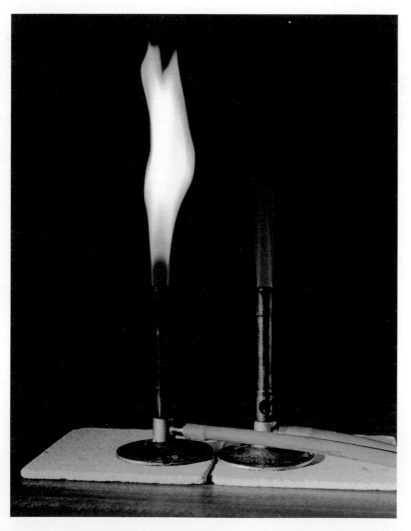

△ Fig. 4.12 Methane is burning in the oxygen in the air to form carbon dioxide and water.

1. Alkanes are saturated hydrocarbons.

   a) What is meant by the word *saturated*?

   b) What is meant by the word *hydrocarbon*?

2. a) What is the chemical formula for the alkane with 15 carbon atoms?

   b) What products would you expect to be formed if this alkane were burned in a plentiful supply of oxygen?

## Combustion of alkanes

In a plentiful supply of air, alkanes burn to form carbon dioxide and water. A blue flame, as produced by a Bunsen burner, indicates complete combustion:

| methane | + | oxygen | → | carbon dioxide | + | water |
|---|---|---|---|---|---|---|
| $CH_4(g)$ | + | $2O_2(g)$ | → | $CO_2(g)$ | + | $2H_2O(l)$ |

When the oxygen supply is limited, as when a Bunsen burner burns with a yellow flame, incomplete combustion occurs:

| methane | + | oxygen | → | carbon | + | water |
|---|---|---|---|---|---|---|
| $CH_4(g)$ | + | $O_2(g)$ | → | $C(s)$ | + | $2H_2O(l)$ |

The incomplete combustion of hydrocarbons such as methane can be very dangerous. It can produce carbon monoxide, which is extremely poisonous.

| methane | + | oxygen | → | carbon monoxide | + | water |
|---|---|---|---|---|---|---|
| $2CH_4(g)$ | + | $3O_2(g)$ | → | $2CO(g)$ | + | $4H_2O(l)$ |

Carbon monoxide is difficult to detect without special equipment, because it has no colour or smell. Gas and oil heaters or boilers must be serviced regularly. This is to ensure that jets do not become blocked and limit the air supply, or that exhaust flues don't become blocked and allow small quantities of carbon monoxide to enter the room. The flame in such a boiler or heater should always be blue in colour.

△ Fig. 4.13 The gas in this cooker is burning completely.

## THE REACTION OF METHANE WITH CHLORINE

When methane reacts with chlorine in the presence of ultraviolet light, a **substitution** reaction occurs and chloromethane is formed.

| methane | + | chlorine | $\rightarrow$ | chloromethane | + | hydrogen chloride |
|---------|---|----------|---------------|---------------|---|-------------------|
| $CH_4(g)$ | + | $Cl_2(g)$ | $\rightarrow$ | $CH_3Cl(g)$ | + | $HCl(g)$ |

If there is too much chlorine, substitution will continue forming dichloromethane ($CH_2Cl_2$), trichlomethane ($CHCl_3$) and tetrachloromethane ($CCl_4$).

**END OF EXTENDED**

## QUESTIONS

1. How can you tell if a fuel is burning without enough oxygen?
2. Name two products that can form when methane burns in an insufficient supply of oxygen.
3. How does carbon monoxide act as a poison?
4. Suggest some alternative ways of generating electricity that do not involve burning fossil fuels.

## ISOMERISM

The names of hydrocarbons are based on the number of carbon atoms in their molecules. The first part of the name tells you the number of carbon atoms, for example 'meth-' (from methane) has one carbon atom, 'eth-' (from ethane) has two carbon atoms, 'prop-' (from propane) has three carbon atoms, and so on.

△ Fig. 4.14 The bonding and structure of octane.

The carbon atoms in a hydrocarbon molecule can be arranged in different ways. For example, in butane ($C_4H_{10}$) the carbon atoms can be positioned in two ways, while keeping the same molecular formula:

△ Fig. 4.15 Isomers of $C_4H_{10}$.

An **isomer** is a compound with the same molecular formula but different structures to one or more other compounds.

2-methylpropane is a **structural isomer** (same atoms but rearranged) of butane, which has a longer chain of carbon atoms. This feature of alkane structure is called *structural isomerism*. The number '2' in 2-methylpropane tells you which carbon atom the branch attaches to.

Table 4.4 shows the three isomers of the alkane $C_5H_{12}$.

| Isomer | Pentane | 2-methylbutane | 2,2-dimethylpropane |
|---|---|---|---|
| Structure | | | |
| Boiling point (°C) | 36 | 27 | 11 |

△ Table 4.4 Isomers of pentane.

## QUESTIONS

1. What are *isomers*?

2. Write down the structural formula of hexane, the alkane with six carbon atoms. What is its molecular formula?

3. Draw the structured formulae of two isomers of hexane.

4. Would you expect hexane to be a solid, liquid or gas at room temperature? Explain your answer.

**END OF EXTENDED**

# End of topic checklist

## Key terms

alkane, functional group, homologous series, hydrocarbon, isomer, organic molecules, saturated hydrocarbons, structural isomerism, substitution

## During your study of this topic you should have learned:

○ How to name and draw the structures of methane and ethane and the products of some of their reactors.

○ That a chemical with a name ending in 'ane' is an alkane.

○ How to describe a homologous series as a 'family' of similar compounds with similar properties due to the presence of the same functional group.

○ **EXTENDED** How to describe the general characteristics of a homologous series.

○ **EXTENDED** How to describe and identify structural isomerism.

○ How to describe the properties of alkanes (as shown by methane) as being generally unreactive, except in terms of burning.

○ How to describe the bonding in alkanes.

○ **EXTENDED** How to describe substitution reactions of alkanes with chlorine.

# End of topic questions

*Note: The marks awarded for these questions indicate the level of detail required in the answers. In the examination, the number of marks awarded to questions like these may be different.*

**1.** What is a *homologous series*? (1 mark)

**2.** What is the molecular formula for an alkane with 10 carbon atoms? (1 mark)

**3.** Is the compound with the formula $C_{15}H_{30}$ a member of the alkane series? Explain your answer. (1 mark)

**4.** Ethane burns in oxygen.

   **a)** What is the molecular formula of ethane? (1 mark)

   **b)** Name the products formed when ethane burns in excess oxygen. (2 marks)

   **c)** What colour flame would indicate that the ethane was burning in excess oxygen? (1 mark)

   **d)** Write a balanced equation for the reaction. (2 marks)

   **e)** Name two additional products that could be formed if the oxygen supply was limited. (2 marks)

   **f)** What colour flame would indicate that the ethane was burning in a limited supply of oxygen? (1 mark)

**5.** EXTENDED What is *structural isomerism*? (1 mark)

**6.** EXTENDED **a)** Draw a structural formula for octane, an alkane with 8 carbon atoms. (1 mark)

   **b)** Draw a structural formula for another isomer of octane. (1 mark)

   **c)** What will be the physical state of octane at room temperature and pressure? (1 mark)

   **d)** Is octane a saturated or an unsaturated hydrocarbon? Explain your answer. (1 mark)

**7.** EXTENDED Methane will react with bromine.

   **a)** What type of reaction is this? (1 mark)

   **b)** What reaction conditions are needed? (1 mark)

   **c)** What is the name of the product formed? (1 mark)

# Alkenes

## INTRODUCTION

Alkenes are hydrocarbons and burn in air in the same way that alkanes do. However, alkenes are much more reactive due to the C=C double bond they contain. This makes them very useful starting materials for a number of important industrial processes, including the manufacture of synthetic polymers and margarine.

Δ Fig. 4.16 The plastic objects above are made from alkenes.

## KNOWLEDGE CHECK

✓ Understand the sharing of electrons in a double covalent bond.
✓ Know the typical physical properties of compounds that exist as simple molecules.
✓ Know the simple properties of alkanes.

## LEARNING OBJECTIVES

✓ Be able to name and draw the structures of ethene and the products of some of their reactions.
✓ Know that a chemical with a name ending in -ene is an alkene.
✓ Be able to describe the manufacture of alkenes by cracking.
✓ Be able to distinguish between saturated and unsaturated hydrocarbons from their molecular structures and by their reaction with aqueous bromine.
✓ Be able to describe the formation of poly(ethene) as an example of addition polymerisation of monomer units.
✓ **EXTENDED** Be able to describe the properties of alkenes in terms of addition reactions with bromine, hydrogen and steam.

## WHAT ARE ALKENES?

**Alkenes** are another homologous series, so they have similar chemical properties and physical properties that change gradually from one member to the next.

Alkenes are often formed by the catalytic cracking of larger hydrocarbons. Hydrogen is also formed in this process. Alkenes contain one or more carbon-to-carbon double bonds. Hydrocarbons with at least one double bond are known as **unsaturated** hydrocarbons. Alkenes burn

| Alkene | Molecular formula | Structural formula | Boiling point (°C) | State at room temperature and pressure |
|---|---|---|---|---|
| Ethene | $C_2H_4$ | ethene $\overset{H}{\underset{H}{\diagdown}} C = C \overset{H}{\underset{H}{\diagup}}$ | −104 | Gas |
| Propene | $C_3H_6$ | propene or | −48 | Gas |
| Butene | $C_4H_8$ | butene $H-C-C-C=C$ | −6 | Gas |
| Pentene | $C_5H_{10}$ | pentene $H-C-C-C-C=C$ | 30 | Liquid |

△ Table 4.5 Structure and state of alkenes.

well and are reactive in other ways also. Their reactivity is due to the carbon-to-carbon double bond.

A simple test to distinguish alkenes from alkanes, or an unsaturated hydrocarbon from a saturated one, is to add bromine water to the hydrocarbon. Alkanes do not react with bromine water, so the colour does not change. An alkene does react with the bromine, and the bromine water loses its colour.

EXTENDED

The type of reaction is known as an **addition reaction**:

△ Fig. 4.17 The reaction of ethene and bromine water.

The bromine molecule ($Br_2$) splits and the two bromine atoms add on to the carbon atoms on either side of the double bond.

END OF EXTENDED

Ethene can also form poly(ethene) or polythene in an addition reaction, a process known as addition **polymerisation**. Ethene is the monomer and reacts with other ethene monomers to form an addition **polymer**, poly(ethene). Further information about this reaction is included in the *Macromolecules* topic.

EXTENDED

Ethene undergoes other addition reactions. It reacts with bromine in a similar way to its reaction with bromine water, forming 1,2-dibromoethane. It also reacts with hydrogen to form ethane:

△ Fig. 4.18 Ethene reacts with hydrogen to form ethane.

$$C_2H_4(g) + H_2(g) \rightarrow C_2H_6(g)$$

Ethene also reacts with steam to form ethanol, a reaction that is used in the manufacture of ethanol.

ethene     +     steam     $\xrightarrow[\text{phosphoric acid as catalyst}]{300\,°C,\ 70\ atm}$     ethanol

△ Fig. 4.19 Ethene reacts with steam to form ethanol.

END OF EXTENDED

|  | **Properties of alkenes** |
|---|---|
| **General formula** | $C_nH_{2n}$ |
| **Description** | Unsaturated (contain a double C=C bond) |
| **Combustion** | Burn in oxygen to form $CO_2$ and $H_2O$ (CO if limited supply of oxygen) |
| **Reactivity** | High (because of the double C=C bonds); undergo addition reactions |
| **Chemical test** | Turn bromine water from orange to colourless (an addition reaction) |
| **Uses** | Making polymers (addition reactions) such as polyethene |

△ Table 4.6 Properties of alkenes.

Alkenes can also form isomers.

For example, the isomers of butene ($C_4H_8$) are:

but-1-ene                                    but-2-ene

△ Fig. 4.20 But-1-ene and but-2-ene.

**END OF EXTENDED**

## QUESTIONS

**1.** Ethene is an unsaturated hydrocarbon. What does *unsaturated* mean?

**2.** Name a large-scale use of ethene.

**3.** EXTENDED Draw two isomers of pentene.

---

**SCIENCE IN CONTEXT**

### SATURATED AND UNSATURATED FATS

We all need some **fat** in our diet because it helps the body to absorb certain nutrients. Fat is also a source of energy and provides essential fatty acids. However, it is best to keep the amount of fat we eat at sensible levels and to eat unsaturated fats rather than saturated fats whenever possible. A diet high in saturated fat can cause the level of cholesterol in the blood to build up over time. Raised cholesterol levels increase the risk of heart disease.

Foods high in saturated fat include:

- fatty cuts of meat
- meat products and pies
- butter
- cheese, especially hard cheese
- cream and ice cream
- biscuits and cakes.

Unsaturated fat is found in:

- oily fish such as salmon, tuna and mackerel
- avocados
- nuts and seeds
- sunflower and olive oils.

So having a carbon-to-carbon double bond does make a difference.

△ Fig. 4.21 Margarine is made from olive oil, whose unsaturated molecules have been saturated with hydrogen.

Most of the compounds discovered in the world today are organic. There are many of these due to the ability of carbon to form different types of bonds. Alkanes and alkenes are just two examples of homologous series of compounds from the vast number of organic compounds known to date. Use your knowledge of basic organic chemistry to answer the following questions.

## QUESTIONS

1. Alkanes have a general formula $C_nH_{2n+2}$ and alkenes $C_nH_{2n}$. When $n = 5$ the alkane formed is pentane and the alkene is pentene.

   a) Alkanes and alkenes are both hydrocarbons. State why alkanes are called *saturated* hydrocarbons whereas alkenes are *unsaturated*.

   b) Give the formula for the alkane and the alkene where $n = 6$ (hexane and hexene). Draw displayed formulae for hexane and hexene and label the different types of bonds.

   c) Hexene can have a number of isomers. Draw an isomer of hexene and suggest a name for it.

   d) Although both these compounds have six carbon atoms, they undergo different types of reactions with bromine. Name the type of reactions that hexane and hexene will undergo with bromine and draw one product for each reaction. (Hint: hexane reacts with bromine in the same way as it does with chlorine.)

2. These questions are based on combustion reactions.

   a) Alkanes are useful as fuels. What is the reason for this?

   b) Explain why incomplete combustion can be dangerous if the products of this type of combustion are inhaled.

   c) Describe how the products of combustion of a short-chain hydrocarbon differ from those of a long-chain hydrocarbon.

# End of topic checklist

## Key terms

addition reaction, alkene, fats, polymer, polymerisation, unsaturated

## During your study of this topic you should have learned:

○ How to name and draw the structure of ethene and the products of some of its reactions.

○ That a chemical with a name ending in -ene is an alkene.

○ How to describe the manufacture of alkenes by cracking.

○ How to distinguish between saturated and unsaturated hydrocarbons:

- from their molecular structures
- by reaction with aqueous bromine.

○ How to describe the formation of poly(ethene) as an example of addition polymerisation of monomer units.

○ **EXTENDED** How to describe the properties of alkenes in terms of addition reactions with:

- bromine
- hydrogen
- steam.

# End of topic questions

*Note: The marks awarded for these questions indicate the level of detail required in the answers. In the examination, the number of marks awarded to questions like these may be different.*

1. Ethene burns in oxygen.

   a) Name the products formed when there is a plentiful supply of oxygen. (2 marks)

   b) i) Write a balanced equation for the burning of ethene in a plentiful supply of oxygen. (2 marks)

      ii) What colour would the flame be? (1 mark)

   c) When ethene is burned in a limited supply of air, carbon and water are formed.

      i) Write a balanced equation for this reaction. (2 marks)

      ii) What colour would the flame be? (1 mark)

2. a) Draw structural formulae for butane and butene. (2 marks)

   b) Which hydrocarbon is unsaturated? (1 mark)

   c) Which substance could you use to distinguish between butane and butene? (1 mark)

3. Propene gas is bubbled through some bromine water.

   a) Describe the colour change that would occur. (2 marks)

   b) Write a balanced equation for this reaction. (2 marks)

   c) What type of chemical reaction is this an example of? (1 mark)

4. Which type of fat is recommended for a healthy diet – a saturated fats or unsaturated fats? (1 mark)

5. EXTENDED A hydrocarbon has the formula $C_7H_{14}$.

   a) Is the hydrocarbon saturated or unsaturated? Explain your answer. (1 mark)

   b) What is the name of the hydrocarbon? (1 mark)

   c) Draw structural formulae of two different isomers of this hydrocarbon. (2 marks)

6. EXTENDED Octene is an alkene.

   a) Write down the molecular formula of octene. (1 mark)

   b) What state of matter will octene exist in at room temperature and pressure? Explain your answer. (1 mark)

# Alcohols

## INTRODUCTION

Ethanol, or common alcohol, belongs to a homologous series known as the alcohols. There are many more uses for ethanol than for other alcohols, and so its manufacture is very important. Ethanol is produced by a 'natural' method starting with sugar, and by a 'synthetic' method starting with a product of petroleum.

△ Fig. 4.22 The ethanol being made here could be used in alcoholic drinks or as a fuel in cars.

## KNOWLEDGE CHECK

✓ Understand the term homologous series.
✓ Know the typical physical properties of compounds that exist as simple molecules.
✓ Know what products are formed when hydrocarbons are burned.

## LEARNING OBJECTIVES

✓ Be able to name and draw the structure of ethanol and the products of some of its reactions.
✓ Know that a chemical with a name ending in -ol is an alcohol.
✓ **EXTENDED** Know the unbranched alcohols containing up to four carbon atoms per molecule and their structure.
✓ Be able to describe the properties of ethanol in terms of burning.
✓ Be able to name the uses of ethanol as a solvent and as a fuel.
✓ Be able to describe the manufacture of ethanol by fermentation and by the catalytic addition of steam to ethene.
✓ **EXTENDED** Be able to outline the advantages and disadvantages of the two methods of manufacturing ethanol.

## WHAT ARE ALCOHOLS?

**Alcohols** are molecules that contain the OH **functional group**, which is responsible for their properties and reactions.

Alcohols have the general formula $C_nH_{2n+1}OH$ and belong to the same homologous series, part of which is shown in Table 4.7.

| Alcohol | Formula | Structural formula | Boiling point (°C) |
|---------|---------|--------------------|--------------------|
| Methanol | $CH_3OH$ | H<br>\|<br>H—C—OH<br>\|<br>H | 65 |
| Ethanol | $C_2H_5OH$ | H  H<br>\|   \|<br>H—C—C—OH<br>\|   \|<br>H  H | 78 |
| Propanol | $C_3H_7OH$ | H  H  H<br>\|   \|   \|<br>H—C—C—C—OH<br>\|   \|   \|<br>H  H  H | 97 |
| Butanol | $C_4H_9OH$ | H  H  H  H<br>\|   \|   \|   \|<br>H—C—C—C—C—OH<br>\|   \|   \|   \|<br>H  H  H  H | 118 |

△ Table 4.7 The first three alcohols.

**EXTENDED**

Alcohols form structural isomers depending on where the OH group is placed on the carbon chain. For example:

propan-1-ol

H  H  H
\|   \|   \|
H—C—C—C—OH
\|   \|   \|
H  H  H

propan-2-ol

H  OH  H
\|   \|   \|
H—C—C—C—H
\|   \|   \|
H  H  H

△ Fig. 4.23 Propan-1-ol and propan-2-ol.

**END OF EXTENDED**

Ethanol burns readily in air to form carbon dioxide and water:

Ethanol   +   oxygen   →   carbon dioxide   +   water

$C_2H_5OH(l)$   +   $3O_2(g)$   →   $2CO_2(g)$   +   $3H_2O(l)$

## Ethanol – the most common alcohol

Ethanol, commonly just called 'alcohol', is the most widely used of the alcohol family. Its major uses are given in Table 4.8.

| Use of ethanol | Reason |
|---|---|
| Solvent – such as in disinfectants and perfumes | The OH group allows it to dissolve in water, and it dissolves other organic compounds. |
| Fuel – such as for cars | It only releases $CO_2$ and $H_2O$ into the environment, not other pollutant gases as from petrol. It is a renewable resource because it comes from plants, for example sugar beet and sugar cane. |
| Alcoholic drinks – such as wine, beer, spirits | In ancient times, fermented drinks were sometimes considered safer than polluted water supplies. However, alcohol affects the brain. It is a depressant, so it slows reactions. It is poisonous and can damage the liver and other organs. |

△ Table 4.8 Uses of ethanol.

△ Fig. 4.24 Brazilians use *alcool* as vehicle fuel. It is made from the fermented and distilled juice of sugar cane.

## QUESTIONS

1. What would be the formula of the alcohol butanol, which has four carbon atoms?

2. What are the advantages of using ethanol as a fuel in motor cars?

3. Ethanol is commonly used as a *solvent*. What is a solvent?

## Manufacturing ethanol by fermentation

Ethanol is made by **fermentation**. This involves mixing a sugar solution with yeast and maintaining the temperature between 25 and 30 °C. The yeast contains **enzymes**, which catalyse (speed up) the breaking down of the sugar. Enzymes are not effective if the temperature is too low, and they are destroyed (denatured) if the temperature is too high.

Fermentation of ethanol takes place in large vats. However, even with the yeast as a catalyst, the process is slow and it takes several days to be completed. As the concentration of the ethanol increases, the activity of the yeast decreases, so eventually fermentation stops.

The balanced equation for fermentation is:

sugar $\xrightarrow{\text{yeast}}$ ethanol $+$ carbon dioxide

$C_6H_{12}O_6(aq) \xrightarrow{\text{yeast}} 2C_2H_5OH(l) + 2CO_2(g)$

The source of the sugar determines the type of alcoholic drink produced – for example, grapes for wine, barley for beer.

Fermentation takes time because it is an enzymic reaction (yeast) and a batch process. After fermentation, a more concentrated solution of alcohol is extracted by fractional distillation. The mixture is boiled and the alcohol vapour reaches the top of the fractionating column, where it condenses back to a liquid.

thermometer

water out

condenser

fractionating column containing glass beads

water in

almost pure ethanol

ethanol + water

heat

Δ Fig. 4.25 Laboratory apparatus for fractional distillation of alcohol. In large-scale manufacture, different equipment would be used but the principles of separation are the same.

## QUESTIONS

**1.** What does *fermentation* mean?

**2.** What is the optimum temperature for fermentation?

**3.** Why is yeast needed in the fermentation process?

**4.** After fermentation is complete, why is fractional distillation used to obtain pure ethanol?

## Developing Investigative Skills:

A group of chemists needed to carry out the fermentation of sugar in the laboratory to make some ethanol for fuel. They set up the apparatus shown in Fig. 4.27. To prevent the oxidation of ethanol to vinegar, the apparatus was set up so that air could not enter flask. At first there seemed to be nothing happening, but by the next morning the reaction had started. When the reaction had finished, the chemists used fractional distillation to obtain some pure alcohol.

reaction flask containing sugar + yeast + water

limewater containing bubbles of $CO_2$

water bath at 25–30°C (the best temperature for the enzymes in yeast to break down sugar molecules).

△ Fig. 4.26 Fermentation apparatus for making ethanol in the laboratory.

### Evaluating methods

❶ How could the chemists have tried to maintain the temperature of the water bath while the reaction was proceeding?

❷ What was the purpose of the limewater?

❸ What would the chemists have observed to indicate that a reaction had started?

❹ How would the chemists know when the reaction was complete?

❺ In the fractional distillation process, which liquid would be collected first – ethanol or water? Explain your answer.

ALCOHOLS

## Manufacturing ethanol from ethene

On an industrial scale, ethanol is also made from ethene, which is obtained from crude oil. This is an example of an addition reaction. The reaction is:

△ Fig. 4.27 Reaction of ethane and steam to make ethanol.

These are quite extreme conditions in terms of energy (300 °C) and specialist plant equipment is required to withstand a pressure of 70 atmospheres, so the process is expensive.

Unlike fermentation, this process is continuous and produces ethanol at a fast rate.

## The choice of method in the manufacture of ethanol

The best method for making ethanol depends on local circumstances: for example, how much sugar cane or crude oil is available.

|  | Advantage | Disadvantage |
|---|---|---|
| **Fermentation** | Uses renewable resources; produces the flavour of alcoholic drinks | Slow 'batch' process; only small amount of ethanol produced |
| **Ethene + steam** | Fast continuous processes; large amounts of ethanol produced | Uses non-renewable resource; flavours have to be added artificially for alcoholic drinks |

△ Table 4.9 Advantages and disadvantages of methods of making ethanol.

# ETHANOL AS A FUEL

The development of ethanol as a fuel for cars has a long history. In the USA, until 1908, cars made by Ford (especially the Model T) used ethanol as a fuel. Now most cars in the USA can run on blends of petrol/ethanol containing up to 10 percent ethanol.

△ Fig. 4.28 In the USA, the ethanol in gasohol is made from corn (maize).

Brazil and the USA are the World's top producers of ethanol. In Brazil about one-fifth of all cars can use 100% ethanol fuel, known as E100; many other cars use petrol/ethanol blends. Brazil makes its ethanol mostly from fermented sugar obtained from sugar cane; in the USA, corn (maize) is used as the source of the sugar. Starting from sugar cane is much more efficient, and so ethanol is much cheaper to produce in Brazil than in the USA.

One problem with using ethanol as a fuel is that it readily absorbs water from the atmosphere. This causes some problems when transporting the fuel and makes it more expensive than petrol to transport.

A key question is, should food be used to make a fuel? Is it better to use fuel made from crude oil? Some people argue that food is needed for people to eat and should not be used to run cars. They say that using so much land for growing sugar cane and corn to make ethanol means that less land is available for growing food. This leads to food shortages and increases in the price of food. What do you think?

# End of topic checklist

## Key terms

alcohol, enzyme, fermentation, fractional distillation, functional group

## During your study of this topic you should have learned:

○ How to name and draw the structure of ethanol and the products of some of its reactions.

○ That a chemical ending in 'ol' is an alcohol.

○ **EXTENDED** The unbranched alcohols containing up to four carbon atoms per molecule and the structures.

○ How to describe the properties of ethanol in terms of burning.

○ About the uses of ethanol as a solvent and as a fuel.

○ How to describe the formation of ethanol by fermentation and by the catalytic addition of steam to ethene.

○ **EXTENDED** How to outline the advantages and disadvantages of the two methods of manufacturing ethanol.

# End of topic questions

*Note: The marks awarded for these questions indicate the level of detail required in the answers. In the examination, the number of marks awarded to questions like these may be different.*

**1.** What is the general formula of an alcohol? **(1 mark)**

**2.** What are the two main sources of sugar used in the manufacture of ethanol by fermentation? **(2 marks)**

**3.** In the laboratory fermentation experiment to make ethanol from sugar using yeast, explain the importance of the following:

**a)** The reaction temperature is kept between the range 25–30 °C. **(2 marks)**

**b)** Oxygen from the air cannot enter the reaction flask. **(2 marks)**

**4.** In the industrial manufacture of ethanol from ethene:

**a)** What is the source of the ethene? **(1 mark)**

**b)** What is the function of the phosphoric acid? **(1 mark)**

**c)** What conditions of temperature and pressure are used? **(2 marks)**

**d)** Write a balanced equation for the reaction. **(1 mark)**

**5.** Ethanol can be produced by fermentation of sugar or from ethene.

**a)** Give one advantage of using the fermentation process. **(1 mark)**

**b)** Give one advantage of using the process involving ethene. **(1 mark)**

**6.** **EXTENDED** Pentanol is an alcohol with five carbon atoms.

**a)** What is the molecular formula of pentanol? **(1 mark)**

**b)** Draw the structural formula of pentanol. **(1 mark)**

**c)** Three of the isomers of pentanol are pentan-1-ol, pentan-2-ol and pentan-3-ol.

**i)** What is an *isomer*? **(1 mark)**

**ii)** Draw the structural formula of pentan-3-ol. **(1 mark)**

# Acids

## INTRODUCTION

The first member of the organic acid (carboxylic acid) homologous series is methanoic acid, which ants produce when they sting an animal or attack another insect. The most common carboxylic acid is ethanoic acid, or acetic acid as it used to be called, which is the main constituent of vinegar. As well as having properties similar to those of common acids such as hydrochloric acid and sulfuric acid, the carboxylic acids have some very different properties.

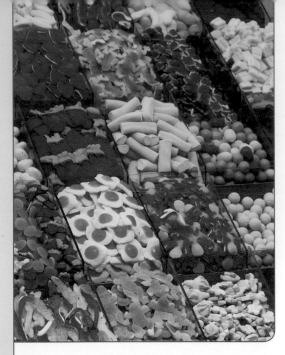

△ Fig. 4.29 Organic acids can be made into esters, which provide the smell and flavour of some sweets.

## KNOWLEDGE CHECK

✓ Understand the term homologous series.
✓ Know some of the typical properties of common acids such as hydrochloric acid and sulfuric acid.

## LEARNING OBJECTIVES

✓ Know that a chemical ending in 'oic' is an acid.
✓ Be able to describe the properties of aqueous ethanoic acid.
✓ **EXTENDED** Be able to describe the formation of ethanoic acid by the oxidation of ethanol.
✓ **EXTENDED** Be able to describe ethanoic acid as a typical weak acid.
✓ **EXTENDED** Be able to describe the reaction of a carboxylic acid with an alcohol in the presence of a catalyst to give an ester.

## EXTENDED

### WHAT ARE ORGANIC ACIDS?

**Carboxylic acids** are molecules that contain the COOH functional group, which is responsible for their properties and reactions. The carboxylic acids have the general formula $C_nH_{2n+1}COOH$ (although $n$ can be equal to zero in the case of methanoic acid).

| Acid | Formula | Structural formula |
|------|---------|---------------------|
| Methanoic acid | HCOOH | $H-C\overset{\displaystyle O}{\underset{\displaystyle OH}{}}$ |
| Ethanoic acid | $CH_3COOH$ | structure of ethanoic acid |
| Propanoic acid | $C_2H_5COOH$ | structure of propanoic acid |
| Butanoic acid | $C_4H_8O_2$ | structure of butanoic acid |

△ Table 4.10 Some common organic acids.

Ethanoic acid is a weak acid because it is only partially ionised when dissolves in water.

$$CH_3COOH(aq) \rightleftharpoons CH_3COO^-(aq) + H^+(aq)$$

## Making ethanoic acid

Ethanoic acid can be made by the oxidation of ethanol. This can happen by accident in the fermentation of sugar if oxygen is allowed to get into the fermenting mixture. Occasionally this process causes wine to taste of vinegar. In the laboratory the oxidation is most easily carried out by heating the ethanol with acidified potassium manganate(VII) solution:

△ Fig. 4.30 Oxidising ethanol to make ethanoic acid.

**END OF EXTENDED**

## The reactions of ethanoic acid

Aqueous ethanoic acid behaves as a typical acid. It has a pH lower than 7 and will react with alkalis and carbonates to form salts. For example, aqueous ethanoic acid will react with sodium carbonate as follows:

△ Fig. 4.31 The reaction of aqueous ethanoic acid with sodium carbonate.

The reaction will not be as vigorous as with dilute hydrochloric acid of the same concentration. Ethanoic acid is a weak acid and has a lower concentration of hydrogen ions, $H^+(aq)$.

## EXTENDED

Ethanoic acid will also react with ethanol, in the presence of concentrated sulfuric acid as a catalyst, to produce an **ester** called ethyl ethanoate. Esters are used extensively as flavourings and have characteristic fruity smells.

ethanoic acid + ethanol ⇌ ethyl ethanoate + water

△ Fig. 4.32 The reaction of ethanoic acid with ethanol.

Other esters can be made from an acid and an alcohol. e.g.

Propanoic acid + propanol ⇌ propyl propanoate + water

Butanoic acid + methanol ⇌ methyl butanoate + water

## END OF EXTENDED

# End of topic checklist

## Key terms

carboxylic acid, ester

## During your study of this topic you should have learned:

○ That a chemical ending in 'oic' is an acid.

○ How to describe the properties of aqueous ethanoic acid.

○ **EXTENDED** How to describe the formation of ethanoic acid by:

  ● the oxidation of ethanol by fermentation
  ● the oxidation of ethanol using acidified potassium manganate(VII).

○ **EXTENDED** How to describe ethanoic acid as a typical weak acid.

○ **EXTENDED** How to describe the reaction of a carboxylic acid with an alcohol in the presence of a catalyst to give an ester.

# End of topic questions

*Note: The marks awarded for these questions indicate the level of detail required in the answers. In the examination, the number of marks awarded for questions like these may be different.*

1. What is the functional group in a carboxylic acid? (1 mark)

2. **a)** What is the name of the carboxylic acid with three carbon atoms in the molecule? (1 mark)

   **b)** Draw the structural formula of this carboxylic acid with three carbon atoms. (1 mark)

3. **a)** What would you observe when solid sodium carbonate is added to an aqueous solution of ethanoic acid? (3 marks)

   **b)** Write a balanced equation for this reaction. (2 marks)

4. **EXTENDED** Explain under what conditions ethanoic acid can be formed during the fermentation of sugar. (2 marks)

5. **EXTENDED** What substance can be used to oxidise ethanol to ethanoic acid in the laboratory? (2 marks)

6. **EXTENDED** Ethanoic acid is a weak acid. Explain what this means. (2 marks)

# Macromolecules

## INTRODUCTION

'Macromolecule' is the term used to describe a very large molecule made up from smaller molecules joined together. The smaller molecules are called monomers and the large molecules (the macromolecules) are usually called polymers. The macromolecules can have different numbers of monomers and have different links or bonds between the monomers. Synthetic polymers are those that are manufactured and some types are often referred to as plastics. Some types of synthetic polymers are used as fabrics and have names such as 'polyester' or 'polyamide'. Other macromolecules occur naturally and include proteins, fats and carbohydrates and are the main constituents of our food.

△ Fig. 4.33 Most tennis rackets have carbon fibre reinforced polymer frames.

**EXTENDED**

## SYNTHETIC POLYMERS

There are two types of synthetic polymers, **addition polymers** and **condensation polymers**.

### Addition polymers

Alkenes can be used to make polymers, which are very large molecules made up of many identical smaller molecules called **monomers**. Alkenes are able to react with themselves. They join together into long chains, like adding beads to a necklace. When the monomers add together like this, the material produced is called an addition polymer. Poly(ethene) or polythene is made this way.

By changing the atoms or groups of atoms attached to the carbon-to-carbon double bond, a range of different polymers can be made.

The double bond within the alkene molecule breaks to form a single covalent bond to a carbon atom in an adjacent molecule. This process is repeated rapidly as the molecules link together.

many small molecules

ethene

catalyst and heat

poly(ethene)

one large molecule

△ Fig. 4.34 Ethene molecules link together to produce a long polymer chain of poly(ethene).

△ Fig. 4.35 Poly(ethene) from ethene.

△ Fig. 4.36 Poly(chloroethene) from chloroethene.

**END OF EXTENDED**

**REMEMBER**

Macromolecules are polymers and are made from monomers. In some cases the polymer is made from just one monomer, in other polymers there are two or more different monomers.

| Name of monomer | Displayed formula of monomer | Name of polymer | Displayed formula of polymer | Uses of polymer |
|---|---|---|---|---|
| Ethene | H H \ / C=C / \ H H | Poly(ethene) | ( H H ) − C − C − ( H H )$_n$ | Buckets, bowls, plastic bags |
| Propene | H H \| \| H−C−C=C / \| \ H H H | Poly(propene) | ( CH$_3$ H ) − C − C − ( H H )$_n$ | Packaging, ropes, carpets |
| Chloroethene (vinyl chloride) | H H \ / C=C / \ Cl H | Poly (chloroethene) (polyvinylchloride) | ( H H ) − C − C − ( Cl H )$_n$ | Plastic sheets, artificial leather |
| Phenylethene (styrene) | H H \ / C=C / \ C$_6$H$_5$ H | Poly (phenylethene) (polystyrene) | ( H H ) − C − C − ( C$_6$H$_5$H )$_n$ | Yoghurt cartons, packaging |
| Tetrafluoroethene | F F \ / C=C / \ F F | Poly (tetrafluroethene) or PTFE | ( F F ) − C − C − ( F F )$_n$ | Non-stick coating in frying pans |

△ Table 4.11 Monomers and their polymers.

△ Fig. 4.37 This pan is coated with PTFE non-stick plastic. How is PTFE made?

1. In what way is a polymer like a string of beads?

2. Name the polymer used extensively to make plastic bags.

3. **EXTENDED** The diagram shows the structural formula of chloroethene.

$$\begin{array}{cc} H & Cl \\ \diagdown & \diagup \\ C \!=\! C \\ \diagup & \diagdown \\ H & H \end{array}$$

  a)  Show how two molecules of chloroethene join together to form part of the polymer poly(chloroethene).

  b) Draw the structure of the repeat unit of the polymer.

4. **EXTENDED** What type of polymer is poly(chloroethene)?

---

**EXTENDED**

### Condensation polymers

Polymers can also be made by joining together two different monomers so that they react together. When they react, they expel a small molecule. Because the molecule is usually water, the process is called condensation polymerisation and the products are condensation polymers.

△ Fig. 4.38 Condensation polymerisation.

Nylon is a common synthetic condensation polymer.

◁ Fig. 4.39 Surfboards are made from a condensation polymer called polyurethane.

Nylon is made from a molecule with a carboxylic acid group (COOH) and another molecule with an **amine** group (NH₂).

They react to form an **amide** link:

△ Fig. 4.40 Nylon is a polyamide.

Another example is Terylene, which is made from two different monomer molecules, one with a carboxylic acid group (COOH) and another with an alcohol group (OH). They react to form an **ester** link:

△ Fig. 4.41 Terylene is described as a polyester.

Note: As a general rule, addition polymerisation is used to make plastics.

By changing the atoms or groups of atoms attached to the carbon–carbon double bond, a whole range of different polymers can be made.

Condensation polymerisation is used for making man-made fibres for clothes, ropes etc. such as nylon and Terylene.

## QUESTIONS

**1.** Nylon is an example of a condensation polymer. How is this type of polymer different from an addition polymer?

**2.** Why is it important that the monomers that join together to make nylon have reactive groups at each end of the molecule?

**END OF EXTENDED**

# THE CHALLENGES OF RECYCLING PLASTICS

△ Fig. 4.42 Waste plastics are lightweight but very bulky.

Plastics are very difficult to dispose of. Most of them are not **biodegradable** – they cannot be decomposed by bacteria in the soil. Currently, most waste plastic material is buried in landfill sites or burned, but burning plastics produces toxic fumes and landfill sites are filling up.

Some types of plastic can be melted down and used again. These are called **thermoplastics**. Other types of plastic harden or decompose when they are heated. These are called **thermosetting** plastics. Recycling them is difficult because the different types of plastic must be separated.

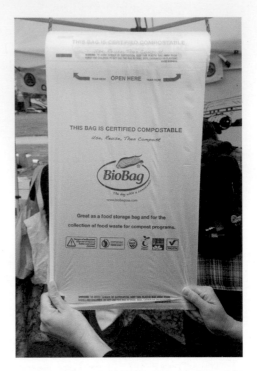

△ Fig. 4.43 Some plastic bags are biodegradable. They are made from polythene and starch. When buried, the starch breaks down and leaves tiny fragments of polythene.

△ Fig. 4.44 Thermoplastics have weak intermolecular forces that break on heating, which allows them to be melted and remoulded. In thermosetting plastics, the intermolecular bonds are strong interlinking covalent bonds. The whole structure eventually breaks down when these bonds are broken by heating.

# NATURAL POLYMERS

There are many natural large, long-chain molecules found in nature – that is, in plants and animals.

The food we eat contains many of these macromolecules and we will look at two in more detail in this section. These macromolecules are some of the main constituents of the foods we eat: **proteins** and **carbohydrates**.

## Proteins

These macromolecules have been formed by condensation polymerisation of **amino acids**.

Amino acids have a carboxylic acid group on one end and an amine group on the other:

$H_2N -$ ☐ $- COOH$

The ends of the molecules react together to form an amide link, as shown here:

△ Fig. 4.45 An amide link.

This is the same linkage as found in nylon, but the amino acid molecules are different from the molecules used in nylon. Proteins can be broken down to amino acids by **hydrolysis** (reaction with water). The protein is boiled in dilute acid to be hydrolysed.

## Carbohydrates

Carbohydrates contain carbon, hydrogen and oxygen atoms. Starch is an example of a carbohydrate macromolecule. It is made of sugar molecules (the monomer) joined together by condensation polymerisation:

△ Fig. 4.46 Starch is a carbohydrate macromolecule.

The carbohydrate linkages in complex carbohydrates, e.g. starch, can be broken down by hydrolysis using acids or enzymes to form simple sugars.

Fermentation is a technique for turning sugars into ethanol.

The products of the hydrolysis of proteins and carbohydrates can be separated and identified using paper chromatography. The products are colourless so need spraying with a locating agent to be seen on the chromatogram.

**END OF EXTENDED**

## QUESTIONS

1. What does it mean if a plastic is described as 'non-biodegradable'?

2. EXTENDED When a protein is made from amino acids, which two functional groups are needed to form an amide link?

3. EXTENDED This question is about carbohydrates.

   a) What does the term *carbohydrate* mean?

   b) What type of polymerisation is needed to make a carbohydrate?

   c) What is the name of the process in which a carbohydrate can be broken down into simple sugars?

# End of topic checklist

## Key terms

addition polymer, amide, amine, amino acid, biodegradable, carbohydrates, condensation polymer, ester, hydrolysis, monomer, proteins, thermoplastic, thermosetting

## During your study of this topic you should have learned:

○ How to describe polymers as large molecules built up from smaller units (monomers).

○ About some typical uses of plastics and of man-made fibres such as nylon and terylene.

○ How to describe the pollution problems caused by non-biodegradable plastics.

○ That proteins and carbohydrates are two of the main constituents of food.

○ **EXTENDED** How to deduce the structure of the polymer product from a given alkene and vice versa.

○ **EXTENDED** How to describe the formation of nylon (a polyamide) and terylene (a polyester) by condensation polymerisation.

○ **EXTENDED** That different polymers have different units and/or different linkages.

○ **EXTENDED** How to describe the differences between condensation polymerisation and addition polymerisation.

○ **EXTENDED** How to describe proteins as having the same (amide) linkage as nylon but with different units or monomers.

○ **EXTENDED** How to describe the structure of proteins.

○ **EXTENDED** How to describe the hydrolysis of proteins to amino acids.

○ **EXTENDED** How to describe complex carbohydrates in terms of a large number of sugar units joined together by condensation polymerisation.

○ **EXTENDED** How to describe the acid hydrolysis or enzyme hydrolysis of complex carbohydrates (e.g. starch) to give simple sugars.

○ **EXTENDED** How to describe the fermentation of simple sugars to produce ethanol and carbon dioxide.

○ **EXTENDED** How to describe, in outline, the usefulness of chromatography in separating and identifying the products of the hydrolysis of carbohydrates and proteins.

# End of topic questions

*Note: The marks awarded for these questions indicate the level of detail required in the answers. In the examination, the number of marks awarded for questions like these may be different.*

1. Explain what is meant by the following:

    **a)** *monomer* (1 mark)

    **b)** *polymer*. (1 mark)

2. **EXTENDED** This question is about addition polymers.

    **a)** What is an *addition polymer*? (1 mark)

    **b)** What structural feature do all monomers that form addition polymers have in common? (1 mark)

    **c)** Use structural formulae to show how propene molecules react to form poly(propene). (2 marks)

    **d)** Explain why a polymer called poly(propane) does not exist. (2 marks)

3. **EXTENDED** Copy and complete the table, giving one use for each of the following addition polymers. (3 marks)

| Addition polymer | Use |
|---|---|
| Poly(ethene) | |
| Poly(propene) | |
| Poly(chloroethene) | |

4. **a)** Addition polymers are 'not biodegradable'. Explain what this means. (2 marks)

    **b)** It is important to recycle polymers or plastic materials. Explain some of the problems associated with recycling plastics. (3 marks)

5. **EXTENDED** This question is about condensation polymers.

    **a)** In what ways is a condensation polymer different to an addition polymer? (2 marks)

    **b) i)** Name an example of a condensation polymer. (1 mark)

    **ii)** Describe a use of this condensation polymer. (1 mark)

**6.** **EXTENDED** This question is about natural macromolecules.

a) i) What is the structure of an amide link? (1 mark)

  ii) In which natural macromolecules would you find the amide link? (1 mark)

b) i) What are the monomer units in a protein? (1 mark)

  ii) How can the protein be broken down into its monomer units? (2 marks)

c) i) What are the monomer units in a carbohydrate? (1 mark)

  ii) How can the carbohydrate be broken down into its monomer units? (2 marks)

# Exam-style questions
## Sample student answer

*The questions, sample answers and marks in this section have been written by the authors as a guide only. The marks awarded for these questions indicate the level of detail required in the answers. In the examination, the number of marks awarded to questions like these may be different.*

## Question 1

This question is about the following organic compounds:

**A** $C_4H_{10}$    **B** $C_2H_5OH$    **C** $C_4H_8$    **D** $CH_3COOH$

**a)** Which compound belongs to the alkene group?

*C* ✔ ①      **(1)**

**b)** Which compound is a saturated hydrocarbon?

*C* ✘      **(1)**

**c)** Which compound can be made by fermentation?

*B* ✔ ①      **(1)**

**d)** Which compound will decolourise bromine water?

*C* ✔ ①      **(1)**

**e)** Draw the displayed formulae of the two isomers of compound A. Name each isomer.

**Isomer 1**      **Isomer 2**

✔ ①      ✘

**Name**      **Name**

*butane* ✔ ①      ✘ ............................ **(4)**

**f)** Name the two products that are formed when compound A burns in a plentiful supply of air.

*carbon dioxide* ✔ ① *and water* ✔ ① **(2)**

## TEACHER'S COMMENTS

**a)** Correct answer, alkenes are hydrocarbons with the general formula $C_nH_{2n}$.

**b)** The correct answer is A. Compound C is an alkene and is unsaturated, it contains a carbon-to-carbon double bond.

**c)** Correct answer, ethanol is made by fermentation.

**d)** Correct answer. The decolourising of bromine water is a test for an alkene.

**e)** Only one isomer has been drawn and named correctly. Both isomers drawn contain a single chain of carbon atoms – they are the same molecule. The missing isomer only has three carbon atoms in a chain and is called 2-methylpropane.

**f)** Correct answers. All hydrocarbons burn in a plentiful supply of oxygen forming carbon dioxide and water.

**g)** Carbon is correct and is responsible for the yellow flame characteristic of incomplete combustion. The missing substance is carbon monoxide, which is extremely poisonous.

**g)** Name two other substances that can be produced when compound A burns in a limited supply of air.

carbon ✓ ① and hydrogen ✗          (2)

Total ⑧/₁₂

## Question 2

The alkanes are a homologous series of saturated hydrocarbons.

**a)** Say whether each of the following statements about the members of the alkane homologous series is TRUE or FALSE.

   **i)** They have similar chemical properties.          (1)

  **ii)** They have the same displayed formula.          (1)

 **iii)** They have the same general formula.          (1)

  **iv)** They have the same physical properties.          (1)

   **v)** They have the same relative formula mass.          (1)

**b)** Define the following terms:

   **i)** hydrocarbon          (1)

  **ii)** saturated          (1)

**c)** The third member of the alkane homologous series is propane.

   **i)** What is the molecular formula of propane?          (1)

  **ii)** Draw the displayed formula of propane.          (2)

**(Total 10 marks)**

## Question 3

Many useful substances are produced by the fractional distillation of crude oil.

**a)** Bitumen, fuel oil and gasoline are three fractions obtained from crude oil.

Name the fraction that has the following property:

  **i)** the highest boiling point (1)

  **ii)** molecules with the fewest carbon atoms (1)

  **iii)** the darkest colour. (1)

**b)** Some long-chain hydrocarbons can be broken down into more useful products.
What is the name of this process and how is it carried out? (3)

**c)** Methane is used as a fuel. When methane is burned in a limited supply of air, carbon monoxide is formed.

  **i)** Write a balanced equation for this reaction. (2)

  **ii)** Explain why carbon monoxide is dangerous to health. (2)

(Total 10 marks)

## Question 4

Propene can be converted into a polymer called poly(propene).

propene

**a)** Which homologous series does propene belong to? (1)

**b)** What is the general name given to an individual molecule that combines with other molecules to make a polymer? (1)

**c)** Use the displayed formula of propene to show how three molecules link together to form part of the poly(propene) molecule. (2)

**d)** Draw the repeat unit in poly(propene). (2)

**e)** What type of polymer is poly(propene)? (1)

**f)** List two uses of poly(propene). (2)

**g)** Why are polymers such as poly(propene) hard to dispose of? (2)

**h)** Nylon is a different type of polymer from poly(propene).

  **i)** What type of polymer is nylon? (1)

  **ii)** In terms of how it is made, how is nylon different from poly(propene)? (1)

(Total 13 marks)

## Question 5

Poly(ethene) is a plastic that is made by polymerising ethene, $C_2H_4$.

**a)** Which one of the following best describes the ethene molecules in this reaction?
Draw a ring around the correct answer.

alcohols, alkanes, monomers, polymers, products (1)

**b)** The structure of ethane is shown below.

```
     H   H
     |   |
 H — C — C — H
     |   |
     H   H
```

Explain, by referring to its bonding, why ethane cannot be polymerised. (1)

**c)** Draw the structure of ethene, showing all its atoms and bonds. (1)

**d)** Ethene is obtained by cracking alkanes.

   **i)** Explain the meaning of the term *cracking*. (1)

   **ii)** What condition is needed to crack alkanes? (1)

   **iii)** Copy and complete the equation for cracking. decane, $C_{10}H_{22}$.

   $C_{10}H_{22} \rightarrow C_2H_4 +$ _____ (1)

**e)** Some oil companies crack the ethane produced when petroleum is distilled.

   **i)** Copy and complete the equation for this reaction.

   $C_2H_6 \rightarrow C_2H_4 +$ _____ (1)

   **ii)** Describe the process of fractional distillation, which is used to separate the different fractions in petroleum. (2)

   **iii)** State a use for the following petroleum fractions:

   gasoline fraction (1)
   lubricating fraction. (1)

**(Total 11 marks)**

## Question 6

Enzymes are biological catalysts. They are used both in research laboratories and in industry.

**a)** Enzymes called proteases can hydrolyse proteins to amino acids. The amino acids can be separated and identified by chromatography. The diagram shows a typical chromatogram.

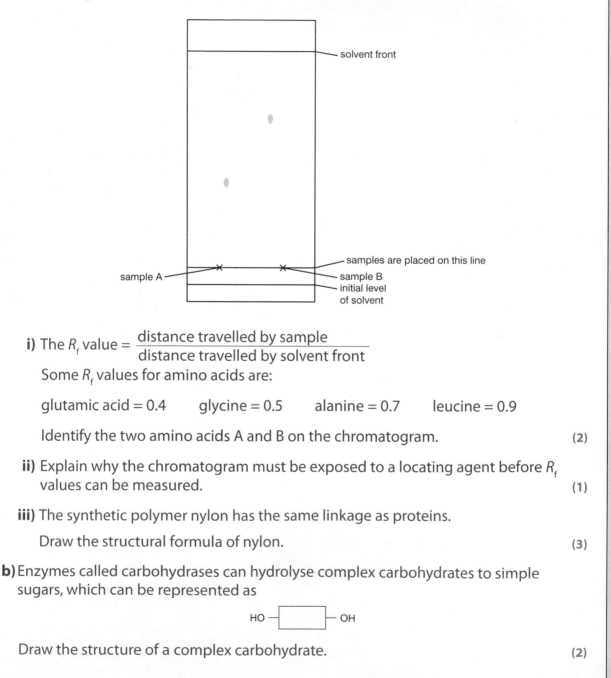

**i)** The $R_f$ value $= \dfrac{\text{distance travelled by sample}}{\text{distance travelled by solvent front}}$

Some $R_f$ values for amino acids are:

glutamic acid = 0.4      glycine = 0.5      alanine = 0.7      leucine = 0.9

Identify the two amino acids A and B on the chromatogram.                    (2)

**ii)** Explain why the chromatogram must be exposed to a locating agent before $R_f$ values can be measured.                    (1)

**iii)** The synthetic polymer nylon has the same linkage as proteins.

Draw the structural formula of nylon.                    (3)

**b)** Enzymes called carbohydrases can hydrolyse complex carbohydrates to simple sugars, which can be represented as

HO —☐— OH

Draw the structure of a complex carbohydrate.                    (2)

**c)** Fermentation can be carried out in this apparatus. After a few days the reaction stops. It has produced a 12% aqueous solution of ethanol.

allows carbon dioxide to escape but prevents air entering

aqueous glucose and yeast

i) Copy and complete the equation.

$C_6H_{12}O_6 \rightarrow$ _____ + _____

glucose    ethanol                  carbon dioxide          (2)

ii) Zymase catalyses the anaerobic respiration of glucose. Define the term *respiration*. (2)

iii) Suggest a reason why the reaction stops after a few days. (1)

iv) Why is it essential that there is no oxygen in the flask? (1)

v) What technique is used to concentrate the aqueous ethanol? (1)

**(Total 15 marks)**

## Question 7

The simplest alcohol is methanol.

a) It is manufactured in the following reversible reaction:

$$CO(g) + 2H_2(g) \rightleftharpoons CH_3OH(g)$$

300 °C

↑

30 atm

   **i)** Reversible reactions can come to equilibrium.
Explain the term *equilibrium*.   (1)

  **ii)** At 400 °C, the percentage of methanol in the equilibrium mixture is lower than at 300 °C. Suggest an explanation.   (2)

**iii)** Suggest two advantages of using high pressure for this reaction. Give a reason for each advantage.   (4)

b)  **i)** Copy and complete the equation for the combustion of methanol in excess oxygen:

   ☐ $CH_3OH$ + ☐ $O_2$ → ☐ + ☐   (2)

 **ii)** Copy and complete the word equation.

   methanol + ethanoic acid → ☐ + ☐   (2)

**iii)** Methanol can be oxidised to an acid. Name this acid.   (1)

**(Total 12 marks)**

# Doing well in examinations

## INTRODUCTION

Examinations will test how good your understanding of scientific ideas is, how well you can apply your understanding to new situations and how well you can analyse and interpret information you have been given. The assessments are opportunities to show how well you can do these.

To be successful in exams you need to:

✓ have a good knowledge and understanding of science

✓ be able to apply this knowledge and understanding to familiar and new situations

✓ be able to interpret and evaluate evidence that you have just been given.

You need to be able to do these things under exam conditions.

## OVERVIEW

Ensure you are familiar with the structure of the examinations you are taking. Consult the relevant syllabus for the year you are entering your examinations for details of the different papers and the weighting of each, including the papers to test practical skills. Your teacher will advise you of which papers you will be taking.

You will be required to perform calculations, draw graphs and describe, explain and interpret chemical ideas and information. In some of the questions the content may be unfamiliar to you; these questions are designed to assess data-handling skills and the ability to apply chemical principles and ideas in unfamiliar situations.

## ASSESSMENT OBJECTIVES AND WEIGHTINGS

For the Cambridge IGCSE examination, the assessment objectives and weightings are as follows:

✓ A: Knowledge and understanding (50%)

✓ B: Handling information and problem solving (30%)

✓ C: Experimental skills and investigations (20%).

The types of questions in your assessment fit the three assessment objectives shown in the table.

| Assessment objective | Your answer should show that you can... |
|---|---|
| A Knowledge and understanding | Recall, select and communicate your knowledge and understanding of science. |
| B Handling information and problem solving | Apply skills, including evaluation and analysis, knowledge and understanding of scientific contexts. |
| C Experimental skills and investigations | Use the skills of planning, observation, analysis and evaluation in practical situations. |

## EXAMINATION TECHNIQUES

To help you to work to your best abilities in exams, there are a few simple steps to follow.

### Check your understanding of the question

✓ **Read the introduction to each question carefully before moving on to the questions themselves**.

✓ Look in detail at any **diagrams, graphs** or **tables**.

✓ Underline or circle the **key words** in the question.

✓ **Make sure you answer the question that is being asked** rather than the one you wish had been asked!

✓ Make sure that you understand the meaning of the '**command words**' in the questions.

### REMEMBER

Remember that any information you are given is there to help you to answer the question.

### EXAMPLE 1

✓ **'Give', 'state', 'name'** are used when recall of knowledge is required – for example you could be asked to give a definition, write a list of examples, or provide the best answers from a list of options.

✓ **'Describe'** is used when you have to give the main feature(s) of, for example, a chemical process or structure.

✓ **'Explain'** is used when you have to give reasons, e.g. for some experimental results or a chemical fact or observation. You will often be asked to 'explain your answer', i.e. give reasons for it.

✓ **'Suggest'** is used when you have to come up with an idea to explain the information you're given – there may be more than one possible answer, no definitive answer from the information given, or it may be that you will not have learned the answer but have to use the knowledge you do have to come up with a sensible one.

✓ **'Calculate'** means that you have to work out an answer in figures.

✓ **'Plot', 'Draw a graph'** are used when you have to use the data provided to produce graphs and charts.

## Check the number of marks for each question

✓ Look at the **number of marks** allocated to each question.

✓ Look at the **space provided** to guide you as to the length of your answer.

✓ Make sure you include at least as many points in your answer as there are marks.

✓ Write neatly and keep within the space provided.

### REMEMBER

Beware of continually writing too much because it probably means you are not really answering the questions. Do not repeat the question in your answer.

## Use your time effectively

✓ Don't spend so long on some questions that you don't have time to finish the paper.

✓ You should spend approximately **one minute per mark**.

✓ If you are really stuck on a question, leave it, finish the rest of the paper and come back to it at the end.

✓ Even if you eventually have to guess at an answer, you stand a better chance of gaining some marks than if you leave it blank.

## ANSWERING QUESTIONS

### Multiple choice questions

✓ Select your answer by placing a cross (not a tick) in the box.

### Short- and long-answer questions

✓ In short-answer questions, **don't write more than you are asked for**.

✓ You may not gain any marks, even if the first part of your answer is correct, if you've written down something incorrect later on or which contradicts what you've said earlier. This may give the impression that you haven't really understood the question or are guessing.

✓ In some questions, particularly short-answer questions, answers of only one or two words may be sufficient, but in longer questions you should aim to use **good English** and **scientific language** to make your answer as clear as possible.

✓ Present the information in a logical sequence.

✓ Don't be afraid to also use **labelled diagrams** or **flow charts** if it helps you to show your answer more clearly.

### Questions with calculations

✓ **In calculations always show your working**.

✓ Even if your final answer is incorrect you may still gain some marks if part of your attempt is correct.

✓ If you just write down the final answer and it is incorrect, you will get no marks at all.

✓ Write down your answers to as many **significant figures** as are used in the numbers in the question (and no more). If the question doesn't state how many significant figures then a good rule of thumb is to quote 3 significant figures.

✓ Don't round off too early in calculations with many steps – it's always better to give too many significant figures than too few.

✓ You may also lose marks if you don't use the correct **units**. In some questions the units will be mentioned, e.g. calculate the mass in grams; or the units may also be given on the answer line. If numbers you are working with are very large, you may need to make a conversion e.g. convert joules into kilojoules, or kilograms into tonnes.

### Finishing your exam

✓ When you've finished your exam, **check through** your paper to make sure you've answered all the questions.

✓ Check that you haven't missed any questions at the end of the paper or turned over two pages at once and missed questions.

✓ Cover over your answers and read through the questions again and check that your answers are as good as you can make them.

---

**REMEMBER**

You will be asked questions on investigative work. It is important that you understand the methods used by scientists when carrying out investigative work.

More information on carrying out practical work and developing your investigative skills are given in the next section.

# Developing experimental skills

## INTRODUCTION

As part of your IGCSE Chemistry course, you will develop practical skills and have to carry out investigative work in science.

This section provides guidance on carrying out an investigation.

The experimental and investigative skills are divided as follows:

**1.** Using and organising techniques, apparatus and materials

**2.** Planning experiments and investigations

**3.** Observing, measuring and recording

**4.** Interpreting observations and data

**5.** Evaluating methods

## 1. USING AND ORGANISING TECHNIQUES, APPARATUS AND MATERIALS

**Learning objective**: to demonstrate and describe appropriate experimental and investigative methods, including safe and skilful practical techniques.

**Questions to ask**:

**How shall I use the equipment and chemicals safely to minimise the risks – what are my safety precautions?**

✓ When writing a Risk Assessment, investigators need to be careful to check that they've matched the hazard with the concentration of a chemical used. Many acids, for instance, are corrosive in higher concentrations but are likely to be irritants or of low hazard in the concentration used when working in chemistry experiments.

✓ Don't forget to consider the hazards associated with all the chemicals, even if these are very low.

✓ In the exam, you may be asked to justify the precautions taken when carrying out an investigation.

**How much detail should I give in my description?**

✓ You need to give enough detail so that someone else who has not done the experiment would be able to carry it out to reproduce your results.

## How should I use the equipment to give me the precision I need?

✓ You should know how to read the scales on the measuring equipment you are using.

✓ You need to show that you are aware of the precision needed.

△ Fig. 5.1 The volume of liquid in a burette must be read to the bottom of the meniscus. The volume in this measuring cylinder is 202 cm³ (ml), not 204 cm³.

## EXAMPLE 2

This is an extract from a student's notebook. It describes how she carried out a titration experiment using sulfuric acid and potassium hydroxide solutions, with methyl orange as an indicator.

$$2KOH(aq) + H_2SO_4(aq) \rightarrow K_2SO_4(aq) + 2H_2O(l)$$

### What are my safety precautions?

*Equipment*

*I will be using a pipette, burette and conical flask all made from glass so I will need to handle them carefully and, in particular, clamp the burette carefully and make sure the pipette does not roll off the bench when I am not using it. I will also be careful when attaching the pipette to the pipette filler so that the pipette does not break.*

*Chemicals*

*I have looked up the hazards*

*Sulfuric acid 0.1M: LOW HAZARD*

*Potassium hydroxide (0.1M approx.): IRRITANT*

**COMMENT**

The student has used a data source to look up the chemical hazards.
There is no risk assessment for methyl orange.

*I will need to handle the chemicals carefully, have a damp
cloth ready to wipe up any spills and wear eye protection.*

**COMMENT**

The student has suggested some sensible precautions.

The student's method is given below

*A pipette and a burette were carefully washed, making sure
they were drained after washing.*

*25.00 cm³ of the potassium hydroxide solution was measured
in a pipette and transferred to a clean conical flask. 3 drops
of methyl orange indicator were then added.*

*The burette was filled with the sulfuric acid solution, making
sure that there were no air bubbles in the jet of the burette.
The first reading of the volume of acid in the burette was
taken.*

*The acid was added to the alkali in the conical flask,
swirling the flask all the time. When the indicator colour was
close to changing, the acid was added drop by drop until the
colour changed. The second reading on the burette was
taken.*

*The whole procedure was repeated twice, making sure that
between each experiment the conical flask was washed
carefully. The results are shown in the table.*

**COMMENT**

The method is well written and detailed. Point 1 could have been
improved if she had said that the burette and pipette had been washed
with distilled water first and then the chemical to be used (burette –
acid; pipette – alkali).

**Precision and accuracy.** Some examples from the notebook are:

*'25.00 cm³ of the potassium hydroxide solution'*

The student has appreciated the accuracy a titration can achieve.

*'making sure that there were no air bubbles in the jet of the burette'*

An air bubble could easily lead to an inaccurate measurement.

*'the acid was added drop by drop until the colour changed'*

Again the student tried to get accuracy to within one drop ($\pm$ 0.05 cm$^3$)

## 2. PLANNING EXPERIMENTS AND METHODS

**Learning objective**: to devise and plan investigations, drawing on chemical knowledge and understanding in selecting appropriate techniques.

**Questions to ask**

**What do I already know about the area of chemistry I am investigating and how can I use this knowledge and understanding to help me with my plan?**

✓ Think about what you have already learned and any investigations you have already done that are relevant to this investigation.

✓ List the factors might affect the process you are investigating.

**What is the best method or technique to use?**

✓ Think about whether you can use or adapt a method that you have already used.

✓ A method, and the measuring instruments, must be able to produce **valid** measurements. A measurement is valid if it measures what it is supposed to be measuring.

You will make a decision as to which technique to use based on:

✓ The accuracy and precision of the results required.

### REMEMBER

Investigators might require results that are as accurate and precise as possible but if you are doing a quick comparison, or a preliminary test to check a range over which results should be collected, a high level of accuracy and precision may not be required.

✓ The simplicity or difficulty of the techniques available, or the equipment required – is this expensive, for instance?

✓ The scale – e.g. use standard laboratory equipment or a microscale- which may give results in a shorter time period.

✓ The time available to do the investigation.

✓ Health and safety considerations.

## What am I going to measure?

✓ The factor you are investigating changing is called the **independent variable**. A **dependent variable** is affected or changed by the independent variable that you select.

✓ You need to choose a range of measurements that will be wide enough to allow you to plot a graph of your results and so find out the pattern in your results.

✓ You might be asked to explain why you have chosen your range rather than a lower or higher range.

## How am I going to control the other variables?

✓ These are **control variables**. Some of these may be difficult to control.

✓ You must decide how you are going to control any other variables in the investigation and so ensure that you are carrying out a fair test and that any conclusions you draw are valid.

✓ You may also need to decide on the concentration or combination of reactants.

## What equipment is suitable and will give me the accuracy and precision I need?

✓ The **accuracy** of a measurement is how close it is to its true value.

✓ **Precision** is related to the smallest scale division on the measuring instrument that you are using—e.g. when measuring a distance, a rule marked in millimetres will give greater precision that one divided into centimetres only.

✓ A set of precise measurements also refers to measurements that have very little spread about the mean value.

✓ You need to be sensible about selecting your devices and make a judgement about the degree of precision. Think about what is the least precise variable you are measuring and choose suitable measuring devices. There is no point having instruments that are much more precise than the precision you can measure the variable to.

## What are the potential hazards of the equipment, chemicals and technique I will be using and how can I reduce the risks associated with these hazards?

✓ You can find out hazards associated with the reactants using CLEAPSS Student Safety Sheets or a similar resource. Visit www.cleapss.org.uk

✓ In the exam, be prepared to suggest safety precautions when presented with details of a chemistry investigation.

EXAMPLE 3

You have been asked to design and plan an investigation to find out the effect of temperature on the rate of reaction between sodium thiosulfate and hydrochloric acid. In a previous investigation you have used this reaction so you are familiar with what happens and how the rate of the reaction can be measured.

## What do I already know?

Previously you have the reaction between sodium thiosulfate and hydrochloric acid to investigate the effect of changing the concentration of sodium thiosulfate on the rate of the reaction. So you know that as the reaction takes place a precipitate of sulfur forms in the solution and makes the solution change from colourless (and clear) to pale yellow (and opaque). The time it takes for a certain amount of sulfur to form can be used as a measure of the rate of the reaction.

## What is the best method or technique to use?

The technique you used in your previous investigation can be adapted. Previously you added 5 cm$^3$ of hydrochloric acid to 50 cm$^3$ of sodium thiosulfate solution in a conical flask, and then looked down the conical flask and measured the time that was taken until a mark on a piece of paper under the flask was no longer visible.

△ Fig. 5.2

## What am I going to measure?

You are investigating the effect of temperature on the rate of the reaction. The independent variable is temperature. The time it takes for the mark to become obscured by the sulfur forming in the flask is a dependent variable as it depends on the temperature you select.

Other independent variables you could measure are the temperature of the sodium thiosulfate or the mixture once the acid has been added.

You will need to be able to measure a **range** of temperatures (e.g. 20 °C to 60 °C). Ideally you will need to repeat the experiment at about five different temperatures (e.g. 20, 30, 40, 50 and 60 °C).

## How am I going to control the other variables?

It is important that you decide on the quantities of sodium thiosulfate and hydrochloric acid (the volumes) you are going to use and then keep these unchanged throughout. As you are familiar with the reaction, you can look back at your previous results and decide which concentrations or combination of reactants would be the most appropriate.

## What equipment is suitable and will give me the accuracy and precision I need?

You now know what you will need to measure and so can decide on your measuring devices.

| Measurement | Quantity | Device |
|---|---|---|
| Volume (sodium thiosulfate) | about 50 cm$^3$ | 100 cm$^3$ measuring cylinder |
| Volume (hydrochloric acid) | about 5 cm$^3$ | 10 cm$^3$ measuring cylinder |
| Temperature | 20–60 °C | Thermometer (1 °C precision) or a thermostatically controlled water bath |
| Time | up to 120 s | Stop watch or stopclock (1 s precision) |

△ Table 5.1 Suitable equipment for experiment.

Choosing a burette accurate to 0.1 cm$^3$, a thermometer accurate to 0.1 °C or a stop clock accurate to 0.01 s would be inappropriate when the technique itself does not have a very precise way of judging when the mark has been obscured.

## What are the potential hazards and how can I reduce the risks?

The hazards are as follows:

✓ Concentrated sodium thiosulfate solution: LOW HAZARD

✓ Dilute hydrochloric acid: LOW HAZARD

These indicate that there are no specific hazards you need to be aware of. However, you will be using an acid so it would be sensible to wear eye protection.

In terms of the equipment and technique, the major hazard will be handling the hot solution. You can limit this hazard by choosing a range of temperatures that do not include very high values (e.g. between room temperature and about 60 °C).

## 3. OBSERVING, MEASURING AND RECORDING

**Learning objective**: to make observations and measurements with appropriate precision, record these methodically and present them in a suitable form.

**Questions to ask**:

**How many different measurements or observations do I need to take?**

✓ Sufficient readings have been taken to ensure that the data are consistent.

✓ It is usual to repeat an experiment to get more than one measurement. If an investigator takes just one measurement, this may not be typical of what would normally happen when the experiment was carried out.

✓ When repeat readings are consistent they are said to be **repeatable**.

**Do I need to repeat any measurements or observations that are anomalous?**

✓ An **anomalous result** or **outlier** is a result that is not consistent with other results.

✓ You want to be sure a single result is accurate (as in example 4). So you will need to repeat the experiment until you get close agreement in the results you obtain.

✓ If an investigator has made repeat measurements, they would normally use these to calculate the arithmetical mean (or just mean or average) of these data to give a more accurate result. You calculate the mean by adding together all the measurements, and dividing by the number of measurements. Be careful though – anomalous results should not be included when taking averages.

✓ Anomalous results might be the consequence of an error made in measurement. But sometimes outliers are genuine results. If you think an outlier has been introduced by careless practical work, you should omit it when calculating the mean. But you should examine possible reasons carefully before just leaving it out.

✓ You are taking a number of readings in order to see a changing pattern. For example, measuring the volume of gas produced in a reaction every 10 seconds for 2 minutes (so 12 different readings).

✓ It is likely that you will plot your results onto a graph and then draw a **line of best fit**.

✓ You can often pick an anomalous reading out from a results table (or a graph if all the data points have been plotted, as well as the mean, to show the range of data). It may be a good idea to repeat this part of the practical again, but it's not necessary if the results show good consistency.

✓ If you are confident that you can draw a line of best fit through most of the points, it is not necessary to repeat any measurements that are obviously inaccurate. If, however, the pattern is not clear enough to draw a graph then readings will need to be repeated.

**How should I record my measurements or observations – is a table the best way? What headings and units should I use?**

✓ A table is often the best way to record results.

✓ Headings should be clear.

✓ If a table contains numerical data, do not forget to include units; data is meaningless without them.

✓ The units should be the same as those that are on the measuring equipment you are using.

✓ Sometimes you are recording observations that are not quantities, as shown in Example 6. Putting observations in a table with headings is a good way of presenting this information.

## EXAMPLE 4

The student from Example 2 has recorded the results in a table as shown in Table 5.2. In this case she needs to get two results within 0.1 $cm^3$ of each other and so has had to do the titration three times to get that level of agreement.

Volume of potassium hydroxide solution = 25.00 $cm^3$

| Burette reading | 1st experiment | 2nd experiment | 3rd experiment |
|---|---|---|---|
| 2nd reading ($cm^3$) | 17.50 | 19.50 | 20.50 |
| 1st reading ($cm^3$) | 0.00 | 2.50 | 3.50 |
| Difference ($cm^3$) | 17.50 | 17.00 | 17.00 |

△ Table 5.2 Readings from titration.

## EXAMPLE 5

In an experiment to measure the volume of a gas produced in a reaction the student has sensibly recorded her results in Table 5.3. Notice each column has a heading *and* units.

| Time (s) | Volume of gas ($cm^3$) |
|---|---|
| 0 | 25 |
| 10 | 45 |
| 20 | 60 |
| 30 | 70 |
| 40 | 74 |
| 50 | 76 |
| 60 | 76 |

△ Table 5.3 Results of experiment.

## EXAMPLE 6

In another experiment, the student has recorded his results obtained in an experiment involving heating magnesium in a crucible to form magnesium oxide.

tongs

pipe-clay triangle

crucible and lid

◁ Fig. 5.3 Apparatus for the experiment.

| Mass of crucible + lid (1) | = 23.00 g |
| Mass of crucible + lid + magnesium (2) | = 24.13 g |
| Mass of crucible + lid + magnesium oxide (3) | = 24.20 g |
| Mass of magnesium (2 − 1) | = 0.13 g |
| Mass of oxygen (3 − 2) | = 0.07 g |

△ Table 5.4 Results of experiment.

## COMMENT

In Table 5.4:

The description of each measurement is clear.

The units are given in each case.

## EXAMPLE 7

In this example, a student has recorded his observations on mixing various metals with dilute hydrochloric acid in Table 5.5.

| Metal | Observations on adding dilute hydrochloric acid |
|---|---|
| Copper | No reaction. |
| Iron | Slow effervescence and a colourless gas is produced, a pale green solution forms. |
| Lead | A few bubbles of gas form on the surface of the metal. |
| Magnesium | Rapid effervescence and a colourless gas is produced, a colourless solution forms. The magnesium disappears. |
| Zinc | Quite rapid effervescence and a colourless gas is produced. A colourless solution is formed. |

△ Table 5.5 Presenting results in a table.

Terms such as 'effervescence' and 'solution' have been used correctly and chemical names have not been included. For example, although the colourless gas referred to is hydrogen you would not actually observe hydrogen – what you see is effervescence. When interpreting or explaining the observations you may identify this gas as hydrogen.

## 4. INTERPRETING OBSERVATIONS AND DATA

**Learning objectives**: to analyse and interpret data to draw conclusions from experimental activities which are consistent with the evidence, using chemical knowledge and understanding, and to communicate these findings using appropriate specialist vocabulary, relevant calculations and graphs.

**Questions to ask**:

**What is the best way to show the pattern in my results? Should I use a bar chart, line graph or scatter graph?**

✓ Graphs are usually the best way of demonstrating trends in data.

✓ A bar chart or bar graph is used when one of the variables is a **categoric variable**, for example when the melting points of the oxides of the Group 2 elements are shown for each oxide, the names are categoric and not continuous variables.

✓ A line graph is used when both variables are continuous e.g. time and temperature, time and volume.

✓ Scattergraphs can be used to show the intensity of a relationship, or degree of **correlation**, between two variables.

✓ Sometimes a line of best fit is added to a scatter graph, but usually the points are left without a line.

When drawing bar charts or line graphs:

✓ Choose scales that take up most of the graph paper.

✓ Make sure the axes are linear and allow points to be plotted accurately. Each square on an axis should represent the same quantity. For example, one big square = 5 or 10 units; not 3 units.

✓ Label the axes with the variables (ideally with the independent variable on the x-axis).

✓ Make sure the axes have units.

✓ If more than one set of data is plotted use a key to distinguish the different data sets.

**If I use a line graph should I join the points with a straight line or a smooth curve?**

✓ When you draw a line, do not just join the dots!

✓ Remember there may be some points that don't fall on the curve – these may be incorrect or anomalous results.

✓ A graph will often make it obvious which results are anomalous and so it would not be necessary to repeat the experiment (see Example 8).

### Do I have to calculate anything from my results?

✓ It will be usual to calculate means from the data.

✓ Sometimes it is helpful to make other calculations, before plotting a graph – for example you might calculate 1/time for a rate of reaction experiment.

✓ Sometimes you will have to do some calculations before you can draw any conclusions.

### Can I draw a conclusion from my analysis of the results, and what chemical knowledge and understanding can be used to explain the conclusion?

✓ You need to use your chemical knowledge and understanding to explain your conclusion.

✓ It is important to be able to add some explanation which refers to relevant scientific ideas in order to justify your conclusion.

### EXAMPLE 8

A student carried out an experiment to find out how the rate of a reaction changes during the reaction. She added some hydrochloric acid to marble chips and measured the volume of carbon dioxide produced in a gas syringe. She took a reading of the volume of gas in the syringe every 10 seconds for 1.5 minutes.

The apparatus she used and the results obtained are shown in Figs 5.4 and 5.5:

△ Fig. 5.4

△ Fig. 5.5 Graph of experimental results.

## What is the best way to show the pattern in my results?

In this experiment both the volume of gas and time are **continuous variables** and so a line graph is needed.

## Straight line or a smooth curve?

With the results obtained in this experiment it is clear that a smooth curve is needed. Drawing a straight line of best fit would not be sensible.

## Do I have to calculate anything from my results?

In this experiment the student had to find out how the rate of the reaction changed as the reaction proceeded. She could do this by looking at the change in steepness/gradient of the curve as the reaction proceeded and so she didn't need to do any separate calculations.

## Can I draw a conclusion from my analysis of the results?

*As the line is steeper at the beginning of the experiment than nearer the end the rate of the reaction decreases as the reaction proceeds.*

### COMMENT

This is a very clear statement. In addition, the student might have referred to 'the gradient of the line' at points 1, 2 and 3 to make her conclusion even more precise.

## What chemical knowledge and understanding can be used to explain the conclusion?

*As the reaction proceeds the reacting particles are converted into products. This means that there will be fewer reacting particles as time goes on, there will be fewer effective collisions and so the rate of the reaction will decrease.*

### COMMENT

This is a good conclusion because it makes direct links to scientific knowledge in relation to collision theory. Reference to 'effective collisions' also indicates a good level of precision. The student might also have mentioned that as the particles react, the concentration of the reactants decrease and with it the rate of the reaction.

## 5. EVALUATING METHODS

**Learning objective**: to evaluate data and methods.

**Questions to ask**:

**Do any of my results stand out as being inaccurate or anomalous?**

✓ You need to look for any anomalous results or outliers that do not fit the pattern.

✓ You can often pick this out from a results table (or a graph if all the data points have been plotted, as well as the mean, to show the range of data).

**What reasons can I give for any inaccurate results?**

✓ When answering questions like this it is important to be specific. Answers such as 'experimental error' will not score any marks.

✓ It is often possible to look at the practical technique and suggest explanations for anomalous results.

✓ When you carry out the experiment you will have a better idea of which possible sources of error are more likely.

✓ Try to give a specific source of error and avoid statements such as 'the measurements must have been wrong'.

Your conclusion will be based on your findings, but must take into consideration any uncertainty in these introduced by any possible sources of error. You should discuss where these have come from in your evaluation.

**Error** is a difference between a measurement you make and its true value.

The two types of errors are:

✓ random error

✓ systematic error.

With **random error**, measurements vary in an unpredictable way. This can occur when the instrument you're using lacks sufficient precision to indicate differences in readings. It can also occur when it's difficult to make a measurement.

With **systematic error**, readings vary in a controlled way. They're either consistently too high or too low. One reason could be down to the way you are making a reading—e.g., taking a burette reading at the wrong point on the meniscus, or not being directly in front of an instrument when reading from it.

What an investigator *should not* discuss in an evaluation are problems introduced by using faulty equipment, or by using the equipment inappropriately. These errors can be, or could have been, eliminated, by:

✓ checking equipment

✓ practising techniques before the investigation, and taking care and patience when carrying out the practical.

## Overall was the method or technique I used precise enough?

✓ If your results were good enough to provide a confident answer to the problem you were investigating then the method was probably good enough.

✓ If you realise your results are not precise when you compare your conclusion with the actual answer it may be you have a **systematic error** (an error that has been made in obtaining all the results.) A systematic error would indicate an overall problem with the experimental method.

✓ If your results do not show a convincing pattern then it is fair to assume that your method or technique was not precise enough and there may have been **random errors** (that is, measurements varying in an unpredictable way).

## If I were to do the investigation again what would I change or improve upon?

✓ Having identified possible errors it is important to say how these could be overcome. Again you should try to be absolutely precise.

✓ When suggesting improvements, do not just say 'do it more accurately next time' or 'measure the volumes more accurately next time'.

✓ For example, if you were measuring small volumes, you could improve the method by using a burette to measure the volumes rather than a measuring cylinder.

### EXAMPLE 9

A student was measuring the height of a precipitate produced in a test tube when different volumes of lead(II) nitrate solution were added to separate 15 cm$^3$ samples of potassium iodide solution:

$Pb(NO_3)_2(aq) + 2KI(aq) \rightarrow PbI_2(s) + 2KNO_3(aq)$

### Do any of my results stand out as being inaccurate or anomalous?

The student plotted her results on a graph. The inaccurate result stands out from the rest. Given the pattern obtained with the other results there is no real need to repeat the result – you could be very confident that the height should have been 3.0 cm. A result like this is referred to as an anomalous result. It was an error but not a systematic error.

△ Fig. 5.6 Student's graph of experimental results.

### What reasons can I give for any inaccurate results?

There are two main possible sources of error – either one of the volumes was measured incorrectly or the height of the precipitate was measured incorrectly.

Perhaps there was some air trapped in the precipitate and it didn't settle like the precipitates in the other tubes.

### Was the method or technique I used precise enough?

You can be reasonably confident that 7.5 cm$^3$ of lead(II) nitrate solution reacted exactly with 15 cm$^3$ of potassium iodide solution (the point at which the height of precipitate reached its maximum value of 3.0 cm).

### How can I improve the investigation?

For example, you could say, 'stir each precipitate to get rid of air bubbles and then let the precipitate settle'.

# Periodic table of elements

**Group**

| 1 | 2 | | 3 | 4 | 5 | 6 | 7 | 0 |
|---|---|---|---|---|---|---|---|---|
| | | | | | | | | 4 He / 2 / helium |
| 7 Li / 3 / lithium | 9 Be / 4 / beryllium | | 11 B / 5 / boron | 12 C / 6 / carbon | 14 N / 7 / nitrogen | 16 O / 8 / oxygen | 19 F / 9 / fluorine | 20 Ne / 10 / neon |
| 23 Na / 11 / sodium | 24 Mg / 12 / magnesium | | 27 Al / 13 / aluminium | 28 Si / 14 / silicon | 31 P / 15 / phosphorus | 32 S / 16 / sulfur | 35 Cl / 17 / chlorine | 40 Ar / 18 / argon |

1 H / 1 / hydrogen

| 39 K / 19 / potassium | 40 Ca / 20 / calcium | 45 Sc / 21 / scandium | 48 Ti / 22 / titanium | 51 V / 23 / vanadium | 52 Cr / 24 / chromium | 55 Mn / 25 / manganese | 56 Fe / 26 / iron | 59 Co / 27 / cobalt | 59 Ni / 28 / nickel | 64 Cu / 29 / copper | 65 Zn / 30 / zinc | 70 Ga / 31 / gallium | 73 Ge / 32 / germanium | 75 As / 33 / arsenic | 79 Se / 34 / selenium | 80 Br / 35 / bromine | 84 Kr / 36 / krypton |
|---|---|---|---|---|---|---|---|---|---|---|---|---|---|---|---|---|---|
| 85 Rb / 37 / rubidium | 88 Sr / 38 / strontium | 89 Y / 39 / yttrium | 91 Zr / 40 / zirconium | 93 Nb / 41 / niobium | 96 Mo / 42 / molybdenum | 99 Tc / 43 / technetium | 101 Ru / 44 / ruthenium | 103 Rh / 45 / rhodium | 106 Pd / 46 / palladium | 108 Ag / 47 / silver | 112 Cd / 48 / cadmium | 115 In / 49 / indium | 119 Sn / 50 / tin | 122 Sb / 51 / antimony | 128 Te / 52 / tellurium | 127 I / 53 / iodine | 131 Xe / 54 / xenon |
| 133 Cs / 55 / caesium | 137 Ba / 56 / barium | 139 La / 57 / lanthanum | 178 Hf / 72 / hafnium | 181 Ta / 73 / tantalum | 184 W / 74 / tungsten | 186 Re / 75 / rhenium | 190 Os / 76 / osmium | 192 Ir / 77 / iridium | 195 Pt / 78 / platinum | 197 Au / 79 / gold | 201 Hg / 80 / mercury | 204 Tl / 81 / thallium | 207 Pb / 82 / lead | 209 Bi / 83 / bismuth | 210 Po / 84 / polonium | 210 At / 85 / astatine | 222 Rn / 86 / radon |
| 223 Fr / 87 / francium | 226 Ra / 88 / radium | 227 Ac / 89 / actinium | | | | | | | | | | | | | | | |

# Glossary

**acid** A substance that contains replaceable hydrogen atoms which form $H^+$ ions when the acid is dissolved in water. It has a pH less than 7.

**acid rain** Rain water that contains dissolved acids, typically sulfuric acid and nitric acid.

**acidic oxide** The oxide of a non-metal.

**activation energy** The minimum energy that must be provided before a reaction can take place.

**addition polymer** A polymer that is made when molecules of a single monomer join together in large numbers.

**addition reaction** The reaction of an alkene and another element or compound to form a single compound.

**alcohol** A molecule with an OH group attached to a chain of carbon atoms.

**alkali** A base that is soluble in water, is a proton acceptor and produces $OH^-$ ions. It has a pH greater than 7.

**alkali metal** A Group I element.

**alkane** A hydrocarbon in which the carbon atoms are bonded together by single bonds only.

**alkene** A hydrocarbon that contains a carbon-carbon double bond.

**allotropes** The different physical forms in which a pure element can exist.

**alloy** A mixture of a metal and one or more other elements.

**amide** The functional group in the polymer nylon (nylon is a polyamide).

**amine** The functional group in amino acids that combines with an acid group when a protein is formed.

**amino acid** An organic compound that acts as a monomer in the formation of protein (a polymer).

**amphoteric oxide** An oxide that reacts with both acids and alkalis to form salts.

**anhydrous** Literally means 'without water' – a compound, usually a salt, with no water of crystallisation.

**anion** A negatively charged ion, which moves to the anode during electrolysis.

**anode** A positively charged electrode in electrolysis.

**atom** The smallest particle of an element. Atoms are made of protons, electrons and neutrons.

**Avogadro constant (or number)** The number of particles in one mole of a substance. It is $6.0 \times 10^{23}$.

**Avogadro's law** Equal volumes of all gases at the same temperature and pressure must contain the same number of molecules.

**base** Substance that neutralises an acid to produce a salt and water.

**basic oxide** The oxide of a metal.

**biodegradable** Can be broken down naturally in the environment (e.g. by bacteria in the soil).

**boiling** The change of state from liquid to gas.

**boiling point** The temperature of a boiling liquid – the highest temperature that the liquid can reach and the lowest temperature that the gas can reach.

**bond energy** The average energy associated with breaking or forming a particular covalent bond (measured in kJ/mol).

**Brownian motion** The random motion of pollen grains on the surface of water (also the random motion of smoke particles in air).

**burning** The reaction of a substance with oxygen in a flame.

**calorimetry** A method for determining energy changes in reactions or when substances are mixed together.

## C

**carbohydrates** Organic compounds containing only carbon, hydrogen and oxygen atoms, usually with a hydrogen: oxygen ratio the same as in water (2:1).

**carbon cycle** The processes which add carbon dioxide to the atmosphere and the processes which remove carbon dioxide from the atmosphere.

**carbonate** A salt formed by the reaction of carbon dioxide with alkalis in solution.

**carbonic acid** An acid formed by the reaction of carbon dioxide with water.

**catalyst** A chemical that is added to speed up a reaction, but remains unchanged at the end.

**catalytic cracking** The process by which long-chain alkanes are broken down to form more useful short-chain alkanes and alkenes, using high temperatures and a catalyst.

**cathode** A negatively charged electrode in electrolysis.

**cation** A positive ion, which moves to the cathode during electrolysis.

**cell** A device for turning chemical energy into electrical energy.

**ceramic** An inorganic non-metallic material usually formed by heating and cooling.

**chemical change** A change that is not easily reversed because new substances are made.

**chemical formula** The combination of element symbols that represents a compound or molecule.

**chemical reaction** A chemical change that produces new substances and which is not usually easily reversed.

**chemical symbol** A unique symbol that represents a particular chemical element.

**chromatogram** A visible record (usually a coloured chart or graph) showing the separation of a mixture using chromatography.

**chromatography** The process for separating dissolved solids using a solvent and filter paper (in the school laboratory).

**collision theory** A theory used to explain differences in the rates of reactions as a result of the frequency and energy associated with the collisions between the reacting particles.

**combustion** The reaction that occurs when a substance (usually a fuel) burns in oxygen.

**compound** A pure substance formed when elements react together.

**concentration** Amount of chemical dissolved in $1 \, dm^3$ of solvent.

**condensation** The change of state from gas to liquid.

**condensation polymer** A polymer formed when two monomers react together and eliminate a small molecule such as water or hydrogen chloride.

**conductor** A material that will allow heat or electrical energy to pass through it.

**contact process** The process in which sulfuric acid is manufactured from sulfur dioxide and oxygen.

**control variable** Something that is fixed and is unchanged in an investigation.

**covalent bond** A bond that forms when electrons are shared between the atoms of two non-metals.

**cracking** Forming shorter alkanes and alkenes from longer alkanes using high temperatures and a catalyst.

## D

**decomposition** Chemical change that breaks down one substance into two or more substances.

**delocalised** Electrons that are not attached to a particular atom (as in graphite or a metallic structure).

**dependent variable** A variable that changes as a result of changes made to value of the independent variable.

**desalination** The separation of salt from sea water by evaporation of the water.

**diatomic** Two atoms combined together (for example in a molecule).

**diffusion** The random mixing and moving of particles in liquids and gases.

**displacement reaction** A reaction in which one element takes the place of another in a compound, removing (displacing) it from the compound.

**dissociation** The splitting of a molecule to form smaller molecules or, in the presence of water, ions.

**distillation** The process for separating a liquid from a solid (usually when the solid is dissolved in the liquid) or a liquid from a mixture of liquids.

**ductile** Describing a substance (such as metal) that can be drawn or pulled into a wire.

**dynamic equilibrium** A situation in which reactants are constantly being converted into products, and products are constantly being converted back into reactants. The rates of the forward and backward reactions are the same.

**E**

**effective collision** A collision between particles with enough energy to cause a chemical reaction.

**electrode** The carbon or metal material that delivers electric charge in electrolysis reactions.

**electrolysis** The breaking down of a compound by passing an electric current through it.

**electrolyte** A substance that allows electric current to pass through it when it is molten or dissolved in water.

**electron** Negatively charged particle with a negligible mass that forms the outer part of all atoms.

**electronic configuration** The arrangement of electrons in an atom, molecule or ion.

**element** A substance that cannot be broken down into other substances by any chemical change.

**empirical formula** The simplest formula of a compound, showing the whole number ratio of the atoms in the compound.

**endothermic** A type of reaction in which energy is taken in from the surroundings.

**enthalpy change ($\Delta H$)** The heat energy change when the reactants shown in a chemical equation react together.

**enzyme** A chemical that speeds up certain reactions in biological systems, such as digestive enzymes that speed up the chemical digestion of food.

**equilibrium reaction** A chemical reaction in which the forward and backward reactions are both likely, shown as: $X \rightleftharpoons Y$.

**ester** a compound that is formed when an alcohol reacts with an organic acid.

**evaporation** When liquid changes to gas at a temperature lower than its boiling point.

**exothermic** A type of reaction in which energy is transferred out to the surroundings.

**F**

**fats** Organic compounds that contain an ester functional group.

**fermentation** The process by which ethanol is made from a solution of sugar and yeast.

**filtrate** The clear solution produced by filtering a mixture.

**formula mass ($M_r$)** The sum of the atomic masses of the atoms in a formula.

**fossil fuel** Fuel made from the remains of decayed animal and plant matter compressed over millions of years.

**fraction** A collection of hydrocarbons that have similar molecular masses and boil at similar temperatures.

**fractional distillation** A process for separating liquids with different boiling points.

**freezing** Changing a liquid to a solid.

**freezing point** The temperature at which a liquid changes to a solid.

**functional group** A part of an organic molecule which is responsible for the characteristic reactions of the molecule.

**G**

**galvanising** The process of coating a metal (usually iron) with zinc.

**gas** The state of matter in which the substance has no volume or shape.

**global warming** The rise in the average temperature of the Earth's atmosphere and oceans.

**greenhouse effect** The trapping of long-wave radiation emitted from the Earth's surface by gases in the atmosphere.

**greenhouse gas** A gas that can trap long-wave radiation emitted from the Earth's surface.

**group** A vertical column of elements in the Periodic Table.

**H**

**Haber process** The process in which ammonia is manufactured from nitrogen and hydrogen.

**halogens** The Group VII elements (F, Cl, Br, I, At).

**homologous series** A group of organic compounds with the same general formula, similar chemical properties and physical properties that change gradually from one member of the series to the next.

**hydrated** Literally means 'containing water' – hydrated salts contain water of crystallisation.

**hydrocarbon** A compound containing only hydrogen atoms and carbon atoms.

**hydrolysis** Breaking down a compound using its reaction with water or steam.

**I**

**independent variable** A variable that is deliberately changed in an investigation and, as a result, causes changes to the dependent variable.

**indicator** A substance that changes colour in either an acid or alkali and so can be used to identify acids or alkalis.

**insoluble** Does not dissolve in water.

**intermolecular force** The force of attraction or repulsion between molecules.

**intramolecular bond** A bond within a molecule.

**ion** A charged atom or molecule.

**ionic bond** A bond that involves the transfer of electrons to produce electrically charged ions.

**ionic compound** A compound formed by the reaction between a metal and one or more non-metals.

**ionic equation** A chemical equation showing how the ions involved react together.

**isomers** Compounds that have the same molecular formula but different structures.

**isotope** Atoms of the same element that contain different numbers of neutrons. Isotopes have the same atomic number but different mass numbers.

**K**

**kinetic theory** The theory describing the movement of particles in solids, liquid and gases.

**L**

**liquid** The state of matter in which a substance has a fixed volume but no definite shape.

**litmus** An indicator that has different colours in acids (red) and alkalis (blue).

**locating agent** A substance used to show the position of a colourless product on a chromatogram.

**M**

**malleability** The measure of how easily a substance can be beaten into sheets.

**mass number** The number of protons and neutrons in an atom (also known as the nucleon number).

melting Changing a solid into a liquid at its melting point.

melting point The temperature at which a solid changes to a liquid.

metal An element with particular properties (usually hard, shiny and a good conductor of heat and electricity).

metalloid An element that has properties characteristic of both metals and non-metals.

mineral A solid inorganic substance that occurs naturally.

mixture Two or more substances combined without a chemical reaction – they can be separated easily.

mole The amount of a substance containing $6 \times 10^{23}$ particles (atoms, molecules, ions).

molecular formula The formula of a compound showing the actual whole number of atoms combined.

molecule A group of two or more atoms covalently bonded together.

monatomic An element composed of separate atoms.

monomer Small molecules that can be joined in a chain to make a polymer.

### N

neutralisation A reaction in which an acid reacts with a base or alkali to form a salt and water.

neutron Particle in the nucleus of atoms that have mass but no charge.

nitrogen cycle The processes by which nitrogen is converted between its various chemical forms – the element, nitrogen oxides, nitrates and ammonium compounds.

nitrogen fixation The process by which nitrogen in the atmosphere is converted into ammonia and ammonium compounds.

noble gas Group 0 elements (He, Ne, Ar, Kr, Xe, Rn). They have full outer electron shells.

non-metal An element with particular properties (usually a gas or soft solid and a poor conductor of heat and electricity).

non-renewable A fuel that cannot be made again in a short time span.

nucleus, atomic The tiny centre of an atom, typically made up of protons and neutrons.

nucleon number (mass number) The total number of protons and neutrons in an atom.

### O

ore A mineral from which a metal may be extracted.

organic chemistry The study of covalent compounds of carbon.

organic molecules Carbon-based molecules.

oxidation state The degree of oxidation of an element.

oxidation The addition of oxygen in a chemical reaction. Electrons are lost.

oxide A product of the reaction of oxygen with another element. For example, oxygen reacts with copper to produce copper oxide.

oxidising agent A substance that will oxidise another substance.

### P

percentage purity The proportion of the pure product compared to the impure product.

percentage yield The proportion of the actual amount of product formed in a chemical reaction, compared to the expected amount as predicted by the equation.

period A row in the Periodic Table, from an alkali metal to a noble gas.

Periodic Table The modern arrangement of the chemical elements in groups and periods.

periodicity The gradual change in properties of the elements across each row (period) of the Periodic Table.

**pH scale** A scale measuring the acidity (lower than 7) or alkalinity of a solution (higher than 7). It is a measure of the concentration of hydrogen ions in a solution.

**photosynthesis** A reaction that plants carry out to make food.

**physical change** A change in a substance that is easily reversed and does not involve the making of new chemical bonds.

**plastic** A synthetic material made from a wide range of organic polymers.

**polymer** A large molecule made up of linked smaller molecules (monomers). Polythene is a polymer made from ethene.

**polymerisation** Making polymers from monomers.

**precipitation** A reaction in which an insoluble salt is formed by mixing two solutions.

**pressure** A physical characteristic of a substance caused by particles of the substance colliding with the walls of the container it is in.

**products** The substances that are produced in a reaction.

**proteins** Organic compounds (polymers) made from amino acids (monomers).

**proton** Positively charged particles in the nucleus of atoms.

**proton number (atomic number)** the number of protons in an atom.

**Ⓡ** ─────────────────────

**radical** An element, molecule or ion that is highly reactive.

**radioactive** A substance that emits radiation (alpha or beta particles or gamma rays).

**rate of reaction** How fast a reaction goes in a given interval of time.

**reactant** The substances taking part in a chemical reaction. They change into the products.

**reactivity series** A list of elements showing their relative reactivities. More reactive elements will displace less reactive ones from their compounds.

**redox** A reaction involving both oxidation and reduction.

**reducing agent** A substance that will reduce another substance.

**reduction** When a substance loses oxygen – electrons are gained.

**relative atomic mass ($A_r$)** A number comparing the mass of one mole of atoms of a particular element with the mass of one mole of atoms of other elements. C has the value 12.

**relative formula mass ($M_r$)** The sum of the relative atomic masses of each of the atoms or ions in one formula unit of a substance.

**relative molecular mass ($M_r$)** The sum of the relative atomic masses of the atoms in a molecule.

**renewable energy** Energy from a source that will not run out, such as wind, water or solar energy.

**retention factor ($R_f$)** The distance travelled by a substance in a chromatography experiment (through the stationary phase) compared to the distance travelled by the solvent in the same time (expressed as a number between 0 and 1).

**reversible reaction** A reaction in which reactants form products and products form reactants.

**rusting** The chemical reaction in which iron is oxidised to iron(III) oxide in the presence of air (oxygen) and water.

**Ⓢ** ─────────────────────

**sacrificial protection** Covering a metal, or ensuring contact, with another metal so that the more reactive metal corrodes instead of the less reactive metal.

**salt** A compound formed when the replaceable hydrogen atom(s) of an acid is (are) replaced by a metal.

**saturated** Describes an organic compound that contains only single bonds (C – C).

**soap** A cleaning agent made from fats or oils using sodium hydroxide.

shell A grouping of electrons around a nucleus. The first shell in an atom can hold up to 2 electrons, the next can hold up to 8.

solid The state of matter in which a substance has a fixed volume and a definite shape.

soluble A substance that dissolves in a solvent to form a solution.

solute A substance that dissolves in a solvent producing a solution.

solution This is formed when a substance dissolves in a liquid. Aqueous solutions are formed when the solvent used is water.

solvent The liquid in which solutes are dissolved.

spectator ions Ions that play no part and are unchanged in a chemical reaction.

state symbols These denote whether a substance is a solid (s), liquid (l), gas (g) or is dissolved in aqueous solution (aq).

structural isomer A compound having the same molecular formula but different structural or displayed formula to another compound.

substitution A reaction in which an atom or group of atoms is replaced by another atom or group of atoms.

surface area The total area of the outside of an object.

## T

thermal decomposition The breaking down of a compound by heat.

thermoplastic A plastic that can be recycled by melting and reforming.

thermosetting A plastic that cannot be melted and recycled (it decomposes on heating).

titration An accurate method for calculating the concentration of an acid or alkali solution in a neutralisation reaction.

transition metal Elements found between Group II and III in the Periodic Table. Often used as catalysts and often make compounds that have coloured solutions.

## U

universal indicator Indicating solution that turns a specific colour at each pH value.

unsaturated Describes carbon compounds that contain carbon-to-carbon double bonds.

## V

valency electrons The outermost electrons of an atom that are involved when the atom reacts with other atoms or compounds.

vapour Another term for gas.

variable A factor that can either be changed in an investigation or changes as a result of other factors changing.

viscous The description of a liquid which does not flow very easily (for example does not flow as readily as water).

volatile Easily turns to a gas.

## W

water cycle The processes that cause the movement of water between the Earth's surface and the atmosphere.

water of crystallisation Water that occurs in crystals.

## Y

yield The amount of substance produced in a chemical reaction.

# Answers

*The answers given in this section have been written by the author and are not taken from examination mark schemes.*

## SECTION 1 PRINCIPLES OF CHEMISTRY

### The particulate nature of matter

**Page 11**

1. (l)
2. Only the solid state has a fixed shape.
3. Fine sand will pour or flow like a liquid; it takes the shape of the container it is poured into (although under a microscope you would see gaps at the surface of the container).

**Page 15**

1. The particles in a solid vibrate about a fixed point.
2. The particles are held together the most strongly in solid water (ice).
3. Evaporation is the process that occurs when faster moving particles in a liquid escape from the liquid surface.
4. Melting is the name of the process when a solid changes into a liquid.

**Page 18**

1. Diffusion is the mixing and moving of particles in liquids and gases.
2. The particles in the potassium manganate(VII) dissolve in the water and diffuse throughout the solution.
3. The particles of perfume vapour/gas diffuse in the air and spread throughout the whole room.
4. All elements contain atoms.
5. **a)** Brownian motion was first observed with pollen grains in water.
   **b)** The random motion is due to collisions between smoke particles and air particles.

### Experimental techniques

**Page 24**

1. A baseline drawn in pencil will not dissolve in the solvent.
2. If the solvent were above the baseline the substances would just dissolve and form a solution in the beaker.
3. The dye may be insoluble in the solvent.
4. The boiling point will be higher than that of pure water/ above 100 °C at normal pressure.
5. $R_f = 1.7/10 = 0.17$

**Page 27**

1. A solvent is a liquid that will dissolve a substance (solute).
2. If a substance is soluble in a solvent it dissolves in that solvent.
3. Distillation
4. Boiling points

### Atomic structure and the Periodic Table

**Page 33**

1. The electron has the smallest relative mass.
2. Atoms are neutral. The number of positive charges (protons) must equal the number of negative charges (electrons).
3. **a)** The nucleon number is 27.
   **b)** 14 neutrons

**Page 34**

1. Isotopes are atoms of the same element with different numbers of neutrons.
2. Radioactive isotopes emit radioactivity from the nucleus (alpha particles, beta particles or gamma rays) and decay.

**3.** Any three uses, for example: sterilising equipment, treating/diagnosing cancer tumours and as tracers to detect leaks in pipes.

### Page 38

**1. a)** Magnesium has two electrons in its outer electron shell.

   **b)** It is in Group II.

**2. a)** Aluminium

2, 8, 3   13p 14n

   **b)** Calcium

2, 8, 8, 2   20p 20n

**3.** The noble gases have full outer electron shells or have eight electrons in their outer electron shells and so do not easily lose or gain electrons.

### Page 39

**1.** In a compound the elements are chemically combined together. In a mixture the elements or components are not chemically combined together.

**2.** A malleable substance can be beaten or hammered into shape.

**3. a)** An alloy is a mixture of a metal and one or more other elements.

   **b)** Brass is made up of copper and zinc.

## Ions and ionic bonds

### Page 45

**1.**

**2.**

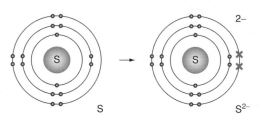

**3.** Both phosphorus and oxygen are non-metals. (A metal is needed to form an ionic bond.)

### Page 48

**1.** The ions are held together strongly in a giant lattice structure. The ions can vibrate but cannot move around.

**2.** Sodium chloride is made up of singly charged ions, $Na^+$ and $Cl^-$, whereas the magnesium ion in magnesium oxide has a double charge, $Mg^{2+}$. The higher the charge on the positive ion, the stronger the attractive forces between the positive ion and the negative ion.

## Molecules and covalent bonds

**1.**

Cl – Cl

**2.**

**3.**

O = O

**4.**

**5.**

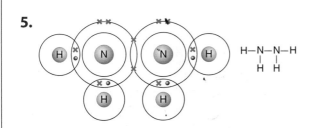

H–N–N–H
 |   |
 H   H

**1.** The intermolecular forces of attraction between the molecules are weak.

**2.** There are no ions or delocalised electrons present.

**1.** Each carbon atom is strongly covalently bonded to four other atoms forming a very strong giant lattice structure. A very high temperature is needed to break down the structure.

**2.** In graphite each carbon atom is strongly covalently bonded to 3 other carbon atoms. The remaining outer shell carbon electron is delocalised and so can move along between the layers formed by the covalently bonded carbon atoms.

## Metallic bonding

**1.** Cation is a positive ion.

**2.** Metals contain delocalised electrons that are not fixed to a particular atom, they can move throughout the structure.

**3.** Metals are not rigid, the ions can move into different positions when the metal is bent.

## Stoichiometry

**1. a)** KBr

**b)** CaO

**c)** $AlCl_3$

**d)** $CH_4$

**2. a)** $Cu(NO_3)_2$

**b)** $Al(OH)_3$

**c)** $(NH_4)_2SO_4$

**d)** $Fe_2(CO_3)_3$

**3. a)** $ZnCl_2$

**b)** $Cr_2O_3$

**c)** $Fe(OH)_2$

**1. a)** $2Ca + O_2(g) \rightarrow 2CaO(s)$

**b)** $2H_2S(g) + 3O_2(g) \rightarrow 2SO_2(g) + 2H_2O(l)$

**c)** $2Pb(NO_3)_2(s) \rightarrow 2PbO(s) + 4NO_2(g) + O_2(g)$

**2. a)** $S(s) + O_2(g) \rightarrow SO_2(g)$

**b)** $2Mg(s) + O_2(g) \rightarrow 2MgO(s)$

**c)** $CuO(s) + H_2(g) \rightarrow Cu(s) + H_2O(l)$

## Page 76

**1. a)** $2C_5H_{10}(g) + 15O_2(g) \rightarrow 10CO_2(g) + 10H_2O(l)$

**b)** $Fe_2O_3(s) + 3CO(g) \rightarrow 2Fe(s) + 3CO_2(g)$

**c)** $2KMnO_4(s) + 16HCl(aq) \rightarrow 2KCl(s) + 2MnCl_2(s) + 8H_2O(l) + 5Cl_2(g)$

## Page 79

**1.** 16

**2.** 46

**3.** 48

## Page 82

**1. a)** To allow oxygen from the air into the crucible.

**b)** To limit the loss of magnesium oxide.

**c)** White.

## Page 84

**1.** $Fe_2O_3$

**2.** ZnO

**3.** $C_4H_{10}$

**4.** $H_2O_2$

## Page 90

**1.** 28 g

**2. a)** 2 moles

**b)** 0.01 mole

**c)** 0.25 mole

## Page 91

**1. a)** 2 moles

**b)** 0.5 mole

**c)** 0.1 mole

**2. a)** 0.5 mole

**b)** 0.1 mole

**c)** 2 moles

## SECTION 2 PHYSICAL CHEMISTRY

### Electricity and chemistry

### Page 108

**1.** The breaking down (decomposition) of an ionic compound by the use of electricity.

**2.** The positive electrode is the anode.

**3.** The substance must contain ions and they must be free to move (in molten/liquid state or dissolved in water).

### Page 116

**1. a)** An inert electrode is an unreactive electrode; it will not be changed during electrolysis.

**b)** Carbon is commonly used as an inert electrode (Platinum is another inert electrode).

**2. a)** Lead and chlorine.

**b)** Magnesium and oxygen.

**c)** Aluminium and oxygen.

**3. a)** Hydrogen (sodium is above hydrogen in the reactivity series).

**b)** Hydrogen (zinc is above hydrogen in the reactivity series).

**c)** Silver (silver is below hydrogen in the reactivity series).

**4. a)** $2O^{2-} \rightarrow O_2 + 4e^-$

**b)** The change takes place at the anode.

### Page 118

**1. a)** Diagram as in Fig. 2.11.

**b)** At the cathode: $Cu^{2+}(aq) + 2e^- \rightarrow Cu(s)$
At the anode: $Cu(s) \rightarrow Cu^{2+}(aq) + 2e^-$

### Page 121

**1. a)** Cryolite is added to lower the melting point of the electrolyte and so reduce energy costs.

**b)** Aluminium forms at the cathode.

**c)** $Al^{3+}(l) + 3e^- \rightarrow Al(s)$

**d)** The aluminium ions are reduced because they gain electrons.

**e)** The oxygen oxidises the carbon anodes forming carbon dioxide.

**2.** High strength-to-weight ratio, low density and resistance to corrosion are all reasons for choosing aluminium for the construction of an aeroplane.

Page 124

**1. a)** $Na^+$, $Cl^-$, $H^+$, $OH^-$ are ions present in sodium chloride solution.

**b)** $Na^+$ and $H^+$ ions will be attracted to the cathode. The reactivity of the metal compared to hydrogen will determine which ion is discharged. As hydrogen is less reactive than sodium, hydrogen will be discharged.

**c)** $2H^+(aq) + 2e^- \rightarrow H_2(g)$

**2.** Sodium hydroxide is used in the manufacture of soap, bleach and paper.

Page 125

**1. a)** The voltage would be higher. Aluminium is more reactive than zinc, and so is further away from copper in the reactivity series.

**b)** Aluminium and copper have the biggest gap in the reactivity series.

## Chemical energetics

Page 132

**1.** A reaction that releases heat energy to the surroundings.

**2.** A reaction that absorbs energy from the surroundings.

**3.** Polystyrene is a very good insulator and so very little energy is transferred to the surroundings.

Page 133

**1.** A high proportion of the energy released transfers to the surrounding air.

**2. a)** Weighing the spirit burner before and after burning the fuel.

**b)** Ethanol 29; Paraffin 33; Pentane 25; Octane 40.

   **i)** Octane

   **ii)** A 10 °C rise would be expected. The same amount of energy is transferred to double the volume of water.

**3.** The group of students using the metal should get more accurate results. The metal conducts the heat from the fuel to the water better than glass does.

Page 134

**1.** The reaction is endothermic.

**2.** The activation energy

**3.**

**Reaction A**

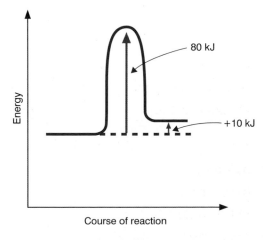

**Reaction B**

1. The sign indicates whether the reaction is exothermic (negative sign) or endothermic (positive sign).

2. Energy is needed to break bonds.

3. In an endothermic reaction more energy is needed to break bonds than is recovered on forming bonds.

4. The units are kJ/ mol.

5. $2H_2(g) + O_2(g) \rightarrow 2H_2O(c)$
Energy needed to break bonds
$= (2 \times 436) + 498 = + 1370$ kJ.
Energy released on forming bonds
$= 4 \times 464 = -1856$ kJ.
Energy change $= (+1370) - 1856 = -486$ kJ.

### Page 143

1. Uranium-235

2. 239 is the nucleon number (the number of protons + neutrons).

## Rate of reaction

### Page 149

1. In a physical change no new substances are made. In a chemical change at least one new substance is made.

2. The apparent change in mass is often because a gas has been either a reactant or a product (and is lost from the reaction vessel).

3. The particles must collide; there must be sufficient energy in the collision (to break bonds).

4. An effective collision is one which results in a chemical reaction between the colliding particles.

5. Student's diagram like Fig 2.36. It is an energy barrier. Only collisions that have enough energy to overcome this barrier will lead to a reaction.

### Page 152

1. A gas syringe will measure the volume of gas produced accurately.

2. No gas is being produced – the reaction hasn't started or it is finished.

3. The quicker reaction will have the steeper gradient.

### Page 156

1. The units of concentration for solutions are $mol/dm^3$.

2. The particles are closer together and there are more of them, so there will be more (effective) collisions per second.

3. Increasing the temperature means the particles have more (kinetic) energy. So more of the collisions will have energy greater than or equal to the activation energy and there will be more effective/ successful collisions per second.

### Page 160

1. A catalyst is a substance that changes the rate of a chemical reaction.

2. A biological catalyst is called an enzyme.

3. A silver halide: silver chloride, silver bromide or silver iodide.

## Reversible reactions

### Page 166

1. Copper(II) sulfate crystals can be converted into anhydrous copper(II) sulfate by heating to remove the water in the crystals. When the water is re-added to anhydrous copper(II) sulfate the copper(II) sulfate crystals are re-formed.

2. The concentrations of each of the products and reactants remain constant unless a change is made to the reaction.

3. Reactants are constantly being converted into products and products are constantly being converted back into reactants. The rates of these two reactions are the same.

Page 168

1. **a)** Low temperature.

   **b)** High pressure.

   **c)** Using a catalyst has no impact on the position of equilibrium.

2. **a)** The catalyst increases the rate of the reaction (but has no affect on the position of equilibrium).

   **b)** The rate of the reaction would be very low.

## Redox reactions

### Page 176

1. Reduction is the loss of oxygen or the gain of electrons.

2. **a)** +2

   **b)** +3

   **c)** +7

3. Reduced, as it has gained an electron.

4. Oxidised, as it has lost electrons.

## Acids, bases and salts

### Page 183

1. Both solutions are alkalis. Solution A is a weakly alkaline whereas solution B is a strongly alkaline.

2. The solution is acidic.

3. Calcium is a metal. The oxides (and hydroxides) of metals are bases.

4. Hydrochloric acid as a strong acid is completely ionised – all the HCl molecules are converted into $H^+$ and $Cl^-$ ions. Ethanoic acid as a weak acid is only partially ionised – only a few of the $CH_3COOH$ molecules are converted into $H^+$ and $CH_3COO^-$ ions.

### Page 186

1. Potassium oxide is a basic oxide. Potassium is a metal and most metal oxides are basic.

2. A basic oxide reacts with acids and not alkalis. An amphoteric oxide reacts with both acids and alkalis (to form salts).

### Page 190

1. A salt is formed when a replaceable hydrogen of an acid is replaced by a metal.

2. Sulfuric acid

3. Potassium chloride will be soluble in water (as are all potassium salts).

4. Calcium nitrate

5. Neutralisation is the reaction between and acid and an alkali or base to form a salt and water.

6. $H^+(aq)$

7. $OH^-(aq)$

### Page 191

1. Precipitation is the formation of an insoluble salt as a result of a chemical reaction taking place in aqueous solution.

2. Filtration

3. Washing with cold water will remove traces of any remaining soluble salts.

4. **a)** lead(II) nitrate + sodium chloride → lead(II) chloride + sodium nitrate

   **b)** $Pb(NO_3)_2(aq) + 2NaCl(aq) \rightarrow PbCl_2(s) + 2NaNO_3(aq)$

## Identification of ions and gases

### Page 198

1. **a)** A white precipitate, which does not dissolve in excess sodium hydroxide solution.

   **b)** A white precipitate, which does dissolve in excess soldium hydroxide solution.

2. Add sodium hydroxide solution. $Fe^{2+}$ produces a green precipitate; $Fe^{3+}$ produces a reddish-brown precipitate.

## Page 202

1. Add dilute sodium hydroxide and heat. An alkaline gas (turns red litmus paper blue) indicates the presence of an ammonium compound.

2. **a)** Carbon dioxide

   **b)** Bubble the gas through limewater. A white precipitate forms.

3. The $Fe^{3+}$ ion is present in solution X.

4. The $Cl^-$ ion is present in solution Y.

5. **a)**

| Name of cation | Colour of precipitate |
|---|---|
| Zinc/lead | white |
| Magnesium/ calcium | white |
| Copper(II) | blue |
| Iron(II) | green/turns brown slowly |
| Iron(III) | rust brown/orange |

**b)** $Ag^+(aq) + X^-(aq) \rightarrow AgX(s)$ where $X^-$ is $Cl^-$, $Br^-$, $I^-$.

**c)** HCl is added to remove any carbonate ions that may be present.

6. Plan needs to check for testing of both anion and cation for each sample and should include practical instructions.

   - Blue compound
   - Test for copper(II) – sodium hydroxide: result blue precipitate
     $Cu^{2+}(aq) + 2OH^-(aq) \rightarrow Cu(OH)_2(s)$
   - Test for sulfate – hydrochloric acid/ barium chloride: result white precipitate
     $Ba^{2+}(aq) + SO_4^{2-}(aq) \rightarrow BaSO_4(s)$
   - White compound
   - Flame test for $Na^+$ – yellow
   - Test for carbonate – add dilute acid – effervescence/carbon dioxide evolved – turns limewater milky
     $CO_3^{2-}(s) + 2H^+(aq) \rightarrow H_2O(l) + CO_2(g)$

## Page 203

1. Ammonia
2. Oxygen
3. Chlorine

## SECTION 3 INORGANIC CHEMISTRY

### The Periodic Table

## Page 218

1. **a)** 20

   **b)** The proton number is the number of protons (which equals the number of electrons) in an atom of the element. Calcium atoms have 20 protons and 20 electrons.

   **c)** Group II

   **d)** Period 4

   **e)** Calcium is a metal.

2. The halogens

3. The halogens are non-metals.

## Page 220

1. Aluminium has 3 electrons in the outer shell.

2. Oxygen will form an $O^{2-}$ ion (the oxide ion) with a 2- charge.

3. Fluorine (F)

4. Barium (Ba)

### Group I elements

## Page 224

1. They react with water to form alkaline solutions.

2. They have one electron in the outer shell.

3. They are soft to cut (also have very low melting points).

4. The potassium atom is larger than the lithium atom so the outer electron is further from the attraction of the nucleus and can be more easily removed.

5. Potassium is more reactive than lithium because of the distance of the outer electron from the nucleus.

Page 226

1. Sodium oxide is white.
2. Hydrogen. The solution formed is potassium hydroxide.
3. The compounds are soluble.
4. a) A period is a horizontal row of elements in the Periodic Table. All the elements in the same period have the same number of electron shells.

   For example: Period 1 elements: hydrogen (1) to helium (2) – 1 electron shell.

   Period 2 elements: lithium (2,1) to neon (2,8) – 2 electron shells.

   Period 3 elements sodium (2,8,1) to argon (2,8,8) – 3 electron shells.

   b) sodium, magnesium, aluminium, silicon, phosphorus, sulfur, chlorine, argon.

   c) 2,8,2; 2,8,3; 2,8,4; 2,8,5; 2,8,6; 2,8,7; 2,8,8.

   d) First element 2,8,1 – 1 electron in the outer shell, easily lost, will form positive ions, reactive metal.

   Last element 2,8,8 – 8 electrons in outer shell, full outer shell, noble gas, unreactive.

5. a) A group is a vertical column of elements having similar chemical properties because of their outer shell electronic structure.

   b) lithium, sodium, potassium

   c) All the elements in Group I have one electron in the outer shell.

   d) The reactivity of these elements depends on the ease with which the outer electron is lost. One electron can easily be lost to form positive ions. The ease with which it can be lost increases down the group because the electron is less tightly held in the atom and therefore reactivity increases down the group.

## Group VII elements

Page 233

1. Seven electrons in the outer shell.
2. The atoms need to gain only one electron to achieve a full outer shell.
3. Chlorine molecules are made up of two atoms combined/ bonded together, $Cl_2$.
4. A displacement reaction is where one Group VII element takes the place of another in a metallic compound.
5. A displacement reaction involves one Group VII element being reduced (gaining electrons) and one being oxidised (losing electrons).
6. Both involve both oxidation and reduction.

Pages 235–236

1. Chlorine kills any bacteria that might be present in the water.
2. Iodine
3. The non-stick surfaces on pans/ frying pans.
4. a)

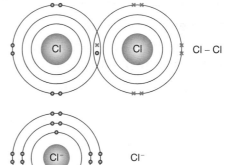

   b) $2Cl^-(aq) \rightarrow Cl_2(g) + 2e^-$. The chloride ions lose electrons.

   c) $2NaOH(aq) + Cl_2(g) \rightarrow NaCl(aq) + NaClO(aq) + H_2O(l)$

   d) Chlorine is a more reactive halogen than bromine. Chlorine will displace bromine from a solution of a bromide ions. (Chlorine will oxidise bromide ions to bromine.)

Observations: chlorine water is pale green. When this is added to a colourless solution of potassium bromide the resulting solution will turn orange due to the presence of bromine.

5. a) The reactivity of fluorine is due to its electronic structure 2,7. Fluorine needs to gain only one electron to form a fluoride ion. This is very easy because of its small size and large attractive force of the nucleus.

b) $F_2 + 2e^- \rightarrow 2F^-$

c) Both chlorine and iodine are less reactive than fluorine. Fluorine could only be displaced from fluoride ions by a more reactive halogen. As there are no halogens that are more reactive than fluorine, fluorine will not be displaced from fluoride ions.

## Transition metals and noble gases

### Page 241

1. No. Copper is very unreactive – it is below hydrogen in reactivity series.

2. The number indicates the oxidation state of the chromium.

3. a) $FeSO_4(aq) + 2NaOH(aq) \rightarrow Fe(OH)_2(s) + Na_2SO_4(aq)$

b) Green

## Metals

### Page 247

1. A ductile metal can be drawn into wires.

2. A malleable metal can be hammered into shape.

3. An alloy is a mixture of a metal with one or more other elements.

4. Cupronickel is used for making coins.

5. The element added in the alloy disrupts the rows of aluminium atoms making them less likely to slide over each other when under strain.

### Pages 250–251

1. No. Copper is below hydrogen in the reactivity series.

2. $2K(s) + 2H_2O(l) \rightarrow 2KOH(aq) + H_2(g)$

3. No. Carbon is below magnesium in the reactivity series.

4. $Mg(s) + PbO(s) \rightarrow MgO(s) + Pb(s)$

### Page 253

1. Potassium hydroxide and sodium hydroxide do not decompose on heating. These are metals at the top of the reactivity series.

2. a) The blue crystals would turn to a black powder; brown fumes would be formed.

b) The gas produced will relight a glowing splint.

c) $2Cu(NO_3)_2(s) \rightarrow 2\,CuO(s) + 4NO_2(g) + O_2(g)$

3. The aluminium reacts with oxygen to form a protective coating of aluminium oxide, which prevents further reaction.

### Pages 257–258

1. Iron ore (haematite), coke and limestone.

2. Iron(III) oxide.

3. Carbon dioxide, carbon monoxide, nitrogen (from the air).

4. $2Fe_2O_3(s) + 3C(s) \rightarrow 4Fe(s) + 3CO_2(g)$

5. a) An alloy is a mixture of a metal and another element.

b) The proportion of carbon is decreased by heating the blast furnace iron in oxygen.

c) The blast furnace iron is brittle – steel is more flexible and more resistant to corrosion.

**6. a)** $2Al(s) + Fe_2O_3(s) \rightarrow 2Fe(s) + Al_2O_3(s)$

**b)** Aluminium is higher in the reactivity series than iron, therefore it is more reactive. Aluminium is able to displace the less reactive iron from its oxide and so form iron and aluminium oxide.

**c)** Any metal that is higher than iron in the reactivity series can be selected theoretically. The higher the metal in the series, the more reactive the metal and the more reactive the reaction will be. If the chosen metal is above aluminium, the reaction is more reactive. In practice this is not feasible.

**d)** Aluminium is displacing iron in iron(III) oxide and becoming aluminium oxide by losing electrons. Iron(III) oxide is gaining electrons to become iron metal.

Redox is when oxidation and reduction occur. Aluminium is losing electrons (oxidation). Iron(III) oxide is gaining electrons (reduction).

**7. a)** oxygen + water

**b)** Chromium protects iron from oxygen and water/used because it is shiny – good decorative effect.

**c)** Aluminium forms a thin layer of aluminium oxide which acts as a protective layer – so it does not react with the air.

Page 260

**1.** Air (oxygen) and water must be present.

**2.** The grease can be easily removed or wiped away.

**3. a)** Galvanising involves coating iron or steel with zinc.

**b)** Because zinc is more reactive than iron, moist air will react with zinc in preference to the iron.

**Air and water**

Pages 273–274

**1.** Anhydrous means without water (water of crystallisation).

**2.** Cobalt(II) chloride will change from blue to pink.

**3. a)** The first filter is coarse gravel. The second filter is fine sand.

**b)** Chlorine is used to kill bacteria.

**4. a)** Nitrogen is 78%.

**b)** Carbon dioxide is 0.04%.

**5.** Oxygen and nitrogen are separated from the liquid air by fractional distillation.

**6.** Photosynthesis removes carbon dioxide from the air.

**7.** In the Haber process the temperature is 450°C and the pressure is 200 atmospheres.

Pages 278–279

**1.** A major source of carbon monoxide is the incomplete combustion of fuels, such as in a motor car.

**2. a)** Methane is the major component of natural gas. It is also produced by decaying vegetable matter and by ruminant animals such as cows.

**b)** Carbon dioxide is another green-house gas.

**3. a)** Sulfur dioxide and nitrogen oxide(s) are gases that cause acid rain.

**b)** Sulfur dioxide forms sulfuric acid; nitrogen oxide forms nitric acid.

**c)** Environmental problems include: harming plants and fish in lakes, damaging buildings made of metal, marble or limestone.

**4. a)** $N_2(g) + O_2(g) \rightarrow 2NO(g)$

**b)** The nitrogen monoxide is converted back into nitrogen and oxygen.

1. In a limited supply of air, carbon will form carbon monoxide.

2. **a)** copper(II) carbonate + sulfuric acid → copper(II) sulfate + carbon dioxide + water

   **b)** $CuCO_3(s) + H_2SO_4(aq) \rightarrow CuSO_4(aq) + CO_2(g) + H_2O(l)$

3. **a)** calcium carbonate → calcium oxide + carbon dioxide

   **b)** $CaCO_3(s) \rightarrow CaO(s) + CO_2(g)$

4. Rust is iron(III) oxide/ hydrated iron(III) oxide.

5. Covering in grease, painting, plastic coating, coating with a metal will all stop air and water getting into contact with iron.

6. Galvanising involves coating iron with zinc.

7. Zinc is more reactive than iron. Air (oxygen) will therefore react with zinc in preference to iron.

## Sulfur

1. A higher temperature is used to give a suitable rate of reaction.

2. The catalyst is vanadium(V) oxide.

3. Increasing the pressure would be uneconomical because the yield is already very high at 98%.

4. Sulfuric acid reacts with ammonia to produce ammonium sulfate:

   $2NH_3(aq) + H_2SO_4(aq) \rightarrow (NH_4)_2SO_4(aq)$

## SECTION 4 ORGANIC CHEMISTRY
## Fuels

1. The supplies of petroleum are limited – it takes millions of years for crude oil to be formed.

2. Natural gas or methane. It is trapped in pockets above the oil.

3. Small chain of carbon atoms.

4. Long chain of carbon atoms.

5. These fractions readily form a vapour.

1. Ethene is a member of the alkene homologous series.

2. The fractional distillation of crude oil produces a high proportion of long-chain hydrocarbons, which are not as useful as short-chain hydrocarbons. Cracking converts the long-chain hydrocarbons into more useful shorter chain hydrocarbons.

3. The conditions required for cracking oil fractions are a temperature of between 600 and 700°C and a catalyst of silica or alumina.

## Alkanes

1. **a)** A compound that has no C=C double bonds.

   **b)** A compound containing hydrogen atoms and carbon atoms only.

2. **a)** $C_{15}H_{32}$

   **b)** Carbon dioxide and water.

1. The fuel will burn with a yellow (rather than blue) flame.

2. Carbon and carbon monoxide.

3. It combines with the haemoglobin to form carboxyhaemoglobin, which prevents the haemoglobin from combining with oxygen.

4. Wind, wave, solar and nuclear power are alternative ways of generating energy.

**Page 323**

**1.** Isomers are molecules with the same molecular formula but different structural formulae.

**2.**

The molecular formula is $C_6H_{14}$.

**3.**

**4.** Hexane will be a liquid. Its physical properties will most closely resemble those of pentane.

## Alkenes

**Page 329**

**1.** It contains at least one C=C double bond.

**2.** The manufacture of polymers (polyethene).

**3.**

**Page 330**

**1. a)** Saturated compounds contain only covalent single bonds. Alkanes contain only carbon–carbon and carbon–hydrogen single bonds and are therefore saturated hydrocarbons. Alkenes contain C=C double bond and are therefore unsaturated.

**b)** Alkane: $C_6H_{14}$, alkene $C_6H_{12}$. The position of the double bond can be between any pair of carbon atoms, but there should be one fewer hydrogen attached to each of the double-bonded carbons.

**c)** The structure drawn needs to have 5 carbon atoms in a straight chain with a carbon as a branch or 4 carbons in a line and two branches (a straight chain should not be written with a bend).

**d)** Hexane undergoes substitution reaction with bromine (any H can be substituted with Br and can have more than one substitution). HBr is also formed in the reaction.

Hexene undergoes an addition reaction with bromine (bromine loses its colour – this is a test for unsaturation). The bromine will add across the double bond.

**2. a)** Fuels are substances that provide heat energy. Alkanes burn readily in air combining with oxygen to produce carbon dioxide and water vapour and large quantities of heat.

**b)** Incomplete combustion leads to the formation of carbon monoxide instead of carbon dioxide. It is a very poisonous gas and particularly dangerous because it has no odour and causes drowsiness. Carbon monoxide is poisonous because it reacts with the haemoglobin in the blood, forming 'carboxyhaemoglobin'. The haemoglobin is no longer available to carry oxygen to the body and death results from oxygen starvation.

**c)** Short-chain hydrocarbons are more likely to form carbon dioxide and water as their main products because there is less carbon per molecule in these hydrocarbons to react with the available oxygen. Long-chain hydrocarbons often burn with a smoky flame and leave black carbon deposits because there is insufficient oxygen to form carbon dioxide, with the many carbons in the longer chains. Carbon monoxide is also formed.

## Alcohols

### Page 335

1. $C_4H_9OH$
2. It is a relatively 'clean' fuel and releases only carbon dioxide and water into the atmosphere. (It does not release sulfur dioxide and nitrogen oxides, as petrol does when it burns.)
3. A solvent is a liquid that dissolves other substances (solutes) to form solutions.

### Page 337

1. Fermentation is the process in which ethanol is made from sugar, yeast and water.
2. The optimum temperature is in the range 25 to 30 °C.
3. The yeast contains enzymes which increase the rate of the reaction.
4. The fractional distillation separates the ethanol from the water.

## Macromolecules

### Page 350

1. The individual beads are like monomer molecules. The string of beads is like a polymer made by joining together many of these monomers.
2. Poly(ethene)/ polythene is used to make plastic bags.
3. a)

   b)

4. Poly(chloroethene) is an addition polymer.

### Page 351

1. Nylon is made from two monomers and a small molecule is eliminated when the two monomers combine. An addition polymer has only one monomer.
2. To produce a polymer chain the monomers need to be able to form amide groups at both ends of the molecules.

### Page 354

1. A non-biodegradable plastic cannot be broken down in the soil.
2. A carboxylic acid (-COOH) and an amine ($-NH_2$)
3. A carboxylic acid (COOH) and an amine ($NH_2$).
   a) A compound containing carbon, hydrogen and oxygen. (H:O ratio 2:1)
   b) Condensation polymerisation.
   c) Hydrolysis.

# Index

# Notes